Greece and the
Inter-War
Economic Crisis

GREECE AND THE INTER-WAR ECONOMIC CRISIS

MARK MAZOWER

CLARENDON PRESS · OXFORD
1991

*This book has been printed digitally and produced in a standard specification
in order to ensure its continuing availability*

OXFORD
UNIVERSITY PRESS

Great Clarendon Street, Oxford OX2 6DP
Oxford University Press is a department of the University of Oxford.
It furthers the University's objective of excellence in research, scholarship,
and education by publishing worldwide in

Oxford New York

Auckland Bangkok Buenos Aires Cape Town Chennai
Dar es Salaam Delhi Hong Kong Istanbul Karachi Kolkata
Kuala Lumpur Madrid Melbourne Mexico City Mumbai Nairobi
São Paulo Shanghai Singapore Taipei Tokyo Toronto
with an associated company in Berlin

Oxford is a registered trade mark of Oxford University Press
in the UK and in certain other countries

Published in the United States
by Oxford University Press Inc., New York

ISBN 0-19-820205-9

*Jacket illustration: detail from 'Athens, 1926', by Ilias Koumetakis.
By permission of the artist's daughter.*

FOR
MY PARENTS

ACKNOWLEDGEMENTS

I could not have written this book without the support of many individuals and institutions. Professors Adrian Lyttelton and Vera Zamagni first encouraged my interest in this area through their teaching in Bologna. I owe an enormous debt to Dr Patrick O'Brien and Dr John Campbell, who patiently supervised my doctoral thesis and then guided its metamorphosis into book form. I am grateful for their tolerance, encouragement, and support, and I hope that I have not, in attempting to satisfy them both, ended up by satisfying neither. In Athens Kostas Kostis provided ideas, friendship, and books. His work forms part of the current flowering of scholarship among Greek historians, without whose insights and discoveries this book would have been much the poorer. In this connection I should also mention my indebtedness to the works of Christos Chadziiosif, Antonios Liakos, and George Mavrogordatos. And I would like to thank Fay Zika, who introduced me to Greece, for her friendship and hospitality.

My research was made possible through the kindness of the staff of the following institutions: the British Library and the Public Record Office in London; the Bodleian Library and the college libraries of Christ Church, Oriel College, and St Antony's College in Oxford; the Firestone and Mudd Libraries at Princeton University; the US National Archives in Washington DC; the Benaki Museum and the Parliament Library in Athens; ASO Head Office in Patras. I would like particularly to express my gratitude to the staff at the library of the Bank of Greece, where the bulk of my research was carried out. Their helpfulness and friendly patience made working there a pleasure.

A year's stay in Athens was facilitated through the generosity of the Leverhulme Trust. In Oxford, St Antony's College provided an environment where modern Greek studies could flourish. I owe a special debt to the Provost and Fellows of Oriel College, and the Dean and Students of Christ Church, whose hospitality and generosity I was able to enjoy over several years, first as Senior Scholar and then as Research Lecturer. Few graduate students can have been offered more beautiful surroundings in which to complete their research. I would also like to thank David Alberman and Brent Isaacs for valuable words of encouragement at critical moments, and my colleagues at Princeton for showing me new ways of looking at the subject. Peter Mandler, in particular, undertook the difficult task of reading the entire manuscript as it neared completion. He, Dimitri Gondicas, and Steve Kotkin suggested a number of improvements. Robert Faber, Tony Morris, and the editorial staff at OUP put up with an infuriating author.

Those to whom I owe the most I have left till last. I want to thank Deb for tolerating, as long as we have been together, my immersion in this work. Apart from her forbearance and encouragement, her tough judgement and instinctive suspicion of academic pretensions have kept me on my toes and become a sort of touchstone for me. For all these things I owe her a debt it is difficult to express. Nor will I try to put into words what I owe my parents. This book is for them.

CONTENTS

Part IV Response, 1932–1936

Part V Towards Dictatorship

Appendices

ABBREVIATIONS

AET	Archive of Emmanouil Tsouderos, Bank of Greece, Athens
AEV	Archive of Eleftherios Venizelos, Benaki Museum, Athens
AKV	Archive of Kyriakos Varvaressos, Bank of Greece, Athens
AOI	*Agrotiki Oikonomia*
AOKE	*Archeion Oikonomikon kai Koinonikon Epistimon*
AOS	Anotaton Oikonomikon Symvoulion
AS	MNE., *Annuaire Statistique* (Athens)
ASO	Avtonomos Stafidikos Organismos
BIS	Bank of International Settlements
DATE	*Deltion tis Agrotikis Trapezas tis Ellados*
DEVE/A	*Deltion Emporikou kai Viomichanikou Epimelitiriou/ton Athinon*
DGFP	*Documents on German Foreign Policy*
DOT	Department of Trade
E	*Ergasia*
EKDO	*Epitheorisis Koinonikis kai Dimosionomikis Oikonomias*
EO	AOS, *Elliniki Oikonomia*
ESG	*Efimeris ton Syzitiseon tis Gerousias*
ESV	*Efimeris ton Syzitiseon tis Voulis*
ETVA	Ethniki Trapeza Viomichanikis Anaptyxis
EV	*Eleftheron Vima*
EX	*Efimeris tou Chrimatistiriou*
FO	British Foreign Office Archives, Public Record Office, London
FRUS	US State Department, *Foreign Relations of the United States*
GD	*Georgikon Deltion*
GPEK	Grafeion Prostasias Ellinikon Kapnon
IBA, YR/HYR etc.	Ionian Bank Archives, Yearly/Half-Yearly Report etc., St Antony's College, Oxford
IFC	International Financial Commission
ILO	International Labour Office
KEPES	Kentriki Epitropi Prostasias Ellinikou Sitou
LLC	League Loans Committee

LN	League of Nations
LNFC	League of Nations Financial Committee
MA	*Messager d'Athènes*
MNE	Ministry for the National Economy (Ypourgeion Ethnikis Oikonomias)
NBG	National Bank of Greece (Ethniki Trapeza tis Ellados)
OA	*Oikonomologos Athinon*
OE	NBG, *Oikonomiki Epetiris*
OT	*Oikonomikos Tachydromos*
P	*Ploutos*
PSV	*Praktika ton Synedriaseon tis Voulis*
RIIA	Royal Institute of International Affairs
RSC	Refugee Settlement Commission
USNA	US State Department files, National Archives, Washington, DC
VE	*Viomichaniki Epitheorisis*

I

INTRODUCTION

I

ISSUES AND MECHANISMS

In November 1929 a young professor of economics, Xenophon Zolotas, noted that everyone in Athens seemed to be asking the same question: was there an economic crisis in Greece or not? A year or so later there could be little doubt: the Governor of the central bank opened his annual report, delivered on Valentine's Day 1931, with a long account of the impact of the world depression on Greece. The following year, after his resignation, his successor Tsouderos was warning his audience of the new 'sinister phase' that the crisis had entered with Britain's abandonment of gold. *Two* years later, in language far removed from the restrained tones generally adopted by central bankers, Tsouderos declared that 'the year 1932, for our country, as well as for the whole world, has been above all a year of agony!'[1]

That the period from 1929 to 1932 constituted a watershed in the life of the country was quite clear to contemporary observers. The nature of this watershed, and its consequences—for the economy, the role of the state, and ultimately for politics—are the subject of this book. It sets out to analyse what happened when, as a consequence of the economic depression, Greece was forced to abandon its traditional reliance on agricultural exports, remittances, and foreign loans and turn instead towards a policy of autarkic development based upon domestic sources of growth. This change of course had as few precedents as the crisis which had brought it about, but one thing was clear: the disintegration of an open international economy left Greece less dependent economically upon the outside world than ever before. By the time that General Metaxas became dictator in August 1936 both the advantages and drawbacks of this new type of development had become apparent.

The structure of the Greek economy between the two world wars would not have inspired the casual observer with confidence: reliant

---

[1] X. Zolotas, *Nomismatikai meletai* (Athens, 1932), 58; Bank of Greece, *Report for the Year 1930 of the Governor of the Bank of Greece* (Athens, 1931), 1–2; *The Economic Situation in Greece and the Bank of Greece in 1931* (Athens, 1932), 8; *The Economic Situation in Greece and the Bank of Greece in 1932* (Athens, 1933), 3.

upon a backward and overcrowded agricultural sector, the country could only pay for vital imports of food and raw materials with the proceeds of a few unreliable export commodities and a stream of invisible earnings from abroad, chiefly from its merchant marine and the remittances of its emigrants. The state had incurred an enormous foreign debt to help pay for ambitious public works and for the extraordinary task of resettling the refugees, more than a million of whom had arrived in Greece from the Near East. In the countryside, fertile land was scarce and in the shadow of the mountains which made communications expensive and difficult. The road and rail network was among the most primitive in Europe. In the towns, small inefficient industries grew where tariffs protected them, unable to sustain an adequate level of employment for a rapidly growing population.

It might seem obvious that such a country would be hard hit by any downturn in the international economy. Few observers would have thought the chances of a swift recovery high. Yet that was precisely what happened. When the Liberal Government reluctantly abandoned the gold standard in 1932, resources which had lain idle in the 1920s, when domestic producers had been unable to compete with imports, were now brought into play. Both agricultural and industrial output grew rapidly; indeed, only the Soviet Union and Japan outstripped Greece's industrial growth rate in the early 1930s. In 1936 a British report on economic conditions in the Balkans stated that 'in Greece there has been an almost spectacular recovery'.[2]

In this book I have sought to analyse both the crisis itself and the mixture of accidents, deliberate policies, and market responses which lay behind this remarkable upswing. One of the earliest and fastest in Europe, it combined impressive short-run growth with increasing structural inefficiencies and social tensions. In many respects Greece's experience in these years can shed light on the way countries outside the developed West took advantage of the international depression to stimulate recovery and further growth from within the domestic economy. Yet this process, which must despite its imperfections be accounted some sort of economic success, coincided with unambiguous political failure. For the years of economic recovery also saw the decline of parliamentary democracy in Greece. The most important and powerful government of the inter-war period, the Liberal administration of Eleftherios Venizelos, collapsed in the aftermath of the financial crisis of

[2] RIIA, *The Balkan States*, 1: *Economic* (London, 1936), 63.

1931-2. Several years of constitutional uncertainty, punctuated by military interventions, culminated in the imposition of Metaxas's dictatorship in 1936. How can we reconcile these seemingly contradictory developments in the economic and political spheres? I have looked for the answer in the new demands which *both* crisis *and* recovery made of the state and the governing class.

Because the study of the economic history of modern Greece is still in its infancy, I have been obliged to provide a broad descriptive backdrop to the events at the heart of my analysis. As recently as 1977 Saul and Milward, casting around for works to recommend on the subject, could find nothing since Zolotas's *Griechenland auf dem Wege zur Industrialisierung*, written in 1926! Since then, though some general studies have appeared in English, including Jackson and Lampe's pioneering and massive *Balkan Economic History: 1550–1950*, and though important monographs have begun to appear in Greek, we still await any detailed work in the area in English. I therefore felt it was necessary to sketch in an account of Greece's economic development from 1912 (when victory in the First Balkan War extended the country's boundaries to roughly their current limits) until the onset of the world depression around 1929. This is to be found in Part II. Readers who wish to move directly to the core of this work should begin with the analysis of the crisis in Part III. Throughout I rely on statistics drawn from bank reports, the publications of specialist agencies such as the Cotton Institute and the Offices for the Protection of Greek Tobacco, as well as the weekly economic Press: this data is generally of a high standard and does not appear to have been much used before. In Appendix 1 I have also provided details of my own crude estimates of agricultural and industrial production in this period. I leave it to others with a better training in statistics to improve on these. The existing estimates of national income, unemployment totals, and certain other variables are so unreliable that I decided to avoid them completely.

Built on such foundations, this book can offer nothing approaching a definitive account of these years. Its aim is rather different: to open up a previously neglected area in the historiography of modern Greece and to show its importance for the history of the country as a whole. It may be regarded as an effort to follow the advice of the late Nikos Svoronos, who once suggested that it was time for historians to turn away from the well-researched theme of foreign interference in Greek affairs towards the study of the interplay of domestic political, economic, and social forces.

Until recently the historiography of modern Greece was dominated, on the one hand, by an emphasis on the importance of foreign influences in Greek affairs, and, on the other, by a narrow concentration upon the activities of the political élite, the so-called 'political world' (*politikos kosmos*). In comparison with political history, social history attracted few scholars, economic history almost none.[3] Within Greece the political conservatism which reigned in the universities for some three decades from the end of the civil war discouraged the critical study of the recent past on any terms; the exciting intellectual developments of the inter-war years were replaced by a sterile and highly nationalistic conformity. Outside Greece history itself as a mode of understanding the country was long overshadowed and deeply influenced by political science and anthropology. During the post-war 'miracle' it was these disciplines which apparently offered the best insights into the supposed transition from tradition to modernity. Anthropological studies of rural Greece, of which perhaps the most influential was John Campbell's *Honour, Family and Patronage*, introduced concepts which became part of the standard vocabulary of many historians of the modern Greek state. Clientelism, for example, became a key to analysing not merely political relations within Greece but also the nature of Greece's relations with foreign powers. Later, the view that presented Greece as the 'client' of more powerful 'patron' states was reinforced by dependency theory: dependency was invoked to explain, not just economic exploitation, but, with greater frequency, political developments such as the civil war or the 1967 coup.

When I wrote this study I was dissatisfied with this way of analysing Greek politics. Who would try to deny the massive influence foreign powers have exerted in Greece's internal affairs since its independence?

---

[3] For comprehensive reviews of recent historiographical trends, see *Synchrona Themata*, 35–7 (Dec. 1988); also, A. Kitroeff, 'Continuity and Change in Contemporary Greek Historiography', *European History Quarterly*, 19(2) (Apr. 1989), 269–98. One of the main beneficiaries of what Kitroeff hails as the current 'revolution in Greek historiography' (p. 274) has been the study of the inter-war period. The following recent works should be mentioned: M. Psalidopoulos, *I krisi tou 1929 kai oi ellines oikonomologoi* (Athens, 1989); H. Fleischer and N. Svoronos (eds.), *I Ellada 1936–44: Diktatoria, katochi, antistasi* (Athens, 1989); G. Mavrogordatos and C. Chadziiosif (eds.), *Venizelismos kai astikos eksynchronismos* (Irákleion, 1988); K. Kostis, *Oi trapezes kai i krisi, 1929–32* (Athens, 1986); *Agrotiki oikonomia kai Georgiki Trapeza* (Athens, 1987). M. Dritsa, *Viomichania kai trapezes stin Ellada tou mesopolemou* (Athens, 1990); K. Kostis and V. Tsokopoulos, *Oi trapezes stin Ellada, 1898–1928* (Athens, 1988); L. Leontidou, *Poleis tis siopis: Ergatikos epoikismos tis Athinas kai ton Peiraia, 1909–1940* (Athens, 1989); D. Tziovas, *Oi metamorphoseis tou ethnismou kai to ideologima tis ellinikotitas sto mesopolemo* (Athens, 1989) came to my notice too late to be used in the preparation of this book.

Nevertheless, in stressing the omnipresence of the 'foreign finger' (as Greeks term it) one runs the risk of underestimating the role played by the domestic political élite. Svoronos has warned us that the view that Greece is 'merely a stage for puppets whose strings are moved by alien hands' is 'naive for a historian, a mortal disease for history itself and an unacceptable alibi for politicians'.[4] It seemed instructive to examine the behaviour of the Greek political world in a period when foreign influence suddenly declined. This is what happened after 1932 as the crisis shifted power from creditor to debtor, from London, Geneva, and New York to Athens, from the international arena to the closed economy. As existing trade and financial arrangements were thrown into disarray, the Greeks were able to renegotiate the terms of their relationship with their former economic partners and patrons—British bankers, French merchants, American business men. Economic pressure from London and Paris could not suddenly be ignored, but it was abruptly curtailed by the collapse of the liberal economic order of the 1920s, and this gave Greek policy-makers new room to manœuvre. The question is: what use did they make of it?

The answer involved examining the way in which the economic crisis transformed the role of the state and the politicians' reactions to these changes; this, in turn, required an examination of economic policy-making. The shift towards import-substitution in agriculture, the acceleration of industrialization and private capital accumulation, the introduction of restrictions on trade, debt default, and currency depreciation all made new demands on Greece's political élite. Their efforts to cope with these changes, and with the social tensions that emerged at the same time, brought them into contact with a world of peasants, workers, and merchants, a world whose boundaries extended beyond the narrow confines of the Athenian political salons and military barracks which in the past have tended to provide the setting for discussions of Greek politics. Viewing the politicians in their social and economic context will, I hope, offer a new angle from which to examine familiar questions about constitutionalism, civil–military relations, and the stability of parliamentary institutions.

The political life of these years is generally portrayed in terms of a deep division between two opposing camps (the *ethnikos dichasmos*, or 'national schism'). Veremis and others have traced out the lines of this conflict on the élite plane between the republican supporters of the

---

[4] N. Svoronos, 'Greek History, 1940–1950: The Main Problems', in J. Iatrides (ed.), *Greece in the 1940s: A Nation in Crisis* (Hanover, NH, 1981), 2.

Liberal politician Venizelos and his royalist opponents. They depict this chiefly as a struggle between competing (and shifting) alliances of civilian and military factions for control of the state apparatus. More recently, in a rich and thought-provoking work, Mavrogordatos has extended the analysis to bring mass politics into the picture; in his view, the *dichasmos* at the élite level mirrored certain fundamental social cleavages.[5] His argument holds up well for certain aspects of Greek society, notably the strong regional differences in the electoral support for the two camps. The *dichasmos* pitted the staunchly anti-Venizelist and royalist territories of the pre-1912 Kingdom of Greece against the Venizelist New Provinces of northern Greece and the islands. But did these regional divisions reflect differences of ideology and class? This is more difficult to prove.

The ideological significance of the rise of Venizelos's Liberal Party has been one of the most hotly disputed issues in modern Greek history. An early view, shared by many Marxists and Liberals alike and dating back to the inter-war years, was that the Goudi uprising and Venizelos's assumption of the premiership in 1910 constituted a sort of Greek 1848, reflecting the triumph of a bourgeois class over conservative, if not aristocratic, élites. But the lack of a substantial land-owning class in Greece, hardly changed by the acquisition of Thessaly in 1881, makes it difficult to accept the argument that the élites in power before Venizelos came from a background very different from that of his supporters. Merchants and local notables provided the leaders for a society which lacked either aristocracy, industrial proletariat, or landless farm workers. What *was* noticeable in the late nineteenth century was the growth of the state bureaucracy, control over which became an important source of power and patronage. To some extent, Venizelos and his *novi homines* were aiming to oust established politicians whose power resided in their jealously guarded hold over the state's resources.

This is why, for Mavrogordatos, the *dichasmos* pitted a 'new' entrepreneurial bourgeoisie led by Venizelos and his Liberals against an established 'state bourgeoisie' loyal to King Constantine. The one, he argues, espoused a 'pragmatic irredentism' allied to plans for state expansion and increased economic power in the Near East; the other a 'romantic and utopian irredentism' based around a 'traditional military–bureaucratic regime under the monarchy'. But such a sharp division—if

[5] T. Veremis, *Oi epemvaseis tou stratou stin elliniki politiki: 1916–1936* (Athens, 1977); G. Mavrogordatos, *Stillborn Republic: Social Coalitions and Party Strategies in Greece: 1922–1936* (Berkeley, Calif., 1983).

it had ever existed in this form at all—was rendered redundant by the 1922 defeat in Asia Minor. In the inter-war period, as Mavrogordatos himself suggests, the distance between the two camps narrowed. In their view of society and their relation to it, Greek royalist and republican politicians had much in common. The two groups overlapped to a surprising degree in terms of economic policy. The Liberals, it is true, were the more imaginative, but their supposed opponents often ended up following their lead once they took power. Only at the margin of the republican camp was there talk of radical socio-economic reform. Otherwise both groups seem to have regarded themselves as representatives and defenders of the *astikos kosmos* (the 'bourgeois world'). Although the economic crisis did reveal some differences of opinion between them, especially over the merits of industrialization, it is difficult in general to argue that the passions of the *dichasmos* stemmed from a serious clash of ideologies.[6]

Until native Greek concepts of class have been further investigated, it is difficult to be sure about the social implications of the *dichasmos*; the evidence available at present suggests that regional loyalties and special interests rather than class differences provided its underpinnings. On the basis of Mavrogordatos's own calculations of inter-war election results, it seems that a close connection between a specific social group and a political camp existed only in the case of the tobacco workers and the small Communist Party; *neither* of the two main blocs, Venizelists and anti-Venizelists, possessed an exclusive base of support in any given class. What was at stake was control of the state apparatus, and in particular of the armed forces, rather than competing visions of society.

Thus in one important respect the emphasis of earlier historians on civil–military relations was fully justified. Most Greek politicians in the inter-war years worried more about the military than they did about broad economic or social questions. In general they preferred debating the future of the Republic, or the responsibility for Greece's defeat in Turkey in 1922, to the more mundane complexities of fiscal policy. In

---

[6] Cf. G. Dertilis, *Koinonikos metaschimatismos kai stratiotiki epemvasi, 1880–1909* (Athens, 1977); K. Tsoukalas, *Koinoniki anaptyxi kai kratos: I synkrotisi tou dimosiou chorou stin Ellada* (Athens, 1981); Mavrogordatos, *Stillborn Republic*, 121–36; data correlating social categories and political camps in *Stillborn Republic*, 138–82; on the implications of Mavrogordatos's statistical findings for his own thesis, cf. the review by Keith Legg in *Journal of Modern Greek Studies*, 2(1) (May 1984), 137–9; see also the illuminating article by C. Chadziiosif, 'I venizelogenis antipolitefsis sto Venizelo kai i politiki anasyntaxi tou astismou sto mesopolemo', in Mavrogordatos and Chadziiosif (eds.), *Venizelismos kai astikos eksynchronismos*, 439–58.

the winter of 1934–5 Venizelos and Metaxas—the former premier and the future dictator—fought out the First World War all over again in the pages of the Athens Press. But the fury of the *dichasmos* between republicans and royalists obscured a more fundamental deficiency of the Greek political élite: their limited conception of the role of politics and the state in a time of social and economic transformation. In other words, we should try to see the *dichasmos* within the context of a more profound crisis of inter-war parliamentary democracy in the face of turbulent economic change. Despite the many specifically Greek ingredients of this story—notably the charismatic and paternalistic flavour of politics—this was part of a more widespread phenomenon. It was closely connected with the tensions of what Hirschman, referring to similar trends in Latin America, has described as the transition from the 'entrepreneurial' to the 'reform' stage of development.[7] In the longer run it was *this* crisis, rather than the old internecine struggles within the political élite, which would shape the new forms of ideological conflict in the following two decades, both in Greece and elsewhere.

The moment of transition, the point at which the extraordinary pace of economic change became visible, was the collapse of the international economic order after 1929. This ended the entrepreneurial growth patterns employed in the underdeveloped world in the preceding decade, and altered the tasks facing politicians and the state. Trade slumps, debt default, import-substitution all formed part of a break with the past. What would come next? To what extent could the political élite secure continued economic growth or greater distributive fairness? What *were* the economic options in the early 1930s for an underdeveloped economy?

Despite an apparent air of prosperity, the international economy during the 1920s rested on insecure foundations. Although reconstruction and stabilization policies had enabled most countries to return to the gold standard by 1928, the international monetary system was weaker than it had been before 1914. The development of fiduciary note issues throughout the world had increased more rapidly than the gold reserves by which they were legally backed. London's position as an international lender of last resort had been weakened by Britain's legacy of war debts to the USA. New York and Paris had amassed large gold reserves, but

---

[7] A. Hirschman, 'The Turn to Authoritarianism in Latin America and the Search for its Economic Determinants', in D. Collier (ed.), *The New Authoritarianism in Latin America* (Princeton, NJ, 1979), esp. pp. 87–97.

were unprepared to take responsibility for management of the international monetary system. The whole quarrel over the link between
inter-Allied war debts and reparations hindered economic co-operation
between Britain, France, and the USA.

In the second half of the decade there was a massive flow of capital
from the creditor nations to the rest of the world, initially for projects
designed to repair wartime dislocation to public finances, but gradually
for a wider variety of schemes, few of which were self-financing.
Countries assumed a burden of debt which could only be sustained by
further borrowing. The position of many primary producers was made
worse by the downward trend in world prices for many primary exports.
In some cases they suffered income losses through unfavourable movements in the terms of trade, but even where these did not occur, falling
export prices meant that the burden of servicing the foreign debt
increased in real terms.

In 1929 the net flow of capital towards the debtor nations was
reversed as funds were attracted back into the USA by rising share
prices and a business boom. This movement back towards the USA was
accelerated during the autumn, when the Wall Street crash produced a
liquidity crisis and forced a repatriation of funds. Controversy rages in
the USA over the causes of the sudden contraction in 1929, but whether
real or monetary factors were responsible, the effect on the international
economy was much the same: many countries faced balance of payments
difficulties and were forced to choose between draconian deflationary
measures at home or abandoning the gold standard.

A number of Latin American countries, which felt the effects of the
cessation of US lending more directly than elsewhere, left the gold
standard in 1930. Those countries that remained on gold pursued
deflationary policies which reduced liquidity, hit business sales, and led
to an increase in the number of bankruptcies. Deflation reduced
producers' incomes and increased real debt burdens. In addition the
general decline in confidence in the stability of national monetary
arrangements led to speculative withdrawals of gold and exchange,
which further weakened domestic banking systems and made the task
facing central banks more difficult.

The next stage of the crisis unfolded in the deflation-prone economies of Central Europe. Commercial banks throughout the region
held substantial assets in local industry; as profits and security prices
fell, many bank loans had to be written off. Bank lending to agricultural
producers created similar problems. At first small banks in difficulties

were taken over by larger ones. But in May 1931 it was revealed that the Credit-Anstalt, a major Austrian bank, was in difficulties, after absorbing the losses of weaker banks. This led to a major financial crisis in Austria, which soon spread through Central and Eastern Europe. In Germany a combination of fears—news of the Anstalt affair, as well as a domestically induced loss of confidence in financial markets—led to a general run on the banks and inspired the Hoover moratorium on all intergovernmental debts in June.

Despite the continuing bank crisis in Germany, the major creditor nations, Britain, France, and the USA, were unable to agree terms for fresh injections of credit to stabilize the situation. Pressure now switched to sterling. The Bank of England had funds tied up in Eastern Europe. Its defence of the gold standard was made more difficult by the publication of the May Report in late July, which gave a bleak forecast of the budget position and recommended that assistance be sought from Paris and New York. In August the Labour Government fell over the question of whether the gold standard should be maintained at the cost of domestic deflation. A national government was formed, but continued withdrawals of foreign exchange put the Bank of England under pressure once more. On 21 September sterling was taken off gold.

Twenty-five countries followed the British example. Devaluation was accompanied by measures to conserve scarce foreign exchange reserves and reduce imports: exchange controls, import quotas, and raised tariffs. As international trade declined, governments switched their attention to reinforcing domestic producers, who were anyway often encouraged by the new constellations of relative prices which emerged as a result of leaving the gold standard. The effect of decreased export earnings on the balance of payments was counterbalanced by lower imports and debt defaults. The significance of the 1929–32 crisis as a watershed in the evolution of the international economy remains beyond dispute. It marked the end of the attempt to return to the pre-1914 liberal order, characterized by attachment to the gold standard and an open trading environment. As the last remnants of this order disintegrated, economic policy became more complex, less the result of automatic adjustment—what one scholar has termed 'the triumph of discretion over automaticity'.[8] Government élites and institutions had to

---

[8] A. Cairncross and B. Eichengreen, *Sterling in Decline* (Oxford, 1983), 4.

operate under new conditions. Uncertainty increased, but so did the room for innovation.

Economists have devoted more attention to the causes of the crisis than to the ways countries recovered from it. Until recently most analyses of the impact of the 1929–32 crisis on the underdeveloped world concentrated on the international transmission of the crisis, chiefly through trends in trade balances. The characterization of countries as 'primary producers', identifying them in terms of their function within the international economy, together with a neglect of their potential for internally generated economic growth, seemed to justify such an emphasis. According to Kindleberger 'in these economies the level of exports is generally a critical autonomous variable in the determination of national income—more important than investment, which is often dependent on export sales, and surely more so than government expenditures, which cannot be independent, because of the lack of a domestic money market at home . . .'[9] Raupach stressed the effect of deteriorating terms of trade and plummeting exports in his article on the impact of the Depression on Eastern Europe.[10] Lee emphasized the vulnerability of primary producers to a reduction in export earnings.

This last scholar, however, introduced some new elements into the debate. He recognized the enormous variety of individual country experiences, and also made the point that income falls were more severe in the USA and Germany between 1929 and 1932 than in many poorer countries. Indeed, he concluded his 1969 article by suggesting that 'it may be . . . that the great depression, generally regarded as one of the main economic disasters of modern times, was in fact a major catalyst, stimulating economic development in some underdeveloped countries by forcibly diverting their resources to more productive purposes . . .'[11]

More recent studies have followed this line of thought, shifting their emphasis to the impact of the international crisis on the domestic economy, examining the mechanisms of recovery in periphery countries, and charting continuities with patterns of development initiated in

---

[9] C. Kindleberger, *The World in Depression: 1929–1939* (London, 1973), 190.

[10] H. Raupach, 'The Impact of the Great Depression in Eastern Europe', *Journal of Contemporary History*, 4 (1969), 77–85.

[11] C. Lee, 'The Effects of the Depression on Primary-Producing Countries', *Journal of Contemporary History*, 4 (1969), 139–155.

the previous decade.[12] Such an approach has several virtues: in the first place, whereas the story of how the crisis was transmitted to and experienced by these countries is well known, this cannot be said of the recovery stage. There were many routes to recovery and many blind alleys: why did some countries flourish while others stagnated? A case-study such as this work may help answer this question. Secondly, policy-makers in these countries reacted to the crisis on the basis of their experience of the previous decade. Their priorities and values can only be understood when seen against the backdrop of what they had striven for earlier in their careers. Thirdly, setting the *domestic* economy at centre stage provides a way of judging the range of policy options available to governing élites; no longer can they plausibly be presented as the helpless victims of international circumstance. What was true during the crisis may no longer have been so during the recovery stage. There were—as this study will illustrate in the case of Greece— advantages as well as disadvantages to backwardness.

Our analysis of recovery processes on the periphery in the early 1930s should begin with the question of the exchange rate. It was this, together with the existing distribution of domestic resources and the ease with which they could be reallocated between and within sectors, *not* the possibility of Keynesian-style fiscal policies (which would have been unacceptable to most ruling élites at the time), which constituted the main determinants of economic outcomes after the slump. The immediate impact on the balance of payments via reduced export earnings and changes in the direction of net capital flows could either be met by stringent domestic deflation or by leaving the gold standard and letting the exchange rate take most of the strain. There can be no doubt that in the 1930s depreciation eased the path to early recovery. Resisting depreciation, as Argentina did, for example, meant waiting for demand in export markets to recover—not entirely desirable in the conditions of the time.[13] The Greek depreciation was the most severe in Europe and

[12] e.g. M. Jackson and J. Lampe, *Balkan Economic History, 1550–1950* (Bloomington, Ind., 1982); M. Kaser (ed.), *The Economic History of Eastern Europe: 1919–1975*, i (Oxford, 1985); R. Thorp (ed.), *Latin America in the 1930s* (London, 1984). Angus Maddison states in a recent study of the international dimensions of the crisis: 'In discussions of the 1930s it is too readily assumed that the whole decade was one of depression, but there was in fact a vigorous recovery process from 1932 to 1937 in Latin America.' See 'Growth, Crisis and Interdependence, 1929–38 and 1973–83', unpublished paper, OECD, Paris, 1985.

[13] B. Eichengreen and J. Sachs, 'Exchange Rates and Economic Recovery in the 1930s', *Journal of Economic History*, 45(4) (1985), 925–46. On Argentina, see Thorp (ed.), *Latin America in the 1930s*, p. 200.

this fact must surely be connected with the speed of her recovery. Devaluation was generally a policy forced upon governments rather than adopted consciously by them for its expansionary effects. The abandonment of the gold standard was regarded by most policy-makers at the time as a mark of economic mismanagement. Yet such a move was capable of stimulating the domestic economy.

This could come about in at least four ways: (1) relative price shifts which altered the structure of domestic output; (2) 'real' devaluations, which were possible, since wages and prices did not always increase to wipe out the effect of the exchange rate depreciation; (3) freer domestic monetary policy; (4) debt default and the consequent windfall gains, which often followed close behind depreciation. Let us examine these in turn.

(1) Devaluation affected relative prices within the domestic economy. Prices of importables rose relative to those of exports and non-traded goods, encouraging producers where they could to adapt accordingly. In the Greek case, this provided encouragement for import-substituting agriculture and for domestic manufacturing, which was almost entirely directed towards the home market. And not only in Greece: in Latin America and the Balkan states the cultivated area expanded considerably in the early 1930s compared with the late 1920s. In Britain and the USA, by contrast, it shrank. Similarly, industrial output grew 35% or more between 1932 and 1935 in Greece, Brazil, Chile, and Mexico. Of the developed economies, only Germany grew more rapidly, and there growth was barely sufficient to bring output back to the 1929 level, whereas this was surpassed by 1935 in many periphery countries. Often this growth resulted in the increased use of capacity which had been laid down but under-utilized in the 1920s.[14]

(2) Policy-makers in many countries had feared the inflationary consequences of leaving the gold standard. To be sure, after a currency was allowed to depreciate domestic prices rose but the positive effects usually outweighed the negative ones. The real value of domestic debts was diminished, relieving indebted peasants and other products. At the same time, of those countries whose currencies depreciated heavily in the 1930s, only Chile experienced a surge in prices which outweighed

---

[14] For various examples see: Thorp (ed.), *Latin America in the 1930s*, p. 150 (Brazil), pp. 233–5 (Mexico); Alice Teichova, 'The Potential and Actual Exploitation of Natural Resources and Industrial Structure, 1919–1949', *Papers in East European Economics*, 41 (Feb. 1974), *passim*; Tore Hanisch, 'The Economic Crisis in Norway in the 1930s', *Scandinavian Economic History Review*, 26(2) (1978), 145–55.

the extent of the depreciation. Several Latin American countries managed to achieve improvements in price competitiveness equivalent to those gained in Eastern Europe through drastic domestic deflation (Table 1.1). Wage data for periphery countries is scarce, but there is evidence to suggest that nominal wages were sluggish, certainly in the early stages of recovery.[15] The leading industrial sectors in the upswing tended to be those which could take advantage of the large pool of available unskilled, low-waged workers; this meant above all textiles —which spearheaded industrial recovery in numerous countries.

(3) Leaving the gold standard also meant that monetary growth could be determined independently of movements in the country's foreign exchange reserves. Although growth in real money supply tended to be higher in countries which remained on gold, this largely reflected sharply falling domestic prices. Increases in nominal money supplies,

TABLE 1.1. *Depreciation and prices on the periphery, 1929–1935 (%)*

Country	Depreciation of national currency	Movement in wholesale price index	'Real' depreciation/ appreciation of national currency
Greece	−44.7	+10.0	−34.7
Czechoslovakia	−16.5	−23.0	−39.5
Hungary	−0.5	−22.0	−22.5
Poland	+0.1	−45.0	−44.9
Romania	−9.9	−48.0	−57.9
Bulgaria	−1.5	−45.0	−46.5
Yugoslavia	−22.9	−35.5	−58.4
Argentina	−53.7	+0.8	−52.9
Brazil	−58.3	(−0.1)[a]	(−58.4)
Chile	−75.0	+79.0	+4.0
Mexico	−65.8	−9.0	−74.8
Peru	−64.8	+0.2	−64.6

[a] Movement in cost-of-living index.

Sources: LN, *International Statistical Yearbook: 1936–1937* (Geneva, 1938), 223–6; LN, *International Statistical Yearbook: 1937–1938* (Geneva, 1939), 231–5; LN, *Public Debt: 1914–1946* (New York, 1946); M. Jackson and J. Lampe, *Balkan Economic History 1550–1950* (Bloomington, Ind., 1982), 472.

[15] Thorp (ed.), *Latin America in the 1930s*, p. 24.

which occurred only in devaluing countries, were often an indication that monetary policy could be made with an eye to the requirements of the domestic economy. In many periphery countries new central banks had been set up in the 1920s as part of more general reconstruction schemes. These newcomers had had to fight for their existence in an unwelcoming world. Not only did they face hostility from the commercial banks they were supposed to supervise and the governments who had agreed to their establishment, but they were also entrusted with the task of defending currency parities at the very time the international monetary system was about to collapse. Perhaps the best example is that of Yugoslavia, where the National Bank was pledged to defend the dinar at a rate set in the very month the Credit-Anstalt's troubles became known throughout Europe.[16] Paradoxically, by liberating themselves from the gold standard system, they were in a better position to strengthen themselves domestically. Thus the 1930s saw many previously weak central banks take control of domestic banking policy and achieve a new authority. If the best way to achieve this was by making credit available to troubled commercial banks, or increasing loans to a straitened state administration cut off from international money markets, then so much the better for the domestic economy.

(4) Exchange rate policy was closely bound up with the question of debt default. Countries which regarded it as important to continue servicing their external debt were reluctant to devalue, since this would increase the domestic currency burden of the debt service. On the other hand, a decline in exchange reserves might make devaluation necessary for ensuring some sort of monetary stability, and, once a currency had been devalued, default was often not far off.

For the debtor country, default had two main merits. Firstly, it eased pressure on the balance of payments by reducing the country's foreign exchange requirements. In effect, it was a form of unilateral reaction to the reversal in international capital flows between the 'centre' and the 'periphery' which had taken place after 1928. Secondly, it improved the position of the public finances of the debtor state, and freed resources which could be ploughed back into the domestic economy rather than transferred abroad. When it became clear that the money-markets of London, Paris, and New York could no longer function—and this was obvious certainly by the ineffectual Lausanne Conference in June 1932—there was little reason not to adopt this course of action. The

[16] RIIA, *The Balkan States*, pp. 84–5.

story of Greece's protracted negotiations with her creditors shows how powerless the latter were. Few countries defaulted on as high a percentage of their debt as did Greece; but most introduced partial suspensions or restrictions on the transfer of funds in blocked accounts—which amounted to much the same thing from the creditors' point of view.[17]

Default, however, also emphasized that the international crisis had forced countries to finance domestic economic development out of their own resources. The stimulus provided by devaluation led to rapid rates of growth through import-substitution over the short term; by the mid-1930s, however, various problems had begun to emerge. The advantages offered by barter trade in the early years began to be eroded as prices spiralled upwards, fuelling domestic inflation. Autarky often led farmers to retreat from the hazards of the market back into self-sufficiency, which—it soon became obvious—was a cul-de-sac rather than a new avenue towards greater prosperity. Many 'reactive' countries—to use Diaz Alejandro's terminology—ran up against a shortage of capital and found that they had encouraged the development of an inefficient, ill-equipped manufacturing base, incapable of competing on world markets.[18] By 1936 shortages of labour, especially skilled labour, increased the pressure on industrialists to grant real as opposed to nominal wage rises. They simultaneously faced rising capital costs as industry and government competed for a dwindling pool of domestic savings.

A second problem was that industrial growth under autarky often displayed the classic symptoms of imperfect competition. Leading manufacturers merged or established cartels, and though governments were rarely enthusiastic about such tendencies, they did not always counteract them effectively.[19] They tried to curb industrial expansion through limiting the amounts of foreign exchange which could be spent on imports of machinery or raw materials. But the effect of these restrictions was to prevent the entry of newcomers into markets dominated by established firms, and to remove the incentives and even the

---

[17] Maddison, 'Growth, Crisis and Interdependence', p. 27.

[18] Thorp (ed.), *Latin America in the 1930s*, pp. 41–2; for the Balkan States, see G. Ranki, 'Problems of South European Economic Development (1918–38)', in G. Arrighi (ed.), *Semiperipheral Development: The Politics of Southern Europe in the Twentieth Century* (London, 1985), p. 66.

[19] Jackson and Lampe, *Balkan Economic History*, p. 492.

opportunity for the latter to modernize increasingly outdated plant and equipment. Hence the move towards autarky had drawbacks as well as advantages.

It would be misleading to conclude this brief discussion of recovery mechanisms without considering the influence of politics and ideology. Few people in authority in 1931 could see beyond the need to defend the gold standard, whilst in Italy and Spain, as well as Greece, governments at the turn of the decade expressed a rather self-congratulatory, if premature, confidence in their ability to escape the worst effects of the crisis.[20] When the Greek Parliament debated the government's handling of the crisis two months after Britain left gold, all the political parties agreed on the need to defend the drachma; none advocated following sterling. The British adviser to the Bank of Greece was almost alone in believing that it was 'not a question of Greece's keeping to the gold standard, but of the gold standard leaving Greece'.[21] We should recall that Yugoslavia only joined the gold standard in 1931, whilst Spanish politicians were seriously thinking of linking up with gold as late as 1934.

Ruling élites viewed defence of the currency as a patriotic duty; monetary (if not fiscal) orthodoxy became part of the nationalist armoury. In addition, of course, many people retained bitter memories of previous inflations, whether of the post-1918 boom, as in the case of Eastern Europe, or of the late nineteenth century, as for several countries in Latin America. Memories of the hyperinflation of the early 1920s explain the Polish decision to cling to gold—at the cost of a highly deflationary domestic policy—until 1936. One consequence of presenting the 'defence of the currency' in terms of national honour was that losing the 'battle'—as Primo de Rivera in Spain and Venizelos in Greece found to their cost—could destroy political prestige. Abandoning gold might make economic sense but it rarely impressed public opinion.

In Greece the economy adjusted rather more successfully than the politicians to the shock of the crisis. Politicians after 1932 were ready to claim the credit for what was in fact due either to good fortune (terms of trade movements; record cereal harvests in 1932–4) or to the unintended consequences of uncertain policies (the benefits of default). But in general the political élite remained wedded to *laissez-faire*, and

---

[20] J. Harrison, 'The Interwar Depression and the Spanish Economy', *Journal of European Economic History*, 12 (2) (Autumn 1983), 295–322; G. Toniolo, *L'economia dell'Italia fascista* (Laterza, 1980), 139.

[21] FO 371/15960 C2951/324, Ramsay–FO, 29 Mar. 1932.

resisted calls for more coherent state intervention in the economy. This
was partly for cultural and political reasons to be explored below; but it
was also true that they were simply far less interested in the economy
than in other matters such as relations with the military or the constitutional question. Their negligence had profound social consequences,
for the recovery brought with it new tensions in Greek society with
unmistakable overtones of class conflict. At the same time as speculators pushed up property prices in Athens suburbs, martial law was being
declared in Salonika and Kalamata, where unemployed tobacco workers
and current growers were protesting at the state's indifference to their
difficulties. Strategies of corporatist mediation, whose appearance in
Western Europe after 1918 has been analysed by Charles Maier, were
not even attempted in inter-war Greece, where strikes, demonstrations,
and other expressions of popular discontent were usually seen as forms
of 'anarchy'.[22] The inability of the politicians to control social conflict
in the early 1930s was an important factor behind the collapse of parliamentary democracy. The reasons for this must be traced to the
priorities and attitudes of the political élite. And so, before going on to
analyse developments in the economy, we should first look briefly at the
turbulent course and character of Greek politics at this time.

[22] C. Maier, *Recasting Bourgeois Europe: Economic Stabilisation in France, Germany and Italy in the Decade after World War* I (Princeton, NJ, 1975).

2

THE GREEK POLITICAL WORLD

Bien qu'on fasse chez nous beaucoup de vaine politique, tous nos partis sont d'accord sur les grands principes.

(S. Loverdos, *Messager d'Athènes*, 13–14 August 1934)

In October 1922 the young Ernest Hemingway, reporting for the *Toronto Daily Star*, witnessed the flight of refugees from eastern Thrace into Macedonia: 'twenty miles of carts drawn by cows, bullocks and muddy-flanked water buffalo, with exhausted, staggering men, women and children, blankets over their heads, walking blindly along in the rain beside their worldly goods'.[1]

To the small country which received them, the refugees were perhaps the saddest part of a legacy of burdens bequeathed by 10 years of fighting. Desperate and bedraggled, they marked the dismal end of Greece's irredentist dreams and the beginning of a new era of domestic challenges and transformations. The arrival of over 1 million new-comers in a country of less than 5 millions enormously complicated the arduous task of post-war reconstruction and worsened the country's long-standing demographic problem. The outlook was not promising: even before 1914 the Greek economy had been unable to provide sufficient work for the existing population, and many young men had crossed the Atlantic and settled in the USA. But in 1921 the USA clamped down on immigration: that safety-valve was no longer open. The post-war state thus inherited a massive social problem.

There was also another wartime inheritance, and this was one which poisoned the political system for the entire inter-war period. The *ethnikos dichasmos* (national schism), which arose over the issue of Greece's stance in the First World War, continued to divide politicians and exhaust their energies after 1918. This *dichasmos* became the most prominent feature of the Greek political landscape, and the responses of policy-makers to the economic crisis cannot be understood without

---

[1] Quoted in K. Andrews, *Athens Alive* (Athens, 1979), 306.

reference to it. It is therefore necessary to take a brief look at its history in order to make sense of the chaotic succession of elections, plebiscites, coups, and counter-coups which filled these years.

Greek politics had been dominated since 1910 by the dapper figure of Eleftherios Venizelos, who had made his name as a leader of the Cretan struggle for union with Greece and enlarged his reputation in the immediate pre-war years by the modernizing reforms undertaken nationally by his Liberal Party. His dramatic diplomatic successes at the post-war peace conferences made him known more widely, and led the young Harold Nicolson in a moment of admiration to rank him alongside Lenin as one of the leading figures in post-war Europe. For the American Henry Morgenthau he was 'this lovable man, whose personality combined all the elements that charm and impress'. Within Greece, his influence was more contentious, polarizing political sympathies into two camps—Venizelist and anti-Venizelist—which roughly corresponded to the division between republicans and royalists.[2]

In late 1914 Venizelos, then Prime Minister, had urged that Greece join the war on the side of the *Entente*, whose victory he believed would pave the way for the fulfilment of Greece's irredentist dreams. But he was opposed by King Constantine, who was no less of an irredentist but had a greater respect for Germany's military strength. This dispute generated constitutional strains which culminated in a virtual civil war in 1916–17 between the provisional government which Venizelos set up in Salonika and the official government in Athens. Venizelos enjoyed the backing of the *Entente* Powers and when the King was finally forced to leave the country, he returned to Athens. Royalist sympathizers in the Army and civil service were removed from their posts and three years of Liberal rule began.

But in November 1920 the Liberal Party quite unexpectedly lost the general election, and a month later the Greeks voted in a national plebiscite to restore Constantine to the throne. The tables were now turned and Venizelist sympathizers were replaced by royalists. However, Dimitri Gounaris's royalist Government continued the policy which Venizelos had initiated of establishing a Greek military presence in Asia Minor, only to collapse in 1922 as this policy foundered on the rocks of Turkish nationalism. In what became known simply as the

[2] H. Nicolson, *Peacemaking 1919* (New York, 1931), 271; H. Morgenthau, *I was Sent to Athens* (New York, 1929), 85.

katastrofi, the Greek population of Asia Minor was uprooted, and while Smyrna burned, thousands of refugees made their way to Greek soil. A group of rebellious junior Army officers with Venizelist sympathies formed a 'revolutionary' committee and seized power in Athens.

Seeking scapegoats for the disaster in Asia Minor, they tried five members of the previous Government—including Gounaris himself —and the former commander-in-chief of the Army before a military court. All six were sentenced to death after a summary trial, and despite widespread protests they were executed in November 1922. It was the shooting of the Six, more than any other event, which ensured that the passions aroused by the *dichasmos* would not easily be laid to rest. Venizelos had been opposed to the executions, but he had not seriously tried to stop them. That even a politician of his stature could not always control the fanaticism of his own supporters was a pointer to the dissension and instability that awaited the country in the inter-war period. As the Greek historian Dafnis put it, the young and dynamic elements of Venizelism 'did not obey the Liberal chief however much they respected him'. Two years later, in March 1924, this was emphasized when radical Venizelists, again acting contrary to Venizelos's wishes, declared Greece a Republic in what one recent scholar has described as a 'scandalous and abnormal manner'. A plebiscite on the constitutional issue was only held *after* King George had been expelled and the Republic proclaimed. Not surprisingly these events left the new Republic with a taint of illegitimacy it would never entirely shake off. A close observer of these events, William Miller, wrote later that when Alexandros Papanastasiou had announced the creation of the Republic from the steps of the Parliament building, he 'could see no more enthusiasm and no more hostility than had been displayed on the expulsion of the King. The people was indifferent; it was weary of changes and accepted the accomplished fact.'[3]

Much of the population seems to have been unmoved by the fanaticism of the extremists in both camps and after 1924 there was an attempt to move beyond the schism. But Venizelos left Greece in disgust, and, while his would-be heirs fought among themselves, Theodoros Pangalos, a short-lived and uninspiring dictator, seized power in 1925 with the announcement: 'There is no longer Venizelism and Constantinism.' This former Army officer and fierce nationalist, the

[3] G. Dafnis, *I Ellas metaxy dyo polemon*, i (Athens, 1955), 19; J. Koliopoulos, *Greece and the British Connection: 1935–1941* (Oxford, 1977), 3; W. Miller, *Greece* (London, 1928), 84.

first of many Greek putschists to model himself on Mussolini, attempted
to remedy an array of disparate concerns, ranging from the length of
women's skirts to the threat posed by communism. But Pangalos's main
achievement, after a brief flirtation with corporatist schemes, was to
disillusion the middle classes with the idea of extra-parliamentary rule.
'We too support parliamentary institutions . . . not out of unconditional
faith in parliamentarianism but from our deep disappointment in
dictatorship, at least as we experienced it here,' stated the conservative
petty-bourgeois daily *Nea Himera*, suggesting something less than
whole-hearted support for democratic processes.[4]

In fact, after Pangalos's downfall in 1926 there was a brief period
when they seemed to be working. Public opinion demanded co-
operation between the political camps, and a succession of coalition
governments uniting republicans and royalists appeared to herald the
end of the *dichasmos*. Venizelos had announced his withdrawal from
politics in 1924 and lived in Paris, ostensibly working on a study of
Thucydides. His main opponents, the Populist Party, led by the colour-
less Panayis Tsaldaris, agreed to co-operate in the workings of government, although they continued to withhold public recognition of the
Republic. Under Georgios Kafandaris, the Liberal Finance Minister,
the coalition government embarked on negotiations with the League of
Nations aimed at restoring the gold standard and encouraging foreign
investment. But this harmonious arrangement was brought to an end by
the news that Venizelos had changed his mind and would be returning to
Greece. In May 1928 an observer reported:

So long as M. Venizelos remained out of the country, the cooperation of the
formerly hostile parties was maintained, albeit in an ever-weakening degree.
Such political changes as took place were due to the fissiparous tendencies of
Greek political life rather than to any definite recrudescence of the Monarchist/
Republican vendetta. M. Venizelos's return to Greece threatens to bring the
political cauldron once more to boiling point.[5]

The opposition now held that by breaking his promise not to re-enter
politics, Venizelos had freed them from the obligation to remain silent
on the constitutional question. In the run-up to the 1928 elections the
new atmosphere of confrontation intensified, as the Venizelist and
anti-Venizelist camps solidified around the two main parties. With
Venizelos himself considerably more conservative in outlook than he

---

[4] Dafnis, *I Ellas metaxy dyo polemon*, i. 291; T. Veremis, *Oikonomia kai diktatoria*
(Athens, 1982), 123.   [5] *Near East and India*, 31 May 1928.

had been before 1920, few ideological differences now separated the Liberals and Populists; indeed, just a few years later, a leading Liberal politician could claim, in all seriousness, that 'all parties here consist equally of the same elements'. It was above all the memories of the *dichasmos* which distinguished them in the eyes of the electorate. By 1932 these had become a powerful rhetorical tool which political leaders in both camps used to cement the allegiance of hesitant supporters.[6]

In August 1928 the Liberal Party won 47% of the vote and 71% of the seats in the Chamber, a massive increase over the 32% vote and the 38% of the seats it had won in Venizelos's absence in 1926. Taking allied minor parties into account, the Venizelists dominated the Chamber, crushing both the anti-Venizelist Populists, and the small Agrarian and Communist Parties. The following year, in the first elections to the new Senate, the Venizelists won a similar victory. Fortified by this massive parliamentary majority, the Liberal Government of 1928–32 was able at first to allay many of the fears aroused by Venizelos's return and to continue the reconstruction policies of his predecessors. There were striking foreign policy successes such as the 1930 pact of friendship with Turkey, which showed that Venizelos had lost little of his diplomatic skill. However, on the domestic front his touch was less sure. His lieutenants began to contest his tight grip on the Liberal Party, while the refugees—an important source of support for him—were unhappy over the *rapprochement* with Turkey.

His mishandling of the economic crisis damaged his image more widely. As he struggled to keep Greece on the gold standard, amidst the turmoil generated by the sterling depreciation in September 1931, much of his former charisma deserted him. One observer reported that he seemed 'rather tired and listless', giving the impression of one 'who had lost his courage'.[7] The British were unable to bail him out of his financial difficulties, the Populist opposition unwilling to assist him politically, rejecting his calls for the formation of a coalition government. In May, as criticism of his leadership mounted from within the Liberal Party, Venizelos resigned as Prime Minister, to be succeeded by a brief minority government headed by Alexandros Papanastasiou, a key intellectual presence on the left of the Venizelist camp. Barely two weeks

---

[6] T. Sofoulis, cited in G. Mavrogordatos, *Stillborn Republic: Social Coalitions and Party Strategies in Greece, 1922–1936* (Berkeley, Calif., 1983), 113 n.7; for an alternative interpretation, see C. Sarandis, 'The Emergence of the Right in Greece (1922–1940)', D.Phil. thesis, Oxford University, 1979.

[7] FO 371/15960 C2951/324, Ramsay–FO, 29 Mar. 1932.

later, worried at the prospect of Papanastasiou profiting from the premiership at the autumn elections, Venizelos brought his administration down and returned to power. That summer he attempted to reassert his authority over the Venizelist camp by deliberately reviving the constitutional issue. In June he stated that the Populists would never be permitted to return to power until they had officially recognized the republic, and he hinted at the existence of an anti-monarchist organization within the Army. Tsaldaris, the Populist Party leader, tried to keep matters calm. In fact the most vigorous protests at Venizelos's inflammatory rhetoric came not from Tsaldaris, but from leaders of Venizelist splinter groups, who realized that these attacks were aimed as much at them as at the Populists. Venizelos's deliberately divisive tactics—put into effect amidst the uncertainty of the economic crisis —were intended to help him reunite the various Venizelist factions under his leadership and to array them against an anti-Venizelist foe. But in pursuit of this goal, which he never managed to attain, he was ready to fuel a fanaticism which would ultimately make Parliament redundant and hand over power to the barracks, the Athenian political salons, and the streets.

At the general election in September 1932 the Liberal majority was sharply reduced—with only three seats separating the two main parties. Although the Venizelist coalition managed to maintain a sizeable lead over the anti-Venizelists, the Liberal Party itself only won 98 seats to the Populists 95. Also disturbing to Venizelos was the impressive growth in support for the Agrarians and the Communists, a phenomenon which suggested that his popularity with the left wing of the Venizelist camp was diminishing. Tsaldaris tried to lay the regime question to rest by recognizing the republic, and then, with Liberal acceptance, he formed a minority government—the Populists' first taste of power for a decade. But the Liberals feared a Populist bid to remove their power base in the Army, and in January, alarmed at the ambitions of General Kondylis, the new Army Minister, they brought the Tsaldaris Government down.

The Populists were soon to return, however. At new elections, in March 1933, the Tsaldaris coalition of anti-Venizelist groups unexpectedly won an outright majority. The result marked the end of a decade of Venizelist control of the state apparatus. Venizelist officers, horrified at the prospect of losing control of the armed forces, attempted a pre-emptive *coup d'état*, but after several days' confusion they were defeated and Tsaldaris was finally able to form a new administration. It lasted for more than two years—no negligible achievement for the times—but its accomplishments were few and its activities over-shadowed by the increasing violence of the political scene. In the aftermath of the 1933 coup attempt, relations between Populists and Liberals plumbed new depths: Venizelos's own part in the coup was far from clear, and extreme anti-Venizelists demanded he be put on trial. Several months later, the tense atmosphere exploded with an assassination attempt against the Liberal leader, involving a dramatic car chase through Athens, in which the Athens chief of police turned out to be implicated. Extremists in both camps now determined the momentum of politics. Tsaldaris, by nature an unassertive personality, found himself caught in the middle: in the Chamber he was effectively in thrall to the extremists in his own camp; the Senate, on the other hand, despite the Government's best efforts, retained a Venizelist majority. The *dichasmos* had produced political deadlock.

Tsaldaris's strategy for appeasing his royalist extremists involved pledges of constitutional and military reform, which if realized would have directly threatened the bases of Venizelist power within the state apparatus. It was the fears aroused by rumours of these reforms which led to the abortive Venizelist uprising of March 1935, involving the Navy and some Army units. Venizelos himself took part, echoing the heady days of 1916 and the 'National Defence' movement; but this time there was no foreign backing for Venizelos and little popular support. The uprising was suppressed by government forces within several days, and was followed by the abolition of the Senate. Venizelos fled into exile for the last time. The extremists, led by the ambitious General Kondylis, were greatly strengthened and, before the year was out, Tsaldaris himself had been ousted by monarchist Army officers and the Republic had been abolished. King George, one of Constantine's sons, returned to Greece from Brown's Hotel in London, where he had spent his years in exile. An ineptly rigged plebiscite provided the necessary varnish of legitimacy, but in fact there was so clearly a longing for some sort of domestic peace throughout Greek society that, despite the pervasiveness of republican sentiment, the King's return seems to have been greeted with resigned acceptance.

But though the demise of the Republic, after its troubled existence of just 11 years, might have closed the constitutional question as a political issue, it did not lead to a new era of stable parliamentary rule for Greece. On the contrary, with the constitutional issue out of the way, the incapacity of the political élite was cruelly exposed.

At first the newly returned King acted with surprising resolve in asserting his authority over General Kondylis and shepherding the country towards new elections in January 1936. Yet their outcome presented him with no easy task: Tsaldaris's Populists and allied anti-Venizelists won 143 seats, the Venizelists 141. The Communist Party, with 15 seats, held the balance of power. Interpreting the results as the expression of popular approval for a coalition of the two main parties, the Liberal leader, Themistoklis Sofoulis, immediately declared that so far as his party was concerned the constitutional issue was now settled, and he thereupon entered into negotiations with the Populists to form a joint government.

The main obstacle to a swift resolution of the impasse were the anti-Venizelists who controlled the upper echelons of the officer corps. Their resistance to the idea of reinstating their former Venizelist colleagues hindered the Populists from reaching an agreement with Sofoulis. But some senior officers went further than this: they informed the King through the sympathetic Minister for Army Affairs in the interim government that they would seize power themselves sooner than permit the formation of any government which was dependent on Communist support. This was, of course, the only alternative for both the main parties if they could not co-operate with one another, and representatives of both were indeed involved in secret discussions with the Communists. Once again, faced with a challenge to his authority, the King acted with dispatch: he dismissed the incumbent Army Minister and replaced him with a man he knew he could trust, Ioannis Metaxas. The stocky Metaxas had been a brilliant and deeply loyal staff officer under the King's father, Constantine, before turning to a rather less successful career in politics after 1922. Despite his well-known dictatorial aspirations and long anti-Venizelist record (Metaxas's antipathy towards Venizelos was exceeded only by his jealousy towards his apparently more successful rival Kondylis), his appointment was hailed by none other than Venizelos himself from his Paris exile. It may be that Venizelos had been led to underestimate Metaxas after the latter's humiliatingly poor performance in the January elections; at all events, he wrote that the King's action had assured the 'definitive return of the country to a normal political life'. It was not one of his better predictions.

Barely one week later, the news reached Athens of Venizelos's death. As the prominent anti-Venizelist journalist George Vlachos immediately realized, it was a political landmark: 'Eleftherios Venizelos is dead, and along with him all of us are dead too: Venizelists, anti-Venizelists, the past, the political camps.' 'The Greeks were born and died Venizelists

and anti-Venizelists. They had ceased to think in political terms . . . ,'
wrote Gregorios Dafnis. 'After his death, the Greeks should have
started thinking politically: to take decisions, study issues, find solutions
to problems. Here lay the impasse.' If Greece's politicians did not start
'thinking politically', if negotiations between Liberals and Populists
remained bogged down, providing an opening for Metaxas, it was partly
because habits do not change so quickly; but it was also because time was
against them.[8]

Venizelos was not the only prominent politician to die that spring:
Kondylis had collapsed unexpectedly in February; in April came the
news of the sudden death of the interim Prime Minister, Demertzis,
whom the King replaced with Metaxas. And the following month
Tsaldaris, too, died. Both of the main parties were plunged into a profound succession crisis. Neither Sofoulis nor Venizelos's son Sofoklis
had the charisma of the great Liberal leader, and the party vacillated
between soliciting support from the Communists and backing Metaxas.
After Tsaldaris's death, the Populist Party split into factions, complicat-
ing still further the process of trying to form a regular government.

The redundancy of the existing party system was now evident. At the
end of April, a few days after Metaxas had been appointed Prime
Minister, Parliament voted to adjourn until the end of September,
permitting him to govern by decree in the interim. He was not slow to
turn the situation to his advantage. Against a backdrop of labour protests
at home, and ideological polarization abroad, his regime acted in an
increasingly repressive manner. Although there is evidence that in July
the main party leaders were on the verge of reaching an agreement, it
seems that King George and Metaxas had decided between them that it
would be better to abolish parliamentary rule completely. The Greek
trade union federation provided a pretext: when the Government
announced its intention of introducing compulsory arbitration procedures by decree, the union movement made plans for a nation-wide
general strike. On 4 August, the day before the strike was scheduled to
take place, Metaxas declared a state of emergency and announced the
indefinite suspension of Parliament and the imposition of martial law.
His dictatorial regime would govern the country without serious
challenge until the Second World War.

[8] H. Cliadakis, 'The Political and Diplomatic Background to the Metaxas Dictatorship, 1935–36', *Journal of Contemporary History*, 14 (1979), 117–38. Dafnis, *Metaxy dyo
polemon*, ii. 406–7, 411; Sarandis, 'Emergence of the Right', 324; Mavrogordatos,
Stillborn Republic, 84–7.

Greece's need for domestic economic growth was a commonplace of educated opinion after 1922. Yet the ruling politicians belonged to a pre-war generation for whom irredentism rather than social or economic policy was the stuff of politics. Even before 1914, political affiliations in Greece had been determined less by policy issues than by considerations of patronage. The *ethnikos dichasmos* was an extreme development in this tradition, creating two rival camps, each attracting its own civilian and military clients. The Army became an important political factor, split between republican and royalist factions who saw their intervention in the political arena as essential for their own professional prospects. The question of the regime, and the allied question of reinstating cashiered royalist or republican officers to active service, were of considerable interest to those factions closely linked to the main political groupings. The paradox was that though these officers used the rhetoric of the *dichasmos* quite shamelessly, and were among the extremists in either bloc, they were at the same time among the least loyal to their political patrons. Strikingly, it was the *same* military officers—Kondylis and Chadzikyriakos—who were responsible both for the foundation of the republic in 1924 and for its demise in 1935. It took them just over a decade to insist on the restoration of the monarch they had earlier deposed. The politicians depended on the military, but the military were unreliable allies. They moved from one camp to the other according to their assessment of where power would lie in the future. In the back of their minds remained a fundamental contempt for the world of civilian politics and the belief that given the chance they would be able to supersede the very factions they enthusiastically promoted, and govern in the name of the people as a whole. This was the dream of Pangalos, Kondylis, and Metaxas.[9]

Wrapped up in these quarrels, Venizelos and lesser political luminaries lost touch with the dilemmas of a society which had changed immeasurably since their entry into politics. By their endless debate of the constitutional issue and by their constant gerrymandering with the electoral system, politicians alienated themselves from their electorate. Venizelos, it is true, was by temperament imaginative and energetic; his period in office between 1928 and 1932 was at least characterized by the attempt to implement a definite set of policies, even if these were largely

---

[9] T. Veremis, 'The Officer Corps in Greece, 1912–1936', *Byzantine and Modern Greek Studies*, 2 (1976), 113–34; Sarandis, 'Emergence of the Right', pp. 37–48.

culled from his predecessors. But Panayis Tsaldaris, his opponent and successor, entered office in late 1932 with few policy aims at all. His election speeches that summer had been marked by 'the absence of any clearly defined, expressed programme of financial and economic recon-struction, and the absence of any statement as to what the Populist Party's internal and foreign policy would be'. Thus economic recovery took place in a policy vacuum. Tsaldaris's sole card had been his refusal to recognize the republic; once that had been conceded, his habitual caution began to look like inertia, or, in the words of US Ambassador MacVeagh, 'the spineless indecision of a temporising Premier'. His Government—according to the British Ambassador in June 1934—was living 'from hand to mouth, with no plans for the future and neither the inclination nor the ability for constructive work'.[10]

Anti-Venizelism, as the pioneering sociologist Georgios Skliros noted in 1919, attracted those who were 'nostalgic for the old, small Greece with its tranquil, even patriarchal life, and fought against the enlargement of the state with its new dire consequences'.[11] As befitted the political expression of this outlook, the Populist Party was a rather traditional coalition of notables, based on local factions. Indeed, the party did not have a central headquarters during the entire lifetime of the inter-war Republic. Venizelos's Liberal Party was not much more cohesive. Though Venizelos was a convinced parliamentarian, he was aware that his quite unprecedented success was due to his personal charisma rather than to the party organization. The conviction that he had come to power in 1910 to rid Greece of the 'old parties' could not always be separated from a hostility to parties in general. Especially after 1928, as his grip on his former lieutenants began to slacken, he was inclined to disregard what he contemptuously referred to as the 'party kitchen'. In an interview given the following year he revealed his belief that 'if (the parliamentary system) wishes to survive, it needs today as never before great personalities, capable of interpreting faithfully and directly the popular will, without being required every minute to submit to party pressures'.[12] Neither Venizelos's paternalism nor the clientel-istic factions of the Populists produced party organizations which were

[10] FO 371/15966 C8029/462, Cavendish-Bentinck–FO, 23 Sept. 1932; J. Iatrides (ed.), *Ambassador MacVeagh Reports: Greece 1933–1947* (Princeton, NJ, 1980), 20; FO 371/18393 R3452/19, Waterlow–FO, 14 June 1934.

[11] G. Skliros, *Ta synchrona provlimata tou ellinismou* (Alexandria, 1919), 36.

[12] T. Diamantopoulos, *Oi politikoi dynameis tis venizelikis periodou*, i(i) (Athens, 1988), 84; S. Stefanou (ed.), *Eleftheriou Venizelou politikai ypothikai anthologitheisai apo ta keimena avtou*, ii (Athens, 1969), 96.

capable of articulating mass demands. Neither produced the 'party of ideas' whose absence from Greece was so lamented by contemporary theorists. Nor—in revealing contrast to the small Communist Party —did they succeed in establishing permanent youth sections. The 'schism' which separated them ran more along regional than class lines—between Old Greece and the Venizelist New Provinces—a division increasingly irrelevant to the needs of a country in the midst of rapid urbanization and industrial growth. Both main parties held fast to the view that the function of a national party was to transcend rather than to represent class interests. Thus in 1920 Venizelos criticized one prominent shipowner for proposing to set up a new party. 'I greatly doubt', he wrote, 'whether such a class party can serve the legitimate interests of the capitalist class.' The Liberal Party could do this, he believed, precisely because of its catholic appeal. The Populists, whose embrace was equally wide, declared themselves to be a 'party of the people . . . whose greatest mass consists of the peasants, the workers, the salaried and all the petit bourgeois class'. There were attempts to found what contemporaries described as 'class parties'—usually situated on the left of the Venizelist camp. But most of these—as in the case of Alexandros Papanastasiou's Farmer–Worker Party—remained grouped around local notables overshadowed by the Cretan 'leader of the nation'.[13]

In some circumstances the state bureaucracy may provide an alternative to weak parties as an agent of change. But in the countries where this occurred—inter-war Japan provides an example—one finds a tradition of respect for an administrative élite which was lacking in Greece. The progressive German-educated civil servants in the Greek Ministry of the National Economy believed in 'state socialism' just as much as their Japanese counterparts, but they had much less influence in shaping policy. The popular distrust of the impersonal state may no doubt be traced back to the experience of Ottoman domination; but there was also a strong vein of anti-state sentiment in the writings of influential Greek political theorists early in this century. The most notable of these—Ion Dragoumis—claimed, for example, that 'states create nothing; they only preserve and support nations, whilst the latter

---

[13] A. Liakos, 'L'Apparition des organisations de jeunesse: Le cas de Salonique', *Actes du Colloque International: Historicité de l'enfance et de la jeunesse* (Athens, 1986), 512–38; Mavrogordatos, *Stillborn Republic*, 67–79, 94–8.

create civilizations'.[14] Nationalism in Greece was far from incompatible with hostility to the idea of a strong state. The civil service was further weakened by the politicization which came with the 'schism', beginning with the mass dismissals from office of royalists by the Venizelos Government after 1917. In the 1920s it was striking how many senior figures in the Ministry for the National Economy moved into university posts, where they had more independence and influence: among them were key personalities such as Kyriakos Varvaressos, the professor of economics who served as Finance Minister when Greece left the gold standard, and two early champions of social security reform, Panayiotis Kanellopoulos and Alexandros Svolos, who held chairs in sociology and constitutional law.

Before the international crisis weakened the prestige of foreign advisers in Greece, crucial support for progressive civil servants came from abroad: foreign economic pressure *could* alter the balance of power within the domestic economy for the better. Bodies like the League of Nations Financial Committee carried much weight with the Greek authorities: they linked approval of Greek attempts to raise loans abroad with institutional reforms, such as the creation of a new central bank. But these tactics did not always work: Venizelos listened to the International Labour Office in 1919, when foreign approval was desirable for diplomatic reasons, but he was less receptive 10 years later, when the labour legislation recommended by the ILO (and Greek civil servants) might have discouraged foreign investment in Greek industry. A social insurance bill was only brought before Parliament by Venizelos in the summer of 1932, once Greece had left the gold standard, wrecking his earlier economic strategy and leaving him in urgent need of working-class votes in the autumn election.[15]

If there was little impetus for reform from above, that was partly because of the lack of organized pressure from below. Neither the urban proletariat nor the peasantry possessed powerful, autonomous organizations to bargain on their behalf. The absence of heavy industry and

<hr/>

[14] For Japan, see S. Garon, *The State and Labor in Modern Japan* (Berkeley, Calif., 1987), 34, 74–119; A. Liakos, 'Apo kratos fylax eis to kratos pronoia?', *O Politis*, 78(6) (Apr. 1987), 34–40; G. Veloudis, *Germanograecia: Deutsche Einflüsse auf die neugriechische Literatur* (1750–1944), i (Amsterdam, 1983), 268–73, 403–7; Sarandis, 'Emergence of the Right', p. 64; M. Psalidopoulos, 'O Alexandros Papanastasiou os oikonomologos', in G. Mavrogordatos and C. Chadziiosif (eds.), *Venizelismos kai astikos eksynchronismos* (Irákleion, 1988), 329–44.

[15] A. Liakos, 'O Eleftherios Venizelos kai to Diethnes Grafeio Ergasias', *Synchrona Themata*, 31 (Oct. 1987), 42.

large plantations or estates removed some of the typical stimuli behind an early awakening of working-class consciousness. Small family businesses predominated in Greece's fledgling manufacturing sector and gave it the strongly petty-bourgeois colouring which was indeed typical of Greek society as a whole. As elsewhere, the early achievement of universal manhood suffrage weakened the politicization of labour along class lines. Taken together these factors help us to account for the lack of a strong national union movement. After 1910 the rapid spread of local labour centres, based on the French model, reinforced the regional loyalties which were also clearly visible in politics. The main national union organization, the Greek General Confederation of Labour (GSEE), formed in 1918, was crippled by internal disputes and was unable to exert control over a highly fragmented and disparate labour movement. By 1928 there were no less than 561 organizations for some 163,000 workers. As the Communist activist Avraam Benaroya, whose outlook reflected the wider perspectives of the Jewish socialists of Salonika, noted shortly after he moved to Athens:

the unstable commercial-intermediary and petit-bourgeois character of the Greek 'proletariat' caused the idea of labour organizations to take the form of an uncontrolled tendency towards the creation of numerous bodies existing only with a president and seals, as occurs also with the organization of the petit-bourgeois class in Greece.[16]

In the villages and small country towns the old patronage systems continued to operate, reflecting the individualistic values which peasant smallholder and provincial notable shared. A number of recent anthropological studies have demonstrated the way in which the similar aspirations and moral values of these groups helped to strengthen clientelistic ties and weakened class tensions. There were analogous developments in the new refugee villages where *prosfygopateres* (refugee fathers) and *agrotopateres* (farmer fathers) acted as intermediaries between their illiterate fellow villagers and the state. Perhaps such factors are part of the reason why, to the disappointment of the Agrarian Party, the Greek peasant (unlike his Bulgarian counterpart) remained susceptible to the appeal of bourgeois politics for most of this period. The Agrarian Party itself was crippled by regional rivalries, which were one of the causes of its chronic in-fighting. In the inter-war period the land reform—one of the most sweeping in Europe—intensified that rural

---

[16] A. Benaroya, *I proti stadiodromia tou ellinikou proletariatou* (Athens, 1986), 111.

conservatism which, in the complacent words of one commentator, 'contributes to a large extent to the non-existence in Greece of the great social problems which are convulsing other countries'. Of course there were sporadic outbursts of peasant discontent, notably in the Peloponnese, but the parliamentary system was capable of managing these. The crisis of Greek agriculture was *politically* critical only in so far as it caused conditions in the cities to deteriorate.[17]

Though no doubt economically secondary to the peasantry, it was the urban proletariat who were the new volatile element in society. 'The rural problem is clearly on the way to solution,' noted one American expert on the refugee question; 'much more serious is the urban problem.' Emmanouil Tsouderos, Governor of the Bank of Greece, observed in 1933 that 'the adaptation of our population to the new economic conditions is easier in the generally moderate and conservative environment of the provinces, than for the inhabitants of the cities, where the economic difficulties are more substantial'. The lack of an organized institutional framework for the Greek work-force, in an era which saw the appearance of 'a numerous working class which has profoundly modified the social character of the country', complicated the task of integrating labour's demands within the existing political system. The view that industry created a 'social chasm between rich and poor, between the few capitalists and the broad working masses'—a chasm threatening the myth of Greek social homogeneity and classlessness—explains why both Venizelist and anti-Venizelist administrations during the inter-war years were happier promoting agriculture than industry.[18]

After 1922 politicians clung to a restricted, pre-war conception of the role of the state in social and economic affairs. Such an attitude, of course, was common enough among the parliamentary élites of Europe in those years; but their predicament—that tension between the memory of pre-war stability and present turbulence—surely pressed with especial harshness on the ruling class in Athens. For only if we bear in

[17] S. Aschenbrenner, *Life in a Changing Greek Village* (Dubuque, Ia., 1986); S. D. Salamone, *In the Shadow of the Holy Mountain* (New York, 1987), 67–76; N. I. Anagnostopoulos, *O kampos ton Serron* (Athens, 1937), 75–6; D. E. Protecdicos, *Greece Economic and Financial* (London, 1924), 17; Mavrogordatos, *Stillborn Republic*, pp. 90–2; K. Karavidas, 'Socialismos kai koinotismos', repr. in *To provlima tis avtonomias* (Athens, 1981), 20–1.

[18] Morgenthau, *I was Sent to Athens*, pp. 308–9; E. Venezis, *Emmanouil Tsouderos* (Athens, 1966), 122; Bank of Athens, *Bulletin Économique et Financier*, 110 (Dec. 1932), 2079; D. Stefanides, *I thesis tis viomichanias en ti koinoniki mas oikonomia* (Thessaloniki, 1938), 5.

mind that the *megali idea*—the dream of re-creating a Greater Greece in the Near East—had been the chief rallying-cry of the political élite for almost a century, can we appreciate the political impact within Greece of the 1922 *katastrofi* at the hands of the Turks. As the young novelist George Theotokas wrote:

> The wars had ended, the 'Disaster' had abruptly and rudely closed the first century of modern Greek independence. The second century was beginning in anarchy and discontinuity. Greece had suddenly found herself without a form of government, without a constitution, without institutions or state organizations, without ideologies, because all had been bankrupted in the conscience of the nation.[19]

How could such pessimism be averted? What new role should the state play now that the road to Constantinople had been blocked? A few Venizelist reformists sought to encourage the idea of a national revival from within. For George Papandreou, the young Liberal Minister of Education, filled during his student days at Berlin with a heady mixture of Nietzsche and German social democracy, 'The Great Idea remains immortal. It simply changes its content. Instead of the increase of territory it aims at the increase and elevation of civilization . . . The nation united strives for its economic, intellectual and moral improvement.'[20] But Papandreou's vision of a united society sounded implausible in an era of unprecedented social turmoil. Venizelos himself, better able than most to adapt to the transition from 'the era of warlike ideals' to a more peaceful age in the international arena, was less sure of his ground domestically. He exhorted Greek youth to keep fit, avoid materialism (a charge to which the Liberals were sensitive), and to learn how to harmonize individual self-interest with the good of the community. But such precepts did not define the role the politicians themselves should play.[21]

For many this came to be seen in terms of their defence of the 'bourgeois' state against its enemies within. Politicians increasingly defined themselves as members of the 'bourgeois world' or 'order' to

---

[19] Cited in T. Doulis, *Disaster and Fiction: Modern Greek Fiction and the Asia Minor Disaster of 1922* (London, 1977), 93.

[20] G. Papandreou, *Politika keimena*, i (Athens, n.d.), 197.

[21] S. Stefanou (ed.), *Ta keimena tou El. Venizelou*, iv (Athens, 1984), 163–4; Venizelos's reasons for asserting that 'the world does not want war' were revealing. In an interview with *Corriere della Sera* he suggested that the 'directing classes dare not risk their prestige before their populations in pressing them on to war, unless they are prepared to accept the results that we see in Russia' (USNA, 868.00/629, Skinner (Athens)–State, 24 Feb. 1930).

point out the contrast with those who were supposed to be plotting its downfall. The language of class, which before 1914 had been used proudly to identify the Liberal Party as a progressive force against the old 'oligarchy', was now deployed defensively, a tacit admission of a social problem by an increasingly conservative political élite. A succession of anti-communist measures culminated in the *Idionymon* (or 'Special Law') passed by the Liberal Government in 1929, which made it possible to punish 'whoever seeks the implementation of ideas whose manifest purpose is the overthrow of the established order by violent means'. A law of early 1931 prohibited civil service organizations not merely from going on strike but even from affiliating with other groups which 'admit the principle of class struggle'. Nominally aimed at the weak Communist Party, both Liberal and Populist Party administrations used these provisions extensively against trade union activists.[22]

But it was not clear that in the pursuit of this basically repressive end parliamentary institutions would be as effective as a more authoritarian regime. The weak and febrile nature of Greek party manœuvring caused many Greek intellectuals, even in supposedly democratic circles, to look with admiration at 'strong men' such as Mussolini and Primo de Rivera. As the brilliant Marxist deputy Serafeim Maximos noted caustically:

The supporters of pure parliamentarianism dwindle daily ... The biggest democratic newspapers in Athens fill their columns with reminiscences and pictures of Mussolini. They admire his achievements and praise him. The republican Army too is full of would-be dictators, who plot and plan how to 'save Greece' with a 'noble dictatorship'.[23]

This was written on the eve of Venizelos's formation of a new government in 1928, ushering in four years of what became widely known as 'parliamentary dictatorship'. Indeed Venizelos himself described his position in these terms.[24] The Greek parliamentary system, with its weak parties and premium on charismatic leadership, had obvious authoritarian tendencies. But many contemporaries appeared

---

[22] Mavrogordatos, *Stillborn Republic*, p. 99; N. Alivizatos, *Les Institutions politiques de la Grèce à travers les crises, 1922–1974* (Paris, 1979), 259–303; *MA*, 21 June 1932; Sarandis, 'Emergence of the Right', p. 370 has an excellent discussion of the meaning of the adjective *astikos*, which, as he notes, lacked the pejorative tone of the English 'bourgeois'; D. Livieratos, *Koinonikes agones stin Ellada (1927–31)* (Athens, 1987), 27, 120–2.

[23] S. Maximos, *Koinovoulio i diktatoria?* (Athens, 1975), 7; G. Milios, 'O Marxismos sto mesopolemo kai o Serafeim Maximos', *Theseis*, 26 (Jan.–Mar. 1989), 102–20.

[24] G. Andrikopoulos, *I dimokratia tou mesopolemou* (Athens, 1987), 40; Sarandis, 'Emergence of the Right', p. 169.

to believe that the charismatic authority of the great Liberal was in fact
one of the main bulwarks *defending* parliamentary institutions: in October 1933 Venizelos was warned by one of his supporters that Greece
'needed a great *archigos* [chief] to lead the country to order' as a defence
against dictatorship!²⁵ It was this authority which the economic crisis
fatally weakened. For if Venizelos was an ambivalent defender of
democracy in Greece, his successors were still less inspiring. Neither
the indecisive Tsaldaris nor the octogenarian President of the Republic,
Alexandros Zaimis, were advertisements for the parliamentary regime.

University professors, civil servants, and intellectuals all advocated
technocratic solutions to the country's economic woes, but inevitably
they ran up against the weaknesses of the political system. At the start of
Venizelos's last extended period in office William Miller, an experienced observer of Greek affairs, noted that 'peace, external and internal,
is the greatest blessing which a statesman can bestow upon Greece, for
her most urgent problems are those of internal administration'.²⁶ But in
the heated atmosphere of Athenian politicking the passions aroused by
the constitutional question left little time for pressing social and economic matters to be addressed. Strikes, demonstrations, and peasant
uprisings were nervously written off as the work of communist agitators.
Yet the Red Peril was a red herring: the significance of communism did
not lie in its numbers. According to a gloomy Comintern report of 1930,
the total membership of the Greek Communist Party was no more than
1,500. As one Liberal observed during the debate on the *Idionymon* in
1929, 'we ought not even to be discussing communism, since in Greece
the only question which remains to be solved is the social question'.²⁷

²⁵ Venezis, *Tsouderos*, pp. 116, 122; Alivizatos, *Les Institutions politiques de la Grèce*, pp.
21–36, 42; the ambiguity emerges even more clearly in the work by the Venizelist
journalist Ventiris, *I Ellas tou 1910–1920*, where Venizelos's rise to power is described in
the following terms: 'The parliamentary oligarchy was dissolved; in its place was
established popular rule. The bourgeoisie, to secure its new regime, gave Venizelos the
powers of a dictator of the people' (i. 75); criticisms of Venizelos's autocratic style of
government were widespread after 1928: see e.g. *Peitharchia*, 29 Dec. 1929, 12 Jan. 1930;
for Venizelos's authoritarian tendencies in the 1930s see Koliopoulos, *Greece and the
British Connection*, pp. 11–12.
²⁶ W. Miller, 'Greece since the Return of Venizelos', *Foreign Affairs*, 7(3) (Apr. 1929),
468–77.
²⁷ A. Elefantis, *I epangelia tis adynatis epanastasis* (Athens, 1976), argues that the
Communist Party failed to become the party of the Greek working class during the
inter-war period (pp. 308–9); the same point is made by R. V. Burks, 'Statistical Profile of
the Greek Communist', *Journal of Modern History*, 27(2) (June 1955), 153–8; Mavrogordatos, *Stillborn Republic*, p. 141; Alivizatos, *Les Institutions politiques de la Grèce*, p. 300;
C. Chadziiosif, 'I venizelogenis antipolitefsi sto Venizelo kai i politiki anasyntaxi tou

Venizelos sought to defuse social conflict by a combination of paternalism and repression, financing economic growth with the aid of foreign capital and cheap labour costs; once on the gold standard, the role of the state in the economy was limited. But the economic crisis of 1929–32 dramatically altered the rules of the game: apart from the political repercussions, it made economics more complicated and thrust the political élite into a new and unfamiliar role. For several years after 1932 the politicians' shortcomings were obscured by the vigour of the domestic recovery. But the recovery too brought new problems in its train and by 1936 the darker social consequences of political inaction had become apparent.

astismou sto mesopolemo', in Mavrogordatos and Chadziiosif (eds.), *Venizelismos*, pp. 447–8; USNA 868.00/673, Sussdorf (Riga)–State, 15 Apr. 1930, also 868.00B/81 Pisar (Salonika)–Athens, 'Communist Activities in Salonica on May 1, 1932', n.d.; police reports sent to Venizelos also discounted the threat of communism, AEV 173/110, Gonatas–Venizelos, 5 Mar. 1932; AEV 173/113, Kalochristoyiannakis–Venizelos, 29 Nov. 1932.

II

THE DEVELOPMENT OF THE GREEK ECONOMY,

1912–1929

3

THE WARTIME INHERITANCE, 1912–1922

It was not just the political situation which was unstable. It was also society generally, the bourgeois class, whose initiatives were smashed to pieces, the state's capital which became the scene of endless uprisings, suddenly now developing into a Hydra-headed cosmopolitan organism.

(A. Terzakis, 1935)

Greece's economic development had followed an uncertain course even before the outbreak of the First Balkan War in 1912. Heavily dependent on earnings from currant exports, the economy suffered when these slumped in the 1890s. Irredentist ambitions directed against Ottoman rule in Crete and Macedonia led governments to spend heavily for military purposes whilst neglecting to improve the country's primitive infrastructure. On the eve of the Balkan Wars there were only 150 cars and 500 miles of carriageway in the entire country. In 1897 Greece was humiliatingly defeated in a war with Turkey and as a result was forced, not merely to pay her enemy reparations, but also to tolerate the establishment of an International Financial Commission intended to ensure the country's repayment of all her foreign debt obligations. The existence of the Commission underlined the failure of the Greek state to free itself from economic dependence on outside forces, for it could effectively veto Greek attempts to raise further loans abroad, and exerted considerable power over domestic financial policy.

Greece was dependent on the outside world not only for capital, but also for food. The nineteenth-century state was unable to feed itself, despite the fact that two-thirds of the population worked in agriculture. Poor export performance kept domestic consumption at low levels. In many areas emigration, especially to the USA, became a demographic safety-valve. The great wave of transoceanic migration gathered force around the turn of the century: from 1,105 departures in 1891 to 5,591 in 1901 and in 1907, the peak year, 37,391—or 14.2 per 1,000 inhabitants. By 1912 over 200,000 people had emigrated, almost entirely young males of prime working age.

The country emerged from a decade of wars (1912–22) completely transformed. The economic problems of Old Greece remained to be solved, but their solution was complicated by the tangle of new difficulties and pressures inherited from wartime. This chapter examines that inheritance.

Territorial and Demographic Changes

'Greece is among the countries of Europe in which the war has left behind it the deepest marks', wrote Alexandros Pallis in 1928, a view which is borne out by a consideration of the dramatic changes in the geography and demography of the country which took place between 1912 and 1922. Between those dates she was involved in five military campaigns, all of which had outcomes which affected her population and/or territorial area.[1]

Greece had expanded in piecemeal fashion from the boundaries laid down in the 1832 Convention which had established the country as an independent state. The Ionian Islands were acquired from Britain in 1864, Thessaly in 1881. On the eve of the First Balkan War the country covered an area of some 65,000 square kilometres, with a population of about 2.8 million inhabitants. As a result of her success in the two Balkan Wars, she acquired part of Macedonia, Epiros, Crete, and the Aegean Islands. Under the Treaty of Sèvres in 1920 she was granted sovereignty over Thrace as far as Chatalja. Including the territory occupied in Asia Minor around Smyrna, the area administered by the Greek state was increased through these additions by 87,600 square kilometres. According to the 1920 census, the population of the entire country was around 5.5 million. And after the Asia Minor *katastrofi* of 1922 there were further changes: the Treaty of Lausanne gave east Thrace back to Turkey, as well as the two islands of Imbros and Tenedos. At the same time, terms were agreed for the compulsory exchange of Greek Orthodox and Muslim populations: Muslims residing in Greece were 'exchanged' for the Greek Orthodox population of Turkey. Only the Greek inhabitants of Constantinople, the Chams of Epiros, and the Muslims of west Thrace were exempted from the provisions of this agreement. Thus at the same moment as Greek territories were diminished her population was swollen by a massive net influx of refugees.

[1] A. Pallis, 'Les Effets de la guerre sur la population de la Grèce', in A. Andreades (ed.), *Les Effets économiques et sociales de la guerre en Grèce* (Paris, 1928), 130.

TABLE 3.1.   *Population change, 1920–1924* (000s)

	No.
Greek population in 1920 (census)	5,536
less	
Loss of east Thrace, Imbros, Tenedos	509
Muslim emigrants	380
Bulgarian emigrants	50
War losses 1919–23	34
TOTAL	4,563
plus	
Immigrants from Turkey and Russia	1,500
Immigrants from Bulgaria	27
TOTAL	6,090
NET INCREASE (excluding natural increase)	554

Source: A. Pallis, 'Racial Migrations in the Balkans during the Years 1912–1924', *Geographical Journal*, 69 (Oct. 1925), 315–31.

These changes transformed the Greek state's relationship with the Greek diaspora. In 1912, only about 2.6 millions of the approximately 7 million Greeks in the Near East actually lived in the Greek state. There were over 1.5 million in Asia Minor, and over 3 million in the Ottoman Empire's European territories. After the Greek successes in the Balkan Wars and the population transfers after the First World War, the diaspora shrank, the rationale for Greece's irredentist ambitions gradually disappeared, and the newly enlarged state became the centre of Hellenism.

Within Greece the exchange of populations was a drastic but largely effective way of eliminating the frictions that had been caused by the multi-ethnic character of certain regions. In Macedonia, where the problem had been especially acute, the non-Greek element of the total population fell from 47.4% of the total in 1912 to 11.7% in 1926. The population of Greece was therefore now almost entirely Greek in terms of both language and religion. On the other hand, inter-war Greece was riven by a new source of tension, between the predominantly refugee Venizelist New Provinces and royalist Old Greece.[2]

The extension of the Greek state northwards had the consequence of making her a Balkan as well as a Mediterranean country. A line drawn from Volos to Arta marks the limit of the relatively rainless

[2] Ibid. 147.

Mediterranean summer; to the north of this, particularly north of the Aliakmon river, climatic and topographic conditions change markedly. Winters are colder than in the south, with snow and frost in upland areas; summers are no less hot, but are accompanied by frequent rains. Such a climate is well suited to the cultivation of cereals and certain fruit.[3]

Topographic factors also form a contrast with the situation in the south. Five major rivers, from the Aliakmon in the west to the Evros in the east, run through the northern territories, providing a supply of water even in the summer months when watercourses in the Peloponnese and central Greece tend to dry up. Adjacent to these rivers are extensive alluvial plains, such as the Campania in the valley of the Axios, and the Strymon Valley by Serres. There is additionally the potentially fertile coastal strip of west Thrace.

Despite being malarial and prone to frequent flooding these northern acquisitions vastly improved Greece's agricultural prospects. The country's ability to feed itself had always been a question of public concern, never more so than in the wake of the Allied blockade in 1916–17. However, the incorporation of the fertile northern plains, combined with the Thessalian plain acquired in 1881, meant that the agricultural sector might now be expected to boost cereal production, perhaps to the extent of making the country self-sufficient. The desirability and feasibility of this aim were to be at the centre of economic policy debate throughout the inter-war period. In addition to boosting cereal output, farmers in the new territories cultivated in certain areas a cash crop which immediately became the most significant source of foreign exchange in the country's balance of trade. This was tobacco, which supplanted the currant as Greece's chief export item.

The immediate increase in Greece's agricultural output may be gauged from the following figures: in 1915, according to Tsouderos, the total area cultivated in New Greece (including Crete and the Aegean Islands) was 581,000 hectares (ha.), and in Old Greece was 1,265,000 ha. In addition to the 657,000 ha. devoted to cereals in Old Greece were now added another 312,000 ha. in New Greece, whilst the area given over to 'industrial and aromatic plants' (in practice chiefly tobacco) expanded from 27,500 to 59,000 ha.[4]

Even more impressive perhaps was the potential for further increase. Table 3.2 shows how the expansion of cultivation in New Greece,

---

[3] M. Newbigin, *The Geographical Aspect of Balkan Problems* (London, 1915), 154, 159.
[4] E. Tsouderos, *Le Relèvement économique de la Grèce* (Paris, 1920), 16–19.

TABLE 3.2.   *Cultivated area in Old and New Greece* (000 hectares)

Year	Old Greece	New Provinces	Total
1914	1,167.5	581.8	1,749.3
1914 (wheat only)	341.4	99.9	441.3
1924	882.7	584.3	1,467.0
1924 (wheat only)	311.2	155.4	466.6
1934	1,100.6	1,043.9	2,144.5
1934 (wheat only)	426.3	365.6	791.9

Sources: E. Tsouderos, *Le Relèvement économique de la Grèce* (Paris, 1920), 108, 110; Ministry of Agriculture, *Etisia Georgiki kai ktinotrophiki statistiki tis Ellados 1931* (1932), 33, 36; ibid. *1934* (1935), pp. 33, 36.

particularly in Macedonia, lay behind the increase in the total cultivated area after 1924.

The wars had a major impact on Greece's population, quite apart from the refugee question. Although there was a slight increase in the population of Old Greece, this barely compensated for the population losses suffered in the new territories, which constituted one of the theatres of war both in 1913 and in 1915–18. According to a study by Andreades, the figure arrived at in the 1920 census for the total population of Greece (excluding Thrace, which was not Greek in 1914) of 4.8 millions was probably slightly less than the total population in 1914. Without the refugee influx, Greece's population would have actually shrunk during the war. Apart from military casualties, mortality rates were also increased by the effects of disease and the disruption to food supplies. Greece generally was affected as elsewhere by the influenza epidemic of late 1918. The casualties among the *Entente* forces in Macedonia bore witness to the prevalence of malaria, which caused more military fatalities than the fighting itself. In Old Greece the population was hit by the Allied blockade, which lasted from December 1916 to April 1917; in Athens itself mortality rates are reported to have doubled, whilst in the Peloponnese there were areas where the peasants were forced to subsist on currants alone.[5]

These afflictions led to shifts in the balance between the sexes and different age groups. For the first time there were more women than men in the total population, a trend later accentuated by the refugee

[5] Marvin Jackson, 'Comparing the Balkan Demographic Experience, 1860–1970', *Journal of European Economic History*, 14(2) (Fall 1985), 223–72; Andreades, *Les Effets économiques*, pp. 84–7.

arrivals from Asia Minor: in 1907 there were 101.4 males to every 100 females, but in 1920 only 99, and by 1928 only 98.3. Among the Asia Minor refugees, according to the 1928 census, the figure was as low as 91. An increasing number of women entered the labour force, where during periods of crisis they tended to replace men at lower wages.[6] Given the limited utility of Greek vital statistics at least before 1925 (no records were kept at all between 1891 and 1920; civil registration was not enforced for births before 1925), one can offer only general observations on long-term population growth. Birth-rates were higher for most of the inter-war period than they had been in the second half of the nineteenth century, while mortality rates fell. Among the refugees, birth-rates were particularly high. As a result the natural rate of increase was almost double what it had been in the earlier period, fuelling demographic pressures in the post-war stage.[7]

Before 1912 the inability of the rural population to support itself on the land available was revealed by the scale of emigration abroad. After 1921, when the US authorities introduced stringent immigration quotas, this escape route from rural poverty was cut off. Over the wartime decade demographic pressure in the countryside actually worsened: between 1911 and 1920 the number of rural inhabitants (those living in settlements with fewer than 2,000 inhabitants) per hectare of cultivated land rose by 10% from 2.37 to 2.63. By 1928 this figure had fallen slightly, but the position remained worse than in 1911. Although Greece was apparently rather under-populated so far as her total land mass was concerned, she was one of the worst-off countries in Europe for arable land.

As Table 3.3 suggests, Greece was poorly endowed in this respect. However, the position was made worse by her low agricultural productivity and by the absence of labour-intensive farming, which might have increased the employment opportunities available in rural areas. The strategies for economic development debated in the inter-war period took as their starting-point the problem of land scarcity. The aim of achieving national self-sufficiency in cereals clashed with the view that extensive cultivation should be replaced by more intensive methods; businessmen argued that land scarcity made it imperative to encourage industrialization.[8]

[6] *AS 1933* (Athens, 1934), 425.

[7] N. Polyzos, *Essai sur l'émigration grecque* (Paris, 1947), 70–92.

[8] Bank of Athens, *Bulletin Économique et Financier*, 122 (Dec. 1935), 2,435–37.

TABLE 3.3. *Rural population density*

Country	No. of inhabitants per sq. km.	Rural population per sq. km. of arable land[a]	% of population dependent on agriculture c. 1938
Greece	48	86.7	60
Bulgaria	59	95.4	80
Yugoslavia	56	100.1	75
Italy	133	53.4	44
Germany	139	52.1	20
England/Wales	264	33.8	5

[a] Density of population dependent upon agriculture per km[2] of 'arable equivalent' land c.1930.

Source: Cited in L. Stavrianos, *The Balkans since 1453* (New York, 1958), 596.

Over this period the trend towards urbanization continued. Since the last quarter of the nineteenth century the proportion of Greeks living in towns of more than 5,000 inhabitants had been gradually increasing: between 1907 and 1928 (the first census to take account of the refugees) it increased from 24% to 33%. Of course many of these towns were largely rural in character, and Greece remained an overwhelmingly rural nation. However, under the population exchange Greece received refugees who tended to be more urbanized than the outgoing Muslims. Refugee encampments were generally situated in the vicinity of major cities, with the result that Athens and other important urban centres grew much more rapidly in size than small provincial market towns. Between 1920 and 1928 the combined population of the five largest cities increased from 12.6% to 21.3% of the country's total population. This unprecedented and uncontrolled urban expansion caught many inhabitants of Old Greece by surprise. 'Life rolled on crazily, amidst a pandemonium which the "petite coquette" provincial town of the old Athenian gentry had never seen before,' wrote George Theotokas of the post-war metropolis. 'The capital whose population had almost doubled changed in appearance from day to day . . . Speed and post-war noises echoed everywhere, destroying the idyllic neglect and humble poetry of Old Athens.'[9]

The American Henry Morgenthau echoed these sentiments. Describing the impact of the refugees in the capital, he recalled that

[9] G. Theotokas, *Argo* (Athens, 1987), 181–3.

the city had been almost somnolent before this irruption. It had been living the staid life of an orderly capital, where business had grown into established channels and where life had settled into an easy and familiar routine. Overnight all this was changed. Now the streets were thronged with new faces. Strange dialects of Greek assailed the ear. The eye was caught by outlandish peasant costumes from interior Asia Minor. Sidewalks were crowded. Avenues that had been pleasantly ample were now filled with peddlers' carts of refugees who were now trying to make a living by selling a few strings of beads . . . The great rock of the Acropolis . . . looked down upon as strange a sight as it had seen since the days when Phidias was adorning the Parthenon at its summit.[10]

The precise number of the refugees who settled in the towns is difficult to ascertain. They pitched their tents in every major town; in Athens their children queued barefoot for bread beneath the Temple of Olympian Zeus. It is scarcely surprising that the fledgling statistical services of the Greek state found it difficult to keep track of them all. We know that around 170,000 settled in Salonika alone, another 300,000 in Athens and Piraeus. Elsewhere the communities were very much smaller. The 1928 census gives a figure of just over 500,000 for the refugee population of the 50 largest towns, but it included in this total only those refugees who had arrived after 1922. The census of urban refugees conducted by the Refugee Settlement Commission (RSC) in September 1927 covered both towns and villages, and arrived at an initial total of 484,747, which for various reasons it regarded as unrealistically low and revised upwards to 'about 615,000'.[11] It is most likely that the true figure for those refugees who settled in towns around 1922 lies somewhere between these two estimates. There is less dispute over their standard of living. Circumstances when they first arrived were truly desperate. 'The large theatre building at Athens housed one family in each box and hundreds more in the aisles and on the stage. Women made a pitiful sight cooking over charcoal braziers and hanging ragged washing from box to box.' Tens of thousands camped out the first winters in makeshift tents on the hills around Athens. Others dug caves or shivered out on the beaches near Piraeus.[12]

There was a high incidence of disease, especially typhus and tuberculosis. Several years after their arrival, over two-thirds of the families

[10] H. Morgenthau, *I was Sent to Athens* (New York, 1929), 50.
[11] E. G. Mears, *Greece Today: The Aftermath of the Refugee Impact* (Stanford, Calif., 1929), 299–300.
[12] Ibid. 52; Morgenthau, *I was Sent to Athens*, p. 50.

visited by RSC staff for the 1927 census were living in temporary dwellings and over one-third were in 'squalid dwellings, mere hovels which should be demolished at the earliest opportunity'. Athens, Piraeus, and Salonika were ringed by overcrowded shanty towns. In comparison with the agricultural resettlement schemes, little was done for the urban refugees. Three-quarters of the rural refugees were resettled within five years while only one-third of the building require-ments of the urban refugees were met.[13]

The arrival of the Asia Minor refugees compounded a long-standing housing problem in the major cities. In 1918 Athens had only 25,000 dwellings for a total population of 250,000. And whilst her population had almost doubled by 1924 her housing stock had increased by only 15,000, much of which was of poor quality. There can be little doubt that the living conditions of the masses deteriorated in the decade after 1912.[14] The political effects of this neglect of urban living conditions became evident in the next two decades. For perhaps the first time there existed in Greece an urban class with no ties with the land. Most Greek politicians, brought up in the more provincial environment of the political world of Old Greece, could not adjust their sights to this new, harsher society. Governments tended to concentrate their efforts, where economic policy was concerned, on the peasantry and did little to regain the sympathies of those city-dwellers alienated by unemployment and inflation.

After 1912 this alienation was expressed in a new and threatening form as the cities became the centre of growing labour militancy. Previously there had been little such activity in Greece. Ottoman Macedonia *had* witnessed a wave of strikes, which had culminated in the formation of the Socialist Workers' Federation of Salonika in 1909. But socialist thought had been propagated chiefly by Jewish and Bulgarian activists, whose expectations had been aroused by the success of the Young Turk movement in 1908; Greek involvement was limited and easily diverted into nationalist channels. In Old Greece, labour milit-ancy in the towns had taken second place to agrarian unrest; the peasant protests at Kililer in 1910 were a more serious disturbance than any contemporary strikes in Volos or Athens. Irredentist aspirations, kept

[13] Morgenthau, *I was Sent to Athens*, pp. 243, 273; D. Pentzopoulos, *The Balkan Exchange of Minorities and its Impact upon Greece* (The Hague, 1962), 114.
[14] George Leontaritis, 'To ergatiko kinima, 1910–20', in T. Veremis (ed.), *Meletimata gyro apo ton Venizelo kai tin epochi tou* (Athens, 1980), 73–4.

alive by the uncertainty over the Ottoman Empire's ability to survive, kept social democracy at the bottom of the political agenda.[15]

After 1912, however, a number of socialist activists from Salonika arrived in Athens and helped lay the foundations for an organized socialist movement. The First Panhellenic Socialist Conference was held in 1915. The Greek Socialist Party was founded in 1918, as was the General Federation of Greek Workers. By 1919 the mobilization of the Army virtually without interruption since 1912 brought about a scarcity of labour which encouraged workers to unionize in order to extract concessions from employers and the government. In addition, labour militancy was stimulated by the appalling working conditions in many factories, and by the scarcity of foodstuffs which pushed up prices. The spread of unionism in Greece was also of course encouraged by the example of organized labour abroad, just as Greek socialists were heartened by the success of the Bolshevik Revolution in Russia. Union membership doubled between 1917 and 1919. During 1919 a British observer noted the increasingly political character of the demands of striking workers, while Venizelos warned Parliament—with considerable exaggeration—that 'we find ourselves today in danger of the dictatorship of the proletariat'.[16]

In the spring of 1920 the Greek Socialist Party joined the Comintern. Then in the general election that winter it rode a wave of war weariness to amass almost 100,000 votes. Never again in the inter-war period would it achieve such success: its own sectarian conflicts, and its commitment to a deeply unpopular policy of espousing autonomy for Macedonia, helped reduce its appeal. Nor did any other socialist party emerge to bid successfully for the labour vote. The Socialist Workers' Union party founded by prominent reformists lasted only a short while before it was dissolved, many of its members joining the Venizelist faction led by George Kafandaris. The truth was that Venizelos's enormous popularity left no room for a moderate socialist alternative. 'So long as we live in a bourgeois state let us live in it without being a revolutionary element opposed to the bourgeois economic policy of the state,' wrote the editor of *Kampana*, a Mytilene newspaper which reflected the thinking of left-wing Venizelism. But Venizelos's charisma

---

[15] G. Leon, *The Greek Socialist Movement and the First World War* (New York, 1976), ch. 7; J. Starr, 'The Socialist Federation of Saloniki', *Jewish Social Studies*, 7 (1945), 323–5.

[16] HMSO, *Report on Commercial and Industrial Conditions in Greece in 1919* (London, 1920); S. Stefanou (ed.), *Eleftheriou Venizelou politikai ypothikai anthologitheisai apo ta keimena avtou*, ii (Athens, 1969), 353–4.

masked the existence of very real grievances among the urban poor in post-war Greece. With demobilization and, of course, the arrival of the refugees, among whom there was a higher proportion of urban workers than in the population as a whole, the cities now had to cope with a massive increase in the pool of labour. Real wage levels rose between 1918 and 1921 and then fell for the rest of the decade; demographic growth (as elsewhere in the Balkans, but not in Western Europe) depressed wages during the 1920s and contributed to rapid industrialization. Together with industrialization came new social tensions. When in 1923 over 150,000 workers came out on a national strike, the largest ever seen in Greece, the 'humble poetry' of pre-war Athens seemed to have disappeared for good.[17]

Agriculture

It is difficult to ascertain the trends in agriculture over this period. Statistics are unavailable for the entire country for 1912 and 1913. There are no data for New Greece before 1914, by which time Macedonia, Epiros, and Thrace had been embroiled in two years of war and were about to witness another four. For Macedonia there are no figures at all for 1915 and 1916; for 1917 and 1918 the data for the *nomoi* (administrative districts) of Drama and Serres are unavailable. For western Thrace there is no information before 1922. This makes it impossible to compare what occurred after 1912 with the pre-war situation, except for the restricted case of Old Greece; for the post-war state the best that can be done is to observe trends during and after the war.

In the early years of the First World War higher producer prices encouraged the peasants to increase the amount of land under cultivation. Prices increased as a result of wartime disruption, the provisioning requirements of the *Entente* forces, and the 1916 *Entente* blockade. Despite the fact that mobilization must have led to labour shortages in the countryside, the cultivated area of Old Greece expanded after 1914. It is worth noting that evidence suggests that the cultivated area had shrunk in the first decade of the century. We know that in Thessaly the area devoted to cereals had shrunk by 17% between 1896 and 1911.[18]

[17] Bank of Athens, *Bulletin Économique et Financier*, 110 (Dec. 1932), 2,081–2; S. Mathaiou, 'I efimerida "Kampana",' *Mnimon*, 10 (1985), 212–35; M. Riginos, 'Oi diakymanseis ton viomichanikon imeromisthion stin Ellada, 1912–1936', *Ta Istorika*, 5 (June 1986), 151–76; Elefantis, *Epangelia*, 23–31.

[18] D. Dakin, *The Unification of Greece, 1770–1923* (London, 1972), 251.

In the Peloponnese male emigration had left many smallholdings to be farmed by women and children. Hence the expansion from 1914 was starting from a historically low base.

According to an article by Simonides, published in 1928, the war had constituted for Greece, as elsewhere, a form of agricultural protectionism. This he welcomed as having guaranteed 'the economic viability of our agricultural production. Without this the development of the war would have brought shortlived benefit to the productivity of Greek agriculture.'[19] However, agricultural productivity seems, if anything, to have suffered during this period. Wheat yields remained well below the 1911 level, as did currants. Tobacco cultivation was completely disrupted by the Bulgarian occupation of eastern Macedonia. As a result, agricultural output fell sharply after 1914. Comparison with the position in 1915–16, when the position may have been relatively healthy, cannot be made because of the lack of figures for Macedonia. But in Old Greece the expansion of cultivation in those years was accompanied by a drop in yields; the overall increase in output was therefore probably small or non-existent. By 1917 overall output at constant (1911) prices had fallen by almost a quarter since 1914, and, although there was a slight improvement in 1918, there was a further decline when the campaign in Asia Minor began. By 1921 output in the whole of Greece was lower than it had been in Old Greece alone in 1911.

The causes of this poor performance are not hard to find. Mobilization was the major factor, removing peasants and their sons from their land for years on end. The fighting in northern Greece and the political turmoil throughout the country brought about by the 'national schism' disrupted normal economic relations. Squads from the rival royalist and Venizelist governments scoured Thessaly and Epiros to requisition scarce food supplies. Similar problems afflicted the islands, which became a vital source of provisions for the Provisional Government in Salonika. The British Consul on the Cycladic island of Syros reported in May 1917 that 'the Provisional Government seems disinclined to do anything for the Cyclades except grabbing all it can (potatoes, eggs, vegetables etc.) and compelling people to enlist.'[20]

In addition, food shortages may have damaged the health of those who had remained on their farms. After 1917 the agricultural sector must also have been affected by the uncertainty over property rights

[19] V. Simonides, 'L'Économie rurale grecque et la crise de la guerre mondiale', in Andreades (ed.), *Les Effets économiques*, p. 180.

[20] Cited in Leon, *The Greek Socialist Movement*, p. 468.

produced by the Liberal Government's proposed land reforms; in Thessaly and northern Greece there were large estates (*chifliks*) which the government planned to expropriate and convert into smallholdings. By 1918 about 150 of the original 466 *chiflik* villages had been expropriated, and opponents of the reforms waged a bitter rearguard action in an effort to improve the terms on which the land would change hands.[21]

War naturally brought about a depletion of livestock herds. Shepherds in the Balkans had traditionally covered vast distances with their flocks in the search for summer pasture. These migrations were disrupted, though not stopped completely, by the establishment of hostilities and the implementation of new national boundaries after the Balkan Wars. The shepherds were also threatened by the break-up of the *chiflik* estates, large areas of which had been leased to them by their owners for winter grazing. Once again there are no figures for the pre-war position in New Greece and gaps in the wartime statistics. However, the general picture is clear: livestock herds in Old Greece were maintained at the 1911 level until the middle of the decade and then declined. Flocks of sheep and goats especially fell between 1916 and 1921. So far as one can tell, depletion was more severe in northern Greece. This is not surprising since Macedonia and Epiros were theatres of war and obvious sources of supply for the occupying forces. By 1921 the number of oxen in Macedonia had fallen by 50% since 1914, with a similar fall in the number of goats. Given that these areas had suffered through the fighting of the two Balkan Wars, the deterioration from the pre-war position must have been enormous.[22]

Industry

Before the Balkan Wars there was little industrial activity in Greece. Stirrings were evident from the 1880s onwards, in the shape of industries based upon the processing of agricultural materials such as flour, olive oil, and grapes. Alongside this existed an extractive sector, which attracted considerable foreign investment, textile factories, and some ship construction and repair. Many of the leading lights of the first generation of entrepreneurs were foreigners, like Adolphus Fix (brewing), Serpieri (the Lavrion silver mines), and Clauss (spirits). Many factories, both in Old Greece and in Macedonia, where Salonika was

[21] Dakin, *The Unification of Greece*, p. 251.
[22] *AS 1933* (Athens, 1934), 442–5.

developing a manufacturing sector, relied heavily on West European managers and technicians.[23]

But around 1900 a number of highly successful Greek industrialists began to make their mark. These included the so-called 'Zürich Circle', named after the city where most of them had studied, who by the time war broke out were involved in soaps, cement, artificial fertilizers, wines and spirits, construction, and banking. Among them were Epaminondas Charilaos, the first President of the Athens Chamber of Commerce and Industry, his brother-in-law Nikolaos Kanellopoulos, and Andreas Chadzikyriakos, President of the Federation of Greek Industrialists and later to become Minister of the National Economy under Metaxas. These men, in the words of a younger colleague, 'created great industries out of nothing' and became the leading spokesmen for Greek industry after 1922.[24] Greek manufacturing thus assumed the dual character which it retained after the war: on the one hand, a large number of small family units of an artisanal nature; on the other, a small number of large, often quite modern companies whose success depended in good measure on the close personal links which their directors maintained with politicians, the military, and the National Bank of Greece. Through the Federation of Greek Industrialists, established in 1907, and the Chambers of Commerce and Industry, the business world developed institutions for publicity and political pressure which stood out in a country where interest group organization was still rudimentary. In the inter-war years, these institutions would provide a strong voice for business interests, carrying across the political divide between Populists and Liberals.

In the absence of statistical information it is impossible to say what industrial output on the eve of the Balkan Wars amounted to. Population censuses show the *combined* industrial and artisanal work-force rising from 15.7% to 25.6% of the total work-force between 1870 and 1907. In Athens and Piraeus the number of large industrial plants rose from 22 in 1880 to 63 in 1900 and 92 in 1910.[25] These indicators of growth may reflect increasing urbanization, but they do not suggest the beginnings of an advanced industrial sector. Even in 1920, after considerable development, Greek industry still had an extremely low ratio of horsepower per worker: 0.72 if we believe the figures in the census, in reality

---

[23] The standard work on industrialization in 19th-cent. Greece is now C. Agriantoni, *Oi aparches tis ekviomichaniseos stin Ellada ton 19⁰ aiona* (Athens, 1986).

[24] ETVA, *Elliniki viomichania apo ton 19⁰ eis ton 20⁰ aiona* (Athens, 1985), 14–15.

[25] Tsouderos, *Le Relèvement économique de la Grèce*, p. 155.

probably lower still. These ratios compare unfavourably with those of other Balkan states: Romania 2.22 in 1919, Bulgaria 2.64 in 1921, Yugoslavia 3.4 in 1918.[26]

The disruption of trade after 1914 had a severe impact on the mining sector—the only area where foreign investment was of any importance before 1912. Output, which in many cases had fallen since 1910, slumped after 1914. The production of magnesite dropped from a peak of 199,494 tonnes in 1916 to under 40,000 tonnes two years later; iron pyrites from 199,000 tonnes in 1914 to under 20,000 tonnes in 1918. By 1922 the labour force employed in mining was half the size it had been in 1910. The war pushed up freight rates and made shipping hard to obtain. Mobilization reduced the manpower available. Output began to recover only after 1923 but both absolutely and relatively the weight of the extractive sector in Greek industry as a whole never regained pre-war levels.[27]

Manufacturing industry, on the other hand, appears to have expanded during the wartime decade. The Balkan Wars did not disrupt trade to any great extent, and those workers who were mobilized were reported to have been replaced without difficulty. Several prominent firms, such as the textile company Kirkinis Bros. and the Greek Gun-Powder Co., benefited from Army commissions for clothing and ammunition. The impact of the First World War was more complex. The import controls introduced by the government from February 1916 obviously benefited domestic producers as did the needs of the military. But Greek manufacturing was dependent upon imports of coal, benzine, and raw materials. The *Entente* blockade of 1916–17 led to fuel shortages. Whilst some factories began to use a mixture of wood and lignite—Greece was known to have reserves of lignite, though they were costly to exploit—others were forced to shut down, and unemployment rose. According to the 1917 census of manufacturing, over 40% of industrial workers in Athens and Piraeus were out of work.[28] However, there seems to have been no shortage of capital, for those with goods to sell were able to realize enormous profits: the US Consul in Athens reported in June 1918 that 'a feature of the last four years here has been the large sums found in the hands of a small group of men and especially

---

[26] Andreades (ed.), *Les Effets économiques*, p. 232, provides census data; M. Jackson and J. Lampe, *Balkan Economic History: 1550–1950* (Bloomington, Ind., 1982), 419–20.

[27] X. Zolotas, *I Ellas eis to stadion tis ekviomichaniseos* (Athens, 1926), 16, 42, provides data.

[28] Cited in Leontaritis, 'To ergatiko kinima', pp. 73–4.

shipowners, side by side with the overwhelming poverty of the masses'.[29]

Indeed many Greek merchants had accumulated substantial wealth during the First World War. The mercantile marine made profits estimated at almost 800 million gold francs between 1915 and 1919, compared with an annual pre-war average of 25–30 million.[30] Although Greek shipping losses during the First World War were substantial, shipowners were able to finance the complete reconstruction of their fleets by 1924 without recourse to foreign capital markets. In addition, emigrant remittances in 1918–21 were at an all-time high: they rose from £1.7 million in 1914 to £14.8 million in 1919 and £22.6 million the following year. There was consequently no shortage of investable capital after the Armistice. In August 1918 the Bank of Industry was founded with 'the principal object of promoting and strengthening home industry'.[31]

If, as seems possible, the period under the Venizelos Government from the summer of 1917 (most especially from the Armistice) until its defeat at the end of 1920 was an important stage in the industrialization of Greece, as wartime profits were invested in manufacturing, this would have contributed to the rapid turn-about in the employment situation: by 1919 severe labour shortages were reported, and factories were having to compete for labour with public works projects on docks and roads. In the same year a law was implemented, which had been passed five years earlier, encouraging the expansion of Chambers of Commerce. These spread rapidly throughout the country. Tariff modifications were introduced to protect textile manufacturers and local distilleries, though protests from importers led the former to be repealed after several months.[32] However, the idea that tariff policy should be shaped by protectionist as well as fiscal criteria had lain behind the formation in September 1917 of a government committee to study the subject. After much delay the committee's proposals bore fruit in the wholesale tariff revision of 1923, which was finally implemented in 1926.[33]

[29] Leontaritis, 'To ergatiko kinima', p. 75.

[30] HMSO, *Report on Commercial and Industrial Conditions . . . 1919*, p. 3; DOT, *Report on Industrial and Economic Conditions in Greece to April 1922* (London, 1923), 33; Zolotas, *Ekviomichaniseos*, p. 33.

[31] P. B. Dertilis, *La Reconstruction financière de la Grèce et la Société des Nations* (Paris, 1929), 224; *The Banker*, 5(25) (Feb. 1928), 286.

[32] HMSO, *Report on Commercial and Industrial Conditions . . . 1919*, pp. 13–14.

[33] A. Andreou, *I exoteriki emporiki politiki tis Ellados, 1830–1933* (Athens, 1933), 139–45.

TABLE 3.4. *The relative values of manufacturing and crop output*

Output	Greece[a]	Bulgaria[b]	Romania[b]
Gross crop output[c]	1,719	2,378	3,978
Gross manufacturing output[c]	1,077	761	2,328
Crop/manufacturing output ratio	1.60	3.12	1.71

Note: Data unavailable for Yugoslavia.

[a] 1921 data.
[b] 1922 data.
[c] In millions national currency units.

Sources: Greece, *AS 1933* (Athens, 1934), 434–8; Bulgaria and Romania, M. Jackson and J. Lampe, *Balkan Economic History 1550–1950* (Bloomington, Ind., 1982), table 10.5.

Although there are numerous contemporary reports of the growth of Greek manufacturing, it is virtually impossible to compute the rate of that growth during wartime. There is no available information concerning industrial output on the eve of the Balkan Wars in either Old or New Greece. According to one estimate, the value of industrial output rose from £8 millions in 1917 to £19 millions in 1925. Despite the statistical lacunae, it seems clear that Greek industry expanded significantly during the wartime decade.[34] Perhaps more importantly, attitudes towards industry changed too. It was now accepted as important to encourage some form of economic autarky even if this aim did not have quite the urgency or comprehensiveness it would acquire after 1932. According to the Governor of the National Bank of Greece, 'the postwar general tendency to create strong self-sufficient industry in each country asserted itself with particular force in Greece'.[35] Although currency instability and the acceleration of inflation during 1920 appear to have encouraged investors to divert their funds into speculating on the foreign exchanges, the expansion of manufacturing continued. By 1921 the gross value of manufacturing output was 1,077 million drachmas, compared with a crop value (excluding olives and olive oil) of 1,719 million drs. Net values are unavailable, but a comparison with Greece's

[34] J. Drosopoulos, 'Industrial Development in Greece', *The Banker*, 5(25) (Feb. 1928), 287; Jackson and Lampe, *Balkan Economic History*, p. 340 and table 10.5.
[35] Drosopoulos, 'Industrial Development in Greece', p. 287; A. Kirkilitsis, *Ai trapezai en Elladi* (Athens, 1934), 85.

Balkan neighbours reveals that in gross terms Greek manufacturing had achieved an unusual weight in the domestic economy (Table 3.4).

Hence even before the refugees from Asia Minor entered the country, Greek industry had expanded significantly.[36]

Yet industrial growth under the conditions of the war years appeared a mixed blessing to many Greeks. On the one hand the poor state of agriculture made it clear that the country's demographic problem could not be solved by farming alone, especially after the restriction of emigration to the USA made that problem even more acute. Industry had shown itself capable of generating new employment opportunities at a rapid rate. Yet it had only done so in the extremely favourable environment brought about by war. Real wages fell whilst supplies of competing imports were, until 1919, reduced to a trickle. The faint odour of profiteering hung around domestic industrialists and made Greek politicians ambivalent about the merits of further expansion. One drawback in the past had been that the state's encouragement of industry had almost always taken the form of increasing import tariffs; this had the advantage of increasing state revenues, but the disadvantage of blunting competition. Writing in 1920, Tsouderos, who was later to become Governor of the Bank of Greece and ultimately Prime Minister, called instead for a policy of supporting industry by improving the country's infrastructure.[37] This method, however, would have cost public funds whilst the other saved them. It is therefore not surprising that even after 1922 state policy towards industry remained based on tariffs and cheap wages. As we shall see, the results of such measures reinforced doubts especially after 1932 about how far industrialization in Greece was desirable at all.

The Balance of Trade

Greece's trading position was, perhaps, her major economic weakness. Since the middle of the nineteenth century she had run a chronic trade deficit. Whilst she depended upon imports for cereals, fuels (chiefly coal), and manufactured goods of all sorts, she exported non-necessary agricultural commodities or minerals. The major export item before 1912 was currants, which earned well over half of all export earnings. The economic vulnerability which such dependence on one commodity

---

[36] Cf. K. Vergopoulos, *Le Capitalisme difforme* (Paris, 1977); N. Psyroukis, *O fasismos kai i 4 Avgoustou* (Athens, 1977), 34–5.

[37] Tsouderos, *Le Relèvement économique de la Grèce*, p. 182.

produced was graphically illustrated when the slump of currant exports in the early 1890s led to a serious financial crisis and debt default by the Greek state.

The size of the trade deficit had gradually been diminishing in the 40 years before 1912, but over the following decade it increased again. Over the period 1880–1910 exports had averaged over 70% of imports (by value); in the following decade this fell to under 50%.

The First World War was a disastrous period for currant exports. These slumped after 1915, and though they recovered slightly at the end of the decade, they never regained their pre-war levels. However, the same years saw tobacco assume a new importance in the Greek trade balance. With the acquisition of Macedonia and later Thrace too, the former heartland of the Ottoman tobacco trade was now Greek. Between 1910–12 and 1914 Turkish exports fell by two-thirds, whilst Greek exports doubled. However, operations on the Macedonian front and the Bulgarian occupation of western Thrace disrupted cultivation before 1919, and the departure of Muslim cultivators and the arrival of refugees meant that it was only after 1923 that the tobacco trade could be conducted under more settled conditions.

Apart from these two crops, the main source of foreign exchange during wartime was emigrant remittances. By 1914 the Greek population of the United States numbered in excess of 400,000. Most of these emigrants had arrived within the previous 20 years and were accustomed to sending remittances to relatives in Greece. This provided a considerable, but fluctuating source of balance of payments income. Remittances rose sharply after 1917 to a peak of $120 million in 1920 before falling to $32 million within two years. At their peak in 1920–1 remittances brought in more foreign exchange than visible exports (see Table A1.5).

Imports were affected less by export instability than by the physical disruption of trade and, in particular, the 1916–17 blockade of Old Greece, which led to a catastrophic drop in the imports of certain crucial commodities. It was above all the suffering caused by the curtailment of cereal imports which underlined the country's inability to feed itself and its economic dependence upon the outside world.

Information on other items in the balance of payments is difficult to obtain. Shipping profits stood at record levels before 1919, but we have no official information regarding the sums that were repatriated to Greece. Even the data discussed above are shaky. It is impossible to find out the precise value of emigrant remittances, since a significant proportion may not have entered the country via the banking system. It follows that it is also impossible to obtain precise estimates of the overall balance of payments position in this period. However, according to the one available study of this subject it appears that certain features of the balance of payments remained constant between the turn of the century and the First World War: throughout this period the capital account showed a chronic deficit. There was also a chronic trade deficit, which grew over time. However, invisible earnings also increased, keeping the current account in surplus for most of the period; indeed, in 1916, receipts from shipping are calculated to have been more than double the value of visible exports.[38]

The Cost of War

From the financial point of view, we can divide the decade before 1922 into two parts: the years until 1920 when the drachma remained at par and the cost of the war was borne chiefly by loans raised through public subscription at home or foreign lending; and the years of the Asia Minor campaign when Greece was excluded from foreign capital markets and financed her military effort largely by means of the printing press.

The two Balkan Wars imposed a strain on the country's finances, but it was a strain the country could withstand. Through the National Bank of Greece the government succeeded in raising loans abroad, chiefly in Paris, to liquidate the debts it had incurred in the course of the fighting. On the outbreak of the First World War, the drachma was at par and financial conditions within the country were stable. Indeed the Venizelos administration regarded 1914 as a 'post-war' year, expanding the civil service in the new territories and granting tax concessions there to persuade the inhabitants of the benefits of Greek rule. Venizelos himself, with his habitual optimism, appears to have assumed that tax revenues from the new territories would naturally increase as the local economy developed.[39]

However, the expenses of the First World War made a mockery of such attitudes. The prolonged mobilization of the Greek Army after 1915 and the cost of operations on the Macedonian front imposed unprecedented burdens on wartime budgets. We should compare the estimated total military costs of the Balkan Wars of 400 million

---

[38] M. S. Eulambio, *The National Bank of Greece* (Athens, 1924), 179–228; T. Kapsalis, *La Balance des comptes de la Grèce* (Lausanne, 1927), 236–8.

[39] Andreades (ed.), *Les Effets économiques*, pp. 22–3.

drachmas with the 904 millions spent for military purposes in 1916–18 alone.[40]

But the structure of the Greek economy made it difficult to increase revenues suddenly. Direct taxation was costly to implement in a country where the bulk of the population lived close to subsistence levels in rural areas. Indirect taxation, upon which government depended for most of its regular revenues, already stood at high levels; further increases were politically unpalatable, and in fact the Venizelos Government had already postponed the implementation of new taxes on farm produce after 1911. But the reduction in trade brought with it a fall in receipts from import duties, which were halved between 1911 and 1917. Between 1915 and 1917 the frequent dissolutions of Parliament, and the growing 'national schism', prevented the formation of a government strong enough to implement new tax measures. The same political turmoil made it impossible to obtain funds through public loans. Governments relied on advances from the National Bank of Greece made on the security of pledged foreign credits—in 1915 from the *Entente* side, in 1916, through Bleichröder's, from the Central Powers! The procedure was based on the 1910 regulation which entitled the National Bank to issue banknotes when they were backed by foreign exchange.

But after 1916, Greece's intensifying military commitment necessitated much heavier borrowing requirements. Despite efforts by Finance Ministers of the Liberal Government to find new sources of revenues once Greece formally entered the war, the explosive increase in military expenditures could not be met through taxation. In 1918/19 the official statistics show the budget in deficit for the first time during the hostilities. This led the authorities to make new demands on capital markets at home and abroad. Negotiations with the Allies led Great Britain, the USA, and France to pledge financial support in February 1918. Credits were to be extended to Greece to meet the cost of Allied military expenditures in Macedonia. The sums involved were considerable, the British pledging £12 millions, the French 300 million francs, and the Americans $50 millions. Although these credits were not immediately made available, the National Bank issued banknotes to the value of 850 million drachmas against them. According to the agreement with her *Entente* allies, Greece could claim reimbursement for the drachma sums she had advanced six months after the end of the war.

[40] Ibid. 26.

However, by the summer of 1920 the franc had fallen against the drachma and insisting upon their repayment in francs would have involved Greece in losses and been awkward for the French themselves, who faced financial turmoil. Hence the settlement was postponed so that by November 1920, when the Liberal Party lost the election and King Constantine returned to the country, the Greek authorities had failed to obtain the bulk of the credits pledged to them. However, the reaccession of the King provided the *Entente* powers with an excuse to withhold these funds permanently and West European capital markets remained blocked to the Greeks until well after the 1922 *katastrofi*.

A comparison of the Greek public debt in 1914 and 1919 (March) before the Smyrna expedition, suggests that the First World War had *not* brought about an unsustainable increase in indebtedness. In nominal terms the debt had almost doubled, from 1,424 million drs. to 2,428 million drs., of which latter sum 939 millions corresponded to the Allied governments' book credits.[41] Such an increase was not unusual among European belligerent states. Tsouderos, writing in 1919, took the view that 'despite this important increase in extraordinary expenditures . . . the situation is far from alarming'.[42] At the time indeed many Greeks regarded the future with assurance: they had ended the war on the victorious side and now looked forward to building on the gains of the Balkan Wars with the aid of Venizelos's inspired diplomacy at the Paris Peace Conference. The American Trade Commissioner later recorded that his 'arrival at Athens in 1919 coincided with post-war Greece's period of unprecedented prosperity and reckless optimism'.[43]

Yet financial pressures did exist. Prices, which had risen almost 400% during the war, fell back only slightly after the Armistice, prompting fears that the money supply had expanded too rapidly. The parliamentary report on the 1918/19 Budget had argued that an expansion of the note issue might be inflationary even in circumstances where it was backed by a corresponding increase in foreign exchange reserves.[44] From 1918 onwards the National Bank increased its short-term advances to the state, beginning a process of pushing upwards at the ceiling of the maximum fiduciary note issue which was to accelerate during the Asia Minor campaign. Another warning sign was that in the

[41] HMSO, *Report on Commercial and Industrial Conditions . . . 1919*, p. 3; X. Zolotas, *I daneiaki epivarynsi tis Ellados* (Athens, 1931), 10.

[42] Tsouderos, *Le Relèvement économique de la Grèce*, p. 90.

[43] Mears, *Greece Today*, p. 48.

[44] Andreades (ed.), *Les Effets économiques*, p. 46.

final results of the 1918/19 Budget, more than half the total revenues were derived from loans. Were military expenditures to increase further, or further loans become unavailable, the financial situation might sharply deteriorate. During 1920 not one but both of these eventualities were realized.

In May 1919 Greek forces disembarked at Smyrna. Their presence was first required to counter Italian ambitions in the region, but Italy soon gave place to the resurgent Turkish nationalists as Greece's foe. Coming to the aid of the Asia Minor Greeks became a military commitment from which withdrawal was unthinkable. Yet this political necessity had to be financed. Even during the final 18 months of the Venizelos Government the task was an onerous one; after November 1920 it was only feasible at the cost of abandoning the pre-war monetary system. In the three years 1920/1 to 1922/3 military expenditures amounted to 4,306 million drachmas, roughly two-thirds of total government spending.[45]

Financing this burden from regular revenues was impossible. In the 1919/20 Budget estimates, two-thirds of total revenues were expected to come from borrowing. The Liberal Finance Minister, Miltiades Negrepontis, warned Venizelos in October 1919 of the difficulties ahead. The Venizelos Government had introduced various fiscal reforms, bringing in an income tax and raising some indirect taxes, but these measures yielded less than new domestic loans, and increased short-term borrowing from the National Bank and new credits from the Allies.[46]

The Venizelos Government had already moved away from the gold standard, with the tacit agreement of the International Financial Commission (IFC), when it increased the fiduciary circulation by 600 million drachmas, issued by the National Bank in two stages. This policy of increasing the maximum note issue permitted to the National Bank as a quid pro quo for further short-term advances was followed by subsequent royalist governments after November 1920.[47] In March 1921 they authorized a further emission of 550 million drs., and in 1922, in two stages, an increase of 1,150 million drs. To a more limited extent, interest-bearing bonds were also issued. The author of a recent study remarks that 'the public budget was the most important of the factors

[45] Ibid. 29, 48.
[46] K. Kostis and T. Veremis, *I Ethniki Trapeza stin Mikri Asia (1919–1922)* (Athens, 1984), 112–13; Andreades (ed.), *Les Effets économiques*, pp. 50–3.
[47] D. G. Bristoyiannis, *La Politique de la Banque Nationale de Grèce* (Paris, 1928), 97–9.

behind the monetary and exchange instability of the years 1919–1922'.[48]

Thus the dramatic growth of the money supply between 1920 and 1922 was very largely government-induced. According to a British report, the government borrowed over 1,200 million drachmas from the National Bank in 1921 alone.[49] By the autumn of 1921 the daily cost of prosecuting the war was estimated at around 8 million drachmas, forcing the Royalist Government to adopt increasingly desperate measures. The Finance Minister, Petros Protopapadakis, introduced an unprecedented makeshift the following spring when he authorized a novel type of forced loan. The public were obliged to hand in their banknotes to the banks where the notes were cut in two: half the note was returned to its owner, the other half was exchanged for 20-year Treasury Bonds. At the same time the National Bank was ordered to credit the state with a sum equivalent to half the value of the existing notes in circulation.[50] The measure was highly regressive, since it was applied only to banknotes and not to deposits or other forms of savings. On the other hand it had the advantage that it was not inflationary: 1,300 million drachmas were raised without expanding the note issue.

In defending the measure before Parliament, Protopapadakis argued that, since the attitude of Greece's wartime allies made it impossible to raise money abroad, a forced loan provided the only way of covering the deficit.[51] Indeed the deficit was so large that even this measure proved insufficient: the 1921/2 Budget ended 1,755 million drachmas in the red, and only 1,265 million were covered by advances from the National Bank.[52] The reduction of the notes in circulation was only temporary since the money withdrawn was reintroduced into the monetary system by government spending. In addition, further fiduciary note issues were permitted to the National Bank in October 1922 and March 1923. By then the circulation amounted to 4.9 billion drachmas compared with 3.1 billion one year earlier.

By this time the Royalist Government had been overthrown, in the aftermath of the Greek defeat at the hands of the Turks in September 1922, and a new government, led by a self-styled 'Revolutionary

[48] Kostis and Veremis, *Ethniki Trapeza*, p. 116.

[49] DOT, *Report on Industrial and Economic Conditions . . . to April 1922*, p. 13.

[50] Andreades (ed.), *Les Effets économiques*, pp. 55–60.

[51] DOT, *Report on Industrial and Economic Conditions . . . to April 1922*, p. 14.

[52] DOT, *Report on Industrial and Economic Conditions in Greece in 1923 and 1924* (London, 1925), 7.

Committee' of republican officers, took power. They introduced a tax on export earnings (which would be used again in 1932) and raised import duties. Certain measures had a radical tinge, for example the decree that holders of bank deposits denominated in gold were to be recompensed with paper drachmas at par, the difference between the parity and the current rates accruing to the government. In March a property tax was introduced. Against the background of increasingly urgent calls for the land reform to be accelerated, these measures led to accusations of Bolshevism. But the new authorities, though republicans, were no Bolshevists: they were simply grappling with a financial problem of colossal proportions. The national debt had increased between 1920 and 1923 from 2,428 million drachmas to 7,912 million. To the purely military costs of the Asia Minor campaign now had to be added the costs involved in accommodating the refugees who had fled to Greece.

The Banking System

During the 1880s, Greek foreign indebtedness had increased rapidly as a result of the military and economic policies of the Tricoupis and Deliyiannis Governments, which alternated in power. The country's ability to service this debt rested largely on its export earnings from currants. When the French introduced high import tariffs in 1892 to protect their own producers, who had by then recovered from the ravages of the earlier phylloxera outbreak, the market for Greek currants abruptly collapsed, triggering off a serious fiscal crisis which would transform the country's monetary system and introduce a new and unprecedented level of foreign supervision into the economy.

The service of the foreign debt was suspended and negotiations began with representatives of the foreign bondholders. After the interruption of the Graeco-Turkish War of 1897 a settlement was reached under which the IFC, representing Greece's bondholders, was set up at Athens to administer assigned revenues for the debt service. Beyond this specific function, however, the IFC also possessed powers which limited the autonomy of the Greek state in monetary affairs. Strict limits were set to fiduciary note issues, and to issues of Treasury bonds, which could only be exceeded with its consent. This was tantamount to a massive restriction of Greek sovereignty. Similar bodies to the IFC existed in Serbia, Bulgaria, and the Ottoman Empire but in no case held such sweeping powers.[53]

---

[53] Tsouderos, *Le Relèvement économique de la Grèce*, pp. 23–31.

The depreciation of the drachma after 1891 had been widely, if erroneously, attributed to an excessive fiduciary note issue, and under the aegis of the IFC this was rigidly controlled. After 1898 the Greek state was obliged to amortize its floating debts to the National Bank by 2 million drachmas annually. But the effects were not wholly negative. From the turn of the century, helped by increasing emigrant remittances, the drachma began to appreciate. Foreign investment, chiefly in the extractive sector, increased and a considerable part of the foreign debt was repatriated.

The banking system in Greece was highly oligopolistic—a fact which may help explain the stability of the commercial banking system after 1929. The National Bank, founded in 1841 by the Swiss philhellene Eynard but controlled from the start by Greek financial interests, was the largest commercial bank, with half of all the bank assets in the country in 1911. It also, of course, had close ties with the state and acted as a central bank. Some years after the *katastrofi*, its then Governor was to wonder 'whether in the whole history of banking there are many examples of banks which have concentrated in their hands business appertaining to almost all the branches of the National Economy, to such an extent as has the National Bank of Greece'.[54] Although there were numerous minor banks, often effectively mere financing arms of commercial operations, domestic banking was dominated by, apart from the National Bank, a handful of large institutions—the Bank of Athens (founded 1893), the Bank of the Orient (1904), the Popular Bank (1905), and the Commercial Bank (1907).

Foreign capital was invested in Greek finance and an English bank, the Ionian, even preserved its right to issue banknotes until 1920—but the Greek banking system remained largely controlled by Greeks. As one writer justly observed: 'once the initial difficulties facing the organization of banks in Greece had been overcome, [banking] proved to offer fertile ground for the special qualities of the Greek character, namely, a close grasp of profitability, entrepreneurial ability, that calculation which make him a force to be reckoned with . . . in commerce and exchange, but which hinder his success in other areas of economic activity which require patience and persistence, such as agriculture and industry'.[55]

Despite the improvement in the country's finances, the 1898 legisla-

[54] Jackson and Lampe, *Balkan Economic History*, p. 223; NBG, *Report of the Governor of the National Bank of Greece for the Year 1927* (Athens, 1928), 51.
[55] G. Charitakis in the preface to Kirkilitsis, *Ai trapezai en Elladi*, p. iv.

tion effectively locked Greece into a highly deflationary monetary policy, which led the money supply to be continuously reduced, and prevented the National Bank from effecting movements in the exchange rate. Increasingly unhappy at this state of affairs the Greek authorities, despite the disapproval of the IFC, determined to bring Greece on to the gold standard. In March 1910, the National Bank was authorized to issue banknotes beyond the legal ceiling in exchange for gold or foreign exchange. The country was put effectively on to a gold exchange standard and the drachma was made convertible and held successfully at par through the Balkan Wars.[56]

The outbreak of the 1914 war had little initial impact on Greek banks. A prohibition on the export of gold was considered but proved to be unnecessary. Deposits with commercial banks continued to increase, as did emigrants' remittances. However, the war made monetary policy 'more complex and less mechanical' than previously.[57]

The first problem the National Bank had to contend with was inflation, which accelerated after 1915. Several factors were primarily responsible: the wartime disruption of trade, submarine attacks on shipping, and the *Entente* blockade all made imports scarce and were largely beyond the reach of policy to influence. But the problem was compounded by the Bank's reluctance to permit the drachma to appreciate against the currencies of the combatant powers. Foreign exchange flowed into the country, causing the domestic money supply to expand. Despite the statement of one scholar that inflationary pressures were caused by excessive state borrowing, it seems clear that this was not a major factor before 1918.[58]

For their part, the commercial banks weathered the First World War with little difficulty. Between 1914 and 1919 the employed capital of the leading six banks increased by 340%, their net profits by 460%.[59] They expanded their activities on a relatively static capital base. Table 3.5 includes figures in current drachmas for bank deposits and their capital and reserves. In real terms (i.e. deflated by the cost-of-living index) the former increased by 23% between 1914 and 1919, whilst the latter fell by 38%.

But despite the apparently privileged position of the drachma, and the expansion of commercial banking activity, inflationary pressures were

[56] Bristoyiannis, *La Politique de la Banque Nationale de Grèce*, pp. 5–14.
[57] Ibid. 17.
[58] X. Zolotas, *Nomismatikai meletai* (Athens, 1932), 45.
[59] Kirkilitsis, *Ai trapezai en Elladi*, p. 60.

TABLE 3.5.   *Monetary indicators, 1914–1922* (million drachmas)

Year	Note issues of the National Bank[a]	Emigrants' remittances	Bank deposits	Bank reserves and capital	(5)/(4 + 2)
(1)	(2)	(3)	(4)	(5)	(6)
1911	159	n.a.	337[b]	126[b]	0.25
1914	265	903	397	99	0.15
1919	1,382	5,566	1,575	199	0.07
1920	1,508	8,476	2,357	237	0.06
1921	2,161	5,650	3,341	351	0.06
1922	3,149	1,840	3,754	464	0.07

n.a. = not available.
[a] Note issues of the other two issuing banks, the Ionian Bank and the Bank of Crete, were negligible.
[b] 1910.

Sources: M. Jackson and J. Lampe, *Balkan Economic History 1550–1950* (Bloomington, Ind., 1982), 219, 380; *AS 1933* (Athens, 1934), 470; A. Kirkilitsis, *Ai trapezai en Elladi* (Athens, 1934), 17, 21, 38, 42.

exacerbating an inherently unstable economic situation. The basic problem lay in the effect of war on the operation of the gold standard. In theory the gold standard was a self-regulating system. When capital inflows produced an increase in the domestic money supply of a given country and pushed up domestic prices, domestically produced goods would become more expensive *vis-à-vis* foreign goods: imports would increase, the country's foreign exchange reserves would fall, and the domestic money supply would fall too, bringing domestic prices down once more. Any balance of trade disequilibrium would be automatically corrected through movements in the exchange reserves and domestic prices.

It is now recognized that in fact the gold standard had not been seriously tested in practice before 1914.[60] It should therefore not be surprising that it failed to operate in the prescribed way in wartime Greece. Capital flowed into the country and prices rose throughout the war; but the disruption of commerce meant that the satisfaction of import demand was postponed until after the Armistice. Even after

[60] See D. Aldcroft, *From Versailles to Wall Street, 1919–1929* (London, 1977), 160–7; A. Bloomfield, *Monetary Policy under the International Gold Standard 1880–1914* (New York, 1959), *passim*.

1918, invisible earnings on current account were so great that they more than offset the visible trade deficit, delaying the inevitable adjustment of Greece's external balance still further. Proceeds from emigrants' remittances stood at record levels in 1919–21, well over double 1914 levels in real terms.

In 1918 the first strains appeared: the trade deficit reached unprecedented levels as import merchants replenished depleted stocks. There was also much speculative investment in imported goods. Late in 1918 the Armistice caught many Greek merchants in possession of large stocks which they had hoped to sell at high wartime prices and upon which they stood to make heavy losses with the reopening of international trade. Only by disposing of these goods in Romania and the Ukraine was a crisis in Athens averted.[61] Even so, according to one commentator, writing at the end of 1919, the enormous increase in the money supply over the past two years had not been excessive; though further increases might give cause for alarm, 'there does not seem to be any fear of inflation for the present'.[62] This view might seem curious in view of the fact that prices had more than trebled since 1914. But then the period had seen a rise in world price levels generally and the Greek experience was not extreme.

However, 1919 turned out to be a year of exceptional financial instability. Although prices actually fell in Greece, while invisible earnings held up well and the drachma appeared, if anything, overvalued against West European currencies, the combination of speculative activity on the foreign exchanges and heavy import demand soon clouded the apparently favourable monetary outlook. Speculation was fuelled by the fact that the National Bank had not permitted the drachma to appreciate as much against major currencies in Athens as it had in West Europe. Arbitrage profits of over 15% could be made by selling francs for drachmas in Athens and then moving back into francs in Paris. The National Bank itself is alleged to have carried out such operations. In common with other Greek banks it had suffered heavy losses on its holdings of sterling and francs when these currencies depreciated. During the war it had therefore moved into dollars. But in 1919, anticipating a recovery of European currencies, it moved back out of dollars in a misguided and unsuccessful bid to recoup its wartime losses. At the same time heavy import demand caused a further diminution of

[61] Kostis and Veremis, *Ethniki Trapeza*, ch. 2; HMSO, *Report on Commercial and Industrial Conditions . . . 1919*, p. 15.
[62] Ibid. 7.

its exchange holdings. In August the depletion of the Bank's dollar reserves necessitated a devaluation of the drachma against the dollar, against which, after a slight rally at the end of the year, it began to fall steadily.[63]

The euphoria evoked by the war's successful outcome soon evaporated. The Greek monetary authorities were forced to abandon the gold standard, and linked the drachma with sterling, which was also depreciating against the dollar. From Paris Venizelos, the Prime Minister, criticized the abandonment of parity and the National Bank's misuse of its dollar reserves. As Greek troops moved into Asia Minor the Government could ill afford a period of financial instability. In September 1919 a public loan of 300 million drachmas was floated with some difficulty. Venizelos, who had persuaded the British Government to hand over the credits it had allocated to Greece in 1918, now sought new facilities. Negotiations resulted in the 1919 Accord and half the amount that Venizelos had requested was pledged by the British and French. But once again not all these sums were immediately realizable.

It is at this point, after the initial strains of post-war adjustment had already made themselves felt, as Greek troops disembarked at Smyrna to occupy their Asia Minor enclave, that state borrowing for military purposes compounded Greece's monetary difficulties: the memory of what followed was to have an important effect on policy-makers' responses to the 1931 crisis.

The drachma, which had remained steady against sterling for most of 1919, began to fall heavily during 1920 as other countries made the transition to peace while Greece became ever more embroiled in Asia Minor. In London, the rate fell from 26.6 drachmas:£ in January 1920 to 140 in mid-1922 and, after King Constantine was ousted by the Revolutionary Government, to 386.9 in December.[64] In the spring of 1922, the Royalist Government's forced loan of 1,300 million drachmas caused the drachma to fall heavily against sterling, losing 20% of its value in one week. Currency instability discouraged the inflow of emigrants' remittances, which fell in 1922 to their lowest value in real terms since well before the war—around one-third of the 1914 level.[65] The Government tried to control the slide by taking measures in April to form a syndicate of leading banks, known as the Consortium, which was given the right to set official exchange rates and the sole right to deal in

---

[63] Kostis and Veremis, *Ethniki Trapeza*, pp. 102–9.   [64] Ibid. 118.

[65] Bristoyiannis, *La Politique de la Banque Nationale de Grèce*, p. 137.

foreign exchange. But currency speculation continued on the black market, as dealers anticipated further depreciation. One difficulty was that a large proportion of Greece's foreign exchange earnings eluded the Consortium's control. Another problem was the limited quantity of funds at the Consortium's disposal: these were exhausted by the summer of 1922. To cap it all, there were suspicions that the members of the Consortium, and specifically the National Bank, were themselves speculating against the drachma![66]

The Revolutionary Government, which seized power after the *kata-strofi*, brought in drastic new measures in November 1922, abolishing the ineffectual Consortium and instead imposing export duties on a wide range of items: exporters were obliged to surrender a proportion of their exchange earnings at an official rate. In addition, the commercial banks were obliged to place 15% of their exchange purchases with the National Bank. The new government also continued the old inflationary practice of raising the legal ceiling for National Bank issues of unbacked banknotes and the fiduciary note issue rose rapidly until 1924. At the same time the official discount rate remained at around 6%, a level which made it easier for the state to service its floating debt.

Up to 1921 the commercial banks benefited from these conditions. Their liquidity position was sufficiently healthy to permit considerable independence of the National Bank, which had in any case no statutory powers over the domestic banking system. Profits on an unprecedented scale allowed them to expand their reserves and to double their deposits in real terms compared with 1914. Net profits of the six main banks, including the National Bank, increased more than five times in real terms between 1919 and 1922.[67] In contrast with the vulnerability of Greece's exchange rate position, her domestic banking system appeared to have emerged from the disastrous Asia Minor campaign in sound shape. While the National Bank had been burdened with the task of financing a decade of wars, the commercial banks had profited from unprecedented capital inflows and then from the opportunities offered for exchange speculation. Such activities suited a system which was traditionally—and increasingly—geared to short-term investment. The question remained: how easily would the Greek banking system adapt itself to the longer-term requirements of financing domestic development once the era of easy profits was over?[68]

[66] Ibid. 131–2.   [67] Kirkilitsis, *Ai trapezai en Elladi*, p. 60.

[68] A. Angelopoulos, 'Ai anonymoi etaireiai en Elladi apo oikonomikis kai dimosiono-mikis apopseos', *AOKE*, 8 (1928), 53; Kirkilitsis, *Ai trapezai en Elladi*, pp. 42–3.

Few Greeks could have anticipated in early 1912 that within a decade their country would have doubled in size and population; the fruits of victory in the Balkan Wars and the First World War should have been sweet. But of course the final, bitter fruit—the Asia Minor disaster —poisoned the taste of the rest. The political world was riven by the *ethnikos dichasmos* between royalists and republicans, which the execution of the royalist Six in November 1922 merely intensified. Most politicians were to spend the next two decades arguing about constitutional issues and ignoring substantive matters. Closely bound to them, part patrons part clients, were groups of Army officers whom the 'national schism' also divided. But while the two camps tussled for political power, major social and economic problems required attention.

The central problem, though it was not couched in these terms at the time, was the need to encourage economic development. Only in part was this a case of 'reconstruction' (the contemporary vogue-word), since, even before 1912, the growth of the economy was inadequate to support the indigenous population, much of which was forced to emigrate. But now, with the closure of traditional transatlantic havens, emigration was no longer a solution and demographic pressure was heightened by the inflow of refugees.

Both agriculture, which had suffered over the decade, and industry, which had prospered, would need to expand. In addition, major expenditure would be required in housing, roads, and harbour works. Although there had been considerable capital accumulation by 1922, it was difficult for the Greek state to appropriate this through taxation. Governments had neither the personnel nor the political strength to implement direct taxation on an adequate scale. In the following decade, an attempt was made to return to the financial relationships of the pre-war world, in the hope of pursuing a policy of economic development financed by foreign capital. The first step on this road was the 1924 League of Nations Refugee Loan, which helped the rural resettlement of the refugees. However, this remained an isolated case for several years. The outstanding dispute with her wartime allies over war debts blocked off the London and Paris money-markets until half-way through the decade, before the eventual settlement of this issue paved the way for Greece's return to the gold standard in 1928. The next chapter charts how the slow process of development and recovery took place as Greece was reintegrated within an open trading and monetary international order.

4

RECONSTRUCTING THE BOURGEOIS
ORDER, 1922–1929

Greece's problem is chiefly a business problem.

(Henry Morgenthau, 1929)

We must all understand this well: that we have, as individuals and as a nation, come out of the unprecedented vicissitudes of the war period poorer than we were . . . Let our motto, both as State and as individuals, be: more work, restriction of expenditure to the minimum possible by means of strict economy, saving and obedience to the law and to the Government of the country.

(John Drosopoulos, 1928)

After 1922, when Venizelist officers toppled the Royalist Government, forced Constantine to leave the country, and established their own 'Revolutionary Committee', the first task to be tackled before Greece's long-term economic problems could be addressed was to reassert civilian control over the military. This did not happen overnight—indeed the creation of the Republic itself in early 1924 owed much to the pressure of fervently republican Venizelist factions in the armed forces, while the following year saw General Pangalos dissolve the Constituent Assembly and establish his own dictatorship. Only with Pangalos's downfall in 1926, itself the outcome of yet another military intervention, was the path cleared for new elections and another, this time rather more successful period of civilian government.

The pressure of public opinion, especially from the business world, forced Venizelists and anti-Venizelists to come together in a coalition, designed to set the Republic on a firmer footing, both politically and economically. Temporarily uniting the two camps, the Zaimis Government finally provided the Republic with a new Constitution in 1927, and also tackled the thorny question of reinstating anti-Venizelist officers within the armed forces. The problem of balancing the demands of various political factions among the military would return to plague the

Republic near its end, but for several years in the interim it faded from view.

What remained then in the late 1920s were the tasks of economic stabilization and reconstruction. The foundations were laid by Finance Minister Kafandaris during Zaimis's premiership. But Kafandaris, one of Venizelos's would-be heirs, was forced to make way for Venizelos himself, after his triumphal return to the political stage in 1928. Following the sweeping Liberal gains in the general election that August, Venizelos continued and extended the reconstruction effort. The role of the state in this reflected the *laissez-faire* orthodoxy of the day as it was applied by the Liberals to a small, open economy in urgent need of economic growth. The state's main function was to act as a conduit for foreign capital entering the country, whether in the form of loans raised abroad, or of direct investment: this meant stabilizing the drachma by joining the gold standard, reassuring foreign investors by creating a new, independent central bank, and confining industrial policy to providing tariff protection and keeping wages low.

The advantages were obvious but so were the drawbacks: closer links to the international economy in the late 1920s implied a readiness to swallow some bitter deflationary medicine and Greek politicians did not like the idea of this. They chose a low rate at which to stabilize the drachma in 1928 to avoid, as far as possible, having to commit the Government to a harsh contractionary regime. For similar reasons they disliked the prospect of a new politically independent central bank whose creation was demanded from Geneva by the League of Nations as a precondition for League backing for Greek forays on to foreign capital markets.

In fact, so far as the Greek state was concerned, the one area where it was heavily and actively involved was agriculture. The rapid growth of industry which occurred in the 1920s owed more to factors such as an abundant supply of cheap labour, tariff protection, and the benefits of a weak currency than it did to a conscious policy of promoting indus-trialization. But for the sake of agricultural development, and in particu-lar of being able to finance a sweeping land reform, Greek politicians, above all in the Liberal Government of 1928–32, were ready to accept the humiliations and restrictions imposed by their growing dependence on foreign capital.

Whether or not it is true, as John Petropulos has suggested, that Venizelos as early as 1923 saw the arrival of the refugees as the chance to push forward a project of economic development on a broad front, it was certainly the case that their arrival presented the Greek authorities with a herculean task which necessitated foreign assistance.[1] Venizelos realized that the creation of a large class of peasant smallholders might defuse peasant radicalism, prevent the formation of a peasant–worker bloc, and do much to secure the social stability of the Republic. This was the thinking which lay behind the land reform of the 1920s, which benefited refugee and indigenous farmers alike, and which provided a cause in which the League of Nations and the Greek authorities combined to provide a notable instance of a decisive and far-reaching reshaping of the economy. Given the centrality of agriculture to the Liberals' political and economic strategy in the 1920s, the land reform provides a good point of entry into a study of the dramatic changes that decade brought to the Greek economy.

Land Reform

Large estates according to the Hungarian, Romanian, or south Italian pattern were never characteristic of Greek farming. During the first 50 years of independence, many large properties were divided up among the peasantry, strengthening the already predominant class of small-holders. However, in Thessaly, acquired in 1881, and in the new territories of northern Greece, large estates cultivated by share-croppers were of considerable importance, and in those regions there was an agrarian problem which caused sporadic peasant unrest.

To the urban bourgeoisie, which was becoming conscious of its political power in the first decade of this century, land reform was a tool in its struggle for popular support against the conservative political class. One of Venizelos's first acts as a new national figure was to pledge his support for the impoverished peasants of Thessaly, arguing that the existing distribution of property was contrary to the 'economic, agri-cultural, humanitarian and national interests of the state'.[2] But although the National Assembly was swift to approve the principle of the compulsory expropriation of large estates, it took the sharp increase in political tensions provoked by the First World War to force the Liberals into realizing their promises. Needing to consolidate his 'Provisional Government' at Salonika against the official Government in Athens, Venizelos was obliged to make further promises of land to the peasants

---

[1] J. Petropulos, 'The Compulsory Exchange of Populations: Greek–Turkish Peace-making, 1922–1930', *Byzantine and Modern Greek Studies*, 2 (1976), 135–61.

[2] G. Ventiris, *I Ellas tou 1910–1920*, 2 vols. (Athens, 1931), i. 78.

of Macedonia. And in December 1917, after King Constantine had left the country, a new Agrarian Law was approved by the now Venizelist Chamber of Deputies in Athens.

This was the legislation which initiated a major process of land reform. On paper the measures it sanctioned were sweeping: all large publicly owned estates and all private properties above an area of 10 hectares in Thessaly and northern Greece, or 30 hectares elsewhere, were subject to expropriation for their redistribution to landless peasants. Any peasant over 20 years old was eligible to receive land. Forest and woodland were exempt from the provisions of the Law, as were larger estates, up to a maximum of 200 hectares, which were cultivated by the proprietors themselves.[3]

The outcome of the Great War both accelerated the reform itself and changed the rationale behind it. No longer was its main purpose the debilitation of landed conservatives. They remained its casualties, of course, but it was now justified by Venizelos himself as 'a conservative measure *par excellence*' designed to forestall the danger 'which has appeared from new theories . . . of seeing the peasants, workers of the fields, and the industrial workers of the towns united in overturning the lawful state [*to kratos ton nomon*]'.[4] This danger seemed the more fearsome as the refugees flooded into Greece: the vast majority of the expropriations were effected between 1923 and 1925. The costs were chiefly borne by the former owners of the land, who were only re-imbursed for their property by the state on the basis of its pre-war drachma value. Since the drachma had lost 90% of its pre-war worth they sustained heavy losses, which were increased by the fact that the interest-bearing bonds with which they were compensated by the state soon depreciated heavily.[5]

But whilst the Greek state took advantage of the wartime inflation in this way to finance the transfer of land under the Agrarian Law, the costs involved in resettling refugee farmers were well beyond it. Unlike indigenous peasants, the refugees lacked homes, tools, or animals. Emergency relief for all refugees had been provided by American charitable organizations, but when it became clear that these would cease their work in the summer of 1923, negotiations began at the League of Nations for a loan to finance longer-term refugee settlement.

[3] V. Simonides, 'L'Économie rurale grecque et la crise de la guerre mondiale', in A. Andreades (ed.), *Les Effets économiques et sociales de la guerre en Grèce* (Paris, 1928), 168–74.

[4] S. Stefanou (ed.), *Ta keimena tou Eleftheriou Venizelou*, iii (Athens, 1983), 82.

[5] Simonides, 'L'Économie rurale grecque', p. 172.

The League had been successfully involved in projects of financial reconstruction in Austria and Hungary, but the Greek refugee problem was of a different nature. In September 1923 these negotiations successfully resulted in an agreement that the League would support the efforts of the Greek Government to raise a sterling loan whose proceeds were to be handled by a specially created institution, the Refugee Settlement Commission (RSC).[6] Land vacated by Muslims who had emigrated to Turkey under the population exchange agreement provided most of the territory initially available to the RSC, but when this began to run out towards the end of 1924 the Government made more available by accelerating the land reform programme. There was thus a close link between the land reform and the work of the RSC. And after subsisting on advances from the Bank of England, the RSC was placed on a more secure financial footing with the flotation of a large loan in London, Athens, and New York, towards the end of 1924.

From the first the RSC concentrated its energies on rural resettlement, and the effect of its activities on Greek agriculture was profound. By 1927 it had been assigned 812,592 hectares—almost entirely in the New Provinces of northern Greece: by 1929 over half a million refugees had been settled, 90% of them in Macedonia and Thrace; elsewhere —especially in the Peloponnese and the Ionian Islands—their presence was small.[7] But the RSC's achievement included more than resettlement alone. Since the lack of a cadastral survey inhibited longer-term investment by the newly settled farmers in their land, the RSC undertook its own survey, which by 1930 had been extended to cover the land of indigenous farmers as well as refugees. In addition it built houses, made various infrastructural improvements, and provided livestock, farming tools, and technical advice.

Contemporaries were struck by the transformation of the landscape in the north. Jacques Ancel, author of a classic study of Macedonia, enthused that 'those miserable Turkish hamlets, nothing but hovels of mud and straw lying in the midst of an uncultivated plain or of unhealthy marshes, are now replaced by large cheerful villages . . . All around one sees sheaves of maize, fields of tobacco, kitchen-gardens, orchards and vines. What a miracle!'[8]

The reality was of course less straightforward. The land reform, one

---

[6] C. Eddy, *Greece and the Greek Refugees* (London, 1931), chs. 3–4, and D. Pentzopoulos, *The Balkan Exchange of Minorities and its Impact upon Greece* (The Hague, 1962), ch. 3, provide full details.   [7] Pentzopoulos, *The Balkan Exchange*, p. 107.

[8] Cited in Pentzopoulos, *The Balkan Exchange*, p. 111.

of the most radical in post-1918 Europe, turned Greece into a nation of smallholders. According to the 1928 census, three-quarters of the cultivated area was farmed in units of less than 10 hectares. Allotments of land made by the RSC varied in size according to the fertility of the soil, from around 1.5 hectares in Thrace to 12 hectares in Thessaly. However, inheritance customs ensured that within several generations even these small plots would become hopelessly fragmented into dispersed strips. Although the need to legislate against such practices was widely recognized, no government in the lifetime of the inter-war Republic succeeded in stopping them. Nor was it true that—as was claimed at the time—the original holding was sufficient to maintain a family if properly cultivated. Land allocations had been made on the basis of prevailing crop values. Around 1924 tobacco prices were high and the land distributed in tobacco-growing areas (like Thrace) was divided into plots so small that only intensive cash crop cultivation was economic. And when tobacco prices began to plummet at the end of the decade, many refugee farmers found themselves unable to turn instead to growing cereals for subsistence, since they could grow no more than one or two months' supply on their land.[9]

An additional difficulty was the legal uncertainty that surrounded the question of property rights. In the first years of the RSC's existence, there were many clashes between refugee settlers and local peasants who claimed the land for themselves. The temporary allocation of plots certainly discouraged farmers from making improvements: 'The provisional work of the partitioning is everywhere detrimental to the progress of the settlement,' wrote League of Nations observers, '. . . many refugees, not feeling sure that their allotment will not be exchanged or diminished, make no improvement on it . . . We have come across some who neglected flourishing vines or refused to manure their land.' Told that their legal title to the land would only be granted once they had repaid their debt to the state in full, many beneficiaries of the land reform looked forward either to returning to Turkey, or to moving to the city. Many of them sold their plots at an early opportunity and sought urban employment as wage-earners or shopkeepers. Farmers had ready access to credit—especially through the credit co-operatives which were promoted by the National Bank of Greece—but they had no incentive to invest in land or equipment, preferring to increase

[9] Pentzopoulos, *The Balkan Exchange*, p. 108; X. Zolotas, *Agrotiki politiki* (Athens, 1934), 126; for a recent discussion of the problem of fragmentation, see J. du Boulay, *Portrait of a Greek Mountain Village* (Oxford, 1979), app. 2.

consumption levels or—influenced by the 'business fever' that swept the country after 1923—to engage in petty trading.[10]

Agricultural Trends

A lengthy debate took place in inter-war Greece over the effects of these changes on the agricultural sector. At its most simplistic it consisted in supporters of the RSC attributing the favourable developments in agriculture to their work, whilst its opponents similarly held it responsible for continued shortcomings. To be sure, the debate did not solely concern economic outcomes: competing visions of Greek society were also at stake. Conservative anti-Venizelists were quite capable, for example, of attacking the spread of co-operatives that accompanied the reform on the grounds that they encouraged financial corruption among the peasantry, or, alternatively, that they pushed the Greek farmer towards an alien communistic ideal which threatened family cohesion and even Greek society itself. In a period of economic instability and new class anxieties, some critics of the reform were even capable of firing off all these arguments at once.[11] Yet here it is the purely economic impact of the land reform which must be our first concern; for, without a clear view of this, we cannot go on to evaluate the impact of the world depression at the end of the 1920s. What were the overall trends in production and yields, and to what extent did they reflect the impact of the land reforms?

The catastrophic effect of the Asia Minor campaign on domestic agriculture was reflected in the diminution of the cultivated area after 1918 (see Table A1.1). In 1922 this area was still smaller than it had been in 1914, despite the addition of western Thrace. In Old Greece less land was cultivated than had been in 1911. After 1922, however, the cultivated area gradually expanded. Here the impact of the land reform was unequivocal, since the rate of expansion was fastest in the new territories, primarily Macedonia and Thrace: at the start of this period they constituted one-third of the overall cultivated area, by its end, almost one-half. In Macedonia the cultivated area expanded between 1922 and 1931 from 275,000 to 550,000 hectares, in Thrace from

---

[10] LN, *Greek Refugee Settlement* (Geneva, 1926), 52–3; N. Theodorou, 'Georgooikonomiki meleti epi tessaron antiprosopeftikon chorion tou lofodous tmimatos tis periferias Katerinis', GD 5 (1939), 63; USNA, 868.00B/39, 'Political and Economic Effects of Refugees in Greek Macedonia', 23 Dec. 1929; A. Angelopoulos, 'Ai anonymoi etaireiai en Elladi apo oikonomikis kai dimosionomikis apopseos', *AOKE*, 8 (1928), 31.

[11] E. Kouloumbakis, in *ESV*, 19 Mar. 1931, 1127–8.

72,000 to 148,000; on the other hand, in central Greece, where few refugees were settled, it rose more slowly from 260,000 to 330,000 ha. The area devoted to tobacco cultivation in northern Greece grew from 50,000 to 138,000 ha., compared with a *drop* from 71,000 to 69,000 ha. in the case of the other main export crop, currants, grown in the Peloponnese.[12]

But the population was growing rapidly too and, by the time of the 1928 census, there were 3.88 inhabitants per cultivated hectare, compared with 3.61 in 1914. Such population growth required an improvement in yields to sustain the pre-war position. This should not have been difficult, for Greek yields, especially in cereals, were among the lowest in the world. A British consular report had noted in 1909 that 'the systems of farming and implements in common use are antiquated. The advantage of growing crops in rotation is almost unknown.' These were problems which persisted well into the post-war period and disease and fluctuating weather conditions remained the major determinants of crop yields. In 1919, for example, bad weather was estimated to have reduced the anticipated cereal harvest by 30%.[13]

In fact the wartime drop in yields was not remedied during the 1920s. On the contrary, in the case of cereals, which took up around 70% of the cultivated area, yields fell still further. At the time the land reform was widely blamed for this. As the agricultural economist Babis Alivizatos remarked, the prevailing conception was that 'the agrarian reform had been perhaps socially necessary, but economically and productively . . . harmful'.[14] Yet there are problems with this argument. The drop in yields did not occur across the board, and was not confined to those areas most affected by the reforms. It was most marked in the case of cereals, which were grown for subsistence throughout the country. On the other hand it was slight in the case of tobacco, whose harvests expanded at the most rapid rate of any crop during the 1920s as a result of intensive cultivation by refugee farmers. Bad weather, high fertilizer prices, primitive crop rotations, and poor seed all depressed cereal yields through the 1920s; this in turn kept overall agricultural output at low levels. It should also be noted that recent research has thrown doubt on

---

[12] M. Dritsa, 'Prosfyges kai ekviomichanisi', in T. Veremis and G. Goulimi (eds.), *Eleftherios Venizelos: Koinonia, oikonomia, politiki stin epochi tou* (Athens, 1989), 41–2.

[13] HMSO, *Report for the Year 1909 on the Trade and Agriculture of the District of Piraeus* (London, 1910); HMSO, *Report on Commercial and Industrial Conditions in Greece in 1919* (London, 1920).

[14] B. Alivizatos, *I metapolemiki exelixis tis ellinikis georgikis oikonomias kai ep'avtis epidrasis tis agrotikis politikis* (Athens, 1935), 15.

the general idea that the breakup of large estates *necessarily* leads to less efficient farming. In northern Greece, as elsewhere in Southern and Eastern Europe, the late nineteenth-century landed estate was often poorly cultivated, whilst absentee landlords often found it more convenient to rent out land for grazing to nomadic pastoralists than to cultivate it themselves. In the 1920s it was the uncertainty over ownership rights and the gradual and dispiriting fall of crop prices rather than land redistribution itself which was the chief constraint to better initial performance. It seems useful to recall Alivizatos's conclusion to his lengthy study of the issue: 'the influence of the agrarian reform on the trend of yields must necessarily be regarded as secondary and less powerful in its effects than other more general factors'.[15]

But there is little doubt that Greek agriculture was in trouble in the 1920s. Gross crop output reached its nadir in 1921–4, but had not even regained the level of 1914 later in the decade. The performance of agricultural production as a whole would have been worse still had not export crops—currants, grapes, and some tobacco—recovered rapidly from their wartime low. In the 1920s export-oriented production accounted for around half the value of total crop output as smallholders responded to the post-war boom. Could the successful performance of these crops herald an era of export-led growth? It seemed unlikely, for all faced increasing competition on world markets and as semi-luxuries were especially vulnerable to any downturn in international trade. In addition, they were associated with a cluster of domestic social and economic problems. Let us now examine these in relation to the two main export crops, currants, a staple of southern Greece, and tobacco, from the Venizelist north.

The Marxist historian Ioannis Kordatos was exaggerating only slightly when he suggested that the Peloponnese 'has all its hopes chiefly in the currant'.[16] There was little else which could easily be substituted for the

---

[15] Ibid. 200; Zolotas, *Agrotiki Politiki*, pp. 97–107; G. Servakis and C. Pertountzi, 'The Agricultural Policy of Greece', in O. S. Morgan (ed.), *Agricultural Systems of Middle Europe* (New York, 1933), 137–201; C. Evelpides' review of N. Anagnostopouios's *I agrotiki metarrythmisis* (Athens, 1930), *Peitharchia*, 2 Mar. 1930; for the Balkan background see F. Adanir, 'Tradition and Rural Change in South Eastern Europe during Ottoman Rule', in D. Chirot (ed.), *The Origins of Backwardness in Eastern Europe* (Berkeley, Calif., 1989), 131–77; M. Jackson and J. Lampe, *Balkan Economic History: 1550–1950* (Bloomington, Ind., 1982), 351–65; D. Mitrany, *Marx against the Peasant* (Chapel Hill, NC, 1951), 115–31; D. Warriner, *Land Reform in Principle and Practice* (Oxford, 1969), 44–57.

[16] J. Kordatos, *Eisagogi eis tin istorian tis ellinikis kefalaiokratias* (Athens, 1972), 123.

TABLE 4.1.　*Currant production and exports, 1890–1929*
(million Venetian lbs.)[a]

Period	Production (average)	Exports (average)	Period	Production (average)	Exports (average)
1890–4	342.4	336.6	1910–14	309.4	246.8
1895–9	348.6	273.2	1915–19	235.6	159.4
1900–4	291.6	227.8	1920–4	260.6	181.2
1905–9	350.6	244.8	1925–9	288.8	165.3

[a] 1 Venetian lb. = 0.478 kilograms.

Source: Data supplied by ASO Head Office, Patras.

vine across the parched mountain slopes of southern Greece. The lack of permanent rivers meant that heavy investment in irrigation works was necessary before citrus fruits or other crops could be cultivated. Farmers were reluctant to experiment, since they would have had to uproot their vines, which took at least five years to grow before bearing fruit and thus represented a considerable investment. Yet the long-term prospects for the currant growers were poor and ever since French vineyards recovered from the ravages of the phylloxera outbreak at the end of the nineteenth century, the Greek economy had been plagued by a chronic imbalance between the production and export of the crop. Harvests, which had trebled in the 20 years after 1870, largely in response to French demand, remained at high levels, whilst exports began a steady decline.

Despite massive emigration from the Peloponnese, the chief area of currant cultivation, in the two decades before 1912, the problem of large production surpluses remained. The stop-gap devised to solve it was the 'retention', an export tax payable in kind by the exporter. As Table 4.2 shows, the amount of fruit removed in this way from the market gradually increased as a percentage of total production. But in the longer term, the task of reducing the surpluses must have seemed particularly intractable to Greek policy-makers. For the emigration that had occurred on a massive scale from the Peloponnese before 1912, no longer offered a solution to the region's problems. And it was difficult to persuade the growers to turn to other crops when they remembered the profits they had enjoyed during boom periods, such as that which followed immediately after the end of the First World War. According to one commentator: 'Among many currant growers one finds the attitude that by growing ten stremmata of currants, they will be able to arrange good marriages for their daughters, to send their sons to study, not have to work either themselves or their children in the fields, being able to pay as many workers as they need.'[17] In the face of such illusions, Greek politicians avoided schemes for the wholesale restructuring of the currant sector and began instead to regard the surplus as an inexpensive source of supply for a domestic wine industry. Since the interests of wine manufacturers and the farmers were opposed to one another, state policy vacillated uneasily between these two poles.

In the nineteenth century, the currant crop had been controlled by the state, directly until 1898, then indirectly through a specially created Currant Bank. When this collapsed in bankruptcy in 1904, it was succeeded by the Privileged Company for the Protection of the Cultivation and Export of the Currant, formed with private capital with rights to administer the currant market for 20 years. Benefiting from the rise in prices during the First World War the new organization was able to realize substantial profits by selling fruit at high prices which it had purchased as part of its support operations at fixed low pre-1914 rates. It sold this surplus fruit to various alcohol manufacturers. But the company had close financial links with the Bank of Athens, and decided to create its own large industrial enterprise, the Wine and Spirits Company, to take advantage of its access to the currant surpluses.[18]

After a parliamentary inquiry in 1914–15 there were persistent calls, especially from growers' representatives, to replace the company with a non-profit-making body. Successive governments too were sympathetic to such calls since the Company continued after the war to pay its annual tax at the old pre-war level originally fixed in 1905, despite the massive

TABLE 4.2. *Surplus production, 1895–1924*

Administration	Period	% total production removed from market
Direct state control	1895–8	10.6
Currant Bank	1899–1904	14.4
Privileged Co.	1905–23	19.1
NBG	1924	18.8

Source: T. Koulas, *H epivarynsis ton foron epi tis stafidos* (Athens, 1948), 49.

[17] D. Nikolaides, *Oi kindynoi tis stafidos* (Patras, 1934), 18.
[18] V. M. Simonides, *O Avtonomos Stafidikos Organismos kai ai ergasiai tou kata to proton etos, 1925–26* (Athens, 1927), 7–9.

subsequent depreciation in the value of the currency.[19] One year before its privileges were due to expire, the Government unilaterally abrogated the agreement, and transferred administration of the currant trade provisionally to the National Bank of Greece.

At the same time, the Ministry of Agriculture undertook a major study lasting one and a half years of the entire currant question. In May 1924 the Panhellenic Farmers' Conference called for the foundation of an organization that would for once reflect the interests of the growers. This was a proposal very much in accord with the inclinations of the then Minister of Agriculture, Alexandros Mylonas, and the Prime Minister, Alexandros Papanastasiou, two key figures on the Left in the Greek political world, both deeply committed to the co-operative movement. When, in the following year, the Autonomous Currant Organization (ASO) was established, it was—as one scholar has recently observed the first time that the state had intervened on such a scale to supplant the private sector. However, the history of both ASO and the co-operative movement would show the variety of motives which lay behind such intervention. Indeed, even from the way the new organization defined itself, one could have predicted the conflicts which would emerge: for ASO, according to the provisions of its charter, was to be 'a mixture of . . . a co-operative organization and a cartel-like type of unified company'.[20] In this body the interests of the growers were represented more heavily than ever before, with five out of the 13 members of the administrative council; but this also included representatives of the merchants, the Government, and the National Bank of Greece, which had been closely involved in the foundation of the new organization.

Council meetings became the scene of frequent struggles which pitted growers against merchants and the National Bank. The growers enjoyed the support of the Zaimis Government, which permitted the new organization to provide various commercial and technical services for them. But this support ebbed away when the 1928 elections diminished the strength of the Populists and Papanastasiou's reformist Republican Union, the two political groups most committed to take the farmers' side. After 1928, as the financial costs of subsidizing the surplus mushroomed, the enthusiasm of the Liberal Government for ASO waned sharply. Vasilis Simonides, ASO's first director, who had aimed to expand operations to the point of developing facilities for the

---

[19] Simonides, *O Avtonomos Stafidikos Organismos kai ai ergasiai tou kata to proton etos, 1925–26.*

[20] T. Veremis, *Oikonomia kai diktatoria* (Athens, 1982), 140 n. 28; K. Kostis, *Agrotiki oikonomia kai Georgiki Trapeza* (Athens, 1987), 193.

manufacture of alcohol, was forced to resign. A parliamentary committee was convened to examine the issue and urged the state to increase its
control over ASO and check the power of the growers. The latter
protested vigorously; public order in parts of the Peloponnese collapsed
in the summer months of 1929 and 1930 as they reacted to news of
lowered levels of subsidy. But in July 1931 the Liberals passed legislation further curtailing ASO's activities: no longer could it make sales on
its own account, auctioning surpluses publicly to wine producers; the
strength of the growers in the administrative council was whittled down.
The powerful Wine and Spirit Company, closely connected with the
National Bank, took over the warehouses that Simonides had built.
Populist Party spokesmen accused the Liberals of oppressing the
growers; Papanastasiou, himself from the Peloponnese, attacked the
Government's 'anti-co-operative spirit'. The Liberal reforms had
turned the producers into the 'slaves' of the industrial and banking
interests. By 1931, according to Kostis, ASO had become the means
whereby the National Bank 'exerted control over the entire currant
sector on the most favourable possible terms'. But Venizelos held out
little hope for the currant producers, most of whom were anyway
staunchly anti-Venizelist—in contrast to the mostly Venizelist merchants. Panayis Vourloumis, the Liberal Minister for the National
Economy, was himself a currant exporter from Patras, and strongly
opposed to the growers' attempts at self-marketing. And he knew as well
as anyone the unfavourable long-term outlook for the crop.[21]

The chief market for Greek currants was the United Kingdom, which
regularly took between 50% and 70% of currant exports, and had held
this position since the turn of the century. On the London market, prices
soared during the post-war boom as importers sought to replenish
stocks. But by 1921 the boom was over and export volumes to Britain fell
27% in two years. Between 1922 and 1929 the British demand for
Greek currants continued to decline: exports fell a further 23% over
this period. Greek sales were not only falling in absolute terms; they
were also losing their share of the British market to raisins from
Australia and California. In both countries production had been stimulated by the post-war boom and their exports rapidly eroded the Greek
producers' former monopoly position. Yet the stabilization policies

[21] A. D. Sideris, *I georgiki politiki tis Ellados 1833–1933* (Athens, 1934), 342–4;
Nikolaides, *Oi kindynoi tis stafidos*, pp. 10–20; Kostis, *Agrotiki oikonomia*, p. 192; *PSV*,
20 June 1931, 1,687–90, ibid., 22 June 1931, 1,769–806; G. Mavrogordatos, *Stillborn
Republic* (Berkeley, Calif., 1983), 164.

TABLE 4.3. *The effect of policy on currant prices, 1926–1929*

Year	Retention (equivalent value)[a]	Export duty[a]	(2) + (3)[a]	Average export price[a]	(4)/(5)(%)
(1)	(2)	(3)	(4)	(5)	(6)
1926/7	1,210	738	1,948	2,848	68.4
1927/8	1,650	795	2,445	4,078	60.0
1928/9	1,950	690	2,640	4,021	65.7

[a] Drachmas per thousand Venetian lbs.

Source: *Eisigiseis tis eidikis proparaskevastikis epitropis epi tou stafidikou zitimatos* (Athens, 1936), table 2.

ASO pursued, under pressure from the growers, to absorb the surplus harvest actually reduced the price competitiveness of the Greek product. By the middle of the 1920s, as Table 4.3 shows, around two-thirds of the export price consisted of the costs of its two export taxes.

Greece was effectively financing the surpluses out of monopoly profits, a strategy which could work only so long as the level of exports held up sufficiently to provide the sums required. When, at the end of the decade, export earnings began to fall, the surplus could only be bought in at lower prices, ASO faced bankruptcy, and the need to find an alternative policy became apparent.

If currants were the export staple of the past, in the early 1920s the future looked to be with tobacco. Oriental tobacco had been cultivated in Macedonia and Thrace since the eighteenth century, involving an export trade which extended from the Levant to Russia and Western Europe via a network of Greek, Armenian, and Jewish merchants. In the second half of the nineteenth century the rapid spread of cigarette smoking stimulated the cultivation of tobacco in the Balkans. 'The excellent cigarette of Macedonian tobacco', enthused an Italian expert in 1905, 'will reign sovereign in a kingdom which has the world as its borders and will enslave civilized and well-mannered persons on account of the delights it alone affords.' This prediction was not far off the mark.[22] The 1919–21 restocking boom was not, as in the case of

---

[22] L. Bacon and F. Schloemmer, *World Trade in Agricultural Products* (Rome, 1940), 373–93; O. Comes, 'Delle razze dei tabacchi', in Reale Instituto d'Incoraggiamento di Napoli, *Atti*, ser. 6, vol. 57 (Naples, 1906), 283.

currants, followed by a period of renewed decline. On the contrary, total export volumes of oriental tobacco remained above the 1919 peak for most of the next decade. And Greece, particularly after the acquisition of western Thrace in 1922, was the largest of the three oriental leaf exporters (the others were Bulgaria and Turkey), exporting just under half of their total sales.

The combination of the buoyant market conditions of the early 1920s, the acquisition of western Thrace, and the resettlement of the refugees in northern Greece increased the importance of tobacco to the Greek economy almost overnight. Initially there had been fears that the departure of Muslim farmers from northern Greece would imperil the cultivation of the crop.[23] But these fears proved unfounded. Refugee farmers, resettled in Macedonia and Thrace, rapidly turned to tobacco, with the encouragement of the RSC and the government. The crop was highly labour-intensive, quickly remunerative (unlike viticulture), and well suited to cultivation on the tiny smallholdings which many refugee farmers were allocated. As exports soared, and money flowed into the previously war-torn region, growing tobacco was soon regarded as a way 'not only to sustain the households of the producers of the region, but to bring those economically and psychologically shipwrecked human-beings, refugees and native-born, to an island of paradise till then unknown, where wealth was as abundant as in a dream'. By 1929 certain areas had become entirely dependent on the tobacco crop: this was said to be the case for 100 out of 131 refugee settlements in the Kavalla region.[24] Average harvests during 1923–6 were double those of 1919–22. Yields fluctuated little, but there was an enormous expansion of cultivation. By the middle of the decade, tobacco constituted almost one-fifth of the total gross crop output, despite being grown on less than one-tenth of the cultivated area, and was responsible for half total Greek export earnings.[25] It had, in other words, become *the* key commodity in the Greek economy.

However, between 1926 and 1929 there were signs of over-cultivation just at the time that export demand finally seemed to have peaked. With the post-war decline in sales to Egypt and the UK, Germany had become the world's major importer of oriental tobacco,

---

[23] M. Mavrogordatos and A. Chamoudopoulos, *Makedonia: Dimografiki kai oikonomiki meleti* (Thessaloniki, 1931), 53.

[24] F. Altsitzoglou, *Oi giakades kai o kampos tis Xanthis* (Athens, 1941), 545; *ESV*, 9 Dec. 1929, 177.

[25] D. Kallitsounakis, *O kapnos* (Athens, 1931), 126–8; AOS, *Epi tou zitimatos tou kapnou* (Athens, 1938), *passim*.

and much of the post-war boom in Greek tobacco exports had been due to the growth there of cigarette smoking. By 1926 40% of Greek tobacco exports were directed to Germany, and other deliveries, nominally consigned to Trieste or Rotterdam, were in fact also destined for the German market.

The downturn in German import demand after 1926 signalled the beginning of a general slump in world oriental tobacco exports. However, in Greece, the high producer prices that had prevailed since 1922 still encouraged an expansion of cultivation. Between 1926 and 1929 the number of cultivators increased by almost one-third, whilst the cultivated area doubled. This trend was most marked in central and western Macedonia, where the land was not so suitable for tobacco cultivation but where smallholders had more land at their disposal than the specialist farmers to the east. The latter found themselves being squeezed out of the market by the cheaper leaf grown by their neighbours. Producer prices in Thrace fell by 45% between 1926 and 1929.[26] Hence even before the 1929 crisis, over-production was pushing incomes down fast in certain areas.

The constraints on any further expansion of export agriculture, at least in the short term, may now be more clearly visible. Export crop production had increased as a proportion of the total crop production of the country from around 40% between 1914 and 1922 to over 50% between 1923 and 1929. Should that proportion increase much more? Both the two leading export crops faced the problem of over-production. Farmers had to be encouraged to diversify, but in what direction? A brief glance at Greece's trade deficit suggested the answer: despite the fact that around 70% of the cultivated area was devoted to cereal cultivation, Greece still relied heavily on cereal imports. The suffering induced by the *Entente* blockade in 1916–17 had highlighted the dangers of such dependence and encouraged calls for a policy of aiming at self-sufficiency in cereals.[27] Indeed one of the objections advanced by opponents of the land reform programme was that it would make this objective impossible. Eftaxias, the elderly conservative who became Prime Minister at the end of the Pangalos dictatorship, believed that as a consequence of the land reform 'we should put off any hope of self-sufficiency in cereals'.[28] Venizelos and his followers believed just

[26] GPEK, *To ergon tou GPEK/Kavallas kata tis dekaetias 1926–35* (Kavalla, 1937), tables 5, 9, 10.   [27] Sideris, *Georgiki politiki*, pp. 274 ff.
[28] Cited in Veremis, *Oikonomia kai diktatoria*, p. 89.

the opposite, and were largely proved correct: by the end of the inter-war period Greece was well on the way to achieving the desired goal.

Indeed, by creating a large class of smallholders, the land reform itself gave a new political rationale for protecting cereal growers. Support for domestic agriculture was associated with the Venizelist camp, and especially with its key figure on the Left, Alexandros Papanastasiou, leader of the small Republican Union party. Papanastasiou was an important figure in the progressive intellectual life of Greece, who had studied in Germany and England before the First World War and tried to bring the influences of Fabianism and post-Bismarckian state social-ism to bear on his countrymen's attitudes towards social issues. Politic-ally he was associated with Venizelos, though he was a more fervent republican and more committed social reformer than the Liberal leader. This was the man who, as Minister of Agriculture in the 1927 Coalition Government, laid the foundations of one of the earliest and most coherent interventionist operations of the inter-war Greek state, a scheme to support wheat production, based on tariff protection and domestic price support. Basing his policy upon legislation which obliged mill-owners to accept one-quarter of their wheat intake from domestic suppliers, Papanastasiou aimed at 'the equating of domestic wheat prices with those of imported wheat plus tariffs in order that farmers should receive a corresponding price for their crop'.[29]

The need for state intervention in support of producer prices was certainly present—even before world prices began to fall. As in the case of other monetized crops, market forces in the wheat trade favoured local merchants at the expense of the small farmers. In Thessaly, for example, whose main port, Volos, was a major milling centre where large surpluses were regularly offered on the market, merchants used to force prices down by buying imports of American wheat in the summer —when peasants had to sell to meet cultivation loans due to the National Bank of Greece—and then waiting for higher prices before selling later in the year. Thus the merchants reaped windfall profits, whilst the peasants suffered through having to sell at a low price.[30]

In the first year of operation the scheme encountered various teething problems, and the eventual amount of wheat collected was less than 10% of the anticipated total. This was partly due to the late implementa-tion of the scheme but mainly to the resistance encountered from flour

---

[29] Sideris, *Georgiki politiki*, pp. 275–7; for a comparative perspective, see M. Tracy, 'Agriculture in the Great Depression', in H. van der Wee (ed.), *The Great Depression Revisited* (The Hague, 1972), 91–119.   [30] Sideris, *Georgiki politiki*. 279.

merchants in Volos, who attempted to renege on their earlier commitments.[31] Despite these set-backs the scheme appears to have succeeded in stabilizing prices in the areas of central and northern Greece where it was put into operation.[32] The following year tougher sanctions were introduced against merchants who refused to participate and a new organization, the Central Committee for the Protection of Domestic Wheat (KEPES), was set up at the Ministry of Agriculture.

The second prong of Papanastasiou's strategy was, as has been mentioned, tariff protection: the 'concentration' of crops could prevent price fluctuations, but the tariff would set relative price levels. In August 1927, Papanastasiou issued a decree raising the tariff on imported wheat by 40%: and although the state benefited from increased revenues, this time the primary motive was clearly protective. Domestic wheat was more expensive than imported, and suffered in addition from high transport costs from the field to the mill. From 1926 gradually falling wheat prices on world markets had strained the position of domestic producers.

The Venizelos Government of 1928–32, after early opposition from the conservative Interior Minister, Konstantine Zavitsianos, continued Papanastasiou's interventionist strategy. While Zavitsianos feared the effects of higher bread prices on urban consumers, Venizelos argued that it was only fair to grant tariff protection to peasants who were forced by the government's policies to buy expensive manufactured goods. In this way considerations of social justice had a ratchet effect on overall tariff levels. Under pressure from Zavitsianos tariffs were lowered in 1929, but raised again in 1930 to a nominal rate of 30%. In 1929 for the first time, KEPES was empowered to intervene actively in local markets, fixing support prices above import prices, giving financial and technical assistance to growers and allocating wheat stocks for distribution to the flour merchants according to their milling capacity. It was also given additional independent sources of finance. These measures reinforced the state control of domestic wheat markets at the expense of the merchants and millers. Moreover, the effect on consumption was expected to be limited, since bread generally contained only 15–20% domestic wheat—so that import price levels would continue to be a determining factor in bread prices.[33]

In the following two years KEPES extended its operations, tightening

[31] *OT*, 1 July 1928.
[32] AOS, *Ta metra pros epavxisin tis enchoriou sitoparagogis* (Athens, 1934), 23–5; *OT*, 20 Jan. 1929.   [33] *OT*, 29 Jan. 1933; IBA/Salonika, YR 1930/31, p. 3.

controls over merchants importing flour from abroad and also taking on increased powers to counteract further falls in wheat prices by raising the margin of support: protection rates for domestic growers rose to a remarkable 73% above import prices in 1931. By this point it had become the most important vehicle for state intervention in the domestic economy: whereas the Autonomous Currant Organization was cushioning an export sector in decline, KEPES, with its close links to the Ministry of Agriculture, marked the Venizelos Government's promotion of agricultural self-sufficiency.

Yet for all the long-term significance of the new institution, KEPES's impact before 1932 was limited. Domestic wheat output actually fell after 1928, whilst there was a steep rise in imports: harvests fell from 356,000 tonnes in 1928 to 264,000 in 1930, while imports rose from 476,000 tonnes to 575,000. Because it only operated in a few areas, KEPES's high support prices remained above producer prices nationally and failed to prevent the latter from following world prices downwards, making cereal cultivation increasingly unattractive: yields were so low that cereal farming was uneconomic for many smallholders. Part of the difficulty lay in poor weather conditions, which reduced anticipated harvests by up to around 40% between 1928 and 1931. It is true that the area sown with wheat increased, but this occurred in a period of general expansion. What is more to the point, this area expressed as a proportion of the total cultivated area declined steadily. By the time that the 1931 financial crisis increased Greece's balance of payments problems, it had become clear that despite the priority placed by the Liberal Government on non-export agriculture, the country faced a severe structural crisis of cereal production.

Industry

In contrast to the difficulties of agriculture, the 1920s were a period of rapid—though not unproblematic—growth for Greek industry. In 1924 an observer noted that there were signs that 'prominent Greek businessmen were shifting capital from commerce to industrial investment'.[34] The young economist Angelopoulos stated disapprovingly that 'from early 1923 an excessive number of firms were created . . . Business fever seized everybody. Each person saw the enrichment of

[34] DOT, *Report on Industrial and Economic Conditions in Greece in 1923 and 1924* (London, 1925), 33.

TABLE 4.4.   *New industrial firms, 1921–1929*

Year	No. of new establishments	Horsepower
1921	56	1,821
1922	46	371
1923	41	1,217
1924	107	2,518
1925	132	4,624
1926	124	3,145
1927	214	6,105
1928	192	6,540
1929	62	3,215

Notes: These figures exclude electricity plants; they include only what are described as 'more or less important' firms; hence they are not comparable with the results of the 1920 or 1930 industrial censuses.

Source: AOS, *EO 1937* (Athens, 1938).

the merchants, which was in reality purely superficial, and wanted to become a businessman.'[35]

Manufacturers, like bankers and merchants, were encouraged by inflation. In addition they benefited from a sharp fall in real wages after 1921, as well as favourable tax concessions and the tariff increases introduced in 1926. A building boom in Athens and Salonika, which had been substantially destroyed by a fire in 1917, encouraged a number of industries: cement output, for example, increased from 28,000 tonnes in 1921 to 86,000 in 1926.[36] The chemical and textile industries expanded, while a number of new industries appeared for the first time, among which the carpet industry—started by refugees from Asia Minor—was the most impressive, expanding output from 60,000 square metres to 200,000 square metres between 1923 and 1928. Table 4.4 charts the establishment of new firms during this decade.

How fast *was* industrialization in this formative phase? Table A1.4 provides alternative estimates of gross rates of manufacturing output growth after 1921. These agree on an average compound growth rate of 6.8% per annum between 1921 and 1929. They also agree that average annual growth rates in the sub-period 1921–5 were around 10.1%,

[35] Angelopoulos, 'Ai anonymoi etaireiai en Elladi', p. 31.

[36] Cf. B. Eichengreen, 'Inflazione e ripresa economica negli anni '20', *Rivista di Storia Economica*, 3(3) (Oct. 1986), 269–303; *OE 1938* (Athens, 1939), 208.

dropping to 3.5% during 1925–9. Overall industrial growth rates (i.e. including the extractive industries) would be somewhat lower, since the extractive sector performed poorly during the 1920s. But the average for the decade of 6.8% per annum was extremely high: it compared favourably with that of Greece's neighbours Yugoslavia and Romania, and was only slightly lower than that of Bulgaria, which was starting from a lower base.[37]

The structure of Greek industry reflected its natural endowments. Heavy industry did not exist: the 'metallurgical' sector was an export-directed refining arm of the Lavrion mines; the 'engineering' sector consisted chiefly of mechanical-repair workshops and traditionally-run shipyards. The major branches were food/drink and textiles, whilst soap and olive-kernel refining, chemicals, furniture, and leather working were also important. The overall impression is of a largely traditional manufacturing sector which contained isolated examples of more modern industrial practices. None the less, in terms of overall importance within the domestic economy, Greek manufacturing achieved an unprecedented prominence during the 1920s. Industrial output was growing twice as fast as crop output through the decade.[38] By 1929 the value of gross manufacturing output was 7,158 million drachmas, compared with 8,462.7 million drachmas for crop output. These figures made manufacturing of greater relative importance in the Greek economy than in any of her Balkan neighbours.[39]

Yet these high growth rates were not accompanied by signs of modernization. Greek industry was split between a large number of small backward firms, mostly self-financing family units, and a relatively small number of larger firms which employed a large proportion of the work-force, had access to bank credit, and were technologically well ahead of the smaller businesses. In many branches a small number of large firms dominated the market. For example, in the case of olive oil processing, only 600 out of approximately 6,000 firms were mechanized, and only eight factories were capable of chemically purifying the oil.[40] In 1932 of the 17 major incorporated olive oil companies in Greece, just two used 62.5% of the total employed capital.[41] Even in a 'non-traditional' branch—electricity generation—the structure of the

---

[37] Jackson and Lampe, *Balkan Economic History*, pp. 340–1.
[38] See Tables A1.1 and 4.
[39] For very similar results cf. Jackson and Lampe, *Balkan Economic History*, pp. 338–9.
[40] MNE, *H elliniki viomichania* (Athens, 1931), 234–5.   [41] *EX*, 30 Sept. 1934.

sector was similar: of 4,350 electricity companies operating under licence in 1932, only 31 were incorporated and of these only six were worth (in total employed capital) more than 100 million drachmas.[42]

This was not a simple case of oligopoly. Poor communications and the largely self-financing nature of the smaller companies meant that large firms could not easily dominate the small ones. What seems to have occurred was a division of the market: the major firms would be located close to their main source of demand, the urban centres of Athens and Piraeus (and to a lesser extent Patras, Volos, Salonika), while the rural areas were supplied by tiny local firms.

To be sure, the decade leading up to 1930 witnessed substantial investment in industry. Comparing the census of 1920 with that of 1930 we find that the number of firms had risen from 33,811 to 76,703, whilst the labour force had increased from 154,633 to 278,855.[43] Yet in most sectors the average number of workers per firm fell over the decade, which tends to confirm the view, commonly held at the end of the decade, that expansion had come about through the appearance of a plethora of *small* firms. The ratio of workers per firm fell from 4.57 in 1920 to 3.64 in 1930. We can understand why contemporaries described industrial growth as 'hypertrophic', the result of indiscriminate protection provided by the state without adequate planning.[44]

Yet the rapid development of industry found few enthusiasts among Greek politicians; there was a surprising consensus right across the political spectrum on this matter. Many Marxists viewed industry with the same suspicion as authoritarian advocates of agricultural self-sufficiency like Metaxas and Kondylis, nostalgic royalists in the Populist Party who harked back to the tranquillity of Old Greece, and even numerous Liberals, who connected the growth of industry with the intensifying class conflicts of post-war Greece, which their paternalistic labour policies had failed to mute. The parliamentary deputy who felt 'genuine national pride' when he visited the 'colossal, titanic works' of the large chemical fertilizer plant outside Athens spoke for a tiny minority. The anti-industrial bias of Greek nationalism was deeply ingrained.[45]

[42] *EX*, 23 Dec. 1934.
[43] MNE, *H elliniki viomichania*, pp. 234–5.   [44] Ibid. 132.
[45] Livieratos, *Koinonikes agones stin Ellada (1927–31)* (Athens, 1987), 184; G. Leontaritis, 'To ergatiko kinima, 1910–20', in Veremis (ed.), *Meletimata gyro apo ton Venizelo kai tin epochi tou*; K. Vergopoulos, *Ethnismos kai oikonomiki anaptyxi* (Athens, 1978), ch. 4; see also D. Stefanides, *I thesis tis viomchanias en ti koinoniki mas oikonomia* (Thessaloniki, 1938), introduction; G. Modis, in *ESV*, 19 Dec. 1930, 424.

TABLE 4.5. *Size of firms according to the 1930 census*

Firm size	No. of firms	No. of workers	Total hp	hp/firm	hp/worker
1–5	70,644	121,198	90,103	1.275	0.743
6–25	4,900	49,665	58,678	11.975	1.181
25+	1,047	109,468	208,559	199.197	1.905
TOTAL	76,591	280,331	357,340	4.666	1.275

Source: *OE 1933* (Athens, 1934), 567.

It was felt that many industries which had sprung up during and after wartime only survived behind high tariff barriers and a favourable fiscal regime. The tax on company profits produced a miserable yield, leading Dimitrios Tantalides, the former Finance Minister who had introduced it in 1919, to confess in 1924 that it was only paid by 'those with a highly developed sense of consciousness of their duty towards themselves and their country or those whose taxable income is too obvious to hide'.[46] Between 1921 and 1926 the contribution of limited-liability companies to total direct tax revenues dropped from 17% to 5.3%. Thus when Epaminondas Charilaos, a prominent industrialist, publicly demanded a reduction in the tax on incorporated companies from the so-called Committee for Economies, which met in 1924 to examine the prospects for budgetary reform, he elicited a hostile response. The conservative chairman of the Committee, Eftaxias, retorted that 'Mr Charilaos seeks tax relief for incorporated companies at the same time that they and their capital are constantly on the increase'. Eftaxias declared himself opposed to the 'unjustified protection of every industry, often kept alive and even thriving unacceptably because of tariffs . . . which lead to the enrichment of a few and higher living costs for the multitude'.[47]

In 1926, the young German-trained economist Xenophon Zolotas, in his book on Greek industrialization, urged that tariff levels be reduced 'so that a healthy industrial sector will develop in the country' rather than the 'unviable' firms that had sprung up in the absence of competition from abroad.[48] The stifling effects of an official industrial policy which awaited results from tariffs alone were underlined in the comments of a government report on the soap industry in 1928: 'The tariff

[46] Cited in A. Angelopoulos, *I ammesos forologia en Elladi* (Athens, 1933), 186.

[47] Veremis, *Oikonomia kai diktatoria*, 88–9; Angelopoulos, 'Ai anonymoi etaireiai en Elladi', p. 80.

[48] X. Zolotas, *I Ellas eis to stadion tis ekviomichaniseos* (Athens, 1926), 118–19.

protection which the State has provided for the soap industry . . . has not unfortunately led to the improvement of its installations, apart from a few exceptions, nor to the production of more varieties nor to the creation of other industries linked to it. Comparing its technical appearance today with that ten years ago, we see no signs of any technical progress, apart from the increase in the number of factories, and the increase in output, which is due to the intervening increase in the population.'[49]

Ironically, in the very year that Zolotas's book appeared, a new tariff schedule was introduced which *increased* the level of protection of domestic manufacturers. Previously exempted items, such as agricultural machines, wool yarn, and wood pulp were now taxed, whilst in other cases duties were doubled. Data included in the Ministry for the National Economy's 1930 survey of Greek industry, but referring to the position in 1928, gave estimates of nominal tariff levels for various manufactured goods (shown in Table 4.6).

Although estimates of effective tariff protection are given in only a few cases, the officials of the Ministry were aware of the importance of allowing for the effect of duties paid on imported raw materials and fuels. Even taking these into account, their conclusion in almost all cases was that existing tariff levels were adequate, if not excessive. Indeed, the state's concern with tariffs stemmed from fiscal motives rather than any desire to promote industry. This was bluntly spelled out by the leading Liberal politician, George Kafandaris, when he was Finance Minister in the 1927 Coalition Government. Speaking to an audience of industrialists, he informed them that 'I am completely indifferent to industry

TABLE 4.6. *Tariff levels on manufactured imports, 1928* (import duty as % c.i.f. price)[a]

Product	Tariff level (%)	Product	Tariff level (%)
Soap	215	Beer	62
Varnish	70–100	Bottles	47
Tiles	60–100	Shoe leather	40–8
Bricks	50–90	Paints	35–50
Cement	60–5	Cotton thread	20–35

[a] c.i.f. = cargo, insurance, and freight.

Source: MNE, *H elliniki viomichania* (Athens, 1931).

[49] MNE, *H elliniki viomichania*, p. 279.

and regard it as useful solely because it is the *raison d'être* for a tariff regime which yields half the budget's revenues.' And he added, 'industry creates obstacles to achieving a balanced budget, for the simple reason that it means that fewer goods are imported and the Treasury receives less in duties'.[50]

Venizelos took a different view. On a visit to one of Greece's largest textile factories in 1930, he admonished his host, Andreas Chadzikyriakos, the President of the Federation of Greek Industrialists, for his reluctance to consider further expansion: 'Listen, my dear Chadzikyriakos, who is going to absorb those 90,000 new Greeks, whom Greek mothers line up for me each year, who, if not industry?' Industrial expansion could be supported by keeping labour costs down, even if this meant renouncing attempts to improve the living conditions of most workers. And yet working conditions in Greek factories were oppressive: a 12-hour day was the norm in some industries, and the employment of women and children was common. The international convention forbidding the employment of children under 14 was not observed and even officials at the Ministry of the National Economy sympathized with the view that the low salaries earned by adult workers made it essential for their children to work too.[51] To a visiting delegate from the International Labour Office, Venizelos confirmed that 'the urgent necessity of securing work for the great mass of refugees, the small proportion among them of male workers, and finally the necessity of dedicating all the available resources to the most urgent task of resettlement, have not permitted the implementation of measures which would be useful but might prevent the creation of new industries—which are anyway often unstable—and halt the development of others'.[52]

The most cogent critics in the late 1920s of Venizelos's policy of industrial expansion were not anti-Venizelist conservatives, but rather proponents of 'rationalization'—a mixed bag of established industrialists, bankers (especially at the National Bank), and young economists. For them, the problem was not the existence of industry *per se*, but the mass of uncompetitive small firms which had sprung up in the post-war decade. Even by 1926 excessive competition between firms founded in

[50] Cited in Vergopoulos, *Ethnismos kai oikonomiki anaptyxi*, pp. 79–80.

[51] FO 371/15960 C2886/324, Venizelos–Simon, 3 Apr. 1932, encloses the ILO report 'Les Conditions du travail des salaires, de l'industrie et de commerce'.

[52] S. Stefanou (ed.), *Eleftheriou Venizelou politikai ypothikai anthologitheisai apo ta keimena avtou*, ii (Athens, 1969), 483; A. Liakos, 'O Eleftherios Venizelos kai to Diethnes Grafeio Ergasias', *Synchrona Themata*, 31 (Oct. 1987), 42; A. Papanastasiou, 'La Politique sociale de la Grèce', *Les Balkans*, 17–18 (Feb.–Mar. 1932), 258–81.

the previous three years was reported to have 'pushed down profits to unsatisfactory levels'.[53] There were increasing calls—as everywhere else in Europe—for a policy of 'rationalization' under which numerous small concerns would be amalgamated into trusts or cartels. Industrialists' organizations themselves called for official encouragement of such a policy and recommended specific sectors—lignite mining, tanning, soap manufacturing—as ripe for mergers. Some economists also recommended 'rationalization' on financial grounds—it might bring down prices 'by the reduction of all useless expenses', thus helping to curb inflation and protect the stabilization programme.[54]

Venizelos's hints that the Liberal Government itself might be prepared to offer financial assistance to 'well-ordered concerns' were, however, greeted by industrialists not with enthusiasm but with alarm. Suspecting a move towards some form of state control over industry, the business world blocked his idea and ensured thereafter that problems of industrial organization and credit were left to the private sector.[55] The National Mortgage Bank, designed to supply credit to industry, always remained a pale imitation of the Agricultural Bank which the Liberal Government created in 1929 to supply credit to farmers. Although commercial bankers criticized the lack of a 'systematic programme for the implementation of industrial and commercial policy' to match what Venizelos had achieved in agriculture, the policy they envisaged for industry boiled down to securing cheap labour, unencumbered by safety legislation or compulsory workers' insurance, and lower business taxes. In their view, it should be left to the banks to provide loan capital and advice on rationalization. The deficiencies of such an approach soon became obvious.

The minor banks retained their old liking for keeping their investments liquid even after the wild exchange rate fluctuations of the early 1920s began to smooth out. Small family firms, especially those based outside the main cities, tended to remain self-financing. Only a rather small number of powerful and well-connected business men were in a position to draw on the resources of the larger banks. Far and away the most important of these was the National Bank, which had begun to expand its portfolio of industrial investments even before it lost its

[53] DOT, *Report on Industrial and Economic Conditions in Greece in 1925* (London, 1927), 8.

[54] *OA* 623, 18 Jan. 1930; P. B. Dertilis, *La Reconstruction financière de la Grèce et la Société des Nations* (Paris, 1929), 218; *Peitharchia*, 3 Nov. 1929.

[55] *MA*, 1 Jan. 1930; ibid., 4 Jan. 1930; C. Chadziiosif, 'Venizelogenis antipolitefsi', in Mavrogordatos and Chadziiosif (eds.), *Venizelismos*, p. 449.

agricultural credit business to the Agricultural Bank and its note-issuing privileges to the new central bank, the Bank of Greece. In 1927 it joined forces with Hambros in London to form the Hellenic Corporation (later renamed the Hellenic and General Trust), a holding company intended to provide capital for specific industries on the condition that they were first 'rationalized'. Rationalization in this context seems to have meant reducing competition and reorganizing production in such a way as to maintain profit margins rather than encouraging greater efficiency or technological improvement. Several mergers took place, which principally had the effect of increasing the National Bank's control over key textiles and cement industries; in addition, a large loan was extended to the Wine and Spirit Company, which the National Bank also influenced through its interest in the Autonomous Currant Organization, whose surpluses had become a cheap source of supply for wine manufacturers. For Hambros, however, the results were disappointing. The Corporation's chairman reported at the first general meeting that investment possibilities in industry were 'hindered by excessive competition among small companies', and he announced that the company would henceforth extend its horizons beyond Greece.[56]

Greek industry seems to have been unattractive not only to the Hellenic Corporation but to foreign investors more generally, and to potential Greek investors too. Even John Drosopoulos of the National Bank argued that 'it is not the work of the banks to take an active share in the management of industrial enterprises, and still less to immobilize funds in such enterprises in a permanent manner'.[57] Drosopoulos was reflecting a very widespread hesitancy which permeated much of the state apparatus. Indeed, when politicians moved from questions of public finance to the broader issue of economic reconstruction, industry was largely left out of the picture. This became increasingly evident after 1926 as negotiations were resumed with the League of Nations for further loans. The broad economic programme which emerged out of these negotiations and which first the Zaimis and then the Venizelos

---

[56] Bank of Athens, *Bulletin Économique et Financier*, (Feb. 1930), 'L'Opinion des grandes banques'; *Peitharchia*, 12 Jan. 1930, 19 Jan. 1930, 9 Feb. 1930; K. Arliotis, *Istoria tis Ethnikis Ktimatikis Trapezis tis Ellados* (Athens, 1979); *Near East and India*, 25 Apr. 1929; *OA* 22 Nov. 1930; on the Hellenic and General Trust, see FO 371/67109 R10692/305, 'Athens Electricity and Transport Undertakings', 27 June 1947; also, M. Mazower 'Economic Diplomacy between Great Britain and Greece in the 1930s', *Journal of European Economic History*, 17(3) (Winter 1988), 603–19.

[57] NBG, *Report for the Year 1929 of the Governor of the National Bank of Greece* (Athens, 1930), 24.

Government began to implement had a heavily agricultural slant. And in a New Year's Day message to the Press, delivered at the beginning of 1930, Venizelos emphasized his intention above all to develop agriculture 'which, improved and increased, will constitute—so the Government firmly believes—the unshakeable foundation of this country's future prosperity'.[58]

Reconstructing the Public Finances

The parliamentary regime that was re-established in January 1924 with the formation of a Constituent Assembly was faced with the daunting task of reintroducing stability into the public finances: one estimate put the combined deficit of the previous three budgets at almost 6 billion drachmas, most of which had been covered by short-term loans.[59] Tax revenues had increased as a result of new fiscal measures—but on nowhere near an adequate scale to enable the Government to reduce its borrowing requirements. These, on the contrary, were set to increase if the mass of refugees were to be resettled and successfully integrated into the economic life of the country. But confidence in the underlying potential of the Greek economy was strong: during 1924 private investors returned to Greece either investing directly in domestic companies, or—more importantly—competing for public contracts. This confidence was strengthened by the decision of the League of Nations to assist the Greek Government with refugee resettlement. An indication of this easing of the situation is provided—in the absence of any comprehensive balance of payments figures—by the movement of foreign exchange through the National Bank of Greece: purchases of exchange rose from £15.1 million in 1922 and £22.3 million in 1923 to £34.6 million (1924) and £32.9 million (1925) before falling back under the Pangalos dictatorship in 1926 to £22.1 million.[60] Because the Government refrained from issuing further quantities of unbacked notes, monetary growth slowed down, the value of government bonds began to rise, and the drachma steadied on the foreign exchanges. By the second half of 1924 it had settled at around 250–60 against sterling.[61]

The market's favourable mood was based on signs of a more determined attitude by the Greek authorities to set their finances in order. A

[58] *MA*, 1 Jan. 1930.
[59] DOT, *Report on Industrial and Economic Conditions . . . in 1923 and 1924*, p. 8.
[60] Bristoyiannis, *Banque Nationale*, 139–42.
[61] DOT, *Report on Industrial and Economic Conditions . . . in 1925*, p. 54.

committee was appointed to recommend economies in government expenditures, and there was closer supervision of purchasing procedures for government supplies. Revenues from direct taxes improved as did those based on increased import and consumption duties. On the other hand the tax on capital was abandoned.[62] But it remained difficult to control expenditures: the military, the civil service, and the public debt all imposed a growing burden.

Attempts to implement the austerity measures urged by the Committee of Economies were met by a wave of strikes which alarmed the political élite. Over the previous two years labour protests on a previously unknown scale had ended in bloodshed. When the leaders of striking civil servants, protesting at the austerity programme, met the Venizelist Prime Minister, Andreas Mikalakopoulos, in 1925, they were told by him that 'such syndicalism is unacceptable to the state as it constitutes anarchy'. That June Mikalakopoulos resigned, leaving none of his political colleagues eager to succeed him.[63]

The politicians' lack of self-confidence—which was to re-emerge with similar results after 1932—opened the way for an ambitious republican Army officer, Theodoros Pangalos, to seize power in a bloodless coup. George Kafandaris, who was in line to succeed Mikalakopoulos, is said to have remarked on hearing of Pangalos's plans: 'Well then, let him become dictator—we'll see what happens!' Initially his regime was buoyed up by a widespread anti-parliamentarianism and by the defeatism of the politicians themselves. The chief economic advisers to Pangalos were men like George Kofinas, who had introduced the radical fiscal reforms of 1922–3 and had condemned his successors' inability to continue in the same vein. But it was soon evident that Pangalos too had neither the prestige nor the inclination for austerity measures and Kofinas resigned in protest. Trying to pose as the protector of the petty bourgeoisie against the high taxes and pro-business inclinations of the Liberals, Pangalos patently lacked the power either to tackle Greece's urgent economic problems or to crush popular dissent through wholesale repression. The public hanging of several unfortunates on charges of embezzlement typified the mixture of violence and ineffectiveness which characterized his regime. On a visit to the town of Patras in December 1925, as the domestic boom showed signs of coming to an end, unrest in the assembled crowd interrupted his

[62] Andreades (ed.), *Les Effets économiques*, p. 47.
[63] G. Dafnis, *I Ellas metaxy dyo polemon, 1923–1940*, i (Athens, 1955), 272; Veremis, *Oikonomia kai diktatoria*, p. 24.

reception and showed how little popularity he had gained. Financial scandals discredited him further and, by the time he fell from power, prolonged political turmoil had served to increase—as his successor Zaimis put it—the public's habitual 'mistrust with respect to everything concerning the Greek state'.[64]

Thus if the politicians had fallen short in the face of the financial crisis, the experience of General Pangalos showed that as an alternative military rule was no improvement: the drachma depreciated heavily, the National Bank's foreign exchange reserves fell from £3.2 millions to £606,000 in seven months, while the sale of exchange caused a credit contraction of over 20%. When Pangalos was bloodlessly deposed and replaced by a civilian coalition government in 1926 the task of economic reconstruction remained to be tackled. The League of Nations in 1924 had already lent assistance to the Greek refugees; as the funds from this loan ran out, the authorities now proposed to approach the League for further help. But economic assistance would not be provided *in vacuo*. Several conditions would have first to be satisfied: the settlement of war debts between Greece and her former allies; financial and monetary stabilization. These issues are discussed below.

On 12 August 1926, ten days before Pangalos was overthrown, a British official at the Foreign Office reminded the Greek Minister in London that 'the market will not any longer lend funds to foreign governments who have not paid their obligations. This rule did not apply when the first refugee loan was issued, but it applies today.'[65] The remark was an indication of the British Government's desire to see the tangled question of Anglo-Greek war debts finally sorted out. Negotiations had been pursued since 1921 without reaching a result, and some of Pangalos's more intransigent associates were expressing the opinion that Greece should abandon the search for a settlement and seek funds elsewhere. The Greek negotiating team in London, however, were well aware of the futility of such talk: Greece urgently required a large foreign loan, and, as the British Foreign Office emphasized, a settlement of the war debt question was a prerequisite to obtaining it.

Moreover, the British side too was keen to reach a settlement, in order to permit British investors to compete with Americans in bids for a number of public works projects which were being discussed. The two

---

[64] Veremis, *Oikonomia kai diktatoria*, p. 24; A. Marasli, *I istoria tis Patras* (Patras, 1983), 135; S. Maximos, *Koinovoulio i diktatoria?* (Athens, 1975), 104–5.

[65] Cited in Veremis, *Oikonomia kai diktatoria*, p. 112 n. 47.

camps differed less over the final total of the debt than over the repayment schedule: from the Greek side came suggestions that the annual repayment should be between £75,000 and £200,000, while the British initially demanded £500,000. According to London, the Greek authorities were exaggerating their economic difficulties and were maintaining a high level of military expenditure, which could be reduced to make way for the service of the debt.[66]

Once Pangalos had left the scene, negotiations proceeded swiftly and a final settlement was signed the following spring. Britain agreed to forgo repayment for *matériel* it had supplied to Greece, whilst Greece would abandon all claims to indemnification and would renounce her claimed right to the balance of the British credits. The total Greek debt to Britain was fixed at £23.5 million, payable over 60 years; in return, British support was pledged for Greek efforts to raise a further loan.[67] At the same time, talks continued with France and the USA, Greece's other creditors. In the American case, settled in December 1927, the Greek authorities renounced claims on unpaid credits of $35 million in exchange for a new loan of around $12 million, which was granted by the US authorities on favourable terms on the condition it was used by the RSC.[68] But negotiations with the French took rather longer, thereby relegating them to a minor role in financing the reconstruction policies that evolved out of the discussions which now began in earnest between Greek officials and League of Nations representatives.

The settlement of Greece's war debts paved the way for her return to foreign capital markets, whose resources were urgently needed to continue the resettlement of the refugees, and to fund the swollen floating debt. To this end, the Zaimis Government, which was formed after the general election in November 1926, decided to solicit the assistance of the League of Nations.[69] A Committee of Experts was appointed by Kafandaris, the coalition Finance Minister, in December, and this shortly afterwards produced a report which condemned the chaotic state of the nation's finances and made a number of recommendations on budgetary procedure, stressing the need to curb military expenditures and advocating various tax reforms. Negotiations now began with the League for a new loan, and in 1927 a financial commission, chaired by the French economist Avenol, visited the

---

[66] Ibid. 102, 110.
[67] Ibid. 114; Andreades, *Les Effets économiques*, pp. 96–7.   [68] Ibid. 95.
[69] G. Pyrsos, *Symvoli eis tin istorian tis Trapezis tis Ellados*, i (Athens, 1936), 27; D. G. Bristoyiannis, *La Politique de la Banque Nationale de Grèce* (Paris, 1928), 231–43.

country. In June, Avenol presented his report to the League's Financial Committee (LNFC) and proposed that a £9 million loan be raised in order to finance the continued work of resettling the refugees, returning Greece to the gold standard, and financing the accumulated budget deficits of previous years. The League approved these measures but set certain conditions: the Greek Government would have to establish an independent central bank; it must take active steps to stabilize the drachma, and it must reform its accounting procedures.

The findings of both Avenol and the LNFC reflected the conclusions of the Greek 'Committee of Experts', which had preceded them. The only new element was the emphasis on monetary reform, but this is perhaps not so surprising: a Greek committee, even had it so desired, would have lacked the authority to suggest major modifications to the role of the National Bank. Experience was to show that such changes would be stoutly resisted even when urged by a powerful foreign body like the League.

The Committee of Experts had emphasized monetary stabilization as the first step towards economic reconstruction. But how best to achieve this? The experts' answer had been sound financial management by the state. It was not perhaps surprising that a committee whose members included the Governor of the National Bank and his two chief coun-sellors should regard the existing monetary system as essentially satis-factory. Nevertheless, when the Avenol Commission presented its findings to the LNFC, discussions centred on the necessity of founding a central bank which would not let commercial considerations distract it from its public duties. The LNFC suggested hiving off the commercial functions of the NBG, turning it into a pure bank of issue. But there was fierce resistance to this idea from within the NBG itself. At first this took the form of disputing the length of time such a transformation would require—two to three months according to the LNFC, at least two years according to the NBG. The authorities at the NBG perhaps believed that the transformation could be indefinitely postponed.[70] But the LNFC demanded that the banking reform precede the stabilization of the drachma.

As an impasse loomed, the Deputy Governor, Emmanouil Tsou-deros, suggested an alternative: turning the NBG into a purely commer-cial bank and creating a *new* central bank, the Bank of Greece, which

---

[70] IBA, General Manager, Annual Report 1926/27, 11.

would be vested with the sole privilege of note issue. This proposal was quickly accepted by both sides and approved by August 1927. When the Geneva Protocol was signed the following month between the Greek Government and the League, it included the charter of the new Bank of Greece, which had been drafted by officials of the League. The League had been involved in several schemes for the creation of new central banks after 1918, and the provisions of the Greek charter reflected the tenets of what had become central-banking orthodoxy: limits to the share capital that could be held by the state, and the advances that the Bank could make to it; a stipulated 'cover ratio', in other words, a stipulation that the reserves were not to fall below a given fraction of the notes in circulation—in the Greek case, 40%; finally, of course, free convertibility of drachmas into foreign exchange at the gold parity rate.[71]

But although the Bank of Greece owed its existence to a belief in the value of central banking, it found few believers in Athens. When it began operations in May 1928, it was tolerated but hardly welcomed by Greek bankers and politicians. To the commercial banks, it was a threatening interloper. Panayis Tsaldaris, the leader of the Populist Party, and Dimitrios Maximos, a close associate of Tsaldaris's and a former Governor of the National Bank, had both opposed its creation and remained opposed to it after they came into office in 1932. Venizelos too had doubts: in fact he returned to power in the summer of 1928 after bringing about the dissolution of the Zaimis Government by criticizing its banking reforms. Strong feeling against the new institution ran across party boundaries.[72]

The Bank, though buoyed up with reserves which covered 80% of the notes in circulation, had been constrained to accept a large quantity of illiquid state debt, which had been transferred from the National Bank and which constituted almost half its assets. Its capacity to control the domestic monetary system was further hindered by the National Bank's refusal to hand over the deposits of a number of state institutions, as had been stipulated in the Geneva Protocol. The National Bank, on the other hand, was freed of all formal obligations to the state and though hurt by the loss of its note-issuing privileges was able now to function as a purely commercial institution, retaining its enormous strength and informal influence with the political and business élite. There seemed some justification for the view expressed by Alexandros Diomedes, who

---

[71] D. Aldcroft, *From Versailles to Wall Street 1919–1929* (London, 1977), chs. 6–7.

[72] Dafnis, *I Ellas metaxy dyo polemon*, i. 381–6; G. Vouros, *Panayis Tsaldaris* (Athens, 1955), 147–62.

moved as Governor from the National Bank to the new central bank, that the National Bank had in fact been strengthened rather than weakened by this new arrival.[73]

Foreign capital began to enter Greece after 1924, with the flotation of the Refugee Loan. The following year the Power and Traction Finance Company Ltd. reached an agreement with the Pangalos Government which gave it the concession to generate and distribute electricity in the Athens area, as well as control of the tram and local rail services. In the next few years British and American capital vied for road-building and other infrastructural projects, and by 1927 the British Commercial Attaché was expressing concern at the scale of foreign lending to Greece.[74] Direct investment in Greece had always been secondary to portfolio investment in government bonds. With the war debt issue settled, British merchant banks could regain their traditionally pre-dominant role in Greece, much to the relief, not only of the Greeks, but of the British themselves, who were alarmed at the appearance of American competition in the area.[75]

It had become obvious by early 1927 that the RSC was running short of funds, and that the first task once public finances had been restored was to float a second refugee loan. In February 1927, Charles Eddy, the Chairman of the RSC, announced that more funds would be needed within several months. Finance Minister Kafandaris made this a priority, stating that he had no intention of seeking other loans at that time, despite approaches from abroad. Prime Minister Zaimis, on the other hand, seems to have envisaged the refugee loan as part of a broader package.[76]

Over the next 12 months even the cautious Kafandaris changed his mind. In January 1928 he declared that the forthcoming League loan, would open the way for 'a series of loans for road-building and drainage projects, which the state has the intention and duty to execute on a large scale'.[77] The so-called 'Tripartite' League loan, whose yield was devoted one-third to monetary stabilization, one-third to paying off old

---

[73] Pyrsos, *Symvoli*, ch. 8; Kostas Kostis, *Oi trapezes kai i krisi, 1929–1932* (Athens, 1986), pt. 2, ch. 1.

[74] D. Stefanides, *I eisroi xenon kefalaion kai ai oikonomikai kai politikai tis synepeiai* (Thessaloniki, 1931), 235–99.

[75] Anglo-American financial rivalry after 1926 is analysed in G. Andreopoulos, 'The IFC and Anglo-Greek Relations (1928–1933)', *Historical Journal*, 31(2) (1988), 341–64; L. P. Cassimatis, *American Influence in Greece, 1917–1929* (Kent, Ohio, 1988), 166–85.

[76] *MA*, 19–21 Feb. 1927.   [77] Ibid., 1 Jan. 1928; ibid., 4 Jan. 1928.

budget deficits, and one-third to continuing refugee resettlement, was floated successfully in London and New York (and in smaller part in Milan, Stockholm, and Zürich) in the spring of 1928. With this success, according to an article written by Kafandaris that March, 'Greece has achieved her financial rehabilitation.'[78]

The international environment now seemed propitious for an attempt to realize more ambitious schemes. 'The terrace of the *Grande Bretagne* in Athens', noted William Miller, 'is often full of businessmen in search of concessions. The drainage of the Vardar and Struma valleys, the Salonika harbour-works, the new port of Candia, the "Power and Traction" convention for the traffic of Athens and suburbs, railways, telegraphic and aerial communications, water-works, and roads—all these have attracted foreigners.' The obvious competition between Hambros of London, and the New York bank Seligman and Co. for the chance to finance further public works encouraged the Greek Government. Skinner, the US Minister in Greece, saw the chance of 'removing Hellenic finances entirely from the domain of European politics'; failure would mean that 'London might manage to exclude New York from the centre of Greek financing.'[79]

Ever since Macedonia and Thrace had been acquired by Greece, developing their agricultural potential had seemed to offer the country one way of freeing herself from her economic dependence on the outside world. Under the Liberal Government of 1917 to 1920, civil servants had drawn up drainage and road-building schemes for the area.[80] The RSC, after 1924, had begun to build roads in eastern Macedonia. From 1925 the American Foundation Company had been involved in negotiations with the Greek authorities over plans to drain the Axios Valley to the west of Salonika, and preliminary work had begun in 1927. The Zaimis Government hoped to finance, not only the drainage of the Axios plain, but also similar works in the Strymon Valley in eastern Macedonia and in Thessaly. These schemes were taken over, with his typical enthusiasm, by Venizelos, when he returned to the Greek political arena in spring 1928. At an election rally in Salonika that July, he outlined his plans for Greece's economic future in a lengthy speech. After the ritual obeisance to the importance of a balanced budget, he turned his attention to the 'great productive works' and to his desire 'to develop all branches of national production'.

[78] Cited in Stefanides, *Eisroi*, p. 245.
[79] W. Miller, *Greece* (London, 1928), 20–1; US State Department, *FRUS, 1928*, vol. 3, pp. 39–41.   [80] *MA*, 31 Mar. 1930.

Although he admitted that projects elsewhere in Greece could not be immediately undertaken, he assured his audience that the completion of the Axios and Strymon works would 'permit us to fulfil the food requirements not merely of the existing population, but also of future ones'. He also underlined his own preference for a development based around agricultural growth, since 'a paternal solicitude in favour of agriculture will help lessen that evil which is the abandonment of the fields and the influx into the towns, where parasitic trades inevitably have the upper hand'.[81]

Such were the views which formed the basis of the Venizelos Government's economic programme over the next four years. In an interview with the *Financial Times*, Venizelos stressed that what he called the 'productive works' were necessary to make the country self-sufficient in wheat, a major priority for his Government in view of the balance of trade and demographic pressures that the country faced.[82] To finance these schemes large loans were floated in late 1928 and again in 1931. In addition, the Venizelos Government floated several smaller loans abroad, and several large drachma loans in Greece.[83]

Venizelos's unexpected return to public life in 1928 had by no means been universally welcomed. His opponent, the Populist leader Tsaldaris, in a pre-election speech had stressed that 'when he was far away, the political world could co-operate and a tranquil political atmosphere prevailed'. And many less partisan observers had also been apprehensive that old wounds would be reopened.[84] Nevertheless, after his resounding victory in the 1928 elections, Venizelos's reconfirmation as the one truly charismatic political figure in the country appeared to inaugurate an era of stability and growth. Anti-Venizelists became more subdued in their criticisms, indeed even welcoming. 'Every Greek in his right mind', remarked the royalist George Streit early in 1930, 'must hope that [Venizelos] would be able to carry through his plan of building up the country economically.'[85] Venizelos promised to work for the

---

[81] *MA*, 28 July 1928; ibid., 6 Aug. 1928.   [82] Ibid., 9 Sept. 1928.

[83] See Stefanides, *Eisroi*, and A. Angelopoulos, *To dimosion chreos tis Ellados* (Athens, 1937), *passim*. A detailed study of the economic policies and achievements of the 1928–32 Liberal Government remains to be written. Kostis, *Trapezes kai krisi*, discusses the monetary reforms; K. Karamanlis, *O Eleftherios Venizelos kai oi exoterikes mas scheseis, 1928–1932* (Athens, 1986), ch. 8, is concerned with financial diplomacy; see also Dafnis, *I Ellas metaxy dyo polemon*, ii, ch. 2.

[84] Marasli, *Istoria tis Patras*, p. 137; W. Miller, 'Greece since the Return of Venizelos', *Foreign Affairs*, 7(3) (Apr. 1929), 468–77.

[85] USNA, 868.00/626, Skinner (Athens)–State, 15 Jan. 1930.

creation of a 'modern state'. In 1929 the Government established a school to train civil servants for the economics ministries, and sent officials from the Ministry of Finance on a mission to England to study fiscal organization and financial administration. In late 1929 the Agricultural Bank was set up, to continue the work begun by the Refugee Settlement Commission, and to take over the task of providing agricultural credit from the National Bank. Former RSC officials staffed a new planning office at the Ministry of Agriculture, which was restructured to help shape a 'unified agricultural policy'.[86] The Senate was finally established, with representatives of the 'professional' organizations among its members, and was greeted as providing a non-partisan, corporatist voice on public issues. In 1930 government spokesmen announced the creation of a Supreme Economic Council, an advisory body composed of bankers, civil servants, business men, and academics. Progressive civil servants looked to a new age of decisive intervention, assisted by a combination of strong government and enlightened foreign support.

It did not work out thus. Outside agriculture the façade of étatism masked a lack of substance or commitment. Take, for example, the plans drawn up at the Labour Section at the Ministry of the National Economy, where a small group, inspired by the example of German state socialism, worked for labour reform in Greece. These civil servants were highly educated, often with foreign degrees, and were situated for the most part on the Left of the Venizelist camp. However, they carried little political muscle, and Venizelos, though sympathetic to their intentions, ignored their proposals for enforcing observation of the eight-hour day and for introducing social insurance for all workers. Even a devastating exposé of domestic working conditions by the International Labour Office did not outweigh in his mind the vociferous objections of Greek industrialists to any form of labour regulation. As we have seen, Venizelos was determined to keep wages low to attract private capital into Greek industry. By no means unsympathetic to the plight of the working classes, the Liberal premier was reluctant to move beyond paternalistic gestures, like arranging temporary work schemes for laid-off miners. Yet the Government was regularly involved in labour negotiations and, as the crisis eroded Venizelos's prestige, his personal interventions would come to be an unsatisfactory substitute for impersonal arbitration procedures. As a result, his star waned, not just in

[86] Ministry of Agriculture (Ypourgeion Georgias), *Ta pepragmena tou Ypourgeiou Georgias kata tin teleftaian tetraetian: 1928–1932* (Athens, 1932), 1–47.

progressive circles, but with the working classes too, who showed diminishing enthusiasm after 1929 for his appeals for social harmony.[87]

But if advocates of social reform complained of the conservative results of the Liberal Government's flirtation with foreign capital, students of public finance feared that heavy borrowing might endanger financial stability. 'The state which realizes a monetary reform must practise a severe monetary policy of restricting expenditure', warned one young French-trained economist.[88] Finance Minister George Maris disagreed, arguing that it was misguided to pay attention solely to such short-term considerations:

Would it truly be an economy to reduce credits to agriculture, public education, and hygiene? If we do not find agriculture the means to develop her produce, how can we obtain a better yield from revenues? And if we do not give the peasant the moral satisfaction of being able to send his children to school and having a doctor to look after his health, would he not then have much more than today the right to complain of the burden of taxation?

The Government defended itself strongly against accusations of over-indebtedness on the grounds that there was all-party support for the schemes and that the money was being used 'productively'. The first point was true: there was surprisingly little criticism from opposition politicians, much more from foreign observers and Greek academics and writers. But the second point was obviously misleading since the Government would have to service the additional debt long before the 'productive works' began to yield revenues. So far as fiscal conservatives were concerned, key members of the Liberal Government, notably the Finance Minister himself, were clearly unready for the rigours of deflation. In November 1930 Maris issued a warning that budgetary spending could not be cut back; on the contrary, increases were to be expected on the grounds that the modern state was 'forced to intervene ever more frequently in different areas formerly regarded as the preserve of private or commercial interests'. By March 1931, he was more defensive, arguing in the debate on the 1931/2 Budget that 'if the national income were adequate, or if the different productive sectors of the country operated in a satisfactory manner, then the present policy of the productive works would be excessive. In that case it would perhaps have been preferable to follow a more cautious policy of restraining

[87] FO 371/13657 C2153/1129 Loraine–Chamberlain, 11 Mar. 1929; FO 286/1052 Urquhart (Piraeus)–Athens, 2 Dec. 1929; A. Liakos, 'Apo kratos fylax eis kratos pronoia?', *O Politis*, 78(6) (Apr. 1987), 34–40; Livieratos, *Koinonikes agones*, pp. 76–85, 114–16; *Peitharchia*, 15 Dec. 1929.   [88] Dertilis, *Reconstruction financière*, p. 218.

productive expenditures and returning the State to its old circumscribed role, in accordance with the tenets of the orthodox school . . . But at present . . . such a conservative policy finds itself in plain contradiction to essential popular and social interests.' This was not an early example of Keynesian thinking; it was traditional populism in a new setting. Here, as so often in inter-war Greece, thoughts of electoral expediency (and these were never far from Maris's mind) overrode the orthodox deflationary prescriptions of the day. But such attitudes suggested an almost deliberate refusal to consider the implications of Greece's worsening debt position.[89]

In the decade after 1922 the Greek foreign debt increased by just under 1 billion gold francs compared with just over 1 billion in the *three* preceding decades; the rate of growth of the domestic debt in this time was similar. Under the Venizelos Government, the foreign debt increased from 27.8 billion drachmas to 32.7 billion drachmas between 1928 and 1932. Officially this growth coincided with a period of balanced budgets. In reality, ordinary revenues peaked in 1929 and budget deficits were only sustained by extraordinary revenues, in other words, the proceeds of loans (see Table A1.2). By borrowing on such a scale from abroad, the Liberal Government threatened to jeopardize the very process of reconstruction it set such store by. At the onset of the world depression, the public debt service as a proportion of public spending was comparable with the position of developed countries rather than Greece's Balkan neighbours.

The budget could only be balanced by improving the yields of ordinary revenues. Since the burden of indirect taxation was already heavy, as Venizelos had himself admitted (in a letter to *The Times* on 31 December 1930), it might have seemed imperative to increase the yield of direct taxation. 'Our fiscal system, we are told, is defective,' agreed Maris, 'but who disputes this? Fiscal justice would evidently require diminishing indirect contributions and an increase in direct ones. Yet in this last category figures among other things the tax on income, which is, above all, a tax on capital. Now, how can we reconcile increasing this tax with the thesis of those who maintain that our policy must be to attract as much capital as possible?'[90] The Liberals shied away from this and the yield from direct taxes actually fell as a proportion of ordinary revenues

[89] Bank of Athens, *Bulletin Économique et Financier*, 92 (Apr. 1930), 1,717; *ESV* 3, 22 Nov. 1930, 41; *ESV* 47, 12 Mar. 1931, 949.

[90] Bank of Athens, *Bulletin Économique et Financier*, 92 (Apr. 1930), 1,717; RIIA, *The Balkan States*, i: *Economic* (London, 1936), 34; RIIA, *The Problem of International Investment* (London, 1937), 223.

TABLE 4.7.   *International comparisons of the Public
Debt Service as a percentage of public spending*
(averages of 1929–1931)

Country	(%)	Country	(%)
UK	56.6	Italy	25.8
Belgium	36.5	Bulgaria	17.6
Greece	35.9	Romania	15.9
France	33.5	Yugoslavia	11.7

Source: X. Zolotas, *I daneiaki epivarynsis tis Ellados* (Athens, 1931), 43.

during the Liberal Government's time in office. Moreover, the sudden increase in the foreign debt threatened more than the budget: higher debt service charges required more foreign exchange to transfer to bondholders abroad, and this added to the pressures which faced the Bank of Greece as did the increased imports sucked in when loan proceeds were spent abroad. Not only was the per capita foreign debt higher in Greece than elsewhere in Eastern Europe, it was also a much higher percentage of her exports: 32% (1928–30 average) compared with 23% in Romania and 15% in Bulgaria.

The strategy for pursuing economic development which was evolved by the Zaimis coalition and adopted by Venizelos from 1928 onwards depended therefore on an open international economic environment. Not only were foreign capital inflows the means chosen to develop domestic resources, but a high level of exports and invisible earnings were required to earn the exchange to service the foreign debt and keep Greece on the gold standard. One might also add, though this was nothing new, that a high level of *imports* was a precondition of budgetary stability.

In May 1930 the Liberal newspaper *Ethnos*, reporting on Greece's high credit standing in London, dismissed as pessimists those critics who warned of impending problems with the balance of payments, and in a eulogistic passage claimed that 'the nation, far from political quarrels and sure of its future, advances with sure and steady tread towards the achievement of its reconstruction. In five years, Hellenism united will have become an important factor in the group of European nations.'[91] But already by this time the first signs were apparent of a crisis in the international economy which would eventually close off Greece from further foreign assistance and force her economic development on to a new path.

[91] Cited in *MA*, 10 May 1930.

III

CRISIS,
1929–1932

5

THE TRADE SLUMP

The word 'crisis' is on everyone's lips.

(the British Vice-Consul at Volos, October 1929)

The period of export growth which had begun with the tobacco boom in the early 1920s ended in 1929. Although it is difficult to fix the point at which the world depression hit Greece, since commodity prices had been falling since the middle of the decade while the stabilization of the drachma may also have had deflationary effects, the year of the Wall Street crash marked a change in mood. The crash itself had little direct impact in Athens where financial strains did not become evident for another year or more, but it made people worried about the general outlook: that autumn there was a spate of articles discussing the economic crisis, debating its origin, or even, in the case of government supporters, whether there was one at all. Then, in December, came news that the French had blocked the import of Greek wines, in violation of a commercial convention which had been signed only a few months earlier. This was a blow to Greek efforts to diversify the country's export activities away from its traditional dependence on the British and German markets. Writing in the weekly *Peitharchia*, Papatsonis demanded retaliation against French goods: 'Of course such measures would be aggressive and contrary to the whole spirit of freedom which Geneva teaches us so insistently. But since the lesson is handed down to us by large liberal states, the very ones who are the pillars and founders of Geneva, there is justification enough for us smaller ones to take similar steps.' Several months later, leading Greek wine companies decided, in an unprecedented move, to form an export cartel to avoid excessive competition among themselves in the remaining markets.[1] In these ways the crisis of world trade began to erode the foundations of the liberal economic order. So far as Greece was

---

[1] *ESV*, 17 Feb. 1930, 655–62; *ESG*, 12 June 1930, 1,118–22; Bank of Athens, *Bulletin Économique et Financier*, 99 (Nov. 1930), 1,846–7; ibid., 104 (June 1931), 1,939; *Peitharchia*, 12 Jan. 1930, 28–9; *EX*, 20 Aug. 1933, 19 Nov. 1933; *Ploutos*, 14 Apr. 1935.

concerned, the ramifications stretched beyond the wine sector. Because just two commodities—tobacco and currants—comprised 60–70% of total exports, the country's balance of trade was heavily affected by their performance. After 1929 neither fared well and export earnings declined until 1933. The most striking collapse was in tobacco sales as German merchants, hit by the onset of the slump there, ran down their stocks and reduced purchases. Between 1929 and 1932 drachma earnings from tobacco exports were halved. Since tobacco was not just the single most important source of Greek export and tax revenues, but was also of vital political importance—with northern Greece a key area of Venizelist support—we should look in some detail at how the export crisis hit the tobacco economy, and how it affected the various groups involved—the state, growers, merchants, and workers.[2]

The Political Economy of Tobacco

'Our tobacco harvest is forty per cent greater than last year's. I do not believe that this fact is so terrible ... In fact, I regard it as quite favourable ... given that what we look for is an annual increase in our agricultural production. The strange thing is that as soon as we achieve it, we begin to wail that there is a crisis!'[3] Thus Panayis Vourloumis, the Minister for the National Economy, summarized the Liberal Government's view of the situation during a lengthy debate on tobacco at the end of 1929. Other speakers were less sanguine. A spokesman for the Communist Party emphasized the indebtedness of the growers which made them vulnerable to exploitation by buyers, and criticized the misallocation of credit, arguing that the commercial banks advanced disproportionate amounts to merchants and little to the growers themselves. The view of the Communist Party was that there was no specific tobacco crisis but rather a general agricultural crisis which could only be overcome through greater state intervention in both financial and commercial markets.[4]

The Government also came under attack from more mainstream voices, such as Anastasios Bakalbasis, a former Minister of Agriculture and chairman of the parliamentary committee that had been set up to examine the tobacco question. Bakalbasis represented a northern constituency and stood on the left of the Venizelist camp, close to Alexandros Papanastasiou. Was there a tobacco crisis, he asked. His answer

---

[2] Cf. MNE., *To kapnikon zitima* (Athens, 1931), intro.

[3] *ESV*, 9 Dec. 1929, 196.   [4] *ESV*, 2 Dec. 1929, 95–112.

was a qualified affirmative. Although it was incorrect to talk of wide-spread over-production—since the total 1929 crop of oriental tobacco was less than in certain preceding years, while consumption was growing—there was an emergent problem for cultivators of the expensive, high-quality varieties which had gained Greek tobacco its reputation. Bakalbasis pinpointed the roots of this problem in a combination of changes in consumer preferences, buying policy by major cigarette manufacturers, and local production.

The unregulated expansion of tobacco cultivation had increased harvests and impoverished quality—but this was only part of the story. In Germany and the USA, cigarette manufacturers were increasingly reluctant to purchase expensive tobaccos. As demand shifted to cheaper leaf, Greece faced increased competition from Bulgaria and Turkey, neither of whom produced comparable high-quality leaf but had cost advantages at the lower end of the market. Also there was a trend towards the exclusion of independent merchants from the market as large tobacco firms and the monopolies directed their purchases through appointed local agents. This put growers in a worse bargaining position when they came to make their sales than they had been previously. Even when organized into marketing co-operatives they were liable to pressure from merchants with easier access to funds than they themselves possessed. In many areas peasants farmed such minute smallholdings that making the switch out of tobacco cultivation was economically impossible for them. Falling tobacco prices meant further indebtedness and, in some areas, starvation.[5]

To these warnings, however, Vourloumis and Venizelos replied that there was little left for the Government to do. It had established the Agricultural Bank to provide agricultural credit, but no swift expansion of its activities was practicable. The Government would allocate funds on a limited scale for the purchase of older and damaged leaf; but it was opposed to a programme of large-scale support buying, or the establishment of a special credit institution for advancing funds to tobacco cultivators. Nor was there any response to widespread calls for the heavy taxation of tobacco leaf to be scaled down. Indeed although tobacco growers numbered about only 10% of all farmers in Greece, they contributed more than half the total revenues from direct agricultural taxation, and this percentage rose when the Government introduced a two-year moratorium on the taxes on most other crops in 1930.

[5] *ESV*, 9 Dec. 1929, 176.

This debate took place at a critical juncture. The 1929 harvest stands out as the moment when the optimism of the 1920s foundered and perspectives changed. This was clear at the time to well-informed observers. Writing his annual report in September 1929, the manager of the Ionian Bank's Kavalla branch (the biggest source of tobacco financing in the commercial centre of the tobacco trade) wrote that 'under the circumstances the year 1927/28 must be considered as marking the high level of profits and the year 1928/29 the high level of employed funds. For many years I do not anticipate such figures.'[6] This judgement was based, not merely on the growth of competition among local banks, but on an evaluation of trends in the tobacco sector generally. One year later the same observer wrote that 'the year 1929/30 marked, as we have seen, a complete revolution in the tobacco trade, and one may say that the period which started in 1919, after the Armistice, now closes'.[7]

In retrospect, it is clear that for various reasons the tobacco sector was coming under increasing strain. The Government's unwillingness to control cultivation in any way allowed it to expand unchecked. By itself the size of the 1929 harvest would have led to a fall in prices in the short term. But so long as demand abroad remained strong the long-run outlook was good. What prolonged and deepened the crisis was a contraction of demand induced by the recession in Germany after 1930.

The repercussions throughout the domestic economy were severe. For Greece, with its rural but highly monetized and commercial society, the fortunes of the urban economy were closely bound up with conditions in the countryside. As the 'communalist' Kostas Karavidas wrote to a socialist critic, in the export areas the chief unit of analysis was not the limited-liability company or other capitalist structures, but 'the personal, classical, provincial Greek community which . . . permits the local Greek peasants to exploit their produce, their personal capital and their own surplus labour, on the spot and indeed not only as producers, but also as traders and manufacturers'.[8] In the northern tobacco-growing regions, growers, merchants, and workers were linked through the provision of goods, labour services, and credit. How did the crisis affect these various groups?

During the boom years of the 1920s tobacco growers—many of them resettled refugees—borrowed heavily from local banks, merchants, and

---

[6] IBA, Kavalla, YR 1928/9, 42–3.   [7] IBA, Kavalla, YR 1929/30, annexe, 1.

[8] K. Karavidas, 'Sosialismos kai koinotismos', repr. in *To provlima tis avtonomias* (Athens, 1981), 13.

money-lenders. Growers began to specialize to such an extent that they now bought their vegetables and flour from the towns, leading commentators to talk of a 'capitalization' of the countryside.[9] By 1927 the National Bank was making more agricultural loans against tobacco than against any other crop.

Many producers' co-operatives were established purely to facilitate the flow of funds to growers. Their members lacked much sense of communal obligation or solidarity, regarding the organization as little more than a new means of obtaining credit. 'Ask producers who are not members if they have enrolled in co-operatives,' wrote one observer, '"I didn't need a loan up till now", they will tell you.' Or consider the definition provided by some refugee smallholders: 'Co-operative is a piece of paper which up to seven guys (*paidia*) sign and take to the bank to get money.'[10] They drew on loans for more than the consumption goods they were frequently accused of buying. As tobacco prices soared and growers increased the area under cultivation, they could no longer tackle the highly labour-intensive tasks of planting and picking the leaves by relying on family labour alone. Not only farmers, but also tradesmen, doctors, and lawyers in the villages of Macedonia joined in the boom, borrowing heavily from the banks and from local money-lenders, and drawing workers from as far afield as Thessaly and central Greece. In September 1930 a bank manager in the northern tobacco town of Xanthi warned that 'to confront the existing tobacco crisis we must regulate cultivation so that money is not heedlessly spent on workers' wages in connection with the various tasks associated with tobacco to the great harm of the growers themselves'.[11]

Once producer prices began to fall this highly monetized economy came under strain. According to information given to the parliamentary committee on tobacco, cultivation of the crop only yielded a positive net income when prices for top qualities were above 43 dr./oke and above 25 dr./oke for poorer qualities. In 1929 prices fell below these levels in many areas.[12] Cultivators were unable to make repayment of existing

[9] *OT* 381, 18 July 1933.

[10] N. I. Anagnostopoulos, *O kampos ton Serron* (Athens, 1937), 72–3.

[11] N. Theodorou, 'Georgooikonomiki meleti epi tessaron antiprosopeftikon chorion tou lofodous tmimatos tis periferias Katerinis', *GD* 5 (1939), 102, 179; IBA, Xanthi, YR 1929/30, 3; K. Kostis, *Agrotiki oikonomia kai Georgiki Trapeza* (Athens, 1987), 205; F. Altsitzoglou, *Oi giakades kai o kampos tis Xanthis* (Athens, 1941), 96–9.

[12] GPEK, Thessaloniki, *To kapnikon zitima* (Thessaloniki, 1929); AOS, *Epi tou zitimatos tou kapnou* (Athens, 1938), table 6, p. 22.

TABLE 5.1. *Tobacco cultivation*

	Harvest (000 tonnes)	Average producer price (drs./kilo)	Average producer income (drs.)	Tobacco as % value of total agricultural production
1928	52.7	34.0	10,706	15.9
1929	79.1	23.9	9,717	22.4
1930	64.2	20.8	8,320	17.2
1931	42.6	17.6	5,798	9.9
1932	27.5	27.1	6,732	6.3

Source: G. Lambrou and M. Jannides, *Ta anatolika kapna* (Kavalla, 1939).

debts and in many cases only survived the winter through falling further into debt by purchasing maize from the newly established Agricultural Bank.[13] Alarmed by the tardiness and difficulty with which the large 1929 crop was absorbed by the market, many farmers sought to abandon tobacco for other crops.

The Government had introduced legislation prohibiting the cultivation of tobacco on 'unsuitable or marshy' ground.[14] This was in belated recognition of the fact that market forces, left to themselves, had widened rather than dampened fluctuations in production and prices. But although there was a decline in the cultivated area after 1929, it appears that once more market forces, not the 1929 legislation, were chiefly responsible.[15] Where it was possible to diversify production, this had happened, whether or not the area had been designated an unsuitable one. As tobacco prices—or more importantly, the ratio of tobacco to cereal prices—fell, the cultivation of wheat spread into what had traditionally been tobacco-growing regions. Around Xanthi, for example, the tobacco area shrank by 50% between 1930 and 1932; as a percentage of the total cultivated area it fell from 37% (1929) to 20% (1932). The extent of impoverishment depended to a large extent on the potential for diversification. For apart from tobacco growers in the Agrinion region in central Greece, who sold to buyers for the domestic industry at reasonable prices throughout the crisis, farmers were faced with a sharp cut-back in demand. In central and western Macedonia, where tobacco cultivation was of recent origin and where landholdings

[13] IBA, Salonika, YR 1931/2, 3; GPEK, Kavalla, *Deltion*, Sept.–Oct. 1932, 32.
[14] GPEK, Kavalla, *Deltion*, Mar. 1930, 35–6.
[15] Ibid., Sept.–Oct. 1932, 14.

averaged a relatively large 2 to 4 hectares, tobacco was swiftly abandoned for other crops. Between 1929 and 1932 the number of growers fell from 56,334 to 18,862, and the area cultivated with tobacco from 32,994 to 8,312 hectares. In eastern Macedonia, on the other hand, over the same period the number of growers fell only from 48,985 to 34,509 and the area sown from 36,243 to 23,134 hectares.[16]

In the latter region, the heartland of Greek tobacco cultivation, conditions varied greatly from one district to another. Fertile plains areas, like Komotini and Drama, had always relied on cereals; encouraged by movements in relative prices this reliance increased, cushioning local communities from the worst of the recession. It was noted that in Komotini cereal growers had—unlike farmers elsewhere in the region—been able to pay off old debts during 1930–2.[17] An observer reported of the Drama district during 1930 that 'it has given proof during the last half year of a remarkable vitality and . . . has not felt as yet the effects of the crisis . . . As a centre of a large agricultural district, which produces not only tobacco, but all sorts of cereals, vines, cheeses etc., Drama has escaped up to now the effects of the crisis.'[18]

Conditions were very different elsewhere. Villages in the foothills around Kavalla and Xanthi found diversification difficult. Because they were centres of good-quality leaf, local land values had been high when the land there had been allocated in the 1920s and landholdings were consequently tiny, 1 hectare or less. Table 5.2 suggests that in a sample of these villages the lack of alternative opportunities restricted the decline in the number of growers despite the fact that incomes slumped and that the grower's income per hectare was not sufficient to cover even cultivation costs. In such villages it is striking that though their incomes had fallen much *more* than the average, the number of growers fell much *less* than the average from the peak in 1929, and in some cases actually rose. The central problem thus remained to be solved. Falling prices had prompted diversification of cultivation over a wide area, but had left unaffected those areas where high-quality leaf had been oversupplied before 1930. There, growers and their dependants faced a stark choice: face heavy income falls or find work elsewhere.

After the First World War, the rapid growth of cigarette consumption led to the appearance of a class of independent merchants who bought

---

[16] GPEK, Kavalla, *To ergon tou GPEK Kavallas kata tin dekaetian 1926–1935* (Kavalla, 1937), table 10. [17] GPEK, Kavalla, *Deltion*, Sept.–Oct. 1932, 23.

[18] IBA, Salonika, HYR 1930/1, 1.

TABLE 5.2.   *High-quality tobacco cultivation trends, 1929–1931*

Village	% change in no. of growers	% drop in gross income per grower	% drop in income per unit area
Pravia	0.0	53.8	45.4
Prosotsani	+9.1	43.1	46.7
Mikros Yiakas	−27.3	58.1	44.8
Sou-Yialesi	+3.1	37.7	32.8
Orta Kolou	−18.4	54.8	28.3
National average	−32.5	10.8	15.0
Regional average[a]	−29.4	36.0	39.5

[a] Eastern Macedonia and west Thrace.

Source: My calculations on the basis of data in GPEK, Kavalla, *To ergon tou GPEK Kavallas kata tin dekaetian 1926–1935*, tables 1–10.

directly from the growers and sold to manufacturers abroad. In many countries—Germany, Holland, Egypt, and Britain, for example—there were numerous small manufacturers, often of Greek descent, who lacked the resources to establish buying agents of their own. These intermediaries thus fulfilled a useful function; in addition they had contact with state monopolies and the large American companies.

As their own capital resources were limited, Greek banks developed an extensive business supplying them with funds to make purchases from cultivators; the merchants in turn would lend these funds at higher rates of interest as short-term loans to the growers themselves. But this precarious financial network depended upon a continual expansion of the market for tobacco. Contraction would reduce the growers' ability to repay their debts to merchants; falling prices could wipe out the margins on the merchants' loans from the banks and force them to sell at a loss.

During the early 1920s market conditions favoured this system. Refugees, with little personal capital, could become brokers with borrowed funds (only to be among the first victims of the 'cleansing' of the market when peasants started defaulting on their debts). Banking profits from such business were so high that they encouraged a growing number of banks, both Greek and foreign, to establish branches in Salonika and Kavalla, the two centres of the tobacco trade.[19] The Ionian

---

[19] IBA, Kavalla, YR 1929/30, 2; Bank of Athens, *Bulletin*, 106 (Dec. 1931), 2,000.

Bank, which became the largest participant in this type of financing, increased the amount of the funds employed by its Kavalla branch from £105,000 in 1923 to £560,000 in 1929. For most of this time, the net yield on these funds was above 8%. By 1929, commercial bank advances to tobacco merchants in Kavalla alone exceeded £3 million.[20] In the context of the Greek economy at that time, these were large sums.

Even before this date, however, developments occurred which were to make the position of these merchants untenable. Chief among these was the decline of the small cigarette manufacturers as the industry became increasingly oligopolistic. This trend appeared most clearly in Germany, Greece's leading customer for tobacco, where smaller firms were taken over from 1924 by the two tobacco giants, Reemtsma and Neuerburg, financed by the Reichsbank and encouraged by the state authorities.[21]

The 'rationalization' of cigarette manufacturing in the long run made most of the independent merchants redundant. Apart from Egypt, all Greece's major customers depended either upon state monopolies or upon giant firms—BAT, Reynolds, Philip Morris. Increasingly such purchasers arranged their deals through one appointed agent who would buy directly from the growers rather than through middlemen. By 1929 75–80% of all tobacco sales were being handled in this way.[22] It was becoming evident that those merchants who lacked links with either manufacturers or growers would gradually be forced out of business.[23] Indeed foreign buyers took advantage of the large size of the 1929 harvest to make direct purchases from the villages rather than buying ready lots from the merchants. The significance of what was happening did not escape local observers:

The decision of big foreign buyers . . . to boycott all intermediaries has ruined all merchants without secured outlets and allowed the big foreign trusts to fix prices in the villages as they pleased . . . The speculators formed in the past the stabilizing factor between the offer in the villages and the demand abroad. A considerable quantity of tobacco was always in their hands . . . Since these speculators were swept from the market, it has become evident that if the State wanted to avoid a fall in prices, it ought to substitute (itself for) the speculators . . . either by taking *in good time* drastic measures to reduce immediately to a very

---

[20] IBA, Kavalla, YR 1929/30.
[21] A. Bakalbasis, *Ta ellinika kapna en ti evropaiki kapnagora* (Athens, 1930).
[22] IBA, Kavalla, HYR 1930/1, 4; G. Lambrou and M. Jannides, *Ta anatolika kapna* (Kavalla, 1939), 112.
[23] MNE, *To kapnikon zitima*, 17.

low level production for one or two crops, or to buy from the market excess stocks and to keep them for disposal at a later date in conjunction with a gradual reduction of the area cultivated.[24]

If foreign buyers had increased their power in the market through new forms of organization—cartels and state monopolies—then should not the Greeks, for the sake of maximizing their earnings, act in a similar fashion? 'We live in an age of group efforts and think there is no better solution than the amalgamation of Greek merchants into one company,' wrote two Venizelist journalists in Salonika. 'The prevailing opinion that Greeks are not good at working together must be set aside. Let us realize that we are living through critical days, which we shall not confront successfully except by co-ordinating our efforts.' Bakalbasis's parliamentary committee, which had been set up to review the entire tobacco question at the end of 1928, was reaching a similar conclusion. In his recommendations, drawn up in 1930 but unpublished till the following year, Bakalbasis demanded decisive state intervention in the market, and an end to the *ad hoc* approaches of the past: because the tobacco trade, he argued, needed to be viewed in the context of the new challenges facing Greek commerce as a whole, a new export organization should be established through which the state would co-ordinate Greece's export trade in conjunction with the private sector. 'Co-ordination' meant an active promotion of trade through diplomatic initiatives, combined with regulation of domestic output. There were civil servants within the Ministry of the National Economy who were sympathetic to such innovations, but they had to contend with the Minister himself, Vourloumis, who, as we have seen already in the case of the currant trade, opposed any infringement of *laissez-faire* principles in commerce. The tobacco merchants too preferred a less aggrandizing role for the state. In the spring of 1930 the Union of Greek Tobacco Merchants in Kavalla appealed for the state to ease the market by purchasing old tobacco stocks at its own expense; these, the Union argued, could be sold off later. And although the parliamentary committee itself had conspicuously *not* recommended such a course of action, this was nevertheless exactly what the Liberal Government opted to do. In the summer of 1931 the Ministry of Agriculture organized the purchase and destruction of low-quality leaf throughout northern Greece. As Bakalbasis had feared, it was the sort of provisional measure

---

[24] IBA, Kavalla, YR 1930/1, 4.

which suggested that the Government was badly underestimating the gravity of the situation.[25]

For despite expectations that excess stocks of the 1929 crop would be sold easily early in 1931, the spreading world crisis led to destocking abroad on a scale which belied any such hopes. By July 1931 more than half the bank funds employed in Kavalla were immobilized in old stocks. Merchants who held 1927 or 1928 stocks faced enormous losses: in addition to price falls of 20–30% there were costs of 40–80% on the original value of the stock from accumulated interest payments and other expenses. The Ionian Bank's manager in Kavalla cited an estimate of £1.2 million for losses in Kavalla on old stocks alone and commented, 'I doubt whether all the tobacco merchants of Kavalla who worked on speculation in the good years [namely, 1926–8] added together possessed enough means to meet this loss, which has eaten up all their capital, and will probably result in losses for the lenders.'[26]

With the financial crisis which began in the autumn of 1931, further obstacles were introduced to the disposal of these old stocks. In the first place, of course, exchange restrictions in client states curtailed export demand. Also, the so-called 'exchange retention' introduced by the Government when Greece abandoned the gold standard in April 1932 obliged exporters to convert 15% of their foreign exchange earnings at the old parity rather than the current rate—the authorities keeping the difference. The effect of this was, on the one hand, to increase the potential losses suffered by export merchants and, on the other, further to depress producer prices, which in turn worsened the position of holders of old stocks.

The small size of the 1932 tobacco harvest brightened the outlook for traders. Just as production had grown far more quickly than export demand in the late 1920s, so between 1929 and 1932 it fell further too. This helped raise producer prices and led commentators to herald the 'first stages of recovery'. But the same report noted that 'of those merchants who found themselves in possession of old stocks of expensive leaf during the crisis, some have been bankrupted and can no longer

[25] M. Mavrogordatos and A. Chamoudopoulos, *I Makedonia: Dimografiki kai oikonomiki meleti* (Thessaloniki, 1931), 77–8; MNE, *To kapnikon zitima*, 28–33; *E* 70, 2 May 1931; *E* 71, 9 May 1931; GPEK, Kavalla, *Deltion*, Apr. 1930, 31; G. Servakis and C. Pertountzi, 'The Agricultural Policy of Greece', in O. S. Morgan (ed.), *Agricultural Systems of Middle Europe* (New York, 1933), 170; Bakalbasis's reservations about the policies of the Liberal Government are expressed in *ESV*, 22 June 1931, 647–51, *PSV*, 8 Apr. 1932, 836–7.

[26] IBA, Kavalla, YR 1930/1, 8.

function as merchants and others have seen their capital enormously reduced'.[27]

Tobacco workers formed one of the most militant sections of the Greek labour force. They worked, not in manufacturing, but in processing the raw leaf prior to export. Repeated strikes and disputes with the merchants during the 1920s turned them into one of the most loyal blocs of support for the Greek Communist Party; thus it was in the tobacco towns of northern Greece that one could first see the popular base of Venizelism splinter under the pressure of class conflict. Several factors lay behind the tobacco workers' tradition of organized radicalism: the urban refugees' lack of ties to the land, and the working environment itself, where several hundred employees worked alongside one another in one of those cavernous warehouses which still impress the visitor to Kavalla or Xanthi. In a country where most of the work-force was slow to develop a sense of the need for collective action, the achievements of the Tobacco Federation of Greece were startling.

This movement drew its strength from the towns of Macedonia and Thrace. Before 1914 peasants had worked in the warehouses for a few months in the year before returning to their fields; Kavalla, for example, would draw workers from the nearby island of Thasos from spring to autumn. But this pattern was disrupted by the refugees, many of whom settled in the towns: the number of workers in Kavalla alone rose from around 2,500 before 1922 to 10,000 in 1925. In the first half of the decade the booming tobacco market enabled the Tobacco Federation to win important concessions from the merchants. Wages were protected against inflation by being tied to the sterling exchange rate, while the use of low-cost methods of tobacco manipulation was outlawed. An unemployment benefit fund was established. Indeed, until around 1930 the tobacco workers were regarded as a privileged part of the labour force.

However, as exports slowed down, major customers began to buy cheaper leaf and turned towards the cheapest processing methods, employing women rather than men. Between 1927 and 1932 the number of men employed fell by a third, while their average income fell from 13,000 to 7,600 drachmas.[28] The maximum permitted 60 days' unemployment benefit was quite inadequate to allow most families to

---

[27] GPEK, Kavalla, *Deltion*, Mar. 1933; IBA, Salonika, YR 1931/2, 9.

[28] Bakalbasis, in *ESG*, 30 Aug. 1933, 344; GPEK, Kavalla, *Deltion*, Aug. 1936, 'To kapnergatikon zitima'; ibid., June 1932, 15–20; ibid., Mar. 1933, 20–2.

bear the enormous reduction in incomes. As the purchasing power of both the workers and the rural population declined, business and commerce in the tobacco towns dwindled, reducing still further alternative sources of employment. In the autumn of 1931 an observer wrote that 'the misery of the working classes in Cavalla is indescribable'. Eighteen months later he observed gloomily, 'Cavalla's future is a very dark one. Communism is rapidly gaining ground, helped by the misery existing among the working classes. In the town of Cavalla the communists have a majority over all the other parties combined.'[29]

The labour problem was one of the trickiest knots in the whole tobacco question for the Government to unravel. Small increases in the unemployment allowance were insufficient to combat the sharp falls in income. The road-building and drainage projects undertaken in the north also soaked up only a part of the growing reservoir of unemployed labourers, and both ground to a virtual halt for lack of funds by the autumn of 1931. Bakalbasis's parliamentary committee argued against increasing dole payments, on the grounds that this would encourage idleness and stimulate hostility among the long-term unemployed towards the 'social order' of the country. It suggested embarking upon a long-term plan to resettle surplus tobacco workers in the countryside. This was not a suggestion likely to appeal to an administration already stretched to the limits by the public works it had undertaken. Instead, as discontent swelled among the workers, the Government turned to police methods to enforce the existing regime.[30]

The shift in political sentiments in Kavalla as the crisis progressed may shed light on the long-term problems facing the Liberal Party and the Venizelist camp in general. In the 1926 general election the Greek Communist Party (KKE) had managed to poll 10–15% of the vote in Kavalla and Salonika, but did far less well in 1928 when Venizelos's triumphant return swung votes back towards the Liberals. A few months earlier, in June 1928, striking tobacco workers had received some support from Venizelos, who criticized the Zaimis Government's handling of a pay dispute and attacked the 'uncompromising' attitude of the merchants. At a pre-election rally in Salonika he had pledged to introduce a labour policy favourable to the workers. However, the

[29] IBA, Kavalla, YR 1930/1, 21; ibid., HYR 1932/3, 8.
[30] IBA, Salonika, YR 1931/2, 9; IBA, Kavalla, YR 1931/2; GPEK, Kavalla, *Deltion*, June 1931, 'I kapnergatiki anergia en Elladi kata to etos 1930', 9; on relations between merchants and the commercial banks, see GPEK, Thessaloniki, *Deltion*, Jan.–Feb. 1932, 'Ta kapna mas kata to etos 1931'; MNE, *To kapnikon zitima*, 22–3.

repressive measures introduced by Venizelos and his Interior Minister Zavitsianos, once in power, ensured that this *rapprochement* was short-lived. Papanastasiou warned Venizelos in 1928 that 'the policy which today is directed against the communist threat, fundamentally and essentially aims against legitimate labour demands'.[31] Indeed the *Idionymon* legislation of 1929 showed quite clearly that the Liberals viewed organized labour as a social menace. Speaking to tobacco workers in November 1929, Venizelos was categorical: 'Let us make it clear. If you are communists, you are enemies of the state and we shall dissolve your organizations as hostile. We do not recognize your right to band together to become stronger and more threatening to the state.' But the extraordinary vagueness of the *Idionymon*'s terms allowed the authorities considerable latitude in decreeing who was a communist. On the island of Samos, police officers sought to dismiss the President of the local Tobacco Worker's Union, despite the fact that his organization was affiliated to the non-communist federation, referring to his 'latent communist principles' and to the fact that he was 'hated by the tobacco merchants'. In 1930 the *Idionymon* was used to dissolve the Tobacco Federation and its affiliates.[32]

As Liberal town councils implemented the new legislation, workers shifted their allegiance back towards the Left. The KKE registered sharp increases in its vote in by-elections in Salonika and in Mytilene in 1931, results which deeply alarmed the Government. When Venizelos visited Kavalla on the eve of the 1932 election, he was greeted with such shouts and cries of disapproval that he was unable to deliver his address. The episode had a symbolic value: Greece's most charismatic political figure no longer had any answer to the demands of a disaffected work-force.[33]

[31] FO 286/1018, 'General Report on Thrace and Macedonia', 22 June 1928; FO 286/1028, 23 July 1928; A. Liakos, 'Apo kratos fylax eis kratos pronoia?', *O Politis*, 78(6) (Apr. 1987), 40; D. Livieratos, *Koinonikes agones stin Ellada (1927–31)* (Athens, 1987), 76–83.
[32] S. Stefanou (ed.), *Eleftheriou Venizelou politikai ypothikai anthologitheisai apo ta keimena avtou*, ii (Athens, 1969), 359; G. Mavrogordatos, *Stillborn Republic: Social Coalitions and Party Strategies in Greece 1922–1936* (Berkeley, Calif., 1983), 146–7; N. Alivizatos, *Les Institutions politiques de la Grèce à travers les crises, 1922–1974* (Paris, 1979), 288–311.
[33] G. Pegios, *Apo tin istoria tou syndikalistikou kinimatos tis Kavallas 1922–1953* (Athens, 1984), 49; USNA 868.00/673, Morris (Athens)–State, 26 Apr. 1932; the political situation in Kavalla is analysed in a report sent by the local prefect to Venizelos, AEV 173/111, 26 Mar. 1932.

Refugees and the Domestic Depression

Kavalla was a refugee stronghold, and Venizelos's unpleasant reception there in 1932 was part of a momentous and, for the Liberals, worrying trend: the gradual erosion of refugee support for the Cretan *ethnarchis* during the depression. Refugee votes had, after all, won Venizelos the 1928 election and would be crucial in its sequel, due in 1932 at the latest. When the newcomers had first arrived in Greece, their intense loyalty to Venizelos had led them to turn a deaf ear to communism and other radical political options. Seven years later in Mytilene, a town where half the inhabitants were refugees, the sharp increase in support for the Communists in the 1931 by-election—up from 7% to 21% since 1928—was a worrying portent.

It is a measure of Venizelos's stature as a statesman that he had not allowed the threat of the refugee reaction to deter him from pursuing a *rapprochement* with the Turkish Government when he returned to power in 1928. This last act of inspired diplomacy culminated in several bilateral agreements signed in Ankara in October 1930. An essential preliminary, however, was the Convention signed that June which provided a definitive solution to the problem of liquidating the properties abandoned since 1922 by the Muslim and Greek Orthodox refugees. Since the Lausanne Convention the two governments had been unsuccessfully negotiating over this issue. Now they agreed to let each government enter into possession of the properties vacated by refugees from its territory: the Greek Government took over formerly Muslim properties, and issued bonds to the refugees which provided for their partial indemnification by the state. The refugees greeted these arrangements with indignation and disappointment. They resented Venizelos's apparent acceptance of the Turkish argument that Greek properties in Asia Minor had amounted to less than those vacated by the Muslims in Greece. They bitterly attacked the Liberal Government for refusing to provide them with full compensation; and perhaps, at a deeper level, they also reacted strongly to the idea that all their hopes of an eventual return to their former homes must now be given up.[34]

Venizelos believed that it was better for the refugees to adapt themselves as quickly as possible to their new life in Greece. The pro-Government *Ergasia* admonished them in the spring of 1930,

[34] I. Anastasiadou, 'O Venizelos kai to ellinotourkiko Symfono filias tou 1930', in T. Veremis and O. Dimitrakopoulos (eds.), *Meletimata gyro apo ton Venizelo kai tin epochi tou* (Athens, 1980), 309–426.

insisting that they 'put an end to their demands and devote all their energy in this new economic environment to the development that would be decisive for their future'.[35] Venizelos could, after all, make the case that, so far as the refugees were concerned, the counterpart to his emollient overtures to Ankara was the land reform and resettlement programme at home. It was not by chance that the year of the Ankara Convention also saw the Greek Ministry of Agriculture and the new Agricultural Bank take over the functions of the Refugee Settlement Commission, which was now wound up: the task of assisting the refugees was henceforth to fall to the Greek Government alone.

'If the patriotism of the ruling classes and the good sense of the refugees', declared the RSC in its final report, 'continue to hold in check those doctrines which claim that the happiness and the progress of a nation can only be acquired by submitting to the rule of a group of fanatics, enemies of all enlightenment, persecutors of all liberties and all initiative; and if, in several dozen years . . . a strong race of peasants, born out of the mixing of all the elements of Hellenism, secures . . . the prosperity of Greece, that result will have been due to the impulse originally given by the RSC.'[36]

But the defensiveness we can discern behind these hopes was to be amplified in the coming years, as the Liberal Government took over its new responsibilities in the midst of a world depression. This struck hard, not only at the tobacco growers, but also at the mainstay of the new agricultural economy of Greece, the cereal farmers, who cultivated over 70% of the land. As world wheat prices plummeted their incomes dropped. In Thessaly, the richest arable land in Greece, the average income of a farming family fell from 19,200 to 12,330 drachmas in one year.[37] The combination of the price support policies enacted by KEPES and more especially tariff increases between 1929 and 1931 successfully insulated farmers from the worst effects of the deflation. Still, since many of them owed debts to the state, commercial banks, and money-lenders, they were saddled with rising real debt burdens. Producers of other crops, who lacked the protection accorded to cereal farmers, fared even worse: the domestic price of cotton, for example, fell 40% between 1928 and 1930 and only in 1931, when Venizelos threw

---

[35] Cited by M. Dritsa, 'Prosfyges kai ekviomichanisi', in T. Veremis and G. Goulimi (eds.), *Eleftherios Venizelos: Koinonia, oikonomia, politiki stin epochi tou* (Athens, 1989), 61.
[36] Bank of Athens, *Bulletin*, 100 (Dec. 1930), 1,868.
[37] *MA*, 13 Mar. 1931.

his weight behind calls for a tariff increase because of its status as an import-substitute, did prices begin to rise.[38]

The slump, and its dramatic effect on farmers' incomes, pushed the whole question of debt relief into the spotlight. It was a problem with which farmers, merchants, and bankers were already grappling long before the Government moved. A bank manager involved in the Mytilene olive oil business offered a vivid description of the fragility of rural financial networks in 1928. There, in the customary pattern, the banks had lent funds to import merchants, who in their turn had used them to buy goods which they advanced to the farmers on credit. Falling crop prices threatened to bring down the whole precarious structure. In his report, the banker explained that temporary difficulties had forced the peasants to postpone payment of their debts to the merchants, and therefore forced the latter to do likewise to his bank. He continued:

This however, cannot be considered as a lack of respect of their engagements. The merchants advancing the funds can at any moment press their debtors to settle, but in order to do this they must proceed with the forced sale of the properties belonging to the villagers. This of course cannot be done for the reason that should all merchants having to receive funds proceed in the above way for the collection of their money they will irreparably ruin the villagers.[39]

Faced with a threat to the banking system, the authorities felt impelled to act. But how, and for whose benefit? On the one hand, it seemed ludicrous to jeopardize the land reform by allowing the new small-holders to be bankrupted; yet debt relief was a potentially enormous expense for a government in no position to take on new commitments.

Refugee farmers were particularly vociferous in calling for government action to scale down the debts they had incurred during the resettlement. Many *prosfygopateres* (refugee 'fathers') had attacked the RSC for supposedly exploiting the settlers financially in the interests of foreign bondholders. Once the RSC had been dissolved, the refugees directed their claims against the Greek state. Negotiations in the spring of 1930 between the RSC and the government did result in a number of decisions favourable to the refugees: the rate of interest on their debts was scaled down, whilst it was agreed they would not be charged various expenses incurred by the RSC. In effect, the Greek Government agreed

[38] *ESV*, 15 May 1931; G. Kordatos, *Eisagogi eis tin istorian tis ellinikis kefalaiokratias* (repr. Athens, 1972), 125.

[39] IBA, Mytilene, YR 1927/8, 4; for a recent anthropological account of how financial ties between farmers and merchants may be seen in a wider social context, see S. Aschenbrenner, *Life in a Changing Greek Village* (Dubuque, Ia., 1986), 75–7.

to shoulder a large part of the settlement expenditure itself.[40] But these concessions did not satisfy refugee leaders, who continued to insist that the Greek state should have met all the costs of resettling the newcomers.

Venizelos was not sympathetic to their demands. Touring northern Greece in May 1930 to explain his new Turkish policy, he made it clear that his Government would insist on the agricultural refugees repaying their debts to the state: it was not merely their moral duty, but also necessary if the remaining homeless refugee families were to be provided for. But this proved to be an extremely unpopular stance in the face of what one anti-Venizelist journalist called the 'great crisis of rural Greece'. Already at the Fifth Tobacco Growers' Congress, held in Salonika in January 1930, it had been obvious that the Liberals had lost a lot of ground among the delegates to other parties, particularly the Agrarians. Despite a lengthy address by Gonatas, Governor-General of Macedonia, defending the Liberal Government's record, the Congress as a whole had displayed a marked anti-Government, indeed anti-capitalistic tone. As support for the Agrarian Party grew in northern and central Greece over the coming months, Venizelos denounced what he described as 'class parties'. But *Peitharchia*, a Venizelist weekly critical of the Liberal leader's rhetorical excesses, pointed out that the problem did not lie in the revolutionary aspirations of the Agrarians:

the farmer of northern Greece is coming to believe that the cause of his misfortune is the insatiable capitalism which all bourgeois governments serve, the present one especially. It is reality as well as the Press which teaches him this. He learns that in the towns lives a mass of rich privileged people who enjoy cinemas, theatres, cars and a thousand other benefits while he works incessantly and goes hungry. Mr Venizelos has promised him, or he thinks he has, wondrous good fortune. Instead of this, however, the support of the RSC has ended, likewise the loans . . . and in their place come failed harvests, the worldwide economic crisis and sheer poverty. What is he supposed to do?[41]

As they watched the 'microbe of politics' spread through the countryside, it was obvious to the Liberals that they would have to do something

[40] S. P. Ladas, *The Exchange of Minorities: Bulgaria, Greece and Turkey* (New York, 1932), 692–6.
[41] M. Notaras, *I agrotiki apokatastasis ton prosfygon* (Athens, 1934), 172–89; for a celebratory Liberal account of Venizelos's reception in northern Greece, see *I istoriki periodeia tou prothypourgou kyriou Eleftheriou Venizelou ana tin voreion Ellada kai to Ayion Oros* (Thessaloniki, 1932); *Proia*, 16 May 1930; *Peitharchia*, 15 Mar. 1931; AEV 173/127, Gonatas–Venizelos, 27 Jan. 1930.

more to retain the support of the smallholders they had helped bring into existence. Natural catastrophe pushed them into action: a series of harsh winters culminated in the storms and floods of 1930–1 which led starving peasants, chiefly shepherds and tobacco growers, to stream into the towns of northern Greece to receive the free maize distributed by the Agricultural Bank.[42] As for the longer-term measures which were clearly required, the first impulse of the Government was to look abroad. In July 1931 the Cabinet decided to seek the support of the League of Nations in raising money for a loan to consolidate the agricultural debt. But they could not have chosen a worse time in view of the chaos in international money markets. As a result they realized that the burden of relieving rural indebtedness would have to be borne by domestic rather than foreign creditors.

In October, on the eve of another bad winter, the Government suspended the direct land tax levied on most crops (though *not* on tobacco), declared a five-year moratorium on agricultural debts owed to private individuals, and also suspended the seizure of farmers' properties against such debts. 'Generally speaking,' wrote an embittered bank manager in Salonika, 'the debtor shows himself as emboldened whereas the creditor only now becomes clearly aware of his disadvantageous position . . . It would not be an exaggeration to add that the only parties succeeding [*sic*], under the circumstances, large collections (and this only thanks to the compulsory measures they dispose) are the Public Treasury and the Agricultural Bank (the latter for the greater part by way of compensations of new advances against old ones).'[43] But provincial merchants, bank managers, and local money-lenders all protested in vain: the Government had resolved to sacrifice their sympathies in order to win back the discontented beneficiaries of the land reform.[44]

The architect of these measures was Ioannis Karamanos, an Italian-trained agricultural expert and formerly a senior official in the RSC who had moved to become the Director-General at the reorganized Ministry of Agriculture. Justifying the debt moratorium, Karamanos argued that

the Government has created a large class whose existence helps to maintain the social equilibrium of the country. In these circumstances, it must necessarily see

[42] C. Evelpides, *I exelixis tis georgikis kriseos* (Athens, 1935), 101; *Peitharchia*, 9 Feb. 1930; AEV 173/110, Gonatas–Venizelos, 17 Mar. 1932, describes the distribution of maize and the plight of the peasantry the following winter.

[43] IBA, Salonika, HYR 1931/2, 2.

[44] USNA 868.00/673, Morris (Athens)–State, 5 Apr. 1932; FO 371/18403 R2908/2908, Waterlow (Athens)–FO, 2 May 1934.

with anxiety the forced sale of many small agricultural properties at low prices, to meet obligations assumed at a time when agricultural prices fetched high prices. The situation thus created may undo all the good done by the Government at such heavy cost.[45]

In particular these policies were felt to be necessary to stem the migration from the countryside into the towns. This exodus from the rural areas had alarmed commentators in Athens for several years. In December 1929, the cartoonist Demetriades published a sketch entitled 'The Last Farmer', showing a villager leading his donkey, wife, and child off to Athens 'to cultivate letters'. According to Karavidas, an employee of the Agricultural Bank, the problem lay in the basic fact that 'the traditional aspirations of our rural population do not lie in farming . . . When the harvest is a success, the surplus is used to open a shop or to send the son to Athens to study law!'[46] For many refugees there were pragmatic reasons for such attitudes: they had no permanent title to their land, and often did not come from farming backgrounds. Many left for the towns to work as labourers or, if they were lucky, to set up a shop with the money they had gained from selling off land and farming equipment.[47] As farm prices fell, the drift from the land continued, alarming many observers, who doubted the capacity of the towns to support them. 'The agricultural workers who go to the towns and cannot find employment in industry', wrote Karamanos, 'would inevitably go to swell the ranks of those who depend for their livelihood on parasitic trades or casual labour. This class is already numerous and its existence precarious, and there is a risk that its members may one day join the extremist elements.'[48]

---

[45] LN, *The Agricultural Crisis*, i (Geneva, 1931), 188; a laudatory portrait of Karamanos is in H. Morgenthau, *I was Sent to Athens* (New York, 1929), 270–2.

[46] K. Karavidas, *Agrotika* (Athens, 1931), 496; this problem had been in the public eye at least as early as 1926, cf. Bank of Athens, *Bulletin*, 54 (Feb. 1927).

[47] Theodorou, 'Georgooikonomiki meleti', pp. 62–3.

[48] LN, *The Agricultural Crisis*, i. 189; L. Polychronis, *Skepseis epi tou georgikou mas provlimatos* (Athens, 1931); cf. the same phenomenon in Italy in A. Treves, *Le migrazioni interne nell' Italia fascista* (Turin, 1976), chs. 7–8. The existence in Italy of a strong industrial lobby associated with the towns meant that the authorities stressed the danger to 'public order' rather than falling back on blanket denunciations of urban 'parasitism' as they did in Greece; M. S. Eulambio, in Bank of Athens, *Bulletin Économique et Financier*, 123 (Mar. 1936), 2,476–81, argued that the scale of internal migration had been exaggerated; the historical background to the problem in Greece and its wider implications are discussed by A. Liakos, 'Problems on the Formation of the Greek Working Class', *Études Balkaniques*, 2 (1988), 43–54.

Conditions in the towns were certainly bad enough to arouse anxiety. The urban refugees had more cause to be restive than their rural counterparts since the assistance they had received from the RSC still left many families living in wretched conditions. According to Morgenthau, the task of housing them had been only partly completed by 1929. In Salonika, he found settlements where malaria and tuberculosis were rife, sanitation and heating arrangements primitive, and privacy impossible to obtain:

Cooking is done in little charcoal braziers improvised out of tin cans and bricks. The roofs of these buildings leak with every rain and the walls are full of gaping cracks that let in the cold damp winds of winter. In visiting this settlement, wherever one's eye turns it is greeted by signs of human misery—death, disease, and bodily suffering and semi-starvation.[49]

Those who lived in these shanty towns received little support from the authorities. Property had been distributed among the refugees on the principle that those in the best position to pay for it would receive most. While this approach may have made sense in view of the extremely limited resources at the disposal of the Greek state, it contributed to the poorer refugees' sense of alienation. 'One would have expected,' wrote Mikalis Notaras, in his detailed study of the problem, 'after the economic overturning of an enormous mass of people, of various social classes . . . that the bourgeois conception of property would have yielded to a more up-to-date, developed and consistent concept of justice, whose balancing influence would have blunted social conflicts and grounded the banner of the post-war state more firmly.'[50]

The crisis hit the urban refugees hard. Many had started out in business during the 1920s as self-employed traders, pedlars and shop-keepers. In fact the RSC and the state had actually promoted the formation of small family firms. The Greek legal system encouraged a tendency to retail-trade fragmentation, which the boom atmosphere of mid-decade also fostered. In Jannina—a town of around 20,000 inhabitants—there were 246 grocers, 137 cafés, and 42 hairdressers. Local observers attributed the 'excessive' number of shopkeepers in the Salonika area to the activity of the refugees, who sought to take advantage of the inflation and easy credit to establish themselves as intermediaries, investing particularly heavily in import goods. Within a

---

[49] Morgenthau, *I was Sent to Athens*, pp. 246–7.
[50] Notaras, *Agrotiki apokatastasis ton prosfygon*, p. 124.

few years refugee traders were supposed to have ousted the Jews as the dominant element in commerce in Salonika.[51]

Several forces combined to jeopardize the position of these small businesses. In the first place, the stabilization of the drachma ended the mild inflation of the mid-1920s; almost immediately after, deflation set in. As early as March 1929 the Ionian Bank's manager in Salonika was reporting that 'the precarious state of commerce in our market becomes apparent from the frequent failures of big merchants and the frequent, almost daily fires in shops, several of which proved to be not casual'. Wholesale prices peaked in the first quarter of 1929, and by early 1930 had fallen almost 10%, dropping a further 10% over the rest of the year. In addition, poor cereal harvests sharply curtailed consumption among peasants. Traders who had tied up funds in stocks of imported goods (or for that matter tobacco) faced immediate losses. The banks, which in towns like Kavalla had been lavish in granting credits to refugee merchants, suddenly took fright after 1929. 'The merchants in your market', a bank manager in Kavalla was informed by London head office, 'have abused through over-trading to an unbelievable extent the facilities foolishly granted to them by Banks in their insane and inexperienced competition with each other and have to pay the price.'[52] The farmers' debt moratorium tied up the funds of urban banks and investors and reduced aggregate demand in the towns. Some commentators also argued that cut-throat competition among new firms had led to a fall in profit rates which together with the eradication of speculative opportunities on the exchanges increased bankruptcies. Stephen Ladas noted in 1932 that while the poorest refugees had benefited from the Liberal Government's large public works outlays, it was 'the class of middlemen and of small traders that seems to be most severely suffering in the large cities'.[53]

The longer-term political implications for Venizelism were critical. Alongside the refugees' shift to the Left which we referred to earlier occurred other realignments. In Salonika, commercial rivalry between Greek merchants and the large Jewish community fuelled growing anti-Semitism. The first prominent sign of this was the appearance of a

[51] A. Pepelasis, 'The Legal System and Economic Development of Greece', *Journal of Economic History*, 19(2) (June 1959), 195; USNA 868.00B/39, 'Political and Economic Effects of the Refugees in Greek Macedonia', 23/12/29.

[52] IBA, Kavalla, General Manager (London)–Ziffo (Kavalla), 24 Mar. 1930.

[53] IBA, Salonika, HYR 1928/9, 1; IBA, Salonika, HYR 1929/30, 1–4; Ladas, *The Exchange of Minorities*, p. 678.

National Macedonian Organization in 1926 which called for a commercial boycott against the Jews. The following year the National Union of Greece (EEE) was founded, with a mostly refugee membership; this organization was responsible for the worst anti-Semitic outrage of the inter-war period, the Campbell riots in Salonika in June 1931, when a Jewish neighbourhood was set on fire. Venizelos's condemnation of these events was lukewarm: he criticized the recourse to violence but expressed his sympathy with what he regarded as primarily an anti-communist nationalist organization.[54]

Venizelos's previously secure grip on refugee loyalties was now slipping and other political leaders made bids for their support. During the parliamentary debate on the Ankara Convention in June 1930, Kafandaris, Kondylis, and the Agrarians proclaimed their rejection of its terms. Most striking of all was the new attitude of the Populists. Tsaldaris, for the first time, added his voice to those who called for greater compensation for the refugees. As the crisis worsened Populist overtures to the refugees met with some success. By the spring of 1932 Tsaldaris was able to deliver a speech at one of the main refugee quarters of Salonika—something which according to the American consul there 'could not have happened a few years ago'.[55]

Yet what needs emphasizing at this point is the sanguine way in which many commentators and public figures interpreted the difficulties facing the urban refugees, and, in particular, those in business. 'Is there an economic crisis in Greece?' asked the *Bulletin* of the Bank of Athens in September 1929. Dimitri Sfikas gave a crisp answer: there was no crisis of any sort. The stabilization of the drachma had, it was true, led to a new 'spirit of economy' which restricted consumption and increased bankruptcies among the small firms which had sprung up over the last few years. But this was, according to him, a welcome development, a symptom of the long-desired 're-establishment' of the economy. In the 1920s there had been 'a truly stupefying growth' of traders, especially after the arrival of the refugees in the towns, virtually all of whom, he added with some exaggeration, had gone into commerce. The current wave of bankruptcies was nothing more than a return to 'the normal order of things'.[56] Another journalist drew the same conclusion, observing that two-thirds of the bankruptcies in the Athens–Piraeus area in

---

[54] Mavrogordatos, *Stillborn Republic*, p. 255; USNA 868.00/660, Skinner (Athens)–State, 12/12/31.

[55] USNA 868.00/673, Morris (Athens)–State, Apr. 5, 1932.

[56] Bank of Athens, *Bulletin*, 85 (Sept. 1929), 1,539–41.

1928 had liabilities of less than 100,000 drachmas, and chiefly involved small merchants.[57] According to the British Vice-Consul there, there was 'properly speaking, no economic crisis, only a surplus of entrepreneurs'. Early in 1930 the British Commercial Attaché reported that 'there is no doubt that the market will adjust itself at no distant date, and if the recent difficulties have had the result of eliminating a large number of unimportant commercial and industrial concerns, they will have served a good purpose'.[58] In similar vein, Liberal Finance Minister George Maris insisted that 'we shouldn't exaggerate our difficulties' —Greece was merely in a period of transition from inflation to stabilization. And the Populists agreed: one senior figure, George Streit, said that the country was passing temporarily through a 'businessman's crisis, due to over-speculation'.[59]

There were several reasons why the slump was viewed with so little alarm. Proponents of business rationalization—and there were many in Greece—saw the crisis as the way in which market forces themselves would 'prune' or 'cleanse' the domestic economy of the inefficient firms founded in the 'period of *gaspillage*' in the 1920s. In an article entitled 'The Crisis and Parasitism' a writer for *Peitharchia* described the need for a 'new equilibrium' in which those business men with adequate resources would survive and begin to operate 'with thrift and good housekeeping [*noikokyrosyni*]'. The Government was keen to play down the impact of the slump in Greece for fear of weakening the country's credit standing abroad. But there was also the fact that before the autumn of 1931 it was quite plausible to argue—as did the pro-Liberal *Ethnos*—that in Greece one saw none of those 'mournful indices which characterize the crisis in other countries'.[60]

There was no downturn in domestic manufacturing until 1932— after the 'battle for the drachma' had been fought and lost. True, ill-advised bank lending to industry had begun to cause liquidity problems for several commercial banks by 1930. But overall lending levels remained surprisingly high. One of the country's most brilliant

[57] Bank of Athens, *Bulletin*, 87 (Nov. 1929), 1,591.

[58] FO 371/13658 C8833/1124, Harvey–FO, 20 Nov. 1929; FO 371/14386 C1035/468, Ramsay–FO, 6 Feb. 1930; C. Chadziiosif, 'Venizelogenis antipolitefsi sto Venizelo kai i politiki anasyntaxi tou astismou sto mesopolemo', in Mavrogordatos and Chadziiosif (eds.), *Venizelismos kai astikos eksynchronismos* (Irákleion, 1988), 448–9.

[59] Bank of Athens, *Bulletin*, 89 (Jan. 1930), 1,641–2; USNA 868.00/626, Skinner (Athens)–State, 15 Jan. 1930.

[60] *Peitharchia*, 19 Jan. 1930; Bank of Athens, *Bulletin*, 85 (Sept. 1929), 1,539; ibid., 101 (Jan. 1931), 1,893.

TABLE 5.3. *Wholesale prices and monetary indicators, 1928–1931*

Date	Wholesale price indices		Notes in circulation (million drs.)	Central bank reserves (million drs.)	Total commercial bank lending (million drs.)
	Import prices	Domestic prices			
31.12.28	100	100	5,690	4,241	19,188
31.12.29	99	104	5,193	3,116	19,645
31.12.30	88	89	4,803	3,011	20,171
31.06.31	83	88	4,254	2,455	18,597
% change 31.12.28– 31.06.31	−17	−12	−25	−42	−3

Sources: Wholesale prices from AOS, *Oi deiktai tis oikonomikis drastiriotitos tis Ellados kata ta eti 1928–1934* (Athens, 1935), 52; monetary data from *AS*, various issues.

economists argued convincingly at the time that, far from cutting credit, the Bank of Greece had pursued a deliberately *expansionary* policy after 1928.[61]

Although the impact of the slow-down in world trade hit export sectors hard, its effect on Greece's overall external account was cushioned for a time by several factors. Invisible earnings held up well; more importantly, import prices collapsed even faster than exports, yielding terms of trade gains to the national economy of around 30% between 1928 and 1932. This was chiefly because Greece, unlike the Danubian states, was a wheat importer on a massive scale and thus benefited from lower world wheat prices. As import volumes did not begin to fall heavily until 1931, the reduction in the trade deficit was very largely due to this rapid fall in import prices.

In turn, however, this suggested that the Liberal Government, which widely publicized the country's terms of trade gains, was little justified in claiming the credit for the smaller deficit. Import consumption was being maintained at surprisingly high levels. Yet Venizelos insisted that there was no cause for alarm. He was optimistic by nature, as he readily

[61] P. Christodoulopoùlos, *Pistotiki politiki kai periodikai kriseis* (Athens, 1930), *passim*; on Christodoulopoulos and other economists in this period see now the excellent book by M. Psalidopoulos, *I krisi tou 1929 kai oi ellines oikonomologoi* (Athens, 1989); for further contemporary evidence on monetary policy, cf. IBA, Patras, YR 1930/1, 11; IBA, Salonika, YR 1930/1, 1–2; Kostis, *Oi trapezes kai i krisi, 1929–1932* (Athens, 1986), 87; AEV 343, Koryzis–Venizelos, 12 June 1931.

confessed, but he also believed that his ability to convey that optimism to his countrymen accounted for much of his past success. When attacked in March 1930 over the budgetary position by his former Interior Minister, Zavitsianos, Venizelos responded: 'I am sure that the Greek people will continue to follow those men who have resolute faith in the future, not those who see everything black and grim.' A few months later, speaking in the Macedonian town of Drama, he reiterated: 'My optimism consists in believing that everything will turn out for the best provided we work—as we are working—systematically.'[62]

But Venizelos's optimism, which had been triumphantly justified in the heady days of the Balkan Wars, rang hollow amid the unmistakable signs of economic depression. Educated circles formerly supportive of the Liberal leader began to distance themselves from his sanguine approach. In October 1929 Venizelist dissidents founded the weekly, *Peitharchia* (Discipline), devoted to promoting 'democracy with disciplined ideals' and outspokenly critical of what they regarded as Venizelos's excessive self-confidence. From its pages came a wide variety of criticisms of the Government, ranging from those who attacked the Liberal premier for his overbearing role in his party, and his failure to organize it on less autocratic lines, to others, like the pro-Fascist Antonios Bernaris, who saw the only solution for a 'disorganized' Greece in 'a system of concentration, tough discipline, a dictator to direct production . . . an economist with the iron will of a Bismarck'.[63]

Perhaps disaffection within the Venizelist camp could have been contained sufficiently to prevent the narrow but critical electoral defections of the following years; but this is only conceivable in the context of a more favourable economic climate. Not even Venizelos's rhetorical skills could withstand certain economic realities. Falling export prices pushed the real debt service burden up by 45% between 1929 and 1931. An analysis of the balance of payments reveals that the shrinking current account deficit was accompanied by a growing deficit on capital account: the two could only be sustained by running down the exchange reserves and relying upon short-term capital inflows. These trends threatened the Achilles heel of the Liberal economic project—the new central bank, the Bank of Greece.

Kostas Kostis has described in detail the Bank of Greece's inability to stand up to such pressures. Widely regarded in Greece as a necessary

---

[62] S. Stefanou (ed.), *Eleftheriou Venizelou politikai ypothikai anthologitheisai apo ta keimena avtou*, i (Athens, 1965), 18–19.

[63] *Peitharchia*, 29 Dec. 1929, 23 Feb. 1930, 7 Dec. 1930.

TABLE 5.4.   *The balance of payments, 1929–1932* ($ million)

	1929	1930	1931	1932
Current account				
Net visibles	−96.7	−84.1	−65.0	−35.5
Net invisibles	+66.6	+62.2	+46.6	+27.9
Balance	−30.1	−21.9	−18.4	−7.6
Capital account	−19.4	−27.1	−31.2	−10.8
Combined current/capital account	−49.5	−49.0	−49.6	−18.4
Balancing items				
Loss of reserves	+14.6	+1.4	+9.8	+11.8
Short-term capital flows	+28.5	+40.0	+35.7	+3.5
Residual	+6.4	+7.6	+4.1	+3.1

Notes: The arrangement of the official data has been amended as follows: (1) 'foreign debt service paid in Greece', entered as a credit item in the source below, has been omitted entirely here since it did not affect the external balance but only the distribution of foreign exchange within the country; (2) 'other State requirements' (i.e. excluding the service of the public debt) has been added to merchandise imports as a deficit item in net income from visibles; (3) 'expenses of Greeks travelling abroad' has been moved from the capital account and included in the estimate of net income from invisibles. The data for 1929–30 have been converted from £ sterling to $US at the rate of £ = 4.86; the data for 1931–2 are expressed in dollars in the original source.

Source: Bank of Greece, *The Economic Situation in Greece and the Bank of Greece in 1932* (Athens, 1933).

evil, tolerated only at the behest of foreign creditors, the Bank was also burdened by its weak balance-sheet and paltry liquid assets. Quite apart from the demand for exchange from legitimate importers and the state, it was forced to meet the less scrupulous claims of the commercial banks, led by its great rival, the National Bank, who hoped to use the withdrawal of exchange from the central bank as a means of engineering its collapse.[64]

For Venizelos the sole *raison d'être* of a central bank was to defend the gold standard. He later recalled in a letter to Tsouderos: 'I remember well that the first time you mentioned abandoning the gold standard to me, I told you in that case there would be no longer any reason to preserve a separate bank of issue.' What could the new Bank's authorities do as their reserves dribbled away? In 1932 Tsouderos, by then the Bank's Governor, wrote how they had hoped, 'strengthened from

[64] Kostis, *Oi trapezes kai i krisi, passim*; AET 48/1, 35, Tsouderos–LNFC, 11 May 1931; this subject is treated in greater detail in the next chapter.

abroad, to hold out until the time when all the planned effort and labour toward the economic reconstruction of the country ... would have begun to yield its fruits'.[65] But such an attitude required a considerable dose of the optimism which Venizelos so valued. When the international financial crisis erupted in the summer of 1931, the vulnerability of Greece's adherence to the gold standard was exposed.

[65] Kostis, *Oi trapezes kai i krisi*, pp. 47–8.

6

THE BATTLE FOR THE DRACHMA

The bourgeois social order in Greece, and in the whole world too,
is today undergoing its severest trial.

(Venizelos, March 1932)

Joining gold in 1928 had heralded the reincorporation of the Greek
economy into the international monetary order, and by opening the way
for foreign capital to flow into the country had lent prestige to the
Liberal Government, and credibility to its ambitious policies of economic development. The effort to use these funds to turn Greece into a
synchronon kratos (modern state) had continued through the commercial
crisis, accompanied by increasingly unconvincing government denials of
any serious economic problems ahead. But though Liberal spokesmen
shrugged off the difficulties of currant growers and tobacco producers,
they too were eventually forced to acknowledge the unprecedented
nature of the international depression.

The shock waves from the European financial débâcle of 1931
reverberated through the Balkans. The collapse of existing international
monetary institutions which followed on the heels of the British sterling
devaluation that autumn dealt the decisive blow to Liberal confidence. It
led to a serious financial crisis in Greece that eventually—after a winter
spent vainly fighting the 'battle for the drachma'—pushed her off the
gold standard.

This was a turning-point. Before the financial crisis it had seemed
that the funds for national economic development could be found
abroad; after it, they would have to be obtained at home. The devaluation of the drachma and default on her foreign debt effectively barred
Greece from Western capital markets, which were anyway no longer
able to go on lending abroad except on a very reduced scale. Because the
use to which domestic capital was put would depend at least in part on
the decisiveness of the fiscal and monetary policies of the state, the
outcome of the financial crisis marked a watershed in the relationship
between state and economy in Greece.

Furthermore, by staking so much on the outcome of his self-proclaimed 'battle for the drachma', Venizelos ensured that his failure to prevent devaluation would precipitate a serious political crisis as well. His ebullient rhetoric would come to sound increasingly hollow, and public opinion would swing towards the view expressed some time later by Dimitrios Maximos, a leading anti-Venizelist, that 'his incorrigible optimism had led him and the country into a dreadful impasse'.[1]

This chapter will chart the course of this second stage of the crisis. We should begin by sketching in the background to existing monetary arrangements in Greece. For relations between the new central bank —the Bank of Greece—and the commercial banks left much to be desired. And as a result, the gold standard operated in Greece in a way which was not to be found in any textbook on banking theory, and which would have rather unexpected effects on the impact of the financial crisis there.

The Gold Standard in Practice

The smooth operation of the gold standard depended in theory upon several monetary mechanisms. The key instruments available to a central bank under the gold standard regime were the discount rate and open-market operations. The Bank of England, for example, used movements in the bank rate both to control domestic credit and to influence short-term capital flows in and out of the country. By open-market operations, involving the purchase or sale of government securities in the open market, the central bank was in a position to regulate the supply of money. Hence, when its reserves fell, it could bring about a contraction in the money supply by the latter method, or attempt to build up its reserves by raising the bank rate.

These were the bare bones of the system which had operated in England before 1914, or rather, which those men responsible for the international stabilization policies of the 1920s believed had existed then. For as de Cecco comments in a recent study:

The international monetary system, as it developed in the course of our period [i.e. 1890–1914] did not however possess—except to a very small degree —those features which were attributed to it by a bevy of postwar economists:

---

[1] Finlayson–Niemeyer, 26 Nov. 1932, AET 46/163.

men who were really seeking a magic formula to resurrect the prewar world from its ruins.[2]

After 1928, when the establishment of a new central bank linked the drachma with gold, this system was supposed to operate in Greece too; but a number of difficulties soon became apparent. The commercial banks were hostile to the Bank of Greece, as they had been since its inception, regarding it as a troublesome upstart. For their part, the authorities at the Bank were under few illusions about the difficulties involved in bringing the commercial banks to accept the Bank's authority over them. The Bank was in a vulnerable position, handicapped by the terms of its foundation—for it was saddled with large quantities of unrealizable government debt, whilst its gold and foreign exchange holdings were barely adequate to maintain the reserve ratio.[3]

The commercial banks were arrayed behind its great rival, the National Bank of Greece, formerly the country's 'unofficial' central bank, which had, as a consequence of the terms of the Geneva Protocol, increased its already considerable domination of the domestic banking system. Venizelos himself described this situation as an 'economic anomaly'. League members in Geneva agreed: at a meeting of the League of Nations Financial Committee (LNFC) in May 1931 there had been lengthy discussion of the 'enormous strength' and 'practical monopoly' exerted by the National Bank, and one speaker had declared that 'the situation might become dangerous, and if the Bank of Greece is not strong enough to cope, the authority of the State should be called in to compel the National Bank not only to reduce its portfolio of drachma bills and foreign exchange, but also to rediscount bills with the Bank of Greece'.[4]

In October 1928—just six months after the Bank of Greece opened its doors—the leading commercial banks established the Union of Greek Banks: this was intended not only to help reduce competition between members, but also to present a common front against the central bank. The Union waged an effective campaign against proposals to compel the commercial banks to keep obligatory deposits with the central bank—a measure which both the Bank's authorities and their

---

[2] M. de Cecco, *Money and Empire: The International Gold Standard, 1890–1914* (Oxford, 1974), 60. LN, *International Currency Experience: Lessons of the Interwar Period* (Geneva, 1944), ch. 4, compares the theory with the inter-war reality.

[3] K. Kostis, *Oi trapezes kai i krisi, 1929–1932* (Athens, 1986), ch. 2.

[4] 'Notes of the discussions of our reports: Geneva', 11 May 1931, AEV 342; E. Venezis, *Emmanouil Tsouderos* (Athens, 1966), 74.

supporters in Geneva regarded as necessary. In the spring of 1931, Parliament debated the introduction of such measures, as part of a bill 'On Limited-Liability Companies and Banks'—designed to revise company law to take account of the enormous changes that had occurred over the previous decade, and in particular to provide greater protection for shareholders and bank depositors. But through the Union the commercial banks succeeded in weakening the force of the bill considerably. Whereas the Bank of Greece, drawing on views Keynes had recently published in *A Treatise on Money*, advocated that the commercial banks be compelled to maintain a liquidity ratio of at least 15% of sight and savings deposits, 7% of which was to be deposited with the Bank, the law as it was eventually passed in July 1931 stipulated only a 12% minimum liquidity ratio, which did *not* have to be held at the central bank. If commercial banks did choose to hold deposits at the Bank of Greece, these only needed to amount to 7% of their sight and savings deposits.[5]

Worse still, the new Bank of Greece had very restricted control over foreign exchange movements. Not only did the commercial banks transact business in foreign exchange within Greece independently of the central bank. They also attracted much of the exchange earned through either exports or invisibles to their branches abroad; indeed, to facilitate this, the National Bank had founded a branch office in New York in 1929. Because of the great importance of invisibles such as emigrant remittances to the Greek balance of payments, the central bank's inability to acquire foreign exchange from these sources would weaken its control of events once the crisis became more acute.

Neither of the two traditional instruments of British domestic credit policy—open-market operations and changes in the official discount rate—worked with the same efficacy in the Greek context. The new Bank's limited capacity to rediscount bills, combined with the fact that short-term government stock was not issued in Greece, meant that open-market operations were not feasible. At the same time, the commercial banks, despite the pressures on them described earlier, were in a considerably healthier financial position than the Bank of Greece; they ignored its advice, and still had sufficient funds to override changes in the Bank's discount rate, which was thus of limited value as

---

[5] Vouli ton Ellinon, *Ekthesis epi tou nomoschediou 'Peri anonymon etaireion kai trapezon'* (Athens, 1931), 50–68; Bank of Greece, *Dyo simeomata epi tou proschediou nomou: 'Peri anonymon etaireion kai trapezon'* (Athens, 1930), 22–36; Kostis, *Oi trapezes kai i krisi*, pp. 52–3, 108–9.

an instrument of credit policy. Nor did movements in this rate affect capital flows, for these were motivated by considerations of security rather than interest rate differentials. In short, the Bank of Greece found it had responsibilities but no power.

The net outflow of foreign exchange was temporarily reversed during 1930, thanks to loan proceeds, but heavy net outflows were resumed in the last quarter of the year and continued through 1931. As its exchange reserves diminished, the Bank should theoretically have attempted to contract the quantity of notes in circulation. In fact it ignored the textbooks and did the opposite: in a bid to establish its control over the commercial banks it began to compete with them directly, expanding its network of provincial branches and offering low interest rates in key local markets such as Kalamata and Patras, where it was reported to have gained 80% of the export business. From Patras, a rival bank manager reported: 'The Bank of Greece embarked upon an open competition towards the other banks, and more especially the National Bank of Greece, with the sole object of acquiring a commercial clientele under the lure of rates and excessive credit facilities . . . A cut-throat competition was started between these two banks into which the other local banks were gradually dragged . . . Naturally the local traders have made the best use of this wild competition.'[6]

Such a policy may have been useful in forcing the commercial banks to recognize the newcomer's authority, but it made the task of defending the drachma more difficult as balance of payments pressures built up. This was exacerbated by the rather apathetic stance of its senior

TABLE 6.1.   *Net foreign exchange movements at the Bank of Greece, 1928–1932* (quarterly, in million drachmas)

	1928	1929	1930	1931	1932
1st quarter	—	−54.7	+289.5	−242.3	−680.0
2nd quarter	—	−248.3	−50.3	−290.7	+477.7
3rd quarter	+37.0	−453.9	+260.5	−13.7	+71.9
4th quarter	+284.6	−357.5	−476.1	−735.0	+32.3
Net annual movement	+321.6	−1,114.4	+23.6	−1,281.7	−98.1

Source: K. Kostis, *Oi trapezes kai i krisi, 1929–1932* (Athens, 1986), 139.

[6] IBA, Kalamata, YR 1930/1, 6; IBA, Patras, YR 1930/1, 10.

management, especially its Governor, Alexandros Diomedes. H. C. Finlayson, the adviser appointed by the League of Nations to the Bank, warned Venizelos at a meeting in 1930 that 'the Bank of Greece, unlike all the other Central Banks in Europe, has been content to play a purely passive role. It has not raised its discount rate nor tried in any way to cut back its advances.' When these problems were extensively debated at the meeting of the League of Nations Financial Committee on 7 September 1931, Deputy Governor Emmanouil Tsouderos defended the Bank against accusations that orthodox monetary policies were not being wholeheartedly applied, declaring that 'in the present conditions, the rigid observation of the strictly orthodox principles governing the conduct of central banks may lead to results contrary to those which were desired'.[7]

But Venizelos's administration appeared oblivious to the weakness of the country's balance of payments position. By the spring of 1931, the fruits of the Liberal Government's programme for economic reconstruction were beginning to appear and the Government had just succeeded in floating a second Public Works Loan abroad.[8] The last three budgets had all officially ended in surplus, and it was expected that the 1931–2 Budget would too. Government spokesmen declared that Greece had managed to avoid the worst effects of the international crisis, and predicted that the public works programme would be completed as planned. The Finance Minister, George Maris, wound up the debate on the 1931–2 Budget with an attack on the 'pessimists' who were always inclined to foresee doom, and defended the Government's 'justified optimism' in the ability of the Greek economy to withstand the crisis.[9]

The Government's insistence on branding all critics of its economic policy as pessimists underlined its own limited understanding of Greece's vulnerability to unfavourable trends in the international economy. Opposition attacks on the Government, it is true, were largely misdirected, concentrating on the high level of taxation and extravagant public spending—arguments countered by the Government's proclaimed budgetary successes—rather than on the public debt position and Greece's dependence on capital inflows. Yet outside Parliament there were warnings of what was to come.

[7] LNFC, 42nd session, procès-verbal, 8, p. 6, AET; Venezis, *Tsouderos*, p. 68.

[8] On the background to the 1931 Public Works Loan, see K. Karamanlis, *Eleftherios Venizelos kai oi exoterikes mas scheseis: 1928–1932* (Athens, 1986), 272–7.

[9] *ESV*, 27 Mar. 1931, 1,296.

Two days after Maris closed the budget debate, Professor Xenophon Zolotas gave a speech to the Thessaloniki Chamber of Commerce, in which he drew attention to the worrying growth in the public debt: 'rather than being curtailed, in order that we may arrive at a healthy state of affairs, on the contrary, through perpetual borrowing we are continually burdened, and there is necessarily a worsening of the existing situation, which holds a danger of throwing the domestic economy into crisis if this policy is not brought to a timely end'.[10]

At the end of June, Finlayson sent Venizelos a report on the preceding nine months, and accompanied it with the warning that 'there is not the least doubt that there is a serious lack of economic equilibrium still persisting in Greece, and that unless remedial measures be taken, a serious situation might develop'.[11] The 1931 Loan had, in fact, only been floated that spring with the greatest difficulty. Three-quarters of the issue had been left with the London underwriters and Montagu Norman, the Governor of the Bank of England, had made it clear to the Greek authorities that London could no longer continue lending on 'the normal scale'.[12]

News of the German financial crisis over the summer finally changed the mood on the Athens Stock Exchange. Government bonds, whose price had risen in the first half of the year, largely owing to the introduction of tax concessions, and heavy support buying by the major banks, peaked in June. Their fall was not so steep as that of industrial shares, but more significant, since these bonds had been regarded as safe investments by the commercial banks, who had increased their holdings of them substantially over the previous 10 months. Outside the stock-market, further financial indicators suggest that conditions were tightening from June onwards. Money market rates rose from 8% to over 11% in the period July–September. The steady withdrawal of deposits from the commercial banks continued, though it is worth noting that a rapid withdrawal of drachma deposits was partly offset by a rise in foreign exchange deposits from 3,998.7 to 4,222.8 million drs.—a trend which suggests that people were worried more about the stability of the drachma than about that of the banking system itself.

[10] Cited in N. Anastasopoulos, *Istoria tis ellinikis viomichanias*, iii (Athens, 1947).

[11] Finlayson–Venizelos, 30 June 1931, AEV 343.

[12] Tsouderos–Diomedes, 2 May 1931, AEV 342. Norman is reported as having said that 'Greece was extremely lucky, first in being able to fund short-term debts at such a time, which England could not possibly do, and secondly in being able to finance a programme of twelve months, when most countries could not do so for twelve weeks'.

Nevertheless, the aggregate trend in deposits was downwards, and the banks, finding it difficult—despite the rise in interest rates—to liquidate their commercial advances, were forced to draw on their reserves. The result was a gradual fall in their liquidity ratio, but the position of the commercial banks at this stage was certainly not critical, and aroused little public disquiet.[13] Banks were able to meet demands for foreign exchange either out of their own reserves, or by purchasing exchange from the Bank of Greece. In this way, they off-loaded the strains of the foreign exchange shortage on to the central bank.

Faced with a steady outflow of exchange, the authorities of the Bank of Greece had foreseen problems during the summer months. Towards the end of July, Tsouderos predicted that the coming weeks would be critical.[14] As the cover ratio slid down towards the 40% legal minimum, it was decided to appeal to the Bank of International Settlements (BIS) for emergency credits. The BIS had already been involved in rescue work of this sort; in May and June it had arranged international credits to shore up the Credit-Anstalt in Austria. On 10 September, Tsouderos was instructed to request a loan of £1 million sterling.[15]

The reply came back from Basle one week later: the BIS was unable to agree to the Bank of Greece's request, in the light of its inability to control the activities of Greek commercial banks. Acknowledging the difficulties the Bank of Greece faced in trying to restrict the note circulation, McGarrah, the BIS President, nevertheless observed that the Bank would have made a better impression if it had made greater efforts to force the commercial banks to co-operate: 'However sound the policy of the Bank of Greece may be, we would face great difficulties in approaching other central Banks, insofar as the commercial banks in Greece appear to be following a different policy.'[16] One of the chief difficulties, the letter went on, lay in the foreign exchange deposits held by the commercial banks. How could foreign bankers be expected to risk their own exchange holdings, when there were still foreign currency deposits within Greece unused by the Bank of Greece?

A few days earlier the same points had been made by the League of Nations Financial Committee, which had advised Governor Diomedes of the need to discourage commercial banks from accepting deposits in

[13] *EV*, 10 Feb. 1932.
[14] Tsouderos–Diomedes, 28 July 1931, AET 101/48.
[15] Diomedes–Tsouderos, 10 Sept. 1931, AET 101/52.
[16] McGarrah–Diomedes, 17 Sept. 1931, AET 65/12.

foreign currency, and also suggested tentatively that the discount rate be raised 'in the near future' and that the Bank of Greece restrict short-term borrowing abroad.[17]

Thus it is clear that the position of the Bank by the third week of September had become exceptionally strained. After the BIS reply, there was no hope in the near future of obtaining assistance abroad, and to have sought help from the commercial banks within Greece would have publicized the Bank's plight, and strengthened the hand of its opponents. Unable to restrict the money supply, the Bank was forced to the expedient of transferring government deposits from sight to time accounts in order to maintain the reserve ratio.

The Onset of the Financial Crisis

In the early autumn, a sense of complacency was still current in government and business circles. To this must be attributed the lack of urgency which marked the initial response to the sterling crisis in London. One of the financial weeklies reported on 20 September that 'State bonds will certainly not fall far or long, given the healthy state of government finances, and that the whole of our economy appears to be in a satisfactory condition . . . Once the unease is past which has been caused in Athens by the tempest on the Stock Exchange in London, Greek shares will quickly and easily again find their correct level, that which in the last word is determined by the true state of affairs.'[18]

But the true state of affairs was to come as something of a shock to many people. On the day the above article appeared in Athens, the decision was taken in London to abandon the gold standard. And the very next day a series of meetings was held in Athens to determine whether Greece should follow the British example.

At this point a brief word may be useful on the nature of Greece's economic ties in this period with Britain. Commercial relations were of secondary importance: in the second half of the 1920s only 12% of Greek exports went to Britain and only 13% of imports came from her. Her previously dominant position in Greek trade was disappearing: Germany took more Greek exports, the United States provided more

---

[17] Suvich (LNFC)–Diomedes, 11 Sept. 1931, AET 'Texts Collected for a History of the Bank of Greece'.
[18] *OT*, 20 Sept. 1931.

TABLE 6.2. *Greece's trading partners* (percentages for the average of trade values in 1925–1929)

Country	Greek exports	Greek imports
Germany	22.1	8.2
USA	21.0	16.4
Italy	19.0	6.9
UK	12.2	13.4
France	5.9	7.7
Others	19.8	47.4
TOTAL	100.0	100.0

Source: LN, *Balance of Payments and Trade: 1927–29* (Geneva, 1930), 309, 331.

imports. British economic influence in Greece was primarily financial. London was the essential source of support for Greek loans, and had been drawn upon to an increasing extent over the previous decade, owing to the borrowing requirements of the post-war reconstruction programme.

In return for credit Britain acquired an ability to intervene in Greek economic affairs through two bodies which supervised Greek finances. One was the International Financial Commission (IFC) which in 1931 had a British chairman, as well as French and Italian representatives. The other was the League of Nations Financial Committee which had begun to monitor economic, and especially monetary policy in Greece at its thrice-yearly meetings. Sir Otto Niemeyer, a director of the Bank of England, was also a member of the Committee, and it was under that body's aegis that he was shortly to go to Greece to write a major report on the state of Greek public finances.

It was no accident that the Bank of England should be represented in this way on the Committee. Greece, like most small countries at that time, was on a gold exchange standard rather than the gold standard proper. In other words, the reserves backing the drachma were not kept exclusively in gold, but rather to a large extent in foreign convertible currencies. In the Greek case they were kept mostly in sterling, which till 1931 had been deposited with the Bank of England. At the time of the crisis, three-quarters of these sterling deposits had been transferred to Paris and New York. Yet neither of the latter two centres rivalled Britain's involvement in Greek affairs. Over half of the Greek foreign debt was held by British subjects, and it was this fact which in the last analysis underlay the depth of British interest in the country.[19]

At the initial meetings called by Venizelos, to which he invited bankers and government officials, powerful voices urged continued adherence to the gold standard.[20] One reason was the authorities' over-confidence, reflected in Diomedes's prediction on the night of the 21st, that Britain's troubles would be 'temporary' and that Greece, though she would be affected, would be less severely hit than other countries.

The commercial banks, too, had good reason to resist a devaluation of the drachma. They had large foreign exchange liabilities, and faced heavy losses if forced to meet these after such a move. Alexandros Koryzis, the Deputy-Governor of the National Bank—a man whose opinion was valued highly by Venizelos at this time—argued strongly in this direction. Moreover, devaluation would also be likely to cause the prices of Greek government securities to plummet, reducing the overall value of the banks' assets.[21]

For the Government too the economic arguments militated against devaluation. Abandoning the gold standard would dramatically increase the drachma cost of servicing the foreign debt. General elections were due within a year: having constantly pledged the Government's commitment to defending the 'national currency' and having frequently praised its success in doing so, Venizelos must understandably have had qualms about throwing his whole achievement into question. One should bear in mind that before stabilization in 1928, Greece had passed through a period of inflation, economic insecurity, and political turmoil; it was natural to fear a return to those conditions if stabilization was abandoned—and devaluing the drachma was regarded as the first step in that direction.

The most outspoken critic of remaining on gold was Kyriakos Varvaressos, at that time an adviser to the Bank of Greece, and one of the outstanding economists and administrators of the inter-war period. A member of that generation which had begun to shape public affairs in Greece under Venizelos before 1914, Varvaressos was a German-

---

[19] Ministère des Affaires Étrangères, *La Grèce et la crise mondiale* (Athens, 1933), 42; G. Andreopoulos, 'The IFC and Anglo-Greek Relations (1928–33)', *Historical Journal*, 31(2) (1988), 341–64, is informative.

[20] *EV*, 24 Apr. 1932, articles by Maris and Tsouderos.

[21] E. Venezis, *Chronikon tis Trapezis tis Ellados, 1928–1952* (Athens, 1955), 100–1; IBA, General Manager, YR, 1932/3, 3–4.

trained university professor who had remained aloof from party politics. Unfortunately he found himself at this critical moment far from the frenetic atmosphere of Athens. From London, where he was meeting officials from the Bank of England, he telegraphed his disapproval: both he and Niemeyer, he wrote, regarded the decision to remain attached to gold as 'hasty and ill-considered', and he warned that despite official announcements from the British Government, bankers expected sterling to remain off gold for well over six months.[22] His advice went unheeded. The drachma was linked to the dollar, which remained on gold, in place of sterling; apart from a prohibition on dealings in sterling, no exchange restrictions were imposed.

Varvaressos's forebodings were soon justified. Already on 22 September, panic selling on the Athens Stock Exchange had forced it to close. A run now began on the foreign exchange holdings of the Bank of Greece, picking up speed as the week progressed: on the 21st it lost $194,660, the next day $432,573, the day after that $726,568. By the end of the week its losses totalled $3.6 million. Combined with other losses she had sustained as a result of sterling's depreciation, this drain forced the Bank into the humiliating position of having to borrow $5.5 million from the NBG and, on the 28th, to announce restrictions on foreign exchange business. Finlayson, the League adviser to the Bank, had recommended such action the previous Tuesday (22 September) but had been overruled by Diomedes.[23]

There was widespread criticism of the manner in which the authorities had handled the crisis. In the Press, expressions of confidence that the crisis would be short-lived soon gave way to accusations that Government action had been inept and ineffectual; not only had it permitted the unrestricted sale of dollars, but its mistaken prohibition on dealings in sterling had caused the Bank to forgo a further £1 million sterling offered to it by panicking sellers. Once again the National Bank had been obliged to bail the Government out.

Attempting to allay the general disquiet, Venizelos gave a speech on the 27th, in which he reaffirmed that monetary stability was a prerequisite for the economic recovery of the country; the productive works would go ahead as planned with the aid of foreign credits which, he assured his audience, would certainly be forthcoming. This was

Venizelos's optimism at its most far-fetched. He insisted that the drachma was stronger than the dollar and indeed stronger than the French franc too! Few countries could match Greece's achievement of balancing the budget three years in a row. He predicted that the budget for the coming year would also end in balance, and expressed faith in the stability of Greek finances. The possibility that there might be difficulties in finding funds to continue the productive works was raised, only to be dismissed: 'The pessimists will say: he talks about productive works—where's he going to get the money for them? I promise you they will be completed as planned. It would be a catastrophe analogous to abandoning the gold standard if we could not finish them. We will surely find abroad the few millions which we need . . .'.[24]

In reality the British crisis had shaken the Prime Minister deeply. He believed it was vital that the Labour Party should lose the forthcoming British election; otherwise it would mean 'the end of today's capitalist democratic order. Britain would sink to a second-rate power, and that would be disastrous for mankind, since the world required leadership and only Britain could provide it.'[25] For Greece, abandoning the gold standard meant at the same time the end of the programme of economic reconstruction. And if that happened, the refugee question would reappear in an acute form. So he, and many others, believed.

In a blatant attempt to find a scapegoat for the mishandling of the September crisis the Liberal premier engineered the resignation of his loyal supporter, Alexandros Diomedes, charging that he had failed to enforce exchange restrictions with sufficient rigour. The result was to leave the Bank leaderless at a critical juncture; and as the politicians fought over the nomination of Diomedes's successor its prestige took a dive. The Governorship was offered first to the Liberal Andreas Mikalakopoulos, whose political ambitions Venizelos mistrusted, and then to Koryzis and to Dimitrios Maximos, a leading Populist and former banker. The first two candidates turned it down. And despite being favoured by Venizelos, Maximos was ruled out when sharcholders voted instead for Diomedes's deputy, Tsouderos. Although Tsouderos's ties to the Liberal Party were close, he quickly realized that these would not be enough to secure either his own position or that of the Bank of Greece. Venizelos's feelings towards him were lukewarm. Maximos, after his rejection, began to step up his attacks through the

[24] *OT*, 10 Oct. 1931.
[25] Karamanlis, *Exoterikes scheseis*, p. 286.

anti-Venizelist Press. Underlining the bad feeling which existed between the new central bank and the commercial sector, the senior management of the National Bank termed Tsouderos's appointment a 'national misfortune'.[26]

For the new Governor and his colleagues, this was a period of flux and improvisation. The restrictions which had come into force on 28 September, supplemented by others on 8 October, were not only a sign of the Government's belated recognition of the gravity of the crisis; in reality they marked the beginning of the end of the gold standard in Greece. The Bank of Greece was released from its obligation to exchange its banknotes for gold or foreign currency. The sale of exchange was only permitted in the case of 'necessary' imports, the criterion for which grew progressively tighter over time: at first only luxury imports were prohibited; then only industrial raw materials and foodstuffs were permitted; finally foodstuffs only.[27] A special committee was set up to examine all applications for foreign exchange. Greek exporters were obliged to surrender their earnings to the central bank, from whom they received drachmas at the official rate. The export of capital from Greece was forbidden.

The uncertainty and experimentation in official policy-making can be seen to good effect in the monetary authorities' handling of interest rates. The central bank was beset, on the one hand, by the League of Nations Financial Committee, which had advocated raising the discount rate to 15% or 20%, and on the other, by domestic industrialists and merchants, who attacked any upward movement in the rate as inflicting further damage upon the domestic economy. On 26 September, the discount rate was raised from 9% to 12%. This belated action had no effect on the demand for exchange, which remained strong after the introduction of restrictions. Nor did it stem the flight of capital. But perhaps its function was intended to be more symbolic than practical, aimed at deflecting criticism at the forthcoming LNFC meeting, where, as the message from the BIS had made plain, offers of assistance would depend upon potential lenders being satisfied that proper banking practice was being observed. On 27 September, Venizelos had declared that he was prepared to see the rate rise to 20% or even 50%, if the safety of the drachma was at stake; but he had come in for criticism from

---

[26] G. Dafnis, *I Ellas metaxy dyo polemon, 1923–1940* (Athens, 1955), ii, 107–11; Karamanlis, *Exoterikes scheseis*, p. 282; FO 371/15230 C8185/18, Ramsay (Athens)–Sargent, 24 Oct. 1931.

[27] N. Pyrris, *La Crise monétaire en Grèce* (Paris, 1934), 173.

business circles for this remark.[28] Barely one month had elapsed before it was lowered again to 11% for reasons which remain obscure. The most likely explanation is that the move represented an attempt by the newly elected Tsouderos to win support from the business community. At the beginning of October a letter had been sent to Venizelos by three influential organizations of industrialists, expressing concern at the consequences of any further tightening of credit. The Prime Minister was asked to request the banks not to withdraw funds from commerce and industry. It was suggested that providing further tax relief on capital assets would encourage the repatriation of Greek capital.[29] Venizelos's reply was non-committal, provoking further outbursts at the October general meeting of the Athens Chamber of Commerce against his Government's over-restrictive credit policy.

In fact it is doubtful whether the business men's complaints about the tightness of credit were justified. The position of the commercial banks remained surprisingly stable in the last quarter of 1931. Drachma deposits actually increased by 3%. Deposits in foreign currencies were provisionally frozen from 29 September, though it is true that the banks must have been anxious at the prospect of losses when these were unfrozen again. There was evidence of only a slight contraction of credit, bills and advances together falling by less than 3%. The central bank, despite a 19% fall in its gold holdings, actually increased its drachma advances by 138 million drs., an increase of 85% on the September figure. In the autumn of 1931, then, there was no severe curtailment of credit. Undoubtedly the banks were worried about the future; many of their assets were either unrealizable or else badly reduced in value. But they were able to improve liquidity by selling off 300 million drs. of their holdings of gold national loans; for them, the real squeeze did not arrive until early 1932.[30]

It quickly became obvious, however, that whilst the domestic money supply was little affected, the measures introduced by the Government were quite insufficient to prevent the Bank of Greece's reserve from draining away. In the final quarter of the year there was a net outflow of 735 million drs., more than double that which occurred in 1929 in the wake of the Wall Street crash. The Bank's purchases of exchange in December were over 700 million drs. down on the same period the

[28] Pyrsos, *Symvoli*, pp. 90–1.
[29] *DEVE/A*, Oct. 1931.
[30] 'Situation of the Commercial Banks in Greece', memo. by Finlayson, Aug. 1932, AET 74/1.

previous year and the smallest monthly purchase since the opening of the Bank in May 1928.

Uncertainty about future exchange rate policy caused a postponement of export orders. At the same time exporters were unwilling to surrender exchange at the official rate when black market rates were much higher. Another problem was that remaining on the gold standard had encouraged importers to keep stocks high, since devaluation would increase import prices. The Bank of Greece, wishing to keep down the cost of living by selling exchange at the official rate, found import demand remaining strong. In its desire to maintain the value of the drachma, the Bank thus found itself pursuing a policy which worsened the trade deficit and increased its own difficulties. To preserve the fiction that the reserve ratio was still above the 40% mark, the Bank moved a number of accounts from sight to time deposits, where they were not counted against the reserve for the purpose of computing the reserve ratio.

In early December, Tsouderos presented Venizelos and the Finance Minister, Maris, with a memorandum in which he examined movements in the Bank's reserves since its foundation. Referring to the current crisis he observed that 'we do not believe that it is realistic to express the hope that by the efforts of the State and the Bank of Greece alone, we can balance our external accounts and at the same time avoid the gradual erosion both of our remaining disposable funds in gold abroad, and of our exchange'.[31] It was, according to Tsouderos, necessary for the commercial banks to be made to surrender their foreign exchange in return for the equivalent in drachmas. In this way the central bank would tighten its control of the available exchange within Greece. To Tsouderos it was surely clear that the crisis could have one of only two possible outcomes for the Bank—either abolition or increased powers over the commercial banks.

But of course the commercial banks were strongly opposed to any legislation which increased the Bank of Greece's control over them. In the Press their supporters renewed their attacks on the Bank, and called for its dissolution. Maximos, at that time economic adviser to the Populist Party, published an article in which he proposed that the central bank be amalgamated with the National Bank.[32] Similar suggestions had gained wide currency in preceding months, but this was the first time they had been publicly expressed by a figure of such prestige.

[31] 'Situation and Development of the Cover', unsigned memo., 4 Dec. 1931, AET 65/1.

[32] *Proia*, 5 Dec. 1931.

Maximos's hostility to the Bank had clearly not been lessened by Tsouderos's actions as Governor. It was, in his view, incapable of functioning as an independent institution. As events had shown, it could not survive without the support of the National Bank, and this fact ought to be recognized.

The article in which his proposed reform of the Bank appeared described a package of measures for dealing with the crisis. The Bank reform was not the most controversial of these. To keep Greece on the gold standard Maximos urged two further measures: firstly, the drawing up and application of a comprehensive economic policy; and secondly, the declaration of an immediate suspension of all foreign debt payments, in order to save the Bank of Greece's reserve.

Both proposals ran contrary to current government policy. In Parliament ministers insisted that because of the unpredictable way in which the crisis was evolving, it was best to introduce temporary measures, as the Government had done, rather than an overall plan which might have to be scrapped as circumstances changed. As Venizelos announced after meeting Maximos and rejecting his proposals, Greece was waiting for the Great Powers to co-operate in a strategy for international recovery, and was confident that an offer of assistance would be made.[33] Such expectations not only made it unnecessary to formulate a plan along Maximos's lines, they also precluded unilateral action to reduce the foreign debt burden, for this would rule out all chances of a sympathetic hearing abroad.

The Government's position was not easy. Committed by their entire strategy to dependence upon foreign capital inflows, they were now, in effect, forced to sit and wait in the hope that these would eventually be resumed. The confidence of a few months earlier was fast disappearing. The budgetary outlook had changed completely as a result of import restrictions, which, though vital to save exchange, had the effect of curtailing a major source of government revenue. Maris had been forced to admit this to Parliament in the debate on the economy on 18 November, though he would not state publicly that there was a chance of the Budget ending in deficit. However, the Bank of Greece informed Venizelos that, according to its estimates, revenues from import duties would fall at least 20% below the predicted level and that the Budget would close with a deficit of over 300 million drs.[34]

[33] Dafnis, *Metaxy dyo polemon*, ii. 111–13.

[34] *PSV*, 18 Nov. 1931, 10; also Bank of Greece–Venizelos, 17 Oct. 1931, AEV 344; Tsouderos–Venizelos, 5 Dec. 1931, AEV 180.

Speaking in the same debate as Maris, representatives of the mainstream political parties reaffirmed their commitment to the gold standard. Papanastasiou asserted that *all* parties agreed on the need to remain on gold, and he directed his criticisms at the Government's inability to do more to reduce consumption! The conservative Venizelist Zavitsianos attacked the Government for its lack of calm in handling the early stages of the crisis, whilst for the Populists all their leader Tsaldaris could come up with was to reproach Venizelos for not adopting the new exchange restrictions earlier. There was a good reason for the Populists' caution: Venizelos had threatened to call new elections early if they challenged his own handling of the crisis without putting forward recommendations of their own. Equally alarmed by the prospect of victory or defeat, Tsaldaris hastened to affirm his basic approval of Liberal policy. Venizelos himself raised for the first time the possibility that foreign credits might not be forthcoming. His view, typically, was that it would make little difference: 'with the English crisis, and the fall of the English pound, I do not know when we will be able to obtain a foreign loan for the completion of the productive works. The Government is convinced that even without a foreign loan, it will manage to continue the productive works. They may proceed a little more slowly, but not much.'[35]

But foreign loans were not required for the public works alone, nor were the works the most urgent item on the agenda. This was the solvency of the Bank of Greece, where despite the restrictions the reserve was diminishing daily. The Government planned to wait for internationally co-ordinated action. But the next few months were to show that events could not wait that long.

The Second Stage

The period from January to March 1932 marked a second stage in the financial crisis, when the authorities explored the possibility of obtaining assistance from abroad. The Government's search for help centred around two missions: a visit by Venizelos to the states represented on the IFC in January, and the later Niemeyer mission to Athens.

In the middle of January, Venizelos made a much-publicized journey abroad, flying first to Rome, then on to Paris and London. In each capital he had talks with the Prime Minister and the Minister of Finance. With him he brought a memorandum which spelled out the difficulties confronting Greece, 'surprise par les effets de la crise mondiale en pleine reconstruction économique', outlined the Government's economic programme and the prudence with which it had so far conducted its affairs, and concluded with a request for a five-year suspension of the debt amortization payments administered by the IFC and, in addition, a $50 million loan over four years. The Governments were warned that if no assistance were forthcoming, Greece would be compelled to leave the gold standard, and give herself up to inflation and social turmoil. They were invited, in the event that they disagreed with the proposals contained in the memorandum, to empower the IFC or the LNFC to make alternative suggestions.[36]

Niemeyer met Venizelos during the latter's stay in London and discussed the Greek proposals with him. To Finlayson he declared confidentially that in his opinion they were 'contradictory and, I fear, mistaken'.[37] Neither he, nor the IFC, whose views had also been solicited, ruled out a moratorium on amortization payments if it proved to be necessary. But the problem was how could one then hope to raise further loans? The Greek Government sought a long-term recovery scheme, but there was a danger of making unrealistic demands on creditors' sympathy. The point was to recur in the coming months, as the LNFC tried to persuade the Greeks that a gradual approach might carry a better chance of success than the ambitious plan embodied in Venizelos's memorandum.

But if the Greeks approached matters with what seemed a rather unrealistic confidence, the involvement of the Powers was characterized by considerable uncertainty and a reluctance to be seen to get involved. This becomes apparent when one looks at the circumstances in which the Niemeyer mission was arranged.

The original idea to invite an expert to Athens to report on the state of the economy seems to have come from the Bank of Greece. After the rebuff from the BIS the previous autumn, some other authoritative backing was required before overtures could begin anew for economic aid. The question was discussed when Tsouderos visited the Bank of England in December. He reported that Niemeyer planned to visit

---

[36] 'Memorandum remis par le Président du Conseil aux Gouvernements anglais, français et italien', n.d., AET 8/1.

[37] Niemeyer–Finlayson, 29 Jan. 1932, AET 65/15.

Greece, but wished to attract as little publicity as possible, pretending that the visit was a simple holiday, with no official character. The date of arrival was to be 'around the middle of January'.[38]

The absurdity of this idea must quickly have become evident and after a week Niemeyer himself changed his mind, suggesting that it would be preferable to channel matters through the LNFC: the Greek Government should make a request to the Committee for an expert to be sent, and if this was approved, he would be prepared to go.[39]

Bringing the mission under the auspices of the League of Nations had important consequences. Unlike the Bank of England, it had no funds of its own and little political influence. The Greek Government was aware of the Financial Committee's reluctance to depart from its traditional role as policy adviser and find itself actively helping the Greeks to obtain loans. Yet such help was exactly what the Greeks wanted, or at the very least a report which would give strong support to their case.

For these reasons the Greek application to the Financial Committee was ambiguous. Tsouderos, in his letter to the President of the Committee, phrased the request in the most general terms: 'In our desire that our co-operation with you for the opportunity [sic] facing of the situation should be based on a precise and complete knowledge of the situation by both sides, I request you to send here a member of your Committee who should study on the spot the actual position of the Bank of Greece, and of our public finances, and confer with us upon the policy to be adopted.'[40]

A few days later, at a regular meeting of the Committee in Geneva, Varvaressos was asked to explain the purpose of the mission. He was franker than Tsouderos, who had mentioned neither the intended report, nor plans to use it in requesting help from abroad: 'the expert could perhaps give us useful advice of an alternative policy to follow. He could draw up an objective report which might be useful to us in the event that the Government believes it necessary to seek international assistance.'[41]

The Greek request was approved, but it was not until the middle of February when Niemeyer finally arrived in Athens. Moreover, despite mutual goodwill, it became clear that the two sides held different views about what the mission could achieve, and this disagreement, reflected

[38] Tsouderos (Paris)–Bank of Greece, 12 Dec. 1931, AEV 179.
[39] Niemeyer–Tsouderos, 22 Dec. 1931, AET 56/2.
[40] Tsouderos–LNFC, 1 Jan. 1932, AET 56/4.
[41] LNFC, 44th session, 11 Jan. 1932, procès-verbal, 2, p. 32.

in two differing approaches for dealing with the crisis, ultimately led to the breakdown of co-operation.

Niemeyer arrived in Athens on 16 February, where he remained two weeks gathering material for the report before leaving to draft it in consultation with the other members of the Financial Committee. On the eve of his departure he warned Venizelos of the difficulties that might be caused by a unilateral suspension of amortization payments. He emphasized the necessity, if the damage to Greece's credit was to be minimized, of having the support of the League, which would be conditional upon the suspension being for one year only (rather than the five years Venizelos had suggested). He also repeated his objections to the proposed fusion of the central bank with the National Bank, concluding his remarks with the observation that such a move would 'involve the exclusion of Greece from international relationships in the sphere of Central Banking'.[42] It was a threat which was rapidly losing its force.

Within Greece, conditions worsened markedly in the first quarter of 1932. From December onwards, import restrictions began to bite and—in Finlayson's words—'brought commerce to a standstill'.[43] There was increasing unrest from business men and merchants, who had previously accepted the need to support the Government. State policies were accused of being improvised and makeshift, reflecting the 'hostile stance of the State towards commerce'.[44] Import merchants were embittered by rumours that they might be supplanted by official import-distribution agencies. Exporters criticized the lack of official encouragement for exports, which were penalized both by the relative appreciation of the drachma and by the 'tax' imposed on exporters by virtue of their obligation to surrender foreign exchange at the official rate. Dissatisfaction among the urban poor also increased. When import restrictions caused textile works at Naoussa, in northern Greece, to close, workers and their families demonstrated, demanding bread. Unemployed men smashed the windows of a bakery in Xanthi. In Nigrita gendarmes opened fire on a crowd of demonstrating workers who had tried to stop lorries loaded with tobacco leaf leaving the town;

---

[42] Niemeyer–Venizelos, 29 Feb. 1932, AEV 345.

[43] Bank of Athens, *Bulletin Économique et Financier* (Dec. 1931), 2,000–1; Finlayson–Venizelos, 10 Feb. 1932, AET 65/20.

[44] Charilaos to Athens Chamber of Commerce, 16 Feb., 1932 in *DEVE/A*, Apr.–May 1932.

the Liberal Minister of the Interior put the blame on a 'few communists' in the crowd. In Salonika there were similar tensions. By February the gendarmerie, supported by an infantry and a cavalry regiment, were patrolling the streets of the city to prevent further demonstrations there. A local eyewitness reported the 'widespread and terrible distress through lack of food, firing, housing and clothing, especially in such a cold and prolonged winter'.[45]

Industrialists demanded a reduction in interest rates and an expansion of credit, claiming that they could not increase output to take advantage of import restrictions if credit was tight. From this quarter too there were complaints at the lack of co-ordination in official policy, and calls for a 'dictator of production'. The Athens Merchants' Federation appealed for greater economic and monetary co-ordination, declaring that these demands were 'neither republican nor royalist, neither liberal nor anti-liberal'. And the ex-Governor of the Bank of Greece, Diomedes, gave a speech on the effects of the crisis, in the course of which he stated that 'the crisis had at least brought this benefit, that it opened many people's eyes, and demonstrated that those nations which genuinely wish to make progress, should not shrink from undertaking a comprehensive economic programme'.[46]

As factories were forced to shut down for lack of funds, the commercial banks came under fire. Predictably, they were held responsible for much of the trouble 'having originally been far too generous in granting credits, and now being over-cautious, exacerbating our difficulties'.[47] In fact the commercial banks, especially the smaller ones, were in no position to increase their lending. Their situation which had already been precarious, worsened in early 1932, with the liquidity ratio of four major banks dropping from 16.8% in December to 9.7% in April, and from 17.8% to 12.5% for the system as a whole. In February public confidence slumped further with the news that the Cosmadopoulos Bank, closely associated with the Thessaly grain trade, had been forced to suspend operations. The withdrawal of deposits accelerated, outpacing the banks' efforts to liquidate their commercial advances. From their point of view, credit was not tight enough: their cash base (cash in

---

[45] FO 371/15966 C2092/462, Ramsay–FO, 'Salonica Monthly Report no. 23', 7 Mar. 1932; *PSV*, 17 Feb. 1932, 294–5; Gonatas–Venizelos, 5 Mar. 1932, 17 Mar. 1932, AEV 173/110.

[46] *DEVE/A*, Mar. 1932; *EV*, 21 Mar. 1932; A. Diomedes, *Meta tin krisin* (Athens, 1935), 66.

[47] *EV*, 16 Jan. 1932.

till + cash with other banks + cash at the Bank of Greece) fell by one-third between December and March. Saddled with a large amount of illiquid assets, they turned for assistance to the Bank of Greece.[48]

Thus in the first quarter of 1932 the central bank came into its own as a lender of last resort. It was an important turning-point. Given the exigencies of the crisis, the commercial banks were obliged to reconsider their previously hostile attitude towards the newcomer. In the first four months of the year, the Bank increased its commercial advances from 300 million drs. to 733 million drs.; of the latter sum, some 500 million represented direct advances to the commercial banks. In Finlayson's judgement 'the Bank of Greece . . . in its quality as lender of last resort, intervened at the proper time and adopted the wisest course'.[49]

But supporting the domestic banking system inevitably affected the Bank of Greece's own balance-sheet. In the first quarter of the year, the quantity of notes in circulation fell only 2.5% despite a 19.5% drop in the Bank's cover.[50] The reserve ratio was now well below the minimum 40% laid down in the Bank's charter.

Rediscounting bills held by the commercial banks was not the only cause of the increase in the Bank's advances. It had also been obliged to extend advances to the state, and those drachma advances were in large part immediately converted into exchange to meet the state's external obligations. In January and February $5 millions were sold to the state, out of a total sales of $14 millions; over the same period the net outflow from the Bank's reserve was $8.4 millions.[51] By the first week in March the reserve was down to £6.5 millions.[52] Unless foreign credits were quickly forthcoming, adherence to the gold standard could not last long.

Defeat

In March attention switched to Paris where the LNFC was due to meet to discuss the findings of the Niemeyer mission at one of its regular meetings. The outlook was grim. Tsouderos had talks at the Bank of

[48] 'Situation of the Commercial Banks in Greece', unsigned memo., 9 Mar. 1933, AET 74/1; USNA 868.00 Gen. Cond./13, Morris (Athens)–State, 21 Mar. 1932.
[49] 'Situation of the Commercial Banks in Greece', AET 74/1.
[50] 'The Policy of the Bank of Greece and the Situation of the Commercial Banks', memo. by Finlayson, 31 May 1932, AET 72/5; 'The Extension of Credit and Exchange Restrictions', unsigned memo., 16 May 1932, AET 46/168.
[51] Tsouderos–Niemeyer, 16 Mar. 1932, AEV 173.
[52] Tsouderos–Niemeyer, 19 Mar. 1932, AET 56/36.

France, but reported that the French were unlikely to provide help.[53] All depended on getting a favourable report from the League. Without this approaches to London or Paris were destined to fail. Venizelos appears to have been confident that with the Committee's support he would be able to find the money abroad. 'Leave it to me,' he assured Finlayson. But he also hinted that lack of assistance might force him to resign.[54]

At the Bank of Greece there were again worries over renewed calls in the anti-Venizelist Press for the Bank's dissolution: the Bank had shown itself incapable of managing the monetary system; the inevitable abandonment of the gold standard would make its position redundant. Venizelos should stop 'making comic speeches about his optimism' and withdraw the privilege of note issue from the Bank. Tsouderos was alarmed by these attacks and suggested that the Committee include in its report a defence of the Bank to serve 'as a sort of guiding basis to all Greek Governments'.[55]

On 10 March the LNFC session opened with a presentation by the Finance Minister, Maris. He traced the origins of the crisis back to the previous September when 'our resistance gave way at its weakest point, that is, our monetary stability'.[56] Efforts to combat the exchange shortage had created new strains on the Budget, whilst failing to halt the diminution of the Bank's reserves. The prospects for the 1932–3 Budget were not good—even after every possible economy, a deficit of 1300 million drs. seemed unavoidable. He repeated the Government's request for a long-term loan, rejecting short-term credits as destabilizing and inadequate.

He was followed by Tsouderos, who concentrated upon the immediate problems caused by the fall in export earnings and the scarcity of foreign exchange. Estimated exchange requirements for the coming six months, he warned, exceeded the reserve at the Bank by some $2 millions.[57] Without assistance very soon, stabilization was doomed, and with it all hope of balancing the current budget. There would also be 'another tragic consequence', namely, 'the incapacity of the country to continue to honour its obligations towards foreign countries'. Should Greece's problems be considered within the context of the overall recovery plan for Central and Eastern Europe that the League was about

[53] Tsouderos–Niemeyer, 10 Mar. 1932, AET 56/14.
[54] Finlayson–Niemeyer, 8 Mar. 1932, AET 56/6.
[55] Tsouderos–Niemeyer, 8 Mar. 1932, AET 56/11.
[56] LNFC, 44th session, 10 Mar. 1932, procès-verbal, 6, p. 4.
[57] Ibid., 11 Mar. 1932; see under AET 54/2.

to debate? No, said Tsouderos, the formulation of this plan would be a lengthy matter, and Greece's problems were urgent. Thus at the outset, the Greek delegation made it plain that only a massive transfusion of funds swiftly provided would, in the Government's opinion, be of any use.

But the members of the LNFC were by no means satisfied that the Greek authorities were willing to make sufficient sacrifices on their own part; they regarded the proposals as an effort to throw the burden of the crisis on to their foreign creditors, and to enlist the help of the Committee in doing so. At further meetings both Niemeyer and de Chalendar, the French delegate, closely interrogated Maris about his budgetary policy, and urged the importance of further cuts—de Chalendar in a draconian vein recommending the closure of schools and 20% cuts in public employees' salaries—if there was to be any chance of persuading foreign Governments to give the go-ahead for another loan. But Maris insisted on questioning his own Budget Director's estimates of yields from possible tax increases, and continued to demand that the Committee accept a lengthy suspension of amortization payments, whilst ruling out major increases in taxation. The Committee's sympathy for the Greek case began to wane.[58]

On the Greek side there were differing reactions to the way events were turning out. The contrast between Tsouderos and Maris—two representatives of the Venizelist élite—is instructive. The former, despite an indecisive meeting of the League's Banking Sub-Committee, continued to remain in favour of working through the League. As a key figure in Greece's economic negotiations with the West over the past decade, Tsouderos combined loyalty to the Liberals with a strong belief in the benefits of internationalism. At a time when the central bank was under attack within Greece, the League was an indispensable protector and ally. Moreover, Tsouderos was a cautious man, by nature inclined to prefer formulating policy and protecting his interests within an established framework.

Maris, on the other hand—a 'good political boss, but neither a financier nor a statesman'—saw advantages in intransigence. He was much closer than Tsouderos to Venizelos, and formed part of his inner circle of advisers. Placating the League for Maris took second place to ensuring continued Liberal rule at home. The likely political repercussions of carrying out the deflationary policies demanded by the

---

[58] LNFC, 45th session, 15 Mar. 1932, procès-verbal, 14, pp. 7–8.

LNFC were not difficult to foresee. The Government's term expired in the autumn, and during the coming electoral campaign it risked sacrificing considerable popularity if it tried closing schools and raising taxes.[59] At the end of the 15 March debate, Maris angrily withdrew, warning the Committee that it was endangering the entire economic programme of the Government, and that Venizelos might feel compelled to resign.[60]

In Athens relations between the major parties were marked by growing bitterness. Venizelos wanted to resign and pave the way for an all-party government. His ostensible reason, that such a government would be free to take the steps that he was honour-bound not to take (i.e. suspending debt repayments from 1 April), prompted the accusation that he was trying to evade responsibilities that were properly his. But in reality his strategy had weightier motives behind it. The opposition Populist Party, with its monarchist past, had denied the constitutionality of the Republic since its inception in 1924. By inviting the opposition to join the Government, Venizelos hoped to gain whatever the outcome. Acceptance would bring the Populist Party within the republican fold, as well as giving them a share of the blame if unpopular measures needed to be taken. Refusal could be interpreted as cowardice and indecision. In the event, the opposition leader, Panayis Tsaldaris, turned the idea down and, in so doing, reinforced the popular image of himself as a weak and unimaginative politician who lacked concrete proposals for handling the situation.[61]

Having failed to secure Tsaldaris's co-operation, Venizelos dramatically changed tack. At the end of March he attacked the Populist leader fiercely, criticizing his failure to defend the 'bourgeois world' and accusing him of waiting to complete the destruction of the country which his side had crippled in 1922. He thus deliberately recalled the question of responsibility for the Asia Minor *katastrofi*, provoking an uncharacteristically sharp reply from Tsaldaris. Yet whilst both sides sought to pin the blame for the crisis on the crimes and errors committed by their opponents a generation earlier, Venizelos continued to project a confidence which the realities of the situation were far from justifying. One of his messages to the public boasted defiantly: 'Despite defeatist cries, our country can victoriously face the world crisis and develop its

[59] Maris–Venizelos, 15 Mar. 1932, AET 2/24; USNA 868.00/675, Morris–State, n.d.

[60] LNFC, 45th session, 15 Mar. 1932, procès-verbal, 14, p. 8.

[61] FO 371/15959 C956/324, Ramsay (Athens)–Sargent, 23 Jan. 1932; USNA 868.00/672, Morris–State, 31 Mar. 1932.

economy: even if the foreigners give us no aid, there is no danger of disaster.'[62]

But urgent decisions awaited him. Even if the Financial Committee's report recommended credits, these would not be immediately forthcoming: the next two months were critical. Maris wanted an immediate suspension of the debt service payments, but there was little chance of the Committee agreeing to this. French offers of credits to tide Greece over the April payments were made and then withdrawn. On 23 March, one day before the Committee published its report, the Government still had not decided whether or not to make the April transfer. It was also pondering removal of its gold holdings in Paris out of the country, perhaps anticipating their seizure by the French in the event of repudiation.[63]

Foreign advisers were pressing the reluctant Venizelos to accept that the 'battle for the drachma' was lost, in the hope that depreciation would take the strain off the exchange reserves. Finlayson had recommended this course to Venizelos as early as February. The following month in Paris Tsouderos was advised by a member of the League's Financial Committee to 'abandon stabilization and postpone the debt service'. Back in Athens Tsouderos passed on these thoughts to the Prime Minister 'with circumlocutions, so as not to make him angry right away. He listened with annoyance but without expressing an opinion.' The advice in fact so angered him that his first thought was to dismiss the new Governor until it was pointed out to him what a poor impression this would make. Cooler counsels prevailed and by early April Venizelos seems to have resigned himself to the inevitable.[64]

The Financial Committee's report, when it appeared in late March, emphasized the severity of the crisis in Greece, and the need for rescue action. It stated that 'the problem to be solved in Greece is . . . first and foremost one of a transfer of exchange, but it is also a budgetary one. Of the two problems, the more difficult, and more urgent, in the Committee's opinion, is undoubtedly the exchange problem.' The Committee had evidently tried to make concessions to the Greek position without encouraging excessive expectations of foreign assistance.[65]

[62] *EV*, 20 Mar. 1932, 30 Mar. 1932.

[63] Ibid., 15 and 24 Mar. 1932; Tsouderos (Paris)–Bank of Greece, 23 Mar. 1932, AET 2/40–2.

[64] Tsouderos–Venizelos, 21 Mar. 1932, AEV 345; Venezis, *Tsouderos*, pp. 88–9.

[65] *Ta prota peninta chronia tis Trapezis tis Ellados* (Athens, n.d.), app.; 'Unofficial Notes of a Meeting held in Geneva', 13 Apr. 1932, AET 62/9.

They did not want to provoke Venizelos into resignation. On the other hand there was little point in promising what could not be delivered. In the event, their recommendations were much as had been predicted: suspension of the transfer of all foreign debt amortization payments for one year, the drachma equivalents being deposited with the Bank of Greece, and made available to the Government for necessary expenditures connected with the public works programme. As Tsouderos had requested, there were emphatic expressions of disapproval for plans to abolish the Bank of Greece. The report urged that public spending be curtailed and conveyed a clear rebuke to Maris in the demand that there should be 'greater efforts to secure a properly balanced budget'. Government spending abroad, apart from the debt service, had to be restricted, if Greece was to appeal successfully to foreign lenders. The terms on which the Committee was ready to support such an appeal were left to the end. Venizelos's long-term solution was implicitly rejected. Rather, Greece was to be included in the League's general recovery plan. The Committee recommended that Greece receive 'in the near future, a loan of no more than $10 millions, guaranteed by international supervision'.

At first the Government reacted hesitantly. According to Maris, the report was 'in many respects better than had been expected'.[66] Yet the possibility of holding back the April transfer was not immediately discarded.[67] When eventually the payment was made, Venizelos warned that 'we cannot make any further interest payments from the dwindling reserve of the Bank of Greece, unless the Council of the League of Nations responds more fully to our requests than the Financial Committee has done'.[68]

Rather than break with the League at this point, the Government chose to wait for the Lausanne Conference in June.[69] Venizelos hoped to gain a sympathetic hearing for Greece at the Council meeting in April, and there were rumours, though they proved nothing more, of emergency credits to tide Greece over till the summer.[70] Maris told Parliament that even if the Council meeting did not produce an improvement in terms, there was still the likelihood of a satisfactory solution being reached at the proposed Conference in June.[71]

[66] *EV*, 24 Mar. 1932.
[67] Bank of Greece–Tsouderos (Paris), 24 Mar. 1932, AET 2/47.
[68] Dafnis, *Metaxy dyo polemon*, ii. 125.
[69] *EV*, 25 Mar. 1932.
[70] Ibid., 26 Mar. 1932.   [71] *PSV*, 31 Mar. 1932, 645.

But the pledges of support for the League were chiefly for public consumption. Behind the scenes, official opinion in Greece was now following the foreign lead and shifting in favour of devaluation. The leading commercial banks, whose views had been solicited by the Government, were almost unanimous in advocating abandonment of the gold standard. Continued adherence to gold after September had led—according to one major bank—to 'withdrawals of bank deposits, an increase in the circulation of banknotes in its most unfavourable form, stagnation in the export trade, signs of difficulty among agricultural producers, excessive profits for certain importers at the expense of the community as a whole, etc.'.[72]

Only the National Bank, which had suffered far less than the other banks, dissented. For the National Bank devaluation would mean heavy losses on its foreign exchange deposits, which had risen during the crisis at the same time as they had fallen with the other banks. By April, the NBG held two-thirds of the sight and time deposits in foreign exchange. Having used its strength in the foreign exchange markets as a weapon against the central bank, it now found the tables turned. What the National Bank desired, not unnaturally, was a continuation of the system in force, where a free market in exchange was unofficially tolerated, and it held the whip hand.[73]

But the National Bank now represented the minority view. On 8 April, Epaminondas Charilaos, a leading industrialist, called for Greece to leave the gold standard even if Venizelos returned from Switzerland with the desired help.[74] For industrialists, devaluation was seen as a way to stimulate exports and permit a more relaxed credit policy. According to one business man, the money supply could be increased by 25% without inflationary consequences.[75] It was pointed out that Greece had *de facto* abandoned gold when exchange controls and import restrictions were introduced the previous autumn, and that she was now suffering all the disadvantages and reaping none of the benefits that full devaluation would have offered. The state—it was argued—should embark upon a coherent economic programme to achieve external balance, and, as part of such a plan, the Bank of Greece should become the chief regulator of foreign exchange, with increased powers over the commercial banks.[76]

---

[72] 'Memorandum' by the Popular Bank, 2 Apr. 1932, AET 60/3.
[73] 'Memorandum' by the NBG, n.d., AET 60/1.
[74] *DEVE/A*, June 1932, minutes of the council meeting of 8 Apr.
[75] Ibid.
[76] *EV*, 23 Apr. 1932.

Events in Geneva, where the League of Nations Council was meeting in the second week of April, finally cleared the way for devaluation. On 13 April, Venizelos met the British and French Foreign Ministers and warned them that payments due on 1 May could not be made without immediate foreign assistance. Sir John Simon made no comment, while Tardieu objected weakly.[77] Venizelos also met unofficially with members of the Financial Committee, to whom he hinted that Greece might be forced to leave the gold standard, rather than exhaust the central bank's reserves by transferring the May and June interest charges. Far from protesting, the Financial Committee seems to have recognized that this was the only practicable option. Caught between the ambitious schemes of the Greek authorities and the caution of their own superiors at home, they had simply run out of time. At Geneva they counselled Finlayson that departure from the gold standard was the only way out.[78] He noted that 'it is indeed curious to reflect that the same persons who had advised Greece to stabilize its currency in 1928 should have been compelled to advise departure from gold in 1932, but I am certain that they were right in each case; stabilization was necessary in 1928 to surmount an inflation crisis, the opposite course is indicated today to meet a deflation crisis'.[79]

The utter inconsequentiality of the Council's deliberations, when it met on 15 April, served to emphasize that the limits of international co-operation had now been reached. The Greek Prime Minister warned the Council in sombre tones to 'bear in mind that if you leave the small states without assistance, a black future awaits Europe'.[80] But his oratory had little effect: a decision on the general part of the Financial Committee's report was deferred until the following month. The Council's verdict on the matter of a debt moratorium was that this was something to be settled between the Greek Government and the foreign bondholders alone. No opinion was given as to whether Greece ought to suspend the May debt payments, nor did it mention the need to raise a further loan.[81]

This was taken in Greece as an indication that default would be tolerated. Venizelos remarked: 'We have crossed the Rubicon.'[82] Maris

[77] D. Kaiser, *Economic Diplomacy and the Origins of the Second World War* (Princeton, NJ, 1980), 40–52; Karamanlis, *Exoterikes scheseis*, p. 306.

[78] 'Greece's Departure from the Gold Standard', memo. by Finlayson, 9 May 1932, AET 77/1, p. 4.

[79] Ibid.   [80] Karamanlis, *Exoterikes scheseis*, p. 306.

[81] Dafnis, *Metaxy dyo polemon*, ii. 126.

[82] Karamanlis, *Exoterikes scheseis*, p. 307.

resigned as Finance Minister, after failing to persuade Venizelos to hold the immediate elections which he argued were necessary if the Liberal Party was to avoid being blamed for abandoning the gold standard. He was succeeded by Kyriakos Varvaressos, who now had the doubtful satisfaction of seeing his criticisms of government policy borne out. On 25 April Varvaressos brought before Parliament the legislation which marked the official abandonment of the existing parity. The Bank of Greece was henceforth relieved of the obligation to exchange its notes for gold, and was given greatly increased powers to supervise all gold and foreign exchange transactions. New measures now came into force altering the terms on which export earnings had to be surrendered to the central bank. A further law announced sweeping ministerial powers to enforce further import restrictions. Management of the exchange rate was henceforth to be left to the central bank's discretion.

On Wednesday, 27 April, the new system came into force and Greece officially departed from the gold standard. Because this event had been widely predicted, it caused little surprise. The measures were implemented at the beginning of Holy Week, so most of the banks remained closed for a week. When they reopened business was calm and there was no panic. But on the exchanges the drachma fell swiftly, dropping against sterling from 456 to 539 on 5 May; it continued its downward movement for the rest of the year, bottoming at 628 in January 1933.

Consequences

The persistent struggle of the Liberal Government to keep Greece on the gold standard raises the question: was it worth it? Was it not clear, as one author argued later, that devaluation was inevitable, and that the best policy would have been to protect the Bank of Greece's reserves as soon as possible?[83]

[83] Pyrsos, *Symvoli*, pp. 90–1. It is instructive to set the Greek 'battle for the drachma' in a comparative context. In Sweden a combination of destabilizing speculative outflows and intellectual backing (from Myrdal and others) for the abandonment of gold led the Swedes to devalue just one week after the British: see B. Thomas, *Monetary Policy and Crises: A Study of Swedish Experience* (London, 1936), *passim*. In most other countries the intellectual and policy consensus was, as in Greece, in favour of defending existing parities. This point is made forcefully for Germany by K. Borchardt, 'Could and Should Germany have Followed Great Britain in Leaving the Gold Standard?', *Journal of European Economic History*, 13(3) (Winter 1984), 471–99. The lack of support for devaluation in France emerges from Tom Kemp, 'The French Economy under the Franc Poincaré', *Economic History Review*, 24(1) (1979), 82–99. The variety of country experiences in Latin America

The situation was rich in ironies. Venizelos, who had been lukewarm about the merits of the original monetary stabilization scheme, became the drachma's staunchest defender. The members of the LNFC, who had insisted in 1927 that Greece join the gold standard, realized by the winter of 1931 that devaluation was a necessary step if the new central bank was to survive. Hence in the spring of 1932 banking experts at Geneva found themselves urging Venizelos to abandon gold.

Venizelos's reluctance to take their advice seems to have been prompted by three concerns. Firstly, he hoped that the disruption of the London money market would be short-lived—when it reopened Greece would be able to resume borrowing with greater ease if the drachma remained at par. Secondly, if Greece left gold, it was difficult to say where the exchange rate should be fixed: the earlier experience of floating rates in the early 1920s had not been encouraging. For most Greek policy-makers, depreciation was a step backwards—with potentially hazardous domestic consequences. Thirdly, and this was perhaps uppermost, adherence to the gold standard had been invested with political significance: the defence of the 'national currency'—as elsewhere in Europe—became a test of political virility, which explains why *no* party in Greece recommended leaving gold. In the parliamentary debate on 18 November 1931, there was unanimity over the need to defend the drachma and Tsaldaris even felt obliged to deny that he had suggested the gold standard should be abandoned.[84] In a country where appeals to the sense of national honour found a ready response, abandoning the gold standard would have been (and was to be) interpreted as a mark of Liberal weakness.

It is easy to be wise after the event. Nevertheless, the Liberal Government's indifference to strains in the international economy, and in the country's balance of payments, blinded it to unpleasant truths. There had been no shortage of commentators, from Montagu Norman downwards, to warn the Greek authorities that their borrowing policies

---

is surveyed in Diaz Alejandro, 'Latin America in the 1930s', in R. Thorp (ed.), *Latin America in the 1930s* (London, 1984), 23–4. It is clear that in almost all cases those advocating devaluation or depreciation were a tiny minority—the Swedish economists being an exception. Policy-makers insisted on remaining on gold unless or until they were pushed off it. Greece was exceptional in European terms in the extent of her devaluation though this was matched in Japan and Latin America.

[84] FO 371/15229 C8807/18, Ramsay–Simon, 20 Nov. 1931; the application of martial slogans to economic crises was, of course, common outside Greece. For striking South European parallels see S. Ben-Ami, *Fascism from Above* (Oxford, 1983), 338; A. Lyttelton, *The Seizure of Power: Fascism in Italy, 1919–1929* (Princeton, NJ, 1988), 333, 342.

would have to be drastically revised. In the Greek case, the chronic balance of payments deficit and the idiosyncratic functioning of the banking system made devaluation inevitable; even had the political will been present, the Bank of Greece could not have enforced a deflationary policy on a sufficiently severe scale to bring the external current account into surplus.

The fact that ultimately Greece did abandon gold, unlike a number of other countries in Europe, does not indicate that policy-makers had woken up to the advantages of this policy. On the contrary, they were pushed into it by fear of the alternatives, notably the domestic implications of severe deflation in an election year. Ironically the extent of Greece's indebtedness, and the strain this put on the balance of payments made leaving gold inevitable if the country's exchange reserves were not to be totally depleted. Other countries, less in debt, or with political élites less sensitive to popular pressure, faced a more difficult choice. Once the drachma was allowed to fall, the sudden increase in the drachma cost of servicing the foreign debt made some form of default inevitable. And default in turn precluded an eventual return to the resources of Western capital markets. Thus the financial crisis of 1931–2 marked the end of the reconstruction strategy of the 1920s.

The culmination of the financial crisis in the spring of 1932 was regarded as signalling the bankruptcy of the Liberal Government's economic policies. In fact it did more: it made the charismatic Venizelos look ineffectual. The US Consul in Salonika reported on 6 April that 'considerable discontent with the present government prevails, not only among those who are opposed to Venizelos in principle, but amongst the Liberals who supported him in 1928 . . . Even the refugees, who have always supported Mr. Venizelos to the full have begun to show dissatisfaction with his present policies.'

If the failure of the 'battle for the drachma' had disappointed many staunch Liberals, on the Left of the Venizelist camp there were others who remained unconvinced that the battle should have been fought at all. The Communist Party argued that Venizelos's defence of the gold standard had been at the expense of the labouring classes. Dimitris Pournaras, the theoretician of the increasingly popular Agrarians, took a similar line:

The majority of working Greeks were literally proletarianized and yet the Liberal Party insisted that only fiscal normalcy would save the country. The drama of the provincial or the peasant was unimportant compared with the danger facing those friends who stood to lose from a fall in the drachma. The economic policy of the bourgeois state ceased long ago to have even superficially a popular basis. It rests openly and brazenly on native capitalism and party cronies.

Thus the financial crisis forced wider the fissures that had already begun to open up between radical and moderate forces within the Venizelist camp. For the Liberal Prime Minister, his charisma waning, a turbulent summer lay ahead.[85] On 21 May he resigned exhausted amid a wave of strikes, insisting that he would not return unless Parliament approved far-reaching measures to increase the powers of the executive and curb Press freedoms. But when the minority government of Alexandros Papanastasiou started to court working-class popularity by announcing plans to bring in long-awaited legislation on social insurance, Venizelos performed a quick volte-face. He brought down the Papanastasiou Government on the grounds that it had been formed by a 'social class party', and formed a new Liberal administration to lead the country into the autumn elections.[86] All this suggested that Venizelos's 'four years' were ending in anxiety rather than triumph. Yet the sense of failure was at least partly self-induced. The abandonment of gold ironically turned out to pave the way for an unexpectedly swift upturn, based on the domestic economy. With the collapse of international trade, the Greek economy moved uncertainly towards autarky.

[85] USNA 868.00/673, Morris–State, 26 Apr. 1932; FO 371/15966 C3474/462, Ramsay–Simon, 23 Apr. 1932; D. Pournaras, *I oikonomiki thesis ton agroton* (Athens, 1932), 95.
[86] FO 371/15966 C4868/462, Ramsay–Simon, 5 June 1932.

IV

RESPONSE, 1932–1936

7

DEPRECIATION AND DEFAULT

The State finds itself in difficult circumstances, and is obliged to
tell its foreign creditors not that it will not pay them, but that it is
absolutely impossible at the moment to fulfil its obligations without
exposing itself to complete financial and social ruin.

(Venizelos, April 1932)

Ah, ti mystirio / pou'n'i Ellada / daneio pairnei / fragko
de'dinei . . .
(Ah, what a mystery is Greece, she takes a loan, gives back not a
penny . . .)

(Attik, lyrics from early 1930s)

Abandoning gold fundamentally changed the relationship between
Greece and the international economy. That change was all the greater
for the extent of Greece's earlier dependence on Western capital.
We have seen how Venizelos—unlike, for example, Ataturk, who had
not dissimilar choices to make—had decided to pursue a policy of
reconstruction which involved relying heavily on foreign loans.[1] One
consequence of this policy was that it meant accepting considerable
limitations to national sovereignty, since bodies such as the LNFC and
the RSC (not to mention the IFC, which was already in existence)
acquired statutory rights to intervene in domestic affairs in defence of
the interests of foreign creditors.

Almost overnight, as it became obvious that Greece had run out of
foreign exchange, the balance of power tilted from creditor to debtor.
The Greek authorities confronted a poorly organized assortment of
private companies, individual bondholders, and foreign governments,
and the drawn-out bargaining began. The British bondholders were so
unprepared for such a calamity that it was not clear whether they had any
body legally entitled to represent them. With little likelihood of new

---

[1] Cf. J. A. Petropulos, 'The Compulsory Exchange of Populations: Greek–Turkish
Peacemaking, 1922–1930', *Byzantine and Modern Greek Studies*, 2 (1976), 135–61.

loans forthcoming in the near future, they held a poor hand, and could do little to push their interlocutor faster than it wanted to go.

Domestic political pressures in Greece turned out to be instrumental in dictating how much successive governments would concede. The Populist Government which was formed, briefly in the winter of 1932, then more enduringly after new elections in March 1933, was unwilling for obvious reasons to appear more compliant with the wishes of Greece's creditors than its Liberal predecessor. The Populists were happy to play the nationalist card, and, since their opponents were always ready to play it against them, they anyway had little choice. Expressing the new mood most forcefully, Koryzis, at the National Bank of Greece, is reported to have expostulated: 'je m'en fiche des relations internationales'.[2]

Leaving the gold standard had another consequence: it made monetary policy a matter of the discretionary judgement of the authorities at the Bank of Greece. In other words, the very institution which was so closely connected in the minds of many Greeks with Geneva found that the collapse of Venizelos's economic strategy actually opened up the possibility of its playing a new, more active part in domestic affairs. 'Generally,' wrote Kirkilitsis in 1934, 'in the last two years the Bank has acted more decisively and extensively than in the first years after its foundation.'[3] Supervising exchange rate movements, managing the domestic money supply, the Bank became a key institution behind the transformation of the role of the state in the economy.

Monetary Management

As it became obvious that Greece would have to abandon the gold standard, the question arose as to what currency regime should take its place. There were two aspects to the problem: the exchange rate and credit policy. The gold standard supposedly linked the two since the flow of exchange at any given rate theoretically determined movements in the domestic money supply. Under a different system, however, the connection between the two might be looser.

By late March 1932 financial experts in Greece accepted that there were two alternatives for the drachma: it could either be pegged at a lower rate, or allowed to float.[4] It seems that Varvaressos supported the

[2] FO 371/19517 R4179/646, Waterlow–FO, 29 June 1935.
[3] A. Kirkilitsis, *Ai trapezai en Elladi* (Athens, 1935), 184.
[4] FO 371/15960 C2951/324, Ramsay–FO, 1 Apr. 1932.

first possibility. The problem there, however, was to assess a defensible rate. In a climate of uncertainty the wrong choice might wipe out the entire exchange reserves of the central bank. The co-operation of the commercial banks would be vital, since there were suspicions that the drain of exchange had been deliberately exacerbated by them. In the early stages of the crisis they had been unwilling to draw on their own exchange holdings and ready to make life difficult for the Bank of Greece. Were they to pursue this line of attack, stabilization at any rate would be precarious and expensive.

The problem with allowing the drachma to float was that no one knew how far it might depreciate, and what the consequences might be for domestic monetary stability. On the other hand, the pressure would temporarily be removed from the central bank's reserves. During the conversations in Geneva in April between LN representatives and Greek officials, the Greeks were urged to let the drachma float provided that they guarded against inflationary pressures arising from excessive central bank lending to either the Government or the private sector.[5] Their advice seems to have swayed Venizelos, who made his preference for this course apparent in a crucial meeting with Greek industrialists and bankers on his return from Geneva.

The proposed new regime raised the question of how the money supply was to be determined. Finlayson put forward three possibilities: (1) a maximum fiduciary circulation beyond which notes could only be issued with 100% gold backing; (2) complete freedom from all forms of control; (3) comparative freedom under important restrictions. Finlayson suggested to Venizelos that (2) was out of the question, given the fears that leaving the gold standard would excite. (1) had been successfully applied in Greece before 1914; however, it was difficult to know where to fix the maximum *plafond*. In addition, once that maximum had been reached, the central bank could no longer directly influence the domestic money market. An additional worry was that political pressure might always be brought to bear on the Bank of Greece to alter the *plafond*. Thus the last course seemed the most advantageous, subject to restrictions on state borrowing from the Bank, on exchange movements across the borders, and on transactions in exchange by the commercial banks.[6]

Venizelos repeated most of these arguments in his speech to the

[5] 'Greece's Departure from the Gold Standard', memo. by Finlayson, 9 May 1932, AET 77/1, p. 5; FO 371/15961 C3426/324, Ramsay–FO, 22 Apr. 1932.
[6] AET 77/1, *passim*.

Chamber on 25 April when he summarized the course of his discussions at Geneva and announced the abandonment of the gold standard. Tsaldaris, speaking for the Populists, had little to add apart from fears that inflationary pressures would build up. Replying for the Government, however, Varvaressos emphasized that allowing the drachma to float would not necessarily lead to 'monetary anarchy'. He claimed that the country's external accounts could be balanced even off the gold standard. And when the new legislation was brought in at the end of the debate, it closely resembled the regime that Finlayson and he had outlined.

Government borrowing from the Bank remained constrained by the limit which had been laid down in the Geneva Protocol. Foreign exchange transactions were permitted to the commercial banks under specific conditions, designed to ensure that they encouraged commerce rather than speculation, under the supervision of the Bank of Greece's Foreign Exchange Control Committee. The same Committee was to supervise the gradual repayment of private commercial debts contracted in foreign currencies. Buying and selling rates were not fixed by law: each bank could set its own rates, and the published rates of the Bank of Greece were described as being 'merely indicative'. Exporters were forced to surrender 30% of export earnings (the percentage was soon reduced to 25%) to the Bank at the old rate.

However, these measures, though formally they laid the foundations for a new domestic monetary order, gave the central bank only a rather insecure grip on exchange flows in the early summer months. Following the abandonment of gold, the drachma depreciated heavily, falling against sterling from 305 on 31 March to 552 on 31 May. The Bank itself intervened in the black market, ordering brokers to purchase exchange on its behalf. This highly irregular tactic indicates how desperate the outlook appeared to the Bank's authorities. Unfortunately we do not know how much exchange was acquired in this way. Nor are we in a position to assess the extent to which it contributed to the depreciation of the currency. But until the position became more stable after January 1933, the Bank of Greece's rates probably followed those on the black market rather than the other way about.[7]

The Bank of Greece only managed to improve its exchange position —and its control over the commercial banks—by the resolution of a

[7] *Ta prota peninta chronia tis Trapezis tis Ellados* (Athens, n.d.), 148; FO 371/16763 C20/2, Ramsay–FO, 24 Dec. 1932.

problem which had arisen when Greece left gold. Greek commercial banks had traditionally accepted deposits and made advances in foreign currencies. After September 1931 borrowers hastened to repay the banks at the stabilization rate while depositors kept their funds with the banks in the hope of eventually realizing gains when the drachma was devalued. An important determinant in the commercial banks' attitude to future exchange rate policy was the question of the terms on which these accounts were to be settled. The National Bank, which held the lion's share of such deposits, stood to make the greatest losses in the event of depreciation and argued as late as April 1932 that the gold standard should be preserved. The National Bank, however, was isolated on this point. It received no support from the other commercial banks, and encountered strong opposition from industrialists and, to some extent, merchants, who argued strongly that the gold standard had been abandoned in all but name the previous autumn.

Although the Bank of Greece had undertaken to cover the exchange losses incurred by the commercial banks as a result of the move off gold, it lacked the resources to do this. Consequently, further legislation was introduced at the end of July (1932) ordering the compulsory conversion of all foreign exchange liabilities into drachmas at a rate of $ = 100 drs. Although this rate was reportedly arrived at by adjusting the stabilization rate to take account of the rise in the cost of living, in fact it implied a considerable over-valuation of the drachma.[8] At the same time the Bank took over the foreign exchange previously held by the commercial banks against payment of these deposits, thereby appropriating $6.5 millions in foreign exchange. Largely as a consequence gold and foreign exchange reserves at the Bank rose from 783.5 million drachmas at the end of May to 1,866.1 million by the end of July. For their part the commercial banks were recompensed in drachmas. In other words, the drachma gains arising from the revaluation of foreign exchange accrued to the state rather than to its former owners.

It is worth noting that the National Bank's prediction that this measure would lead to a run on the banks was not borne out: total commercial bank deposits remained steady in the second half of 1932 and grew steadily in nominal terms over the next two years. 'We Greeks can be proud of our banks and the results of their activities; indeed one may assert without hazard that they were in part responsible for the fact

---

[8] Bank of Greece, *The Economic Situation in Greece and the Bank of Greece in 1932* (Athens, 1933), 24–7.

that the country did not feel the effects of the international crisis more harshly,' observed George Charitakis in April 1934. When we set the relative stability of the commercial banks in Greece against the major failures which occurred in Romania and Yugoslavia (to look no further afield), we may appreciate the justice of Charitakis's remarks. And yet the chief reason for the solidity of the Greek system, the unquestioned hegemony of the National Bank of Greece, was something of a mixed blessing. The National Bank itself emerged from the crisis with its domination of the other commercial banks reinforced; it took over the ailing Bank of the Orient and maintained a controlling interest in many large industrial companies; according to one estimate, by the end of the 1930s it was providing four-fifths of all bank loans to industry. Its size gave depositors confidence and there was a gradual shift of deposits into it from the medium-sized banks. As the memoirs of a prominent industrialist attest, the Bank's authorities—especially Drosopoulos and Koryzis—maintained close ties both with leading business men and with politicians, who drew on its resources for ventures not always of the most orthodox kind. Its overwhelming power led to calls for the creation of a counterweight through the merger of several smaller banks; but this never materialized. And though its strength was one of the main reasons why the Greek commercial banking system survived the crisis without a major collapse, what was an advantage during the crisis became a drawback in the recovery, as its conservative emphasis on short-term lending deprived the economy of badly needed long-term investment capital.[9]

One striking feature of the inter-war Greek monetary system was its resistance—often for political reasons—to any form of sustained contractionary pressure. This was not without its dangers during periods of upswing, when its inflationary tendencies became clear, but it did cushion the economy during slumps.

In the summer of 1932 the Bank of Greece found that in its new more managerial role in the economy, it had a chance to bargain for the

[9] Kirkilitsis, *Ai trapezai en Elladi*, p. v; M. Dritsa, 'Pisti kai viomichania sto mesopolemo', in G. Mavrogordatos and C. Chadziiosif (eds.), *Venizelismos kai astikos eksynchronismos* (Irákleion, 1988), 183–92; K. Kostis, *Oi trapezes kai i krisi 1929–1932* (Athens, 1986), 68–9; Bodosakis Athanasiades, unpub. MS of untitled memoirs, 136–9, describes Kondylis's request for the National Bank to finance the costs of rigging the 1935 plebiscite; *Ta deka eti tis Trapezis tis Ellados, 1928–1938* (Athens, 1938), 122–3; Karl L. Rankin Papers, box 2, 'Projected Fusion of Greek Banks', 6 Apr. 1933.

political recognition it still badly needed from the Government. If Venizelos indeed believed that the sole function of a central bank was to keep Greece on the gold standard, it was important to show him that he was mistaken. Tsouderos's opportunity came in connection with a highly controversial issue: the convertibility of the IFC's deposits. The institution which symbolized the tyranny of the foreign bondholder over the Greeks had had its wings clipped by the debt default and exchange restrictions. Unable to make hard currency transfers, the IFC had continued to pile up large drachma balances from the proceeds of its assigned revenues in blocked accounts with the Bank of Greece. These deposits had stood at 432 million drachmas in September 1931, and 592 million in April 1932; by the end of 1932 they had reached the incredible figure of 2,856 million drachmas. Without countervailing action the withdrawal of these sums from circulation—equivalent at the end of 1932 to 60% of the note issue—would have exerted an enormously powerful deflationary stranglehold on the economy. For both political and financial reasons, however, the Bank of Greece took action to neutralize such effects. During 1932—and especially in the second half of the year—there was a remarkable expansion in its lending activities. Central bank lending as a percentage of commercial bank advances rose from 4.3% in January 1932 to 17.2% that December and 20% one year later.

In the first half of the year, central bank advances were directed chiefly to the private sector—merchants and commercial banks. Thereafter, lending to the state predominated. This was a clear response to the IFC's refusal to relend its frozen drachma balances to the state without a prior resolution of the whole debt question. The Bank's policy was not without dangers, for not only was it technically illegal—something only remedied in June 1934—but it also depended upon the state utilizing funds that the IFC might eventually transfer to it, to repay its floating

TABLE 7.1. *Bank of Greece lending, 1931–1932*
(million drachmas)

Date	Commercial advances	State advances	Total
23.09.31	235.4	—	235.4
23.04.32	768.9	187.4	956.3
31.12.32	858.9	1,825.5	2,684.4

Source: AET 69/2, p. 11.

debt to the Bank. Otherwise the Bank risked generating the sort of inflationary pressures that Finlayson had foreseen.[10]

By the end of 1932 the monetary outlook was therefore uncertain. On the positive side, the Bank had succeeded against a background of political crisis in rebuilding its reserves and in stemming the initially rapid fall of the drachma. Moreover, this had been achieved without jeopardizing the position of the commercial banks and without a credit squeeze. Indeed it had actually lowered the discount rate from 11% at the beginning of the year to 9% by its close. On the other hand the drachma was still falling, pushed further by political uncertainty towards the end of the year.

Just before Christmas new legislation was introduced tightening Government control over foreign exchange movements in an attempt to curb the activities of the black market.[11] Although it is unlikely that this legislation by itself achieved much, it may have had a beneficial effect on public confidence. Towards the end of January 1933, the market appears to have felt that the drachma had fallen too far. Heavy offers of exchange were noted and in the second half of the month the Bank's reserves increased by almost 20 million Swiss francs.[12] These first inflows were mostly funds which had been withdrawn during the early stages of the financial crisis—which according to one estimate amounted to as much as £6 millions.[13] From the end of March, the authorities at the Bank unofficially pegged the drachma to the French franc. Declaring their intention of henceforth supporting the drachma and preventing any further depreciation, they hoped to attract available exchange. They were helped in April by the dollar devaluation, which encouraged the repatriation of large sums from the USA and restarted the flow of emigrants' remittances which had dried up in 1932. Most of the Bank's exchange holdings were converted immediately into gold, with the aim of minimizing the losses that might be caused by any further devaluations. From March 1933 the drachma was held at a rate equivalent to about 43% of its 1928 gold parity value, and over the next three and a half years this rate remained remarkably stable. When the French and Swiss francs left gold in September 1936, the drachma was linked instead to sterling.

[10] *Ta deka eti*, p. 74; USNA 868.00 Gen. Cond./17, Morriss (Athens)–State, 2 June 1932.   [11] FO 371/16763 C20/2, Ramsay–FO, 24 Dec. 1932.
[12] 'Annual Report of the Governor of the Bank of Greece for 1933', *MA*, 17 Feb. 1934; LN, *Report of a Mission Sent to Greece* (London, 1933), 97.
[13] *Ta deka eti*, p. 55; USNA 868.00/675, Morris–State, n.d.

The Bank's successful management of the exchange rate took place at a time when its political prospects seemed set to change for the worse. In November 1932 Tsaldaris's short-lived minority Populist Government announced its intention to revive Maximos's plans for amalgamating the central bank, which it regarded as a Venizelist institution, with the National Bank. Although this administration barely lasted into the new year, it returned after the unexpected anti-Venizelist victory in the March 1933 elections. Venizelos had misguidedly based his campaign on the issue of the Liberals' record of economic management, and the result showed how his claim to leadership had been thrown into question by the crisis.[14] Maximos himself became Tsaldaris's Foreign Minister, and he was strongly supported by Spiros Loverdos, another banker, who was appointed Finance Minister. The watchful League of Nations Financial Committee was forced to put heavy pressure on the Populist ministers to protect the integrity of the central bank. Although in April Tsaldaris publicly repudiated any possibility of a merger of the two banks, Maximos continued to raise the plan at intervals. Needing the support of his two key ministers to balance other, more politically extreme elements in the Government, Tsaldaris's support for the Bank of Greece remained weak.[15]

Fortunately for Tsouderos, neither an abortive *coup d'état* by desperate Venizelist officers nor the attempted assassination of Venizelos himself that summer could prevent 1933 from being an exceptionally favourable year for the Bank. The repatriation of funds, particularly from the USA, gave Tsouderos the opportunity to increase domestic support for the Bank by pursuing a more expansionary monetary policy—though within limits since he was anxious to preserve the margin between the internal and external values of the drachma in order to encourage a revival of domestic output. This meant maintaining a competitive advantage for domestic producers by preventing inflation and keeping the currency stable. His annual report for 1933 was an avowal of pragmatism, a recognition of the primacy of the needs of the domestic economy. Considerations of 'actually prevailing economic conditions', according to Tsouderos, had been crucial in shaping monetary policy.[16]

In statements to representatives of the bondholders, Greek officials

[14] G. Mavrogordatos, *Stillborn Republic* (Berkeley, Calif., 1983), 332–5.
[15] E. Venezis, *Emmanouil Tsouderos* (Athens, 1966), 102–13.
[16] Bank of Greece, *The Economic Situation in Greece and the Bank of Greece in 1933* (Athens, 1934), 10–21.

claimed that the country's good fortune was fortuitous, the consequence of monetary instability abroad. On this reading, Greece's financial system remained as sensitive as before to international fluctuations, only in 1931–2 it had suffered whilst in 1933 it had gained. But to domestic audiences, the emphasis was altered: wise policy had taken advantage of favourable circumstances. Whatever the causes, the signs of recovery were there—increased shipping activity, tourist and building booms. By April 1934 Loverdos, the Finance Minister, was able to present a rosy picture of the future: 'We do not suffer the pressure of unemployment, we have no crisis of output and we can gradually arrive at managing for ourselves out of our own resources.'[17]

The following year, however, with the recovery well under way, the outflow of foreign exchange resumed once more. Its initial cause appears to have been an increase in imports over previous years, including—despite Greece's three successive bumper harvests—a high proportion of foodstuffs. Indeed in the first seven months of the year foreign exchange payments for wheat imports stood at twice the amount transferred over the equivalent period in 1934.[18] But on top of the growing trade imbalance there was the problem of further political instability, as the attempted Venizelist revolt in March ushered in a period of tension and constitutional uncertainty. March itself saw a sudden drop in the Bank of Greece's reserves, though panic subsided fairly quickly. But the dramatic events at the end of the year—above all, General Kondylis's coup, which marked the end of the Republic and brought back King George—rekindled alarm. Moreover, the Bank itself did not escape the turmoil. In Parliament the royalist Ioannis Rallis accused Tsouderos, whose Liberal sympathies were common knowledge, of having used the Bank's funds to finance the Venizelist uprising. To what degree Tsouderos really was involved in Venizelos's plans remains obscure; but with anti-Venizelists now using the uprising as a pretext for a thorough purge of their rivals from the state apparatus there was no need for solid evidence. Prime Minister Tsaldaris opposed the idea of forcing Tsouderos's resignation but eventually allowed himself to be overridden by the more extreme opponents of the Bank among his ministers. Varvaressos, who was Deputy Governor, refused to be promoted in such circumstances and the governorship remained vacant

---

[17] FO 371/18397 R4450/79, Waterlow–FO, 3 Aug. 1934; Bank of Athens, *Bulletin Économique et Financier*, 116 (June 1934), 2,245.

[18] FO 371/19517 R6531/646, Waley (Treasury)–FO, 30 Oct. 1935.

until after King George's return, when the caretaker Demertzis Government reinstated Tsouderos in March 1936.

While Tsouderos was on the sidelines, Populist Ministers again started to drop hints that they would revive Maximos's schemes to curb the influence of the central bank. They criticized its direct interventions in the market through its branch offices and tried to get them closed. This would have confined the Bank to rediscount business which was 'practically non-existent' in Greece. In other words, the Bank of Greece would have been prevented from having any impact on interest rates, let alone from shaping the 'national economic programme' that many non-partisan commentators were now calling for.[19] However, such a policy would have brought the Populists into direct conflict with the Bank's powerful foreign supporters, notably the British. As the story of their debt negotiations will show, the Populists mixed defiance towards their creditors with a desire to avoid outright confrontation: so far as anti-Venizelist extremists were concerned, Tsouderos's scalp was sufficient. By the autumn of 1935 their interest lay elsewhere, in the impending crisis of the Republic itself. The Bank of Greece survived; but the whole shoddy affair showed how experienced politicians had let the passions of the *dichasmos* paralyse the administration of the country.

Negotiating a Foreign Debt Settlement

In the spring of 1932 Venizelos stated publicly that the shortage of foreign exchange at the Bank of Greece would make it impossible to continue paying the full monthly debt service charges. The Greek authorities asked the International Financial Commission to authorize a suspension of amortization payments. However, the IFC representatives in Athens disclaimed the power to make such a concession and suggested that the Greeks approach the guarantor powers directly.[20] On 1 April the Government announced that it was suspending amortization payments and making only limited interest payments.

The attitude of the British authorities—who were certainly the most important of the creditor powers in this context—was that this was a matter for the bondholders themselves, rather than either their Governments or the IFC. At the Treasury, for example, the initial reaction was

[19] FO 371/15917 R4179/646, Waterlow–FO, 29 June 1935; FO 371/15917 R4809/646, Waley–FO, 30 July 1935; Kirkilitsis, *Ai trapezai en Elladi*, p. 184; T. Galanis, *Trapezai meletai* (Athens, 1946), 121.

[20] 'Greece's Departure from the Gold Standard', AET 77/1, p. 5; FO 371/15960 C2442/324, Ramsay–FO, 29 Mar. 1932.

one of resignation: there was little hope of avoiding a 'total or partial default on our foreign debt'.[21] When Venizelos discussed the matter with Sir John Simon, the British Foreign Minister, in Geneva on the eve of the League of Nations Council meeting, the latter simply reiterated the Treasury line and warned that the Financial Committee's recommendation of assistance to Greece might even be adjourned to the next Council meeting in May.[22] Given the urgency of Greece's financial problems this leisurely approach seemed to invite default.[23] When the Government announced that it would make no payments after April, the Treasury's private response was that 'protests are not going to do any good'.[24] The protests of both the IFC and the British authorities were tempered by the fear that they might undermine Venizelos's already precarious standing in Greece and usher in a period of instability in which accommodation would become unattainable.

Meanwhile, events were pushing the Greek authorities into a more extreme position. As it became increasingly unlikely that financial assistance would be forthcoming at the Lausanne Conference, there was ever less incentive to conciliate foreign creditors. After late April the rapid depreciation of the drachma increased the Government's budgetary problems. By the middle of May the Treasury had borrowed to the legal limit from the Bank of Greece and had begun to eye the frozen IFC balances which were accumulating at the Bank. The new Finance Minister, Varvaressos, complained of the IFC's intransigence and warned that the Greek authorities might take over the IFC revenues at source. This elicited a stiff protest from Roussin, the British representative on the IFC; privately, however, Roussin feared that his position was rapidly becoming untenable, and urged that a settlement be reached quickly.

The attitude of the Greek authorities was one of despair mingled with a desire for reconciliation. Politis, the Greek delegate to the League of Nations, told the Council at its May session that the default was only a temporary measure, and that the Greek authorities desired an impartial assessment of Greece's capacity to pay as a preliminary to a settlement. Varvaressos took a similar line in his Budget speech to the Chamber of Deputies on 20 May. Roussin himself, in a memorandum on the 1932/3

[21] FO 371/15960 C2664/324, Leith-Ross–Roussin, 2 Apr. 1932.

[22] FO 371/15961 C3043/324, 'Report of a Conversation between Foreign Minister Sir John Simon and Monsieur Venizelos on 12 April', 13 Apr. 1932.

[23] Finlayson–Niemeyer, 18 May 1932, AEV 183.

[24] FO 371/15961 C3360/324, Waley–Ramsay, 25 Apr. 1932.

Budget, acknowledged that the departure from the gold standard had exacerbated the initial transfer problem and that even 'without depreciation of the currency, the Government would have found great difficulty in meeting the situation'.[25]

The Greek authorities, however, hesitated to defy the IFC further before seeing what negotiations with the bondholders produced. Initial results were unpromising. Early in June the Governor of the National Bank of Greece, John Drosopoulos—a man with close connections with British financial interests—visited London and suggested that the Council of Foreign Bondholders send a delegation to Athens to examine the financial situation. This idea was rejected. So was a Greek proposal at the end of the month for a package deal comprising a five-year suspension of amortization payments, a payment of 25% of the interest due in cash (though not necessarily in exchange), a further 25% in Funding Notes and a cancellation of the remaining 50%. Not surprisingly this scheme, which guaranteed no payments in foreign exchange, was not accepted by the British as a basis for discussion.[26]

The transfer problem had now been replaced by a 'budgetary problem of the first magnitude'.[27] The rapid depreciation of the drachma had effectively doubled the cost of servicing the foreign debt at the very time when revenues were diminishing. By the middle of July the IFC balances at the Bank of Greece had risen to 1,200 million drachmas, and the Finance Ministry informed the Treasury that as Treasury resources were exhausted the Government required the co-operation of the IFC.[28] Roussin, the moving spirit on the IFC, realized the importance of achieving a provisional settlement but felt unable to take the necessary steps without authorization from London. In turn the British authorities, who were trying to keep out of the entire imbroglio, urged the Greeks to come to London and reopen negotiations directly with representatives of the bondholders rather than advancing proposals to the IFC in Athens.

In Athens the Press debate focused on Government budgetary policy. During the summer, the Opposition pressed for further economies, while government papers defended the need to maintain living standards in Greece. In fact—as we have seen—the Government had found

---

[25] FO 371/15962 C4563/324, Ramsay–Simon, 28 May 1932; FO 371/15963 C5970/324, 'Greek Public Debt and the IFC', memo. by Roussin.

[26] Council for Foreign Bondholders, *Annual Report for 1932* (New York, n.d.), 35.

[27] FO 371/15963 C5970/324, 'Greek Public Debt and the IFC'.

[28] FO 371/15963 C6223/324, Cavendish-Bentinck–FO, 21 July 1932.

a temporary way out of its difficulties: the Bank of Greece simply (though illegally) increased its advances to the state in line with the growth of frozen IFC balances. Political prospects too made an early settlement desirable for the creditors. Elections were due in September under a system of proportional representation. Leaders of the main opposition Populist Party informed the British that they foresaw the formation of a weak coalition government which would find it difficult to obtain ratification of any agreement it had negotiated itself. On the other hand, if an agreement was concluded before the new Chamber had assembled, a Populist government would protest at the *fait accompli* but ratify it all the same.[29]

Serious negotiations only got under way in mid-August when Varvaressos and Mantzavinos, the Director-General of the Finance Ministry, came to London for talks with the Council of Foreign Bondholders and the League Loans Committee. Their discussions lasted until the middle of September and resulted in the so-called Varvaressos Agreement, whose main provisions were: (1) 30% of the interest for 1932/3 in foreign exchange; (2) suspension of amortization payments for 1932/3; (3) release of the drachma balances held by the IFC after payment had been made, and after further retention of another 35% of the annual interest due by the IFC in drachmas. But the terms of the Agreement were not immediately implemented, since the Venizelos Government was defeated at the elections, to be succeeded after some delay by a Populist minority government under Tsaldaris.

The omens for the new administration were not good. It existed on Liberal sufferance and was initially expected to fall within two weeks. Tsaldaris himself was an indecisive figure who had never previously been Prime Minister. Though personally a moderate and reconciled to the Republic, he found it difficult to control party extremists, who demanded an unequivocal repudiation of the Liberal Party's policies. He was reluctant to implement the Varvaressos Agreement if he could help it, since this would remove a stick to beat the Liberals with in the future. In his party, and in the Press generally, there was vociferous opposition to carrying out the Agreement and in conversation with the British Ambassador, Patrick Ramsay, he avoided promising that he would do so.[30]

Tsaldaris's introductory speech to the Chamber in early October

---

[29] FO 371/15963 C6785/324, Cavendish-Bentinck–FO, 3 Aug. 1932.
[30] FO 371/15965 C9574/C10517/C10541/324, Ramsay–FO, 7 Oct.–14 Dec. 1932.

contained few concrete proposals or commitments: he acknowledged
the need to reach agreement with the bondholders but gave no indication of how he intended to do this. A contemporary observer noted that
the debate that followed revealed only that Tsaldaris was not anxious to
remain in office and that the leaders of other parties were not anxious to
replace him.[31] Press attacks on the IFC and Roussin in particular
continued. When, at the end of November, the Government proposed a
watered-down version of the Varvaressos Agreement, Roussin recommended immediate acceptance. But in London the Council of Foreign
Bondholders and the League Loans Committee, recently formed by the
Bank of England, stood fast and insisted on the original terms.[32] In early
December Tsaldaris promised that Greece would pay 30% as originally
agreed, but he remained extremely pessimistic about the general outlook, predicting famine and financial collapse. In the end it took over a
month before the transfer was finally effected, while in return the IFC
handed over 1,400 million drachmas to the Greek authorities.

The stance adopted by the Tsaldaris Government cannot simply be
explained by domestic political weakness. It also reflected a body of
opinion—especially strong in established banking circles—which resented the League of Nations' interference in Greek economic affairs
and looked back nostalgically to the days before the Bank of Greece
supplanted the National Bank. Tsaldaris's first choice as Finance
Minister, Constantine Angelopoulos, had resigned after making clear
his opposition to making any budgetary provision for the foreign debt
service. Loverdos, his successor, was a former director of the National
Bank and brother of the Governor of the Popular Bank. In Geneva it had
been noted that the Tsaldaris Government had shown little inclination
to maintain friendly relations with the LNFC and had sent no ministers
to the Financial Committee's winter session.[33] Although Foreign
Minister Maximos's proposals to merge the Bank of Greece with the
National Bank aroused hostile comment in Geneva, Geneva's stock had
fallen in Athens. In reply to remonstrations from Finlayson, the
League's Adviser to the Bank, that the Financial Committee should be
consulted about any changes, Maximos retorted that 'he would not ask
that Committee which in his opinion was largely responsible for the
present mess in Central Europe nor would he ask the views of the Bank

[31] FO 371/15967 C9646/462, Ramsay–FO, 16 Nov. 1932.
[32] FO 371/15965 C9846/324, Ramsay–FO, 28 Nov. 1932.
[33] FO 371/16763 C608/2, Ramsay–FO, 13 Jan. 1933; USNA 868.00/704, Gade–State, 12 Jan. 1933.

of England nor the Bank of France. He was not asking them for assistance and he was convinced they would provide no help anyway.'[34]

The Varvaressos Agreement had recommended that an independent survey of the Greek economy be undertaken before the next round of negotiations began. In the run-up to new elections in March both sides vied in presenting gloomy assessments of the country's economic prospects. There was general agreement on the need to continue expenditure on the public works and other domestic items; but so far as the foreign debt was concerned, it was alleged that the economic situation had deteriorated since the previous autumn, that Greece's capacity to pay had shrunk, and that her debts should be readjusted to take account of the fall in prices. A number of Greek financial comment- ators argued that debt repayment should be linked to exports of goods and services.[35]

In the spring of 1933, the newly victorious Tsaldaris Government announced its willingness to accept a fact-finding mission, and in early May a group of experts from the LNFC arrived in Athens to collect data. Their arrival coincided with the first indications of economic revival since the first quarter of 1933 showed an increase in revenues over the previous year.[36] When the Chamber assembled on 11 May for the first time since the elections, Venizelos greeted the new Government with the news that in his opinion the financial situation was much better than had been anticipated the previous September.[37] This may have been true but for political reasons it was unlikely that the new Government would agree to more favourable terms with the bondholders than their predecessors had done. When a large Greek delegation, including both the Finance Minister and the Minister for Foreign Affairs, arrived in London for the next session of the LNFC and negotiations with the League Loans Committee, the stage was set for another round of lengthy bargaining. Yet agreement did not seem impossible. At the British Embassy in Athens it was reckoned that the Greeks would improve on their initial offer of 20% of the interest due, and could be expected to go up to 25%. At the same time the bondholders would probably come down from their opening bid for 40% to settle for around 30%. On this reckoning a settlement should have been practicable. But

[34] Finlayson–Niemeyer, 26 Nov. 1932, AET 46/163.
[35] FO 371/16763 C2088/2, Ramsay–FO, 21 Dec. 1932.
[36] FO 371/16764 C4276/2, Waley–FO, 10 May 1933.
[37] FO 371/16764 C4516/2, Ramsay–FO, 13 May 1933.

the Greek side proved less yielding than the Embassy had expected. When the two ministers—Loverdos, the Finance Minister and Maximos, Minister for Foreign Affairs, both of them bankers—met Sir John Simon, the British Foreign Minister, they made an initial offer of 15% and voiced their disagreement with Simon when he expressed the view that conditions were better than the previous year.[38]

According to Simon the report prepared by the LNFC the previous month showed that Greece was 'poor but not hopeless' and had emphasized the increase in the central bank's reserves and the generally improved financial outlook. He argued that transfer of 30% was possible and that in view of the improvement in conditions the settlement for 1933/4 should be at least as good as that for 1932/3. The Greek response was to offer a two-year arrangement—22.5% in the first year, 27.5% in the second. The Treasury rejected this 'on behalf of the bondholders' and on 17 June negotiations were broken off after just two weeks' discussions.[39] It is worth noting that for all the British authorities' declarations of non-involvement, they were obviously as heavily involved in the negotiations as were the bondholders' organizations.

Part of the problem lay in the fact that political weakness gave the Tsaldaris Government little room to manœuvre. None of the leading personalities in the Populist Party was able to control the party extremists with the grip Venizelos displayed over the Liberal Party. This was a constant difficulty. It was compounded in July by an unfavourable by-election result in Salonika, which left the Government badly needing a 'victory' over the bondholders. There was now a bipartisan consensus in the Press, which found its strongest expression in Venizelist papers, that Greece should repay only a small fraction of her obligations. At a meeting of party leaders at the beginning of August, Venizelos insisted that the Government should stick to the final offer it had made in London, while other party leaders argued that the Government should make no payment at all.[40]

However, contrary pressure now came from another quarter. A large portion of the foreign debt, perhaps as much as a third, was held by Greek subjects who had frequently in the late 1920s invested in issues floated in London, Paris, and New York. They too demanded consideration. The Government began privately to make new approaches to the

[38] FO 371/16764 C5272/6144/6197/2, Cavendish-Bentinck–FO, 2 June 1933; Waley–FO, 6 June 1933; Simon–Ramsay, 6 June 1933.
[39] FO 371/16764 C6209/2, LLC–FO, 10 June 1933.
[40] FO 371/16765 C6868/2, Cavendish-Bentinck–FO, 2 Aug. 1933.

bondholders but was hamstrung by the strength of public feeling against further concessions. Yet as the upswing continued, the official line that Greece was in worse shape than the previous year began to look makeshift.[41] The Government advanced the view that record cereal harvests actually worsened the fiscal position since the cost of agricultural support schemes rose while revenues from cereal imports fell! It also claimed that the striking increase in the central bank's reserves had no connection with the financial situation in the country but simply reflected lack of confidence in the dollar and other currencies. In both cases there was a grain of truth in the Greek view but little more.[42] By the autumn the Populist Government had improved its offer considerably, authorizing the Greek Minister in London to offer the bondholders 27.5%–32.5% over two years. This could be represented as preserving the 30% agreed with Varvaressos in 1932. But the bondholders continued to demand more in view of the recovery in Greece and succeeded in obtaining improved terms—27.5%–35%—at the beginning of October.[43]

If only the matter had ended there! As had occurred the previous year, friction now arose between the chief representatives of the bondholders. The British bondholders' organizations were willing to accept the new arrangement. However, the French Government again insisted on payment in gold whereas the Greek offer had stipulated dollars or sterling payment. The French also wanted to make agreement contingent upon the settlement of a dispute over Greece's share of the Ottoman Debt. In Whitehall there was considerable irritation over these French demands and neither the Foreign Office nor the Treasury were willing to support them. On the other hand any settlement legally required the consent of the French representative on the IFC.

This impasse weakened still further the authority of the IFC. For the Greek Government, under attack from two sides, sought ways of implementing the Varvaressos Agreement as quickly as possible and now found itself in the ironical position of being prevented by its creditors from repaying part of its debt. Seeking to bypass the French veto, it announced its intention of making unilateral repayments on the interest, leading Waterlow, the new British Ambassador, to warn the Greeks against a course which would have violated the statutes of the IFC. However, in London there was tacit support for their proposed

---

[41] IBA, General Manager, YR, 1932/3.
[42] FO 371/16765 C6868/2, Cavendish-Bentinck–FO, 2 Aug. 1933.
[43] FO 371/16766 C9678/2, Waley–FO, 31 May 1934.

action; the attitude of the French Government made this the only practicable procedure and Treasury officials uttered their usual refrain: 'there is no point in protesting . . .'.[44] The threat of unilateral Greek action was in itself enough to resolve outstanding difficulties with the French. Early in July 1934, exchange to meet the payment of 27.5% of the 1933/4 interest was transferred to the account of the IFC, which in its turn transferred 3,000 million drachmas of its frozen balances—then standing at over 4,200 million—to the Greek Government.[45]

This proved, perhaps unsurprisingly, to be the last settlement agreed during the lifetime of the Greek Republic. At the end of 1934 Loverdos was replaced as Finance Minister by a younger man, George Pesmazoglu, who combined his new job with his existing position as Minister for the National Economy. He did not try to hide his ambition, as the US Ambassador reported, 'to eclipse his predecessor . . . talking loudly about "being master in his own home" and telling the foreigners what is what'.[46] Such an attitude, combined with the political upheavals of 1935—which led Pesmazoglu to resign *twice* within seven months—help to explain why no payments were made to bondholders in 1935. In fact negotiations remained bogged down until the regime of John Metaxas was established midway through 1936.

The implications of abandoning the gold standard seem to have dawned belatedly on both debtor and creditors. Failing to co-ordinate their response, the bondholders and allied governments found there was little they could do to sway a recalcitrant debtor. Within Greece politics rather than economics precluded a more satisfactory settlement: good harvests and the flow of funds from the USA improved the country's financial position within a year of devaluation. What constrained the Tsaldaris administration was the difficulty of being seen to give away more to foreign creditors than the Liberal Government had been prepared to do. Nor were Liberal politicians shy about attacking their opponents on these grounds. This explains the Government's constant emphasis to the bondholders on the parlous state of the economy—an emphasis which has been accepted for many years as a reliable assessment of conditions at the time. In fact the recovery had begun by early 1933, fuelled at least in part by gains to the state from debt default. It seems worth finding out what these gains amounted to: just how

---

[44] FO 371/18394 R1469/26, Waley–FO, 9 Mar. 1934; FO 371/18395 R3105/26, Waley–FO, 31 May 1934.
[45] FO 371/18395 R3745/4240/26, IFC–FO, 23 July 1934.
[46] USNA 868.002/206 MacVeagh–State, 24 Jan. 1935.

advantageous, in purely financial terms, was defaulting on the foreign debt to the Greek state after 1932?

The Benefits of Default

Britain's abandonment of the gold standard was what first alerted the Greek authorities to the possibility of budgetary difficulties ahead. As early as October 1931 Venizelos confided to Finlayson that the 1932/3 Budget might be 'endangered'.[47] Having staked everything on its policy of public works, the Liberal Government now faced a dilemma: should it attempt to keep its credit intact by meeting its obligations in full at a time when further loans were unlikely to be forthcoming, or should it reduce debt payments in an effort to maintain spending on the public works?

In the spring of 1932 Venizelos characteristically continued to hope for the best of both worlds: a five-year moratorium on amortization payments plus a new loan to complete the public works.[48] This day-dreaming got short shrift in London, where one Treasury official described the proposed combination as 'quite impossible'. As Leith Ross at the Treasury saw it, 'the problem to be solved is what steps should be taken by Greece so that she can carry on out of her own resources'.[49] To put the matter in these terms, of course, was to resolve the Greek dilemma. Against a background of international financial dislocation and an acute foreign exchange shortage at home, there was only one likely outcome: default. What were the budgetary gains from this policy, and what changes in expenditure patterns resulted?

Table 7.2 gives a picture of the last pre-crisis Budget and of the five that followed it. After 1931/2, total expenditures and revenues dropped sharply; on the other hand, the drop in ordinary revenues was shallower, despite falling import revenues, and so too was the drop in non-debt spending.

The drop in extraordinary revenues after 1931/2 was due to the curtailment of loan income. However, the effects of this were more than offset by the reduced spending on the external debt service, which allowed spending on most other items to be sustained at pre-crisis

---

[47] FO 371/15230 C8185/18, Ramsay–FO, 24 Oct. 1931.
[48] FO 371/15959 C869/926/324, 'Notes of a Conversation between the Chancellor of the Exchequer and M. Venizelos at the Treasury on 26 January 1932', 27 Jan. 1932.
[49] FO 371/15959 C926/1005/324, Leith-Ross–Roussin (IFC), 30 Jan. 1932.

TABLE 7.2. *Greek Budgets, 1931/2–1936/7* (million drachmas)

Revenue and expenditure	1931/2	1932/3	1933/4	1934/5	1935/6	1936/7
Revenues						
Ordinary	8,936	7,969	8,284	9,154	10,299	11,166
Extraordinary	2,525	1,365	329	328	654	2,225
Total effective revenue	11,461	9,334	8,613	9,482	10,953	13,391
Untransferred external debt interest	—	—	1,496	1,333	1,208	1,194
Total gross revenue	11,461	9,334	10,109	10,815	12,161	14,585
Expenditure						
External debt service	2,657	1,198	642	929	995	1,038
Domestic debt service	511	442	707	719	847	783
Defence	1,767	1,813	1,900	2,029	2,433	4,545
Public works	1,776	1,377	603	440	674	558
Roads	118	112	120	215	239	213
Pensions	665	661	683	797	915	1,188
Education	669	686	698	872	940	940
Other	3,398	3,232	3,270	3,320	3,898	4,026
Total (excluding external debt service)	8,904	8,323	7,981	8,392	9,946	12,253
Total effective expenditure	11,561	9,521	8,623	9,321	10,921	13,291
Untransferred external debt interest	—	—	1,496	1,333	1,208	1,194
Total gross expenditure	11,561	9,521	10,119	10,654	12,129	14,485

Source: FO 371/22358 R1265/169.

TABLE 7.3.   *Budgetary trends, 1931/2–1936/7*

	1931/2	1932/3	1933/4	1934/5	1935/6	1936/7
Domestic surplus/ deficit[a]	+0.4	−4.4	+3.7	+8.3	+3.4	−9.7
Overall surplus/ deficit[b]	−29.4	−19.5	−4.1	−1.8	−6.0	−19.0
External debt service/ordinary revenues	29.7	15.0	7.7	10.1	9.7	9.3
External debt service/total effective expenditure	23.0	12.6	7.4	10.0	9.1	7.8
Direct government expenditure[c]/ total effective expenditure	37.5	41.9	38.5	38.2	39.2	47.1

[a] Ordinary revenues − total effective expenditures, excluding external debt service/ ordinary revenues (%).
[b] Ordinary revenues − total effective expenditures/ordinary revenues (%).
[c] Spending on defence, public works, roads, education (%).

Source: Based on data in Table 7.2.

levels, at least in nominal terms. The only other item to be significantly cut back, from 1933/4 onwards, was spending on the public works. Pensions, defence, and education were all protected, as after 1932/3 was spending on the domestic debt service.

Table 7.3 indicates how far the external debt service bore the brunt of budgetary retrenchment. It fell significantly as a percentage of both revenues and expenditures. Overall the budget remained in deficit throughout these years. However, this was certainly not deliberate, since all parties were agreed on the desirability of preserving budgetary equilibrium. There is no evidence that Keynesian-type ideas had attracted a following in Greece. On the contrary, all Finance Ministers attempted to avoid budget deficits. The declaration of economic principles by the Tsaldaris Government contained as an appendix to the LNFC report of June 1933 included pledges to maintain budgetary equilibrium, follow a cautious spending policy, and exclude any new schemes of capital expenditures.

If we leave aside the external debt service and attempt to calculate the size of public spending within the domestic economy and its relation to revenues, official efforts to preserve a balanced budget appear more successful. The budget was in surplus between 1933/4 and 1935/6. Only in 1936/7, with the introduction of Metaxas's ambitious rearmament programme, funded largely by borrowing, did it move back sharply into deficit.[50] In fact the impact of fiscal policy in the four years after the crisis was broadly neutral, since budget surpluses were too small to exert a significant effect on the domestic economy. Only by the second half of 1936, when the upswing was on the verge of petering out, did the government pursue a more expansionary policy. However, it is important to point out that this fiscal neutrality was only made possible by the decision to default on the external debt. Default made available savings which counterbalanced the lack of fresh sources of foreign funds.

What was the magnitude of these savings? Estimating this amount involves a comparison between what Greece paid and what she might have been expected to pay. The depreciation of the drachma doubled the drachma burden of the full debt service and there was clearly never any chance that this sum could have been paid, since it came to around two-thirds of total expenditures in 1932/3. There are two more realistic bases for comparison. One is to assume that the percentage of total effective expenditure which had been spent on the public debt in 1931/2 might have been spent in successive budgets; the other, to assume that

TABLE 7.4. *Budget savings from debt default, 1932/3–1936/7*
(million drachmas)

Year	Constant percentage assumption	Untransferred external debt assumption
1932/3[a]	969	—
1933/4	1,014	1,496
1934/5	906	1,333
1935/6	1,150	1,208
1936/7	1,821	1,194
TOTAL	5,860	5,231

[a] The 1932/3 budget omitted any figure for untransferred external debt service.

Source: Based on data in Table 7.2.

[50] FO 371/21143 R3166/94, Waterlow–FO, 'Economic Annual Report on Greece for 1936', 29 Apr. 1937.

the savings involved comprised the non-transferred part of the external debt service entered in budget accounts after 1932/3. Table 7.4 presents both calculations.

These estimates both suggest that the savings to the Greek budget from default on the external debt amounted annually to over 1 billion drachmas—roughly equivalent to around 10% of state expenditures in this period, or—more contentiously—around 2% of GNP. These were very large sums, and their non-transfer averted a potentially contractionary source of pressure on the domestic economy. External debt service requirements dropped from 44% of export earnings in 1931 to just over 9% in 1935 and 16% the following year. It is difficult to disagree with the conclusions of a League Loans Committee report —written in 1938—which stated that 'post-default budget figures show a healthy underlying condition and a growing measure of prosperity . . . but the external debt has had little share of expanding revenues'.[51] Not that this was surprising: default exemplified the type of recovery mechanism which contributed to the early upswing in Greece—to couch it in terms of the jargon, a response to the falling opportunity costs of defiance. It was a strategy which reflected the passivity of the Tsaldaris Government as the rules of the economic game changed. But passivity—as we shall see—had drawbacks as well as advantages.[52]

[51] FO 371/22358 R1265/169, Bewley (Treasury)–FO, 'Greek Budget Default' (Note by the LLC), 11 Feb. 1938.
[52] Venezis, *Tsouderos*, p. 123.

8

THE NEW TRADE REGIME

Dear Minister, in Greece all temporary measures become permanent!

(Senator Anastasios Bakalbasis, August 1933)

The 'Simple Policeman'

'The exceptional aptitude of the Greek for commerce is universally recognized,' stated Tsaldaris in a speech in 1933, and few of his listeners would have disagreed. It was a commonplace that trade was an activity particularly suited to the individualism of the Greeks. But here lay the heart of the problem, for it was precisely this individualism which in the eyes of many commentators now needed to be shaped and restrained by a more collective response. To those who held this shift to be the necessary outcome of the post-war process of industrialization were added others who saw it as the required response to the world economic crisis.[1] What gave this issue its urgency of course was the trade balance's chronic deficit, the need to reduce which had been behind Venizelos's encouragement of cereal and cotton producers. As Greece began to feel the effects of the crisis, it became obvious that more direct state intervention in trade, whether to promote exports or restrict imports, was required. The political élite recognized this with reluctance, well aware of the depth of opposition of that electorally crucial Greek *Mittelstand* of shopkeepers, petty traders, and merchants to any move against entrepreneurial freedom. Thus Tsaldaris's Minister for the National Economy, George Pesmazoglu, reassured assembled representatives of the Chambers of Commerce in September 1933: 'State intervention is not due to the rejection of free trade, but has been imposed by events.'[2] Intervention could take many forms, however, ranging from the complete state monopolization of trade in certain

---

[1] G. Vouros, *Panayis Tsaldaris* (Athens, 1955), 293.
[2] *DEVE/A*, Sept. 1933, 26.

commodities at one extreme to support for the private merchant at the other. Neither Liberals nor Populists were politically or ideologically prepared to abandon free trade in principle; as a result, the evolution of commercial policy showed rather clearly the equivocal way in which the economic crisis altered the balance of power between the state and private enterprise.

A key figure in commercial policy before 1932 was Panayis Vourloumis, Minister for the National Economy in the Liberal Government. A leading currant merchant from the port of Patras, Vourloumis held the *laissez-faire* attitudes typical of that milieu. We have mentioned earlier how the Liberal Government restricted the activities of the Autonomous Currant Organization, worried by the possibility of a 'national marketing organization . . . not conceived as a capitalistic trust, nor as a state monopoly in the Soviet style, but as a monopoly where the peasant is master and controller of his own wealth'. Many peasants regarded Vourloumis himself as a tool of the merchants.[3] But though currant and tobacco exporters were opposed for obvious reasons to the creation of alternative marketing organizations, they too increasingly sought the state's assistance, not just through reductions in export taxes, but via some linkage of exports to imports. In May 1931 it was announced that the Ministry of the National Economy was preparing a bill for the 'organization of exports' which would give state support to the private sector, but by September, when the financial crisis began, this bill had still to appear.

With the onset of the financial crisis, of course, the promotion of commerce became a more urgent matter, though the Government seemed unwilling to admit the fact: implementing the first measures to restrict imports and ration foreign exchange, Venizelos insisted that these measures were purely temporary. But Papanastasiou attacked the Government for its 'antiquated economic views', and dissident Liberal deputies like Stavros Kostopoulos opposed Vourloumis by calling for import monopolies of key consumption goods against which Greek exports could be bartered. The Agrarian Alexandros Mylonas insisted that 'free competition must give way to the managed economy' while even Tsaldaris recognized the need for more barter trade.[4]

Early in 1932, when it became evident that existing exchange controls would not save the drachma, Venizelos invited Alexandros Koryzis,

---

[3] D. Nikolaides, *Oi kindynoi tis stafidos* (Patras, 1934), pt. 3; A. D. Sideris, *I georgiki politiki tis Ellados 1833–1933* (Athens, 1934), 342.

[4] *E* 107–9, 16–30 Jan. 1932.

Deputy Governor of the National Bank of Greece, to prepare a plan for the organization of Greece's foreign trade. Koryzis, whose career ended tragically when he committed suicide as Prime Minister in April 1941, was one of the most influential figures behind the scenes in inter-war Greek economic affairs. Starting as a junior clerk in 1903, he had spent his entire career in the National Bank; by the 1920s he was one of the most forceful proponents of a 'reorganization' of the Greek economy across a broad front which ranged from establishing credit co-operatives in rural areas to encouraging the formation of cartels among groups of leading manufacturers. Critics claimed that the primary purpose of such schemes was to consolidate the power of the National Bank. The prominent Populist, Constantine Angelopoulos, decried 'the efforts which the NBG has been making systematically for several years to concentrate in its own hands . . . all the economy of the country'.[5] It seems difficult, however, to disentangle such motives from the feeling which Koryzis undoubtedly shared with other prominent bankers, economists, and intellectuals, that short-term economic stability and long-term growth required some form of intervention in the market. And it is not entirely surprising that Koryzis, who went on to accept ministerial office under Metaxas, appears to have gradually lost faith in the ability of the Republic's politicians to implement this. As the fate of his proposals for trade reform would show, there was ample justification for such disillusionment.

Responding to Venizelos's invitation, in April 1932 he submitted his plan in the form of a draft bill which envisaged establishing monopolies of vital imported goods under State control, explicitly linking such organizations with the need to promote exports.[6] But Vourloumis refused to introduce measures which he regarded as opening the way to a planned economy. Here in miniature was the emerging conflict between the merchant community, and those étatists who for institutional and ideological reasons welcomed the shift towards autarky. Vourloumis threatened resignation, and Venizelos went so far as to offer the Ministry of the National Economy to Koryzis himself, in order to implement his plan. On hearing this news, the Patras Chamber of Commerce ordered shops to close for two hours in protest—and many of the businesses in the town did so. The British Consul there noted that 'as Venizelos's political position has been gradually weakening over the

---

[5] K. Angelopoulos, *Politikoi agones: 1892–1934*, iii (Athens, 1934), 81.

[6] N. Chadzivasileiou, *Katefthynseis tis exoterikis emporikis mas politikis* (Athens, 1936), 17–21; Koryzis–Venizelos, 16 May 1931, AEV 343.

past few months, it is certain that if the Government decides to institute Trade Monopolies, there will be . . . very great dissatisfaction among all classes of the population'.[7] Koryzis declined Venizelos's invitation and though the Liberal Government's major legislative response to the crisis, Law 5426, called for the establishment of a 'Council of Foreign Trade', that part of the law remained a dead letter.

But Alexandros Papanastasiou, who briefly succeeded Venizelos late in May 1932, differed from his predecessor in holding that the economic crisis was far deeper and more far-reaching than just another cyclical downturn, and that it therefore called for a radical change of policy.[8] During his brief period in office, Papanastasiou resuscitated the Koryzis plan and sent it to the Supreme Economic Council for further consideration, thus bringing that body directly to the policy-making process for the first time. In the summer the Council responded with a report, written by its Vice-President, Spiros Loverdos (subsequently Finance Minister in the Tsaldaris Government), which drew heavily on Koryzis's ideas.[9] This called for the creation of a foreign trade organization which would, however, be a limited-liability company with shareholders, rather than a body under direct state control. But before such proposals could be taken further there intervened a period of political uncertainty dominated by the two general elections of September 1932 and March 1933, which eventually brought the anti-Venizelist camp, led by Tsaldaris's Populists, a majority for the first time in more than a decade.

In a private memorandum written shortly before his victory in the 1933 election, Panayis Tsaldaris described his party as being 'conservative with a progressive tendency'. The latter component had originally been not insignificant, and the party's founder, Dimitrios Gounaris, was a trenchant if somewhat aloof critic of Greek society. But under Tsaldaris the elements of progressive thinking were diluted to an anaemic 'anti-plutocratic' populism and subordinated to a constant preoccupation with tactical party manœuvring. It is therefore not surprising that Gounaris's brilliant nephew, Panayiotis Kanellopoulos, one of Greece's leading younger intellectuals (and the first lecturer in sociology at Athens University), soon distanced himself from the Populists. Tsaldaris found it difficult to reconcile the urgent calls for state

---

[7] FO 371/15962 C4167/324, Ramsay–FO, 17 May 1932.

[8] *ESG*, 22 Jan. 1934, 2,004.

[9] AOS, *To exoterikon emporion tis Ellados kai ai symvaseis antallagis emporevmaton* (Athens, 1933), 20–1.

intervention he heard around him with his traditional support for the petty bourgeoisie: the trade issue brought this dilemma to the surface. At a pre-election rally in March 1933 he stressed that any involvement of the state in trade would have to be temporary: 'the policy of the state must be based on freedom of trade . . . (though) more general necessities may require the temporary monopolization by the state of certain goods of mass consumption'.[10] Then, in his opening address to the newly elected Parliament, he tentatively committed the Government to a more active commercial policy. By this time bilateral agreements were playing an increasingly important part in Greece's trade, whilst it was clear that the dramatic closing of the trade deficit was almost entirely due to a fall in imports rather than a rise in exports, as George Pesmazoglu, the Minister for the National Economy, admitted to the Supreme Economic Council.

The Koryzis plan, in slightly altered form, was resuscitated yet again at the end of July 1933, when Pesmazoglu published details of a bill 'On the Organization of Greece's Export Trade'.[11] The same plan had now been considered, in the space of little more than a year, by Liberals, left Venizelists, and anti-Venizelists alike! According to the Minister, existing arrangements needed to be replaced by a systematic development of Greek exports under the aegis of the state. The proposed new organization would be responsible for publicity and propaganda on behalf of Greek exports, and for the creation of import monopolies in certain cases. This latter measure was introduced because Greece's suppliers of cereals, in particular, insisted on being paid in foreign exchange and took negligible quantities of Greek exports. In November 1931 the Venizelos Government had unsuccessfully attempted to pressure these countries by introducing a tenfold increase in maximum import tariffs on goods from countries with whom Greece had no commercial treaty. However, the relative insignificance of the Greek market to her suppliers and the political sensitivity in Greece of high bread prices meant that this legislation had little practical effect.[12] Nor were cereal imports affected by quotas or exchange controls. In other words, despite the regulation of other goods, so far as imports of vital necessities were concerned, trade was unrestricted, and there existed no means by which they could by law be tied to exports.

From the point of view of exporters, the new policy had much to

[10] Vouros, *Tsaldaris*, pp. 289, 293; P. Kanellopoulos, *I zoi mou* (Athens, 1985), ch. 3.
[11] *Proia*, 29–30 July 1933.
[12] Chadzivasileiou, *Katefthynseis*, pp. 49–55.

commend it since many major suppliers—Argentina, Canada, Brazil —represented badly needed new markets which might dilute Greece's dependence on the UK and Germany. However, the announcement that Pesmazoglu was considering the establishment of official import monopolies aroused great disquiet in the commercial community, which was not appeased by being told that recognized importers would be able to participate. In April merchants from Crete publicly attacked the idea of any centralizing organization, insisting instead that private initiative should be sustained and supported. A similar message came in August from Senator George Stringos, the President of the Piraeus Chamber of Commerce; he advised Pesmazoglu that merchants were not demanding Manchester-style *laissez-faire*, but rather a private sector *supplemented* by the State, such as—according to him—had been introduced by Roosevelt and Mussolini. With a nod towards Koryzis and the National Bank he attacked the proposed import monopolies as benefiting only 'capitalists living off the interest of capital'.[13] In the same month Pesmazoglu attended a meeting of assembled representatives of the Chambers of Commerce, where the merchants' opposition to such measures was made clear. The assembly passed a resolution opposing 'any measure of an interventionist character regarding imports or exports'.[14]

By the time that the bill was debated in Parliament in November 1933, this pressure had intensified, forcing the Government on to the defensive. Even the Populist chairman of the committee which examined the bill expressed reservations about import monopolies, declaring that 'I don't want the Populist Party to vote in such legislation, since the Populist Party is above all the party of working people, [and] of the good bourgeois world.' To which the Prime Minister, Tsaldaris, responded with his characteristic mastery of evasiveness that 'no one can say of the Populist Party that it is abandoning its liberal principles and introducing measures to restrict Greek commerce; on the contrary, should it be necessary to monopolize a given good, say cereals or coal etc., . . . I shall not deprive the world of commerce of its freedom'. A little further on he emphasized, 'I insist, I remain an adherent to the principle of the free market . . . Even when we are forced to create a monopoly, we shall leave commerce free.'[15]

Such Delphic utterances failed to satisfy other members of the

[13] *OA* 791, 8 Apr. 1933; 811, 26 Aug. 1933.
[14] *DEVE/A*, Sept. 1933, 27.
[15] *ESV*, 10 Nov. 1933, 71–3.

governing coalition. For anti-Venizelist radicals—for whom the Populist Party was the party of 'petty bourgeois and farming elements' as opposed to the 'big capital' represented by the Liberals—the bill reflected a 'plutocratic policy' because it failed to give enough support to smallholders producing for export markets, whilst it opened the way for import monopolies to dominate domestic producers. From another angle, a spokesman for the provincial merchants insisted that 'this bill is the result of a group in the Ministry of National Economy, not unknown to us or to the world of commerce. The Ministry has taken up arms on behalf of state intervention, the planned economy, the "sovietization" of the market. Greece above all other countries should not fall under the banner of state intervention.'[16]

Pesmazoglu defended himself against this barrage of accusations, retorting that the market by itself had failed to find new export customers, and that the aim of the bill was to bring this about through bilateral trade. But while true, this ignored two factors: firstly, the Populists' need to present themselves as the defenders of the lower middle classes against the supposed 'plutocratic' étatism of the Liberals, and secondly, the easing of exchange pressures from 1933 onwards. Pesmazoglu, a man with little influence in his party, was running too far ahead of his colleagues. Before the debate passed to the Senate two months later, concerted pressure from the merchants' lobby led the Government to drop the contentious articles from the bill. The proposed organization was now little more than a type of chamber of commerce, something which pleased the first government speaker in the debate but brought a detailed attack from Senator Anastasios Bakalbasis, a respected figure close to the reformist Papanastasiou, who argued that something more powerful than that was required: 'What I want is not what the socialist states are introducing. Here all states—even the most conservative —who want above all to combat the drift into anarchy and to preserve the bourgeois state, have recognized and implemented a "planned economy".'[17] But a Populist speaker criticized Bakalbasis's 'capitalist' ideas, arguing that it was the excessive 'concentration of capital' which had made other countries especially vulnerable to the international recession: 'The Greek, gentlemen, is an individualist, and his individualism is a great quality and virtue. Would you destroy the small trader and the livelihood of many people to place it all in the hands of an irresponsible few men?' Pesmazoglu was forced once more to stress the

---

[16] Ibid., 82–3, 86, 92.
[17] *ESG*, 22 Jan. 1934, 2,011–12.

provisional nature of his proposals. Admitting that the articles on import monopolies had been withdrawn because of the criticism they had aroused, he responded that 'both Senator Bakalbasis and the Government support the idea of State intervention in commerce, with the difference that while he supports it on principle, i.e. whatever the circumstances, we regard it as necessary only when circumstances dictate'. Bakalbasis agreed: the Minister for the National Economy viewed the present measures as the 'least of all evils', whilst he held that the crisis was so profound that a change in economic principles was required. The proposed legislation would change nothing. He particularly criticized the fact that the Minister saw no place for civil servants in the new organization where, in his own view, they should have been placed as arbitrators among differing interests. Instead, 'we continue in 1933 to give the State the role of simple policeman'.[18] But Bakalbasis's protests had no effect: the Koryzis plan was finally buried and the Populist Government fell back on to the two less ambitious methods of regulating trade which had been hastily introduced in 1932—import quotas and clearing agreements.[19]

Quotas and Clearings

The original rationale for the introduction of exchange controls and multiple exchange rates late in 1931 had been the need to protect the exchange reserves of the Bank of Greece. Exchange had been made available to merchants at the official rate for imports of foodstuffs, raw materials, and essential manufactured products, and at higher rates for non-essential imports. Even so, the trade deficit grew wider rather than narrower. Comparing the period of the crisis (October–April) with the equivalent period one year earlier, we find that while export values fell by 41%, imports fell by only 17%. This was partly because the Bank's control of exchange movements was very weak, and partly because import merchants kept stocks high as a hedge against the expected devaluation of the drachma.[20] By the spring the inadequacy of the existing measures was widely appreciated. At a meeting of the Council of the Athens Chamber of Commerce in January 1932, various speakers stressed that official policy required more effective legislation. The following month, hoping to offer an alternative to the dreaded trade

[18] *ESG*, 22 Jan. 1934, 2,013–19.
[19] Chadzivasileiou, *Kateflhynseis*, pp. 54–5.
[20] *OE 1932* (Athens, 1933), 369.

monopolies, the Chamber issued a report advocating sweeping import restrictions.[21]

According to this, it was possible to reduce the 1931 import bill by 2.5–3 billion drs.: foodstuffs, fuel, and raw material imports could be cut by around 20%, imports of manufactured goods by virtually 50%. The report raised the question of the effects these restrictions would have on domestic industry—an issue that was increasingly to embitter relations between merchants and industrialists. Whilst it called for relatively small cuts in imports of fuel and raw materials, it proposed restrictions of up to 40% on imports of machinery, arguing that competition in industry was already excessive.

When new legislation was introduced by the Venizelos Government in April 1932, it bore a close resemblance to the report's recommendations. The need to increase official control over exchange flows led to the introduction of Law 5422 (26/4/32) which provided—*inter alia* —that exchange could only be sold for legitimate commercial purposes. This was followed by Law 5426, which introduced sweeping import restrictions and gave extremely wide discretionary powers to the Minister for the National Economy and the Finance Minister: Article 2 of Law 5426 referred specifically to restrictions on imports of machinery, whilst Article 3 supported efforts to increase trade through clearing agreements.[22]

Two weeks later quotas for the next six months were announced for a wide range of goods. The quotas were divided among the different regions on the basis of commercial activity in those regions during 1931, and in each area the local Chamber of Commerce allocated individual quotas on the basis of the activity of individual importers between 1929 and 1931. Each importer was issued with an 'import book' which carried his name and specified the nature and quantity of the goods he was entitled to import over a given period. The severity of the restrictions varied: luxury items, livestock, certain types of industrial and agricultural machinery were cut by up to 75% of the 1931 level of imports. Fuel and raw materials, on the other hand, were only marginally reduced. Nor did the quotas cover Greece's entire import bill: on the contrary, major items such as wheat and coal were left unaffected. Partly this reflected the importance of tariff revenues from these items for the budget. At the same time, the Government feared the political

[21] *DEVE/A*, Mar. 1932.
[22] AOS, *Exoterikon emporion*, pp. 37–8; *DEVE/A*, Apr.–May 1932, 50–1.

consequences of sharp increases in the prices of essential goods. It was estimated that only 57% of the total import bill for 1931 would have been affected by the new measures. Even so, the Government believed that it would achieve savings of 2.5 billion 'stabilized' drs.— exactly in line with the recommendations of the Athens Chamber of Commerce.[23]

Quotas were accompanied by increases in nominal (though not real) tariff protection. The Greek system was based upon specific tariffs whose effective protection obviously fell after devaluation: despite the nominal increases, lowest tariffs were effectively halved in value as the drachma plummeted, whilst the highest were still lower than they had been before April. The reasons for the adoption of such a policy were clear: to keep down the cost of living, even at some cost to the Greek Treasury. This, at any rate, was the explanation given by the senior civil servant at the Ministry of Finance in an article published one year later. In this aim the policy was certainly successful, since the internal value of the drachma fell more slowly than its external value.

During 1932 Greece's trade balance improved remarkably. Imports were more than 3 billion drs. down on 1931 and the trade deficit dropped from 4.5 to 2.4 billion drs. Yet the story was not one of complete success: exports too fell sharply. Moreover, it was debatable to what extent the drop in imports stemmed from the introduction of the new measures. In the seven and a half months of 1932 that import restrictions were in force, import volumes were generally down on the previous year's levels. Yet the significance of the quotas varied among items: they were greatly exceeded in the case of sugar, coffee, livestock, building timber. On the other hand, they were not fulfilled in the case of textiles, where domestic output was expanding rapidly, nor in other instances. It is also noteworthy that imports were down on 1931 in the case of items not subject to quotas, such as rice, fish, coal and benzine, whilst wheat imports rose—perhaps thanks to lower real tariffs— despite the record 1932 cereal harvest. Overall import *volume* was only down 6.7% over the entire year.

An article examining the results of the first year of quotas (May 1932–May 1933) showed that comparing 1932/3 with 1931, goods subject to quotas were down 40% in volume, whilst goods imported under licence from the Ministry of National Economy were down 56% and non-essential goods imported without restriction were down 70%.

[23] AOS, *Exoterikon emporion*, p. 38.

Yet goods of prime necessity, also freely imported, were down by only 19%—hence the argument over the need for import monopolies.[24]

Merchants had initially supported the introduction of import restrictions. As early as May 1932, however, they expressed discontent that the Government had not reduced trade controls upon devaluation.[25] By 1933 they appear to have been increasingly concerned that existing legislation was putting numerous small traders out of business without providing an adequate control on import movements overall. The Chambers of Commerce demanded greater freedom from the Ministry of National Economy in administering controls themselves. The Ministry was criticized for delays—for example in distributing the 'import entitlement' books—or for the difficulties it put in the way of merchants seeking to arrange private barter deals. Law 5426 had sought to encourage these but they tended to give rise to more serious price distortions than did official clearing agreements, and the Ministry subjected traders' invoices to close scrutiny. There was also the matter of commercial debts: the depreciation of the drachma had of course increased Greek merchants' indebtedness to foreign supplies in drachma terms. Yet at the same time, by the so-called 'drachmification' decree passed in the summer of 1932, the state had taken over at the old (i.e. 'stabilization') rate the commercial banks' foreign exchange liabilities, which included assets held by Greek merchants as collateral against foreign obligations.

But while some merchants faced bankruptcy as a result of the quota system, others were able to exploit the situation. Those who qualified for import entitlements found that they could sell their entitlements at a profit. According to one source the price of imported textiles was raised by the equivalent of a 50% increase in the tariff as a result of such sales. A black market in 'entitlement books' arose and began to turn public opinion against 'profiteering' merchants.[26] During 1933 this became a major political issue. When the Ministry of the Interior prosecuted several traders in an effort to curb 'excessive' price increases, merchants' spokesmen complained, arguing that the Ministry was erroneously basing its estimate of a 'fair price' on original costs rather than replacement costs.[27]

While importers argued that restrictions were no longer necessary

[24] *DEVE/A*, Aug. 1933.
[25] FO 371/15962 C3999/324, Ramsay–FO, 19 May 1932.
[26] *DEVE/A*, Nov. 1933; Dec. 1934, 65–7; *OT* 501, 18 Nov. 1934.
[27] *DEVE/A*, Mar.–Apr., June, Sept. 1933.

once the financial crisis had passed, civil servants and politicians feared the consequences of an abrupt liberalization of the market. Merchants argued that since import quotas had not been the cause of the drop in imports, there was no longer any need to keep them in place.[28] But it was anticipated that replacing quotas with higher tariffs, one favoured solution, might attract speculative capital into investment in import stocks and more generally lead to renewed balance of trade difficulties.[29] Also, quotas had had the greatest effect on imports of luxuries; liberalization might cheapen these and pave the way for a consumer boom for the upper classes.[30]

Yet ministers in both Liberal and Populist governments retained their allegiance to the tenets of liberalism. George Pesmazoglu, Minister for the National Economy in the Tsaldaris Government, in a speech to the Athens Chamber of Commerce in November 1934, stated that 'the commercial policy we follow today was forced upon us by the international economic situation and our object is the return to a free market which alone corresponds to our country's geographical position, its natural situation and the character of its inhabitants'.[31] Pesmazoglu, like his Liberal predecessor, Vourloumis, recognized only with reluctance the short-term need to continue a policy of restrictions and this strong 'second-best' attitude explains why under the Tsaldaris administration quotas had at the most a six-month horizon. Most politicians seem to have felt a greater affinity with the liberalism of the merchants than with the *dirigisme* of many of their civil servants. In the two main parties, only Spiros Loverdos, Tsaldaris's Finance Minister, was unreservedly in favour of import controls and a policy of autarky. The Liberal Vourloumis wrote sarcastically of 'the economists, both Greek and foreign, who celebrate the demise of economic orthodoxy and hail the "planned economy"', and he asserted that 'the international crisis has been drawn out precisely because the laws of economics are violated by state intervention'.[32]

Of course the merchants saw matters differently; the Government may have been forced to retreat over the idea of import monopolies, but its policy was still—so far as they were concerned—unjustifiably

---

[28] *Ploutos*, 6 May 1934.
[29] Chadzivasileiou, *Katefthynseis*; *EKDO*, Jan.–Apr. 1934; S. Kostopoulos in *OT* 353, 15 Jan. 1933.
[30] *DEVE/A*, Feb. 1936, 1.
[31] *DEVE/A*, Dec. 1934, 19–20.
[32] *E* 524, 9 Apr. 1934; Chadzivasileiou, *Katefthynseis*; *OE 1934* (1935), 84.

interventionist. The Athens Chamber of Commerce pointed out that quotas were not sufficiently sensitive to fluctuations in domestic demand and supply, so that in the first eighteen months, many quotas had not been satisfied whilst others had been exceeded. Nor were those in business in 1929–31 necessarily still in the import trade after 1934.[33] Civil servants realized that the 'ration book' system had the effect of 'freezing' entitlements, and their view was that the only fair system of distribution would be through a central trade organization. In the words of one, 'any solution within the context of the free market would be full of imperfections'.[34] To the Chambers of Commerce this was, of course, anathema. The trade journals proliferated with daily ministerial decrees on every conceivable topic—from licences for asphalt imports to quotas for sunshades.[35] Their experience of bureaucratic incompetence, mismanagement, and understaffing at the Ministry of the National Economy did not dispose them favourably to any extension of state involvement in trade. The Press carried strident attacks on the Ministry's anti-commercial bias, exemplified by the following extract from the *Athens Economist*:

for a year and a half now the State apparatus has been working actively with one and only one purpose: to bind more tightly the shackles of commerce . . . to erect as rapidly as they can the tombstone on the grave of Greek commerce. The entire effort of the State, with the Minister responsible at the helm, has been devoted to this end.[36]

There were accusations of a deliberate effort to diminish the merchants as an independent class by allocating ration books to state organizations and industrialists rather than permitting the latter to be supplied via professional importers. Merchants from Corfu, for example, protested that by providing the peasants with cheap imported maize and fertilizers the Agricultural Bank was trying to supplant them. Senator Stringos railed against the 'real dictatorial power of the Ministry for the National Economy', arguing that the state had taken on an interventionist role without sufficient preparation.[37]

At the end of 1934 Pesmazoglu, sensitive to criticisms of the profiteering that accompanied the existing procedures, announced that a new system for distributing import entitlements would be formulated. The 'ration books' were to be abolished at the end of the current

[33] *DEVE/A*, May 1934, 5–10. [34] *EKDO*, Jan.–Apr. 1934.
[35] *DEVE/A*, Sept. 1934, 19–20. [36] *OA* 870, 13 Oct. 1934.
[37] *DEVE/A*, Dec. 1934, 23; *OT* 417, 25 Mar. 1934.

six-month period; in their place the Ministry would administer and issue import licences on an *ad hoc* basis. In addition, he introduced a new system of quota classifications with the intention, after having been defeated on the trade monopolies issue, of encouraging exports through an increase in barter trade.[38] Despite the fact that the new legislation legitimized the activity of importers who had entered commerce after 1931, the Chambers of Commerce angrily opposed the new system. Evangelos Leonardos, President of the Merchants' Association of Athens, asserted that 'the Minister wishes to replace the "ration books" with licences simply to humiliate us'.[39]

These changes caused enormous inconvenience to importers, who had now to make applications for each transaction, strained the resources of the Ministry of the National Economy, and continued to provoke outbursts of resentment at meetings of the Chambers of Commerce. On the other hand, it began to be appreciated that the restrictions were becoming less and less significant as an increasing proportion of imports was allowed in unhindered. By July 1936 one observer, himself from the commercial community, was arguing that

> if we want to reduce our imports in total, we must extend the restrictions to the most important items, or take those measures domestically which will reduce consumption of them or replace them in part by domestically produced goods. Otherwise we are maintaining psychological rather than real barriers—since it is clear that if we were to halve imports of those goods [now] subject to restrictions, apart from the problems we shall cause a large number of firms, we shall provide no real benefit to our balance of trade.[40]

This raises the question, which naturally preoccupied professional importers, of how successful import quotas had been. Their own view tended to be that the fall in imports and the consequent improvement in the trade balance had owed relatively little to the restrictions. So were these regulations and restrictions a mere nuisance, an example of state intervention in the economy run wild? What in fact was the impact of import restrictions upon the trade balance?

In terms of 'stabilized' drachmas (i.e. at the 1928 parity), imports fell 5,112 million drs. between 1931 (when controls were first instituted) and 1933, before rising again, especially in 1935. Import controls were not, of course, the only cause of this fall; there were others including: (1) the downward fall in world prices; (2) reduced imports of foodstuffs not

[38] *DEVE/A*, Jan. 1935, 16–17.   [39] *DEVE/A*, Jan. 1935, 17.
[40] *DEVE/A*, July 1936, 2.

TABLE 8.1. *Import decline, 1932–1936*

Year	Overall fall in imports[a]	% of the total fall attributable to			
		Lower world prices	Lower imports: foodstuffs	Lower imports: other non-restricted goods	'Residual' fall
1932	3,679	54.6	7.3	n.	38.1
1933	5,112	52.4	14.5	2.5	30.6
1934	4,965	62.8	17.2	1.5	18.5
1935	4,181	79.2	10.6	0.9	9.3
1936	3,691	84.7	5.9	n.	9.4

n. = negligible.

[a] In constant drachmas (millions) compared with 1931.

subject to restrictions; and (3) reduced imports of other goods not subject to restrictions. What portion of the original fall in import values should be attributed to these factors? Once we have attempted to evaluate—in approximate terms—*their* impact, we can go on to assess the quantitative significance of the import quotas.

The detailed calculations used to answer this problem may be consulted elsewhere. But the results, summarized in Table 8.1, to some extent bear out the merchants' views: they suggest that quotas were never as important a cause of the drop in import values as movements in world prices, and, moreover, became increasingly *unimportant* with time. The percentages in the final column provide a rough possible *maximum* for the contribution of import quotas to the overall drop in imports. They constitute a maximum because the 'residual' may include the effect of a number of factors, of which the quotas are only one. I have not attempted to calculate, for example, possible changes in the propensity to import or in aggregate income generally. Such calculations must await the elaboration of more reliable national income aggregates for the period than we possess at present. Nor have I tried to allow for the effect of changing commercial practices; we know, for example, that after the abandonment of the gold standard there was an increase in the amount of import business conducted on a cash basis, which naturally had the effect of reducing sales.[41]

[41] Details of these calculations may be consulted in M. Mazower, 'Towards Autarchy: The Recovery from Crisis in Greece: 1929–36', D.Phil. thesis, Oxford University, 1987, pp. 237–42. On cash sales see IBA, Patras, YR 1933/4.

But in any event a calculation of this sort only provides very approximate results. From the data above we may infer, firstly, that at the time of the greatest fall in imports, the quotas were not responsible for more than around one-third of the overall fall; and secondly, that their impact fell away rather quickly, to less than 10% of the overall fall by 1935. Thus the import merchants' protests that quotas were no longer effective were justified, even if the corollary, that they were not needed, remained more debatable. The fall in imports was much more due to price movements, and to a lesser extent to increased domestic agricultural production, than it was to the quota policy of post-1932 governments. Quotas disenchanted and inconvenienced the merchant community without having a serious effect on the trade balance.

But import quotas were not the only new regulatory element introduced into Greek commerce as a result of the crisis. The shortage of foreign exchange also stimulated the spread of clearing agreements of various kinds, which were encouraged, especially after 1934, as a way of increasing exports. These arose initially between states in the Danubian region in the aftermath of the 1931 financial crisis, when a representative of the Austrian Government suggested such a procedure at the Prague Conference, sponsored by the Bank of International Settlements, in November 1931. In the same month, the Austrian authorities concluded an agreement with the Bank of Greece to facilitate purchases of Greek tobacco by the Austrian State Tobacco Monopoly.[42] Austria, Czechoslovakia, and other Central European states which faced exchange shortages were among the principal buyers of Greek tobacco, and other customers followed the Austrian example. The other major early agreement was concluded in the summer of 1932 with the French authorities, who negotiated imports of Greek wines through a clearing as a means of obtaining partial repayment of Greek commercial debts to French merchants. Czechoslovakia and Sweden also followed the French example during 1932.

These agreements soon multiplied in a haphazard and complicated fashion. Apart from full clearing agreements, which channelled all trade through accounts at the central banks of the two countries concerned, there were three main other types of clearing agreements employed by Greece. In some cases, certain imports from specific states were prohibited except as part of a barter transaction, although other imports of

---

[42] *OE 1931* (Athens, 1932), 373–6; A. Basch, *The Danubian Basin and the German Economic Sphere* (London, 1944), 82–8.

identical provenance might be paid for in foreign exchange. These so-called 'partial clearing' agreements were generally imposed by the Greek authorities in an effort to pressure the trading partner into negotiating a full clearing agreement. They were applied to more than 10 countries, including major suppliers of basic imports such as wheat (Argentina, Russia) and coffee (Brazil). However, Greece lacked the clout which would have enabled her to obtain full clearings with these states, since her market was too insignificant to make them fear the prospect of losing it. More to the point, they were uninterested in the goods she had to offer in return. Although in December 1931 Law 5313 raised tariffs tenfold against Australia, Canada, Argentina, and all other countries with whom no commercial convention had been reached, this unsubtle attempt to bargain for better terms backfired. Greece's suppliers were no more receptive to Greek entreaties and as a result the Greek authorities were forced repeatedly to exempt wheat imports from these countries from the higher tariffs by a series of *ad hoc* ministerial decrees. For the most part these countries were able to obtain foreign exchange in payment for a large proportion of their goods and the partial clearings remained limited in their scope.

A second potentially more important type of clearing agreement was worked out with Greece's Balkan neighbours. The Bank of Greece issued *bons de caisse*, made out (for example) to the Yugoslav exporter upon payment of the corresponding amount in drachmas, to be withdrawn in exchange for convertible notes used exclusively for the payment of the value of Greek goods imported into Yugoslavia. The Yugoslav central bank would exchange these notes for dinars. The Greek/Yugoslav treaty of September 1932 was the first to incorporate this innovation, which was later included in treaties with Turkey (May 1933) and Romania (September 1933). In all these cases, however, a large part of the import bill from these countries—for wheat and coal, particularly—continued to be paid in foreign exchange. The third variant was the 'individual clearing', according to which imports from certain countries were either given preference, or in some cases only permitted, where the importer had arranged barter terms on his own account. As we have already seen, this sort of arrangement, which was a compromise between the authorities' need to conserve exchange and the autonomy of the individual merchant, was not encouraged by the Ministry for the National Economy, and never became widespread.[43]

[43] *OE 1933* (Athens, 1934), 492; *1934* (Athens, 1935), 291.

TABLE 8.2.   *Greece's import trade by type of supplier, 1926–1935*
(million drachmas)

Year	Group 1	Group 2	Group 3	Total	Conversion rates[a]
1926	3,654.3	3,337.0	3,013.6	10,004.9	1.00
1927	4,652.2	3,983.5	3,966.2	12,601.9	0.98
1928	4,485.0	3,850.9	4,073.2	12,409.1	1.00
1929	4,525.4	4,148.9	4,201.2	13,275.5	1.00
1930	3,488.5	3,682.1	3,353.6	10,525.2	1.00
1931	2,397.7	3,100.3	3,265.3	8,763.3	1.00
1932	1,623.0	1,584.5	1,876.0	5,083.5	1.55
1933	994.0	1,172.1	1,503.0	3,669.1	2.31
1934	1,144.5	1,358.8	1,241.1	3,744.4	2.31
1935	1,332.8	1,442.3	1,763.3	4,538.4	2.33

Notes: Group 1: Bulgaria, Egypt, India, The Netherlands, UK, USA; group 2: Austria, Belux, Czechoslovakia, France, Germany, Italy, Norway, Switzerland; group 3: Albania, Argentina, Brazil, Canada, Hungary, Poland, Romania, Sweden, Turkey, USSR, Yugoslavia.

[a] Conversion rates for current/stabilized drachmas.

Source: C. Christides, *Emporikoi sympsifismoi kai antallagai* (Athens, 1937), table 14; conversion rates from *OE 1939*, 13.

Greece's main weakness was that she lacked the bargaining strength to apply the clearing system to her traditional suppliers of imports. The foreign exchange bill for essential imports remained heavy even after 1932. In addition to wheat, fuel imports continued to be transacted through the free market. The British, in particular, refused to countenance a clearing agreement with Greece.[44] In general the most important clearings were not suggested by the Greek authorities but imposed upon them by Central European states which faced exchange shortages of their own but wished to secure supplies of Greek goods, chiefly tobacco. It is noteworthy, however, that in most cases these clearing accounts soon showed an imbalance against Greece. The exception, of course, was Germany, which will be discussed in greater detail later. As a result the effect of clearing agreements on Greece's exchange requirements was rather limited. In Table 8.2 Greece's trading partners are divided into groups (1) without clearing agreements, (2) with full clearings, (3) with partial clearings. Broadly speaking trade with countries in group 2

[44] FO 371/18393 R2383/18, Board of Trade–FO, 27 Oct. 1934.

was conducted without any foreign exchange flows (though only for as long as the agreement operated). Table 8.2 suggests that goods imported under full clearing agreements rarely constituted more than one-third of total Greek imports. If we omit Germany, it becomes clearer that the trend in other cases was for the percentage of goods imported in group 2 to fall. Heavy exports of tobacco to Germany under clearing necessitated corresponding imports of German goods, particularly after 1934. If we assume that at least two-thirds of the goods supplied from group 3 had to be paid for in foreign exchange, then it seems likely that over half Greece's total import bill still had to be met in exchange after 1931.

Nor did clearing agreements lead to any obvious switches in import supply. If we examine the supply of a number of major import items which could be obtained equally from clearing and non-clearing countries, we find no clear trend. British goods held up perhaps surprisingly well (despite the British Commercial Attaché's fears); exports of cotton thread actually increased their share of the Greek market dramatically after 1931, as did wool thread and yarn. On the other hand, British market share in coal and printed cotton textiles dropped precipitously, whilst German goods only began to increase their market share significantly from 1934 onwards.

To what extent did clearing agreements distort import prices? It was frequently asserted in Greece that for obvious reasons they had pushed prices up. The issue was particularly debated when in 1935 Greece's chronic surplus with Germany impelled the authorities to introduce legislation encouraging the import of German goods.[45] A report by the Director-General of the Ministry of the National Economy estimated that during 1935 out of total imports of 10,681 million drs., the overall loss came to 550 million drs.—or approximately 5% of the total import bill.[46] Another commentator, however, stressed that higher prices were observed for both imports and exports.[47] He stated that German goods were overpriced by 'up to 30%' and mentioned other cases, such as that of Czechoslovak sugar where he claimed that Greece agreed— according to the terms of the clearing—to pay 17% above world prices,

[45] FO 371/20388 R7584/87/19, 'Greece's Commercial Policy', H. C. Finlayson, 30 Nov. 1936; see also *MA*, 19 July 1936.

[46] Finlayson (n. 45) cites a figure of 650 million drachmas—this is probably a misprint; cf. AOS, *Peri tou tropou tis rythmiseos ton meta tis Germanias emporikon synallagon* (Athens, 1936), 15.

[47] Chadzivasileiou, *Kateflhynseis*, pp. 145–53.

TABLE 8.3. *Selected import items by supplier, 1931–1935*

Item, country	Drachma price (c.i.f.) 1931	% share of total Greek import volumes (price index for successive years (1931 = 100))				
		1931	1932	1933	1934	1935
Coal						
Germany	515.19	8.0 (100)	9.0 (101)	3.9 (132)	10.5 (123)	25.8 (112.1)
Turkey	325.60	8.5 (100)	14.1 (119)	22.7 (160.5)	17.1 (154)	9.1 (147.6)
UK	465.24	46.9 (100)	27.8 (115)	13.2 (174)	20.8 (144.5)	23.3 (133.3)
USSR	383.62	36.4 (100)	48.9 (125)	50.8 (151)	41.9 (134.5)	33.6 (137.6)
Iron ingots						
Belgium/ Luxembourg	1,855.40	74.8 (100)	86.6 (118)	87.4 (169)	18.2 (178.5)	9.9 (201.6)
France	1,857.50	9.7 (100)	5.7 (136)	3.4 (212)	23.1 (187)	3.1 (170.2)
Germany	2,556.30	14.0 (100)	6.8 (119)	8.3 (163)	55.4 (141)	72.8 (158.5)
Cotton thread						
France	263	16.8 (100)	9.1 (142.5)	9.0 (188)	8.3 (191.5)	2.1 (175.5)
Germany	177.50	8.9 (100)	6.6 (119.5)	2.1 (187)	6.0 (108.5)	5.3 (125.8)
Italy	114	20.5 (100)	15.9 (152)	11.4 (232.8)	10.4 (198)	5.2 (164.1)
UK	209	44.7 (100)	60.1 (115)	64.9 (139)	63.7 (205)	72.1 (111.5)
Printed cotton cloth						
Czechoslovakia	105.60	14.6 (100)	9.5 (135.5)	5.6 (200.5)	9.1 (177.6)	10.4 (190.8)
France	115.20	4.0 (100)	2.9 (143.2)	negl. (172.2)	negl. (161.9)	negl. (112.1)
Germany	100	7.5 (100)	7.8 (136.6)	7.9 (161.3)	15.7 (158.8)	34.8 (124.4)
Italy	93.20	30.7 (100)	23.3 (144.1)	16.9 (160.2)	16.6 (150.0)	18.9 (141.2)
UK	107.20	38.9 (100)	50.4 (102.7)	38.9 (143.4)	34.5 (132.2)	22.0 (135.9)

Item, country	Drachma price (c.i.f.) 1931	% share of total Greek import volumes (price index for successive years (1931 = 100))				
		1931	1932	1933	1934	1935
Wool thread/yarn						
Belgium	93.80	36.4 (100)	26.3 (127.8)	25.0 (186.5)	9.0 (225.7)	4.5 (136.7)
France	121.70	20.2 (100)	15.0 (151.7)	7.6 (197.2)	17.8 (184.6)	1.9 (183.5)
Germany	137.70	4.2 (100)	3.3 (144.7)	2.8 (195.6)	12.6 (153.6)	15.4 (150.5)
Italy	115.70	14.1 (100)	22.5 (157.4)	12.7 (198.1)	10.0 (204.7)	6.2 (153.8)
UK	127.10	15.8 (100)	25.7 (193.6)	44.4 (163.4)	44.8 (174.9)	59.8 (153.5)

Sources: Market shares of import volumes calculated from data in *AS*, various years. Import prices cited in C. Christides, *Emporikoi sympsifismoi kai antallagai* (Athens, 1937), 142–5.

but in practice paid at a rate 40% above world prices.[48] He also referred to imports from Balkan states, where the system of export 'primes' evolved by the Bank of Greece both stimulated Greek exports and encouraged importers to raise their prices.

Any calculation of consumer losses has to take account of the fact that the incidence of price distortion was not uniform. In the case of coal, for example, the British share of Greek imports fell from 96% of the total in 1924 to 13% in 1933. Officially the British protested that this decline reflected the effect of exchange controls and other restrictions on free trade. But privately the Board of Trade recognized that price trends rather than the implementation of clearings were responsible.[49] Even where imports from clearing countries replaced those outside the clearing system, it remains possible that this trend reflected price competitiveness and that import prices under such conditions remained at low levels by world standards.

Table 8.3 illustrates prices and market shares for a small number of key imports which came from both clearing and non-clearing suppliers. The economist Christides observed, on the basis of the price data incorporated in this table, that 'there seems to be no uniform influence of the clearings on prices'.[50] He admitted that in the case of other goods,

[48] Ibid. 146.   [49] FO 371/18405 R6094/5913/19, Board of Trade–FO, 27 Oct. 1934.
[50] C. Christides, *Emporikoi sympsifismoi kai antallagai* (Athens, 1937), 146.

namely industrial products, it was likely that there had been a rise in prices, but denied that this would have had a major impact on the overall import bill. The figures for coal imports seem to bear out the British Board of Trade's contention that price competition was maintained by countries linked by clearings with Greece. German coal in particular was cheap in drachma terms in 1935; Russian and Turkish coal prices, on the other hand, showed a slight increase relative to British prices. Processed iron imports shifted heavily from Belgium and Luxembourg to German suppliers: all three had clearings with Greece but German prices were again competitive. In the case of cotton and wool thread Britain competed successfully against suppliers in clearing countries. The price mechanism seems to have operated without major impediments in allocating market shares. As French and Italian prices rose relatively steeply, so their market share diminished. Germany, on the other hand, was successful in dampening down increases in the drachma price of her goods. In the case of printed cloth, the market appears to have operated even more competitively. The initial advantage British exporters derived from sterling's devaluation had disappeared by 1934, as both Germany and Italy succeeded in sharply reducing their export prices relative to British prices.

These price movements cast doubt on the view that the clearing with Germany was inherently exploitative. It should be pointed out that the Greek trade deficit with Germany in 1932–5 was not much greater than it had been before the crisis—this in contrast with Eastern Europe as a whole where the deficit with Germany superseded an earlier trade surplus. Up to 1936, unit values of German imports into Greece were only significantly above the average for any given commodity in the case of some 25% of the total imports from Germany. Even during 1936 German prices in most instances appear to have been no higher for most goods than those demanded by Greece's other suppliers. Thus it seems that at least before 1936 the price mechanism operated effectively for Greek importers over a wide range of major imports. In a number of instances, where imports through clearings were exorbitantly priced, the importer shifted to a cheaper source of supply. The popular view that clearing agreements led to increased import prices would seem to be exaggerated.[51]

---

[51] F. C. Child, *Theory and Practice of Exchange Control in Germany* (The Hague, 1958), 159–61; AOS, *Peri tou tropou tis rythmiseos ton meta tis Germanias emporikon synallagon*, 11; H. S. Ellis, *Exchange Control in Central Europe* (Cambridge, Mass., 1941), 257–69.

Tobacco and the German Connection

When discussing the implications of commercial bilateralism we need to look beyond its effect on consumer prices. There were good reasons why clearing agreements proliferated, and there *were* costs to be paid. An examination of the Greek–German clearing, which became the most bitterly discussed economic issue of 1935–6, illustrates how clearings could actually increase Greece's dependence on her traditional export markets, instead of yielding new ones, as their proponents had hoped. It may also illuminate the forces at work behind the expansion of German trade with the Balkans at this time. As I hope to make clear, the Greek trade surplus with Germany was due not so much to German cunning as to a combination of factors, among which we should number the rather unimpressive efforts of successive Greek governments to find alternative export markets as well as the need—for political reasons—to preserve by all possible means the export recovery, centred around tobacco, which began in 1934.

Greek tobacco exports had fallen continuously from early 1931 to early 1934. This was a rather longer fall than either of the preceding two downturns—1929–30 (8 months) and 1926–8 (20 months)—and it was deeper too than at any time since before 1925. Looked at over the longer term, the fall between 1931 and 1934 was an unusually prolonged continuation of a downward trend which had begun late in 1926. Since then, each peak had been lower than its predecessor and each trough had been deeper. It is a measure of the severity of the 1931–4 downswing that the upturn which might have been expected in the first half of 1932 was delayed until the second half of the year, and was then so faint as to be virtually imperceptible. Within the group of exporters of oriental leaf, the Greek product lost ground during the crisis to its Bulgarian and Turkish rivals, but recovered further than them in the upswing. This was because Greek tobacco was mainly used in relatively expensive cigarettes with a high positive income elasticity of demand. As consumption was reduced in Central Europe between 1931 and 1933, the Greek share of oriental tobacco exports fell from 49% to 42% of the total.

The Tsaldaris Government passed several measures to assist the tobacco merchants, who were burdened with unsold stocks and uncollectable loans to the growers. Perhaps because the merchants, despite their traditionally Venizelist allegiance, were clearly part of the bourgeois order, Tsaldaris was prepared to ignore criticisms from extreme *laissez-faire* elements within the Populist Party that supporting them was tantamount to state socialism! In 1933 the export tax on tobacco was substantially reduced, while, in the same year, negotiations began between the Ministry for the National Economy, the Bank of Greece, and the commercial banks for the formation of a consortium which proceeded to buy up old tobacco stocks from the merchants. This consortium operated alongside the Tobacco Organization which the Liberal Government had set up for a similar purpose two years earlier. By the end of 1934 both groups had succeeded in selling off a large part of their remaining stocks. In March 1934 the merchants strengthened their hand against the banks when the Government issued a decree suspending the seizure of collateral by the banks and other creditors from them. In vain did bank managers complain about a 'spiritual crisis' expressing itself through a widespread hostility towards 'organized capital': the decree, originally covering a six-month period, was renewed indefinitely. In June this measure was followed by an even more sweeping law which ordered the discharge of anyone declared bankrupt in the previous three years.[52]

TABLE 8.4. *Wages and incomes of tobacco workers, 1929–1935*

Year	Nominal daily wages (drachmas)		Real wages[a]		Nominal annual incomes (000 drachmas)		Real incomes[a]	
	Men	Women	Men	Women	Men	Women	Men	Women
1929	92.7	36.4	96	96	12.1	4.4	78	73
1930	96.6	36.0	113	107	13.8	8.6	93	86
1931	81.8	32.8	103	105	8.5	6.3	62	127
1932	71.2	28.0	82	82	7.6	4.5	50	83
1933	69.6	31.3	78	89	6.5	2.7	43	48
1934	73.8	34.1	82	96	11.1	3.7	71	66
1935	78.6	34.8	83	93	14.6	4.8	89	81

[a] Indices (1928 = 100) deflating nominal data by the cost-of-living index.

Sources: My calculations on the basis of wage and income data in AOS, *Epi tou zitimatos tou kapnou* (Athens, 1938); GPEK, Kavalla, *Deltion*, Aug. 1936; ibid., Dec. 1937; price index from *AS*, various issues.

[52] Angelopoulos, *Politikoi agones*, iii. 22–4; Bank of Athens, *Bulletin Économique et Financier*, 117 (Sept. 1934), 2,297; IBA, Kavalla, HYR 1932/3, 3; YR 1933/4, 8; YR 1934/5, 7; IBA, Salonika, YR 1933/4; 1934/5; FO 371/19517 R1078/1078, 'Conditions in the Patras Consular District during 1934'.

Less satisfactory—and a far greater worry politically—was the position of the tobacco workers whose incomes were more than halved in real terms between 1930 and 1933. Growing social unrest in the towns of northern Greece culminated in the strikes of July 1933 in Kavalla —the most serious such dispute for a decade. The demand for labour had been reduced by commercial stagnation, the suspension of public works in the vicinity, and finally by the small size of the 1932 tobacco harvest. Facing difficulties of their own, merchants took advantage of the workers' weak situation and tried once again to opt exclusively for cheap female labour in the warehouses. Early in July, the manager of the Beneveniste warehouse in Kavalla sacked his male workers and announced that henceforth he would employ only women. The workforce, male and female, responded by occupying the factory; within a day the strike had spread to other firms and Kavalla was placed under martial law. There can be no doubt that these strikes sprang from economic causes: even one of the Communist activists involved later wrote that the unrest had started spontaneously, springing not from party activity but from 'the need for self-preservation'.[53] On the other hand, Kavalla's reputation as a hotbed of labour activism ensured that the unrest would be interpreted in Athens as a challenge to bourgeois rule.

As tobacco workers in Salonika and Volos struck in sympathy, Tsaldaris sent Miltiades Mantas, the Minister for Thrace, to Kavalla to arbitrate between workers and merchants. In the town itself, the strikers were supported not just by other workers and traders but even by the local mayor. As in the strike in Salonika three years later the wide impact of the tobacco crisis over northern Greece made the unrest a reflection of regional as much as of class tensions. Not only did northern Greece—like the other outlying regions—suffer the drawbacks of being ruled from Athens with little administrative autonomy of its own; it was also heavily Venizelist in sympathy yet ruled now by an anti-Venizelist administration. Prominent in this was the renegade Venizelist General Kondylis, who filled the gendarmerie with his belligerent followers, thereby adding the passions of the *dichasmos* to labour disputes. It did not help that Mantas came from an Attic constituency and was also reputed to be a fanatical anti-Venizelist. Thus the Tsaldaris Government, which a few months earlier had pledged to review the

---

[53] G. Pegios, *Apo tin istoria tou syndikalistikou kinimatos tis Kavallas, 1922–1953* (Athens, 1984), 73–82; *Tachydromos tis Kavallas*, various issues.

entire tobacco question, and saw the dispute as an opportunity to contrast the Liberal Party's known ties with the merchants with its own populist credentials, was no better placed to mediate between workers and employers than the Liberals had been.[54]

Indeed although Mantas helped to negotiate an agreement between the workers and the merchants, the Government failed to ratify most of its provisions. The merchants' agreeing to restrict the extent of cheap processing methods had evidently been contingent on the Government pledging a tougher line against the tobacco unions. Indeed no less than this was implied by Mantas himself, who informed the Senate, after accepting that the main cause of the strike had been economic deprivation, that 'I told [the merchants] that as the State under the submitted bill had fulfilled the demands of the workers, it had the power and moral authority, having given something to them, to attack all anarchic elements and to enforce the law. The tobacco merchants accepted that view.'[55] The Government failed to embark on the course of action that it accepted was necessary for a long-term solution to the tobacco problem —the rural resettlement of part of Kavalla's refugee population. Instead that summer, under the provisions of the *Idionymon*, the authorities in Kavalla closed down union offices and made many arrests and deportations. The predictable result of these policies was that political opinion in Kavalla shifted dramatically to the Left. At local elections in February 1934 proponents of a popular front strategy in the KKE received a strong boost when the Communist candidate, a local tobacco worker, was elected mayor.[56]

The news from 'Red Kavalla' (followed by a similar result in the nearby town of Serres) shocked Athens and underlined the seriousness of the tobacco crisis, which by the beginning of 1934 was passing through its worst phase.[57] The Government's immediate response was to use the *Idionymon* to remove Communist members of the Kavalla town council and send them to jail or into internal exile. Some would remain in prison for a decade. More than repression, however, was demanded of the state. After the failure of Pesmazoglu's bill to set up a new trade organization, Populist commercial policy had, as we have

---

[54] FO 371/19519 R5639/5639, 'Leading Personalities'; FO 371/20389 R4167/220, Walker–Eden, 9 July 1936.

[55] *ESG*, 30 Aug. 1933, 352.

[56] Pegios, *Istoria*, 86–7; D. Koutsoulakis, *I defteri dekaetia tou KKE 1929–1939* (Athens, 1984), 70–110.

[57] *EV*, 29 Jan. 1934.

seen, been confined to emergency makeshifts—tax reductions and debt moratoria. Various groups demanded a more systematic response. Growers called for the fixing of official support prices such as existed for currants, and criticized the Government for its failure to promote exports.[58]

In fact at least two initiatives were being pursued in an attempt to improve the position, though both were fraught with difficulties. One was an attempt—spearheaded not by the Government but by Papanastasiou and Bakalbasis—to establish a cartel in oriental tobacco with Turkey and Bulgaria. A conference in Constantinople in 1932 resolved to found a common sales office. However, the Bulgarians were hostile to the idea, and it proved to be no more successful than other schemes for common action by the Balkan states. The spread of diplomatic tensions throughout South-Eastern Europe in the mid-1930s, and the formation of the Balkan Union, which Bulgaria remained outside, undermined any possibility of joint action in the economic sphere.[59]

The second proposal, to link tobacco exports to foreign debt repayments, had first been mooted in March 1932 and taken up by a variety of politicians from across the political spectrum, including Papanastasiou, Mylonas, Kafandaris, and Loverdos. One proponent advocated using a national trade organization as a way of breaking into the British market, warning with some foresight that 'today the fate of our chief product and therefore the fate of the drachma, lies in German hands. In more normal times it is inevitable that German cigarette manufacturers will exploit our producers. At the first moment of crisis in Germany we too will be wrecked.'[60]

Both Venizelists and anti-Venizelists tried to make Greece's creditors aware of the need to link financial and commercial flows, if something was to be salvaged of the pre-crisis pattern of international economic relations. When Loverdos visited the World Economic Conference in London in June 1933 as Minister of Finance he repeated these proposals, but got no further than did his successor, Pesmazoglu, in London two years later, despite the support of the British Foreign Office. The real stumbling block was the British Treasury, always reluctant to sacrifice financial obligations on the altar of long-term

---

[58] Ibid., 1 Feb. 1934.

[59] *OA* 795, 6 May 1933; 875, 17 Nov. 1934; P. Papastratis, 'Apo ti Megali Idea sti Valkaniki Enosi', in Mavrogordatos and Chadziiosif (eds.), *Venizelismos*, pp. 417–37.

[60] D. Filaretos, *Dia tou kapnou i anastatheropoiisis ton ellinikon oikonomikon* (Athens, 1932), 28.

strategic or political interest. As a result the British Government refused
to take measures to raise imports of Greek tobaccos from their very low
level. It was the same story three years later as Britain awoke to the extent
of German economic power in the Balkans, when there were renewed
attempts to link tobacco exports and the debt problem. Despite the joint
pleadings of Metaxas, Neville Chamberlain, and the British Foreign
Office, British cigarette manufacturers refused to consider voluntarily
increasing their purchases of Greek tobacco. It is not surprising then
that Loverdos and Pesmazoglu failed to achieve what Metaxas—in the
more favourable conditions of the late 1930s—was also unable to bring
about.[61]

The story of the Populist Government's attempts to encourage
tobacco exports was thus a catalogue of failures: failure to create a new
mechanism for the promotion of trade, failure to pursue the possibility
of a producers' cartel, and finally failure to find new markets for tobacco
by persuading the British and French Governments to accept a linkage
with the debt question. Only the first of these failures was a matter of
domestic politics alone; the others are largely explicable in terms of
external forces over which the Greeks could have had little control.
However, the strikes in northern Greece emphasized the grave social
implications of a continuation of the slump in the tobacco trade. When
market forces, in the guise of the Greek–German clearing, suddenly
brought the slump to an end, it was not likely that the Populist
Government would do anything to impede them.

The recovery of tobacco exports in spring 1934 was remarkable; in the
first quarter more tobacco was sold than in the whole of 1933. The
following year sales were even higher; as a result, Greek tobacco exports
rose from 34.7 thousand tonnes in 1933 to 50.2 thousand in 1935. The
value of tobacco purchased from the growers rose from 826 to 1,648
million drachmas over this period, and the value of aggregate workers'
incomes from 168.9 to 352.5 million drachmas.[62] In September 1934,
one observer in Kavalla noted that 'the sale at good prices of the 1933
tobacco crops, and two consecutive good crops of cereals have greatly
improved the position of the agrarian population of our district and have

---

[61] M. Pelt, 'Greece and Germany's Policy towards South-Eastern Europe, 1932–
1940', *Epsilon*, 2 (1988), 55–77; M. Mazower, 'Economic Diplomacy between Great
Britain and Greece in the 1930s', *Journal of European Economic History*, 17(3) (Winter
1988), 603–19; D. Kaiser, *Economic Diplomacy and the Origins of the Second World War*
(Princeton, NJ, 1980), 96.
[62] GPEK, Kavalla, *Deltion*, Feb. 1936, 5; May 1938, 19; June 1938, 17.

greatly reduced the indebtedness of the peasants to the Agrarian Bank'. The following year it was reported that 'the districts of Eastern Macedonia and Western Thrace have almost recovered from the wounds caused by the crisis and are now entering into the state of sound health'.[63] The chief causes of the upswing were, on the one hand, the revival of consumption abroad, and, on the other, the cigarette manufacturers' need to replenish stocks, which had been allowed to run down after 1931.

The only disquieting feature of the recovery was the increasing dependence of tobacco on the German market; indeed, the revival of German demand for Greek tobacco was largely responsible for improved export performance overall after 1933. In 1935 Germany took over 40% of Greek tobacco exports, around one-fifth of total export earnings. The growth of trade took place under the Greek–German clearing, which had shown a credit balance in Greece's favour since its establishment in 1932; however, from late 1934 onwards, under the stimulus of Schacht's New Plan, the imbalance began to reach worrying proportions. Many Greeks assumed that this state of affairs had been deliberately engineered by the Germans, buying tobacco at high prices and inflicting over-priced goods on Greece. But this seems to be too simple: the evidence of local buying patterns indicates that before 1936 at least German buyers were not paying especially high prices for tobacco. Nor, as has been shown earlier, do German goods seem to have been overpriced. The problem was rather that, firstly, the Greek authorities were reluctant for domestic political reasons to limit German tobacco purchases, and secondly, the economic recovery within Germany had—as in Greece—diverted production towards the domestic market, limiting the range of goods available for export to Greece. Another important factor underlying these developments was the manner in which the Bank of Greece operated the clearing: by assuming the entire exchange risk (of a depreciation of the Reichsmark), making immediate payment to the exporter in drachmas of the sum corresponding to his claim, the Bank encouraged exports and increased inflationary pressures by swelling the money supply before ensuring a supply of commodities to soak up the demand thus created. Discussing these problems with Economics Minister Schacht in Berlin in 1934, Pesmazoglu and Varvaressos agreed that Greece's credit on the German clearing should be offset under a trilateral arrangement against her

---

[63] IBA, Kavalla, YR 1933/4, 8; YR 1934/5, 1.

deficit in trade with Romania and Yugoslavia. But, as the tobacco market boomed, the imbalance continued to grow.[64]

Practically the only German commodity which could be traded in sufficient quantities for tobacco was armaments. In 1934 the Greek authorities had announced a tender for munitions deliveries payable by Greek goods, and the following year German arms manufacturers promoted a similar idea through a specially formed export consortium. Their task was eased by renewed rumours of an imminent devaluation of the mark (since any devaluation would have reduced the value of Greece's credit balance). In the summer of 1935 German importers were reportedly investing heavily in tobacco stocks to hedge against this eventuality.[65] The devaluation scare also led the Bank of Greece to put pressure on the Government to remedy the situation: in a dramatic move in February 1936 the Bank announced that henceforth it would pay only 60% in cash to exporters to Germany, and would hold over the remainder until compensation, thus threatening to put a brake on the tobacco trade in the coming season. Although the caretaker Demertzis Government supported the Bank at first, it took fright at the immediate reaction from virtually the entire business and commercial world of northern Greece. Tobacco exporters urged that if the Bank was reluctant to assume the exchange risk, then it should be carried by the state itself. From Salonika the Chamber of Commerce, the Merchants' Association, the Federation of Macedonian Industrialists, the League of Agricultural Co-operatives, and others joined in addressing an appeal to the Demertzis Government to recognize that 'from the good or bad fortune of tobacco alone depends the well-being or economic collapse and social turbulence, not only of northern Greece, but of the entire state'.[66]

The exporters' wishes were granted, the Government capitulated and the Bank of Greece was empowered to make drachma advances against state guarantee. In return for a 15-year loan from the Bank, the state acquired the sum of 22 million Reichsmarks. What the episode confirmed was the political impossibility of remedying the clearing imbalance by reducing Greek exports; reflecting this, a report by the Supreme Economic Council argued in May 1936 that the only way out

[64] Chadzivasileiou, *Kateftbynseis*, p. 124; L. Neal, 'The Economics and Financing of Bilateral Clearing Agreements: Germany 1934–38', *Economic History Review*, 2nd ser. (1979), 391–404; Kaiser, *Economic Diplomacy*, pp. 130–69.
[65] FO 371/19517 R4782/646, Waterlow–FO, 26 July 1935.
[66] GPEK, Kavalla, *Deltion*, Feb. 1936; Apr. 1936.

of a dangerous situation was to increase imports. The Council's arguments were reinforced by the series of strikes which swept northern
Greece the same month, underlining the volatility of the region and
exciting fears that the descent into disorder which was being reported in
Spain might be repeated there. By now Demertzis had been succeeded
as Prime Minister by Metaxas, a man more concerned than his predecessor about Greece's military preparedness. When Hjalmar Schacht
visited Athens the following month, the possibility of a devaluation of the
Reichsmark was raised once again, and this time the effect was galvaniz-
ing. Varvaressos was sent to Berlin the following month, where an
agreement was reached on the financing of future arms orders.[67]

The political significance of the German clearing for Greece's
foreign policy orientation turned out to be rather more limited than
worried observers at the British Foreign Office had feared. Even after
the 1937 Greek–German trade agreement, it is doubtful whether the
Germans entertained serious thoughts of removing Greece from the
British sphere of influence. More crucially, Metaxas himself never
questioned the importance of the British connection. However, the
issue did have political overtones: those powers—like Britain and
France—whose economic and political influence had been paramount
in the 1920s proved unable to adapt their financial and commercial
policies to the needs of debtor nations in the following decade. Germany
was simply a better trading partner so far as the latter were concerned: in
commerce, at least, the *laissez-faire* of the Western democracies seemed
outmoded when set against the achievements of the New Plan.

Set in an international context, the impact of the crisis on Greek trade
does not seem especially severe. Greek export volumes fell far less than
in most countries—a peak to trough fall after 1929 of only 21%
compared with 38% for developed economies and 40% for Latin
America. Similarly, the peak to trough fall in her capacity to import was
only 25% against 30% for developed economies and 54% in Latin
America.[68] The recovery in import volumes began in 1934 and within
three years had surpassed the pre-crisis peak. The visible trade deficit

[67] *Documents on German Foreign Policy*, series C, vol. iv (Washington, DC, 1962),
162–3, 908–12, 1,089–93; v (Washington, 1966), 642–6; Pelt, 'Greece and Germany's
Policy towards South-Eastern Europe', pp. 59–61.
[68] A. Maddison, 'Growth, Crisis and Interdependence, 1929–38 and 1973–83',
OECD, Paris, 1985.

fell as a percentage of export earnings from 86.1 in 1929–30 to 56.1 in 1935–6.

It is, however, doubtful whether these achievements were the outcome of official policy. As we have seen, state intervention was limited and faltering. A Ministry of Trade was not formed in Greece until after the Second World War, and in our period commercial questions were chiefly handled by a section in the Ministry for the National Economy with a staff of three men![69] The plans for tighter public control of key commodities were abandoned, while import restrictions, with their six-monthly terms, reflected the Populist Government's reluctance to rule out an early return to free trade. The import quotas themselves put established traders in a powerful position, resulting according to one report 'in a new charge in favour not of the public purse but of a fixed class of merchants, which provokes the indignation of public opinion'. From the port of Volos it was reported in 1934 that 'owing to the restriction of imports the merchants of colonial products had large profits on a rather limited scale of turnover, having an understanding as to the prices of sale'.[70] Or, as another commentator put it, with slight exaggeration, 'the *idea* of the restrictions (which in reality did not exist) influenced consumers and led them to accept without protest a rise in prices which profited import merchants and retailers'.[71] In fact there were protests and import restrictions *did* exist, though their effectiveness in saving foreign exchange was not great: the chief drain on the reserves, cereal imports, remained unaffected due to the Government's fear that quotas would raise bread prices.

Neither government policy nor the impact of the crisis itself had much effect on the structure of Greece's export trade, which remained dependent on too few commodities and too few markets. Domestic industry remained uncompetitive abroad, for reasons to be discussed in the next chapter. Currant exports to Great Britain held up well during the early 1930s, but overall export recovery was linked to the tobacco trade, and in particular to German demand. In effect, despite the complicated machinery of state regulation, the recovery of trade had been left to the market. As, for example, tobacco prices rose again under the stimulus of German demand, cultivation expanded in an uncontrolled fashion reminiscent of the 1920s, and, from the Bank of Greece,

[69] *Proia*, 29 July 1933.
[70] Bank of Athens, *Bulletin Économique et Financier*, 118 (Dec. 1934), 2,350; IBA, Volos, YR 1933/4, 5.
[71] G. Iliades, in *MA*, 9 May 1936.

Tsouderos warned that 'the dangers of over-production have been entirely forgotten'.[72] But by and large it was only an intellectual élite that called for still further state intervention in trade; as the retreat over import monopolies showed, the Tsaldaris Government was less moved by the theoretical criticisms of bankers and university professors than by the prospect of losing its hold over the electorally crucial petty bourgeoisie, who reacted strongly to any infringement of entrepreneurial liberty. It was the thought that the Populists were vulnerable on that score that led none other than Ioannis Metaxas, seeking a way to revive his flagging political fortunes in the summer of 1935, to launch an attack in the Constituent Assembly on the Populists' *excessive* interventionism and to pose as the defender of the economic freedom of the Greek citizen. Acutely sensitive to such accusations, which were directed at their most loyal constituency, the Populists were inhibited from justifying with any vigour the policy that in their halting fashion they felt obliged to pursue. Their trade policy thus revealed a hesitancy and lack of confidence that hostile critics attributed to 'the parliamentary mentality, the endless debating, weakness of will and absence of moral courage' which a more authoritarian form of government promised to eradicate.[73]

[72] Bank of Greece, *The Economic Situation in Greece and the Bank of Greece in 1936* (Athens, 1937), 11.

[73] FO 371/19508 R4305/34, Waterlow–Eden, 8 July 1935; A. Bernaris, *I diarthrosis kai ai prospatheiai prosarmogis tis ellinikis oikonomias* (Athens, 1933), 102; Chadzivasileiou, *Katefthynseis*, p. 86.

9

RECOVERY AND THE STATE

Speaking about the internal situation, Mr Pangalos emphasized
that there would surely appear some future Greek Dostoevsky to
describe our current debacle under the title 'Madhouse or State?'

(*Eleftheron Vima*, 1 June 1935)

The 1929–32 crisis brought to the boil an old question, simmering
since the First World War if not before: how 'viable' (*viosimos*) was
Greece? The economic journals and even on occasions the daily Press
ran articles which debated topics such as 'Can Greece achieve agricultural self-sufficiency?' or 'Is Greek industry viable?'[1] As Greece
moved towards autarky, some differences of approach towards this issue
emerged between Liberals and Populists. The Populists were forced to
clarify their thinking on economic matters, which had previously been
rather unformed and *ad hoc*. Now they attacked Venizelos for his
overestimation of the capabilities of the domestic economy, and argued
that economic development alone could not solve Greece's social
problems; the only real solution to these, they claimed, was emigration.
Populist rhetoric praised the smallholder and trader—though more for
their supposed moral and social virtues than for their economic role
—and lashed out at the 'plutocrats'.

The elderly Konstantine Angelopoulos, briefly Tsaldaris's Finance
Minister in the winter of 1932, may have been one of the more eccentric
members of the Populist Party, but his views on economics reflected
mainstream anti-Venizelist thinking. He denounced the 1928 stabilization of the drachma for its 'pitiful consequences' and the 'total disaster
which it brought to the country'. He was strongly opposed to the idea
that in the aftermath of the crisis 'the state should turn itself into a
merchant, entrepreneur or industrialist' or even that it should interfere
with the workings of the market in any form. Nor, for similar reasons,

---

[1] e.g. *E*, 1 Jan. 1933; *OT*, 16 Apr. 1933; also, C. Chadziiosif, 'Apopseis gyro apo tin
"viosimotita" tis Ellados kai to rolo tis viomichanias', *Afieroma ston Niko Svorono*, ii
(Rethymno, 1986), 330–68.

did he approve of what he described as the 'monstrous, concentrated power' of the major banks.[2]

The main Populist accusation against Venizelos was that he had been too sanguine about the possibilities for industrialization, whose key importance the Liberal leader had again highlighted in his electoral campaign in the spring of 1933. To the Salonika Chamber of Commerce he had stressed that it would have to be industry which helped find a way out of the crisis and provided new employment in the future for the country's rapidly growing population.[3] For the Populists much domestic industry was parasitic, kept alive with tariff protection and other concessions. Thus, when the Liberals lost the 1933 election, they gave way—after the confusion of the Plastiras coup attempt—to a Populist Government which it would be little exaggeration to say was ideologically committed to doing as little as possible to preclude Greece's eventual return to the world of *laissez-faire.*

How ironic then that a striking feature of Greece's economic experience in the early 1930s was the speed of her domestic recovery! Industrial growth rates after 1932 were surpassed only by the Soviet Union and Japan. In agriculture, too, the collapse of world trade redirected production towards the home market. As one observer noted: 'Our agricultural production has been marked by considerable progress, despite the international crisis, which has influenced only—and then provisionally—tobacco production. This progress is due notably . . . to the policy of "autarky".'[4] The country's overall dependence on imports fell sharply: comparing 1928–32 with 1933–7, we find that the import share of domestic consumption fell from 38% to 25% for manufactured goods, 67% to 32% for foodstuffs, and 64% to 27% for wheat alone.[5]

Yet, as the Populist response in its own way suggested, economic growth under autarky was not an unmixed blessing: agriculture became *less* intensive, industrial competitiveness declined whilst the old export ports stagnated and business activity became concentrated in the Athens–Piraeus area. Above all, autarky inevitably altered the role of the state. In the spring of 1932 John Drosopoulos, Governor of the National Bank of Greece, had warned that:

Greece must organize herself as an up-to-date economic state, and tend to the increase of her production by improving the imperfect methods now in use,

---

[2] K. Angelopoulos, *Politikoi agones, 1892–1934*, iii (Athens, 1934), 29, 93.
[3] Chadziiosif, 'Apopseis gyro apo tin "viosimotita" tis Ellados', p. 347.
[4] *OE 1935* (Athens, 1937), 24.
[5] *Ta deka eti tis Trapezis tis Ellados, 1928–1938* (Athens, 1938), 62–3.

in order that she may become as self-sufficient as possible with respect to necessities. Private enterprise is inadequate, under present circumstances, to the task of organizing and bearing the burden of this endeavour. It is therefore clearly the duty of the state.[6]

Import controls involved the state in decisions about the allocation of resources; rising prices led to popular pressure for intervention on behalf of consumers against producers; low wages and high profits posed the question of how the benefits of protectionism should be divided between capital and labour. The collapse of *laissez-faire* led to calls for greater planning from above, replacing the anarchy of market individualism with—in the words of Panayiotis Kanellopoulos— 'concentration, unification of systems, obedience to one central authority'.[7] Yet while the upswing thus set new tasks and created new demands and expectations, the Populist administrations in power were reluctant to respond to them. This chapter charts the dimensions of the recovery, its limitations, and the tensions it created.

The Agricultural Recovery

The rapid depreciation of the drachma after April 1932 provided the chief stimulus for import-substitution, though it affected some commodities more than others: while the prices of exports and non-traded goods remained depressed—thanks to considerable destocking by merchants for largely financial reasons—devaluation pushed up import prices almost immediately. After falling slightly in 1931, import prices rose more than 15% relative to other prices during 1932. Nor was this favourable trend entirely reversed over the next four years—even in 1936 the margin in favour of import prices was still around 5% higher than it had been in spring 1931, before the financial crisis.

  This movement benefited domestic producers of importables, both in industry, which was almost entirely import-substituting in character (industrial exports were negligible, to Venizelos's disgust), and in agriculture. In our discussion of the recovery, let us begin with the latter, for though agriculture is often given a secondary role in discussions of import-substitution, where a high percentage of the population depends on farming, as in most of Southern and Eastern Europe, the recovery of

---

[6] NBG, *Report for the Year 1931 of the Governor of the National Bank of Greece* (Athens, 1932), 44.

[7] P. Kanellopoulos, *Ai koinonikai asfaliseis kai o nearos ellinikos nomos* (Athens, 1932), 14.

TABLE 9.1. *The composition of crop output at constant prices*
(% of total output)

Period (average)	Crop output at 1928 prices		Crop output at 1932 prices		Crop output at 1936 prices	
	Non-export[a]	Export[b]	Non-export[a]	Export[b]	Non-export[a]	Export[b]
1924–30	48.8	51.2	54.3	45.7	53.1	46.9
1931–7	59.1	40.9	66.5	33.5	64.8	35.2

[a] Cereals, pulses, vegetables, cotton, other industrial plants, 80% of olive oil output, 50% of olives.
[b] Tobacco, must, currants, 20% of olive oil output, 50% of olives.

Sources: Output and price data from A. Boyazoglu, *Contribution à l'étude de l'économie rurale de la Grèce* (Paris, 1931), *passim*; *OE 1938* (Athens, 1939).

peasant incomes was a pre-condition for industrial growth in a closed economy. Just as poor harvests depressed the economy before 1932, so higher agricultural output stimulated it. In addition, Greece benefited for two special reasons: the first was that wheat was an import-substitute (as it was not in most of Eastern Europe), which meant it benefited from the move towards autarky; the second was that the beneficiaries were mostly smallholders rather than owners of large estates, thereby fuelling the demand for items of mass consumption rather than luxury goods.

The expansion of the cultivated area under importables from 1932 contrasted with the performance of export crops, which either expanded more slowly or not at all. Scholars have pointed out that the gradual

TABLE 9.2. *Cultivated area of major crops* (1928 = 100)

Crop	1924–30 average	1931–7 average	Increase (%)
Wheat	102.0	149.6	46.7
Other cereals	105.1	135.9	29.3
Vegetables	106.4	171.3	61.0
Cotton	61.6	201.1	146.5
Currants	111.7	139.0	24.4
Tobacco	88.6	82.6	−6.8
TOTAL AREA	101.7	138.8	36.5

Source: Data in *OE 1937* (Athens, 1938), 134.

expansion of the cultivated area was characteristic of the economic evolution of Eastern Europe in the inter-war period, in contrast with Western Europe, where the cultivated area remained virtually unchanged. It was precisely the backwardness of the economies of Eastern Europe which seems to have provided 'reserves' for economic growth. A similar argument can be applied to Greece too.[8]

Land which had previously been left fallow or used for grazing was gradually brought into cultivation. One should also mention the contribution of the reclaimed areas of northern Greece that had been the subject of the Liberal Government's public works programme, though the impact of this was relatively restricted: despite the surprisingly high level of expenditures, which after 1931 were financed exclusively from the regular budget, by 1936 less than 40,000 hectares out of an anticipated total of 276,000 hectares had been handed over to cultivators.[9] Much more substantial was the growing contribution generally of the provinces of northern Greece, which had of course been the focus for the land reforms of the 1920s. In Macedonia and Thrace—the main areas of tobacco cultivation in the late 1920s—import-substitution proceeded more rapidly than elsewhere. In 1933–7 in these two provinces the area cultivated with wheat increased by over 70% compared with the period 1928–32, while yields rose by 35%. Total cereal output there more than trebled between 1930 and 1934. This may help to explain the improvement in the yields of importables in the 1930s, since the land in these areas was more fertile than in the south. Since Greek crop yields were among the lowest in Europe, a low absolute increase in yields looked impressive in relative terms. In this sense too, perhaps, backwardness provided potential for growth.[10]

Wheat yields had been improved, however, by something more significant than expansion into the fertile lands of the north. For some time before 1932, civil servants had urged the Liberal Government to finance the diffusion of more modern farming techniques in the countryside. Although KEPES, the state wheat marketing agency, played an increasingly important role in protecting Greek farmers from the deflationary effects of falling world prices, the failure of the 1930 harvest had led the Ministry of Agriculture to stress that the policy of

[8] I. Berend and G. Ranki, 'L'Évolution économique de l'Europe orientale entre les deux guerres mondiales', *Annales ESC*, 33 (1978), 389–405.

[9] *OE 1936* (Athens, 1937), 199. The outcome was not dissimilar in Fascist Italy where the much-heralded land reclamation schemes also yielded meagre fruits: G. Toniolo, *L'economia dell'Italia fascista* (Bari, 1980), 156–7.

[10] AOS, *Epi tou georgikou provlimatos tis choras* (Athens, 1939), 156, 159.

support purchases alone would not solve the problem of reducing Greece's dependence on cereal imports.[11] The overriding need was to improve cultivation techniques and debate centred upon how best to achieve this. A report written by the Director of KEPES at the request of the Ministry and of Venizelos himself, criticized the existing lack of co-ordination among government departments, and called for a 'weighty, unified and well-researched programme' of agricultural development.[12] An effort should be made to improve yields by changing systems of crop rotation and by supplying improved strains of seed, more closely adapted to the Greek climate. The author also argued that peasants were supporting uneconomically high levels of livestock: they should reduce these, and switch from growing maize for their animals to wheat for themselves. However, the report underlines that improvements might be of limited utility, and that self-sufficiency in wheat should be regarded as the possible consequence rather than the direct aim of an improved system of cultivation: smallholders should diversify rather than concentrate upon wheat production since at current yields the income from the latter was so low.

This document should be seen within a general context of calls for greater state involvement in agriculture. Mussolini's Italy was a powerful symbol in the minds of many interventionist-minded civil servants, who up to 1932 saw Venizelos as a similar guarantor of stability. The agricultural crisis of the late 1920s, they argued, had left the Greek public passive and pessimistic about the future: government action was vital to restore economic health. Commentators appealed to the example of Fascist Italy as a model of the 'active State' and insisted that 'we must concentrate on winning the battle for agriculture'.[13] The low standard of living in the countryside threatened the social fabric of the nation since it led to a great influx into the towns, where 'the social and moral climate was worse' and where newcomers were exposed to 'subversive propaganda'.[14] Moreover, the peasants ignored the widespread unemployment in the towns and the fact that there was no margin for subsistence as there was in the village. From KEPES and the Ministry of Agriculture civil servants called for a 'large and systematic programme'. The lack of such a programme was a common criticism aimed at the

[11] Ministry of Agriculture, *Ta pepragmena tou Ypourgeiou Georgias kata tin televtaian tetraetian 1928–1932* (Athens, 1932), 47–56.
[12] S. Kypriades, *I organosis tis sitoparagogis mas* (Athens, 1931).
[13] L. Polychronis, *Skepseis epi tou georgikou mas provlimatos* (Athens, 1931), 10–13.
[14] Ibid. 59.

Liberal Government, by the Agrarians and Papanastasiou's Farmer-Worker Party on the Left, and by conservative interventionists.[15]

Low yields and poor cultivation techniques left farmers exposed to the hazards of weather and disease: the losses on both accounts could be substantial. In the fertile plain of Serres hail, drought, flooding, and disease led to average crop losses of 40% over a ten-year period. Crops were frequently damaged because of their poor resistance to winter rains and summer drought. From Larissa—a rich farming district—the manager of the local Ionian Bank reported late in 1930 that 'up to May last . . . a very abundant crop was expected and we expected to do good and profitable business on cereals. Unfortunately, the continuous rains during June and the first days of July have nearly destroyed the whole of the crops.' In Tripolis, in the Peloponnese, it was reported that 'this year's crop in cereals . . . was extremely poor, hardly reaching 15% of the average yearly production, while that of vineyards has been entirely destroyed'. The failure of the 1930 harvest drew attention for the first time to the possibility that the quickest and cheapest route to improved cereal yields might be through improved strains of wheat.[16]

The so-called Crop Improvement Centres had been conducting experiments with new wheat strains since 1925, building on work begun

TABLE 9.3.   *KEPES operations, 1930–1937*

Year	Wheat concentrated by KEPES as % of total harvest	KEPES average support price (dr./kg.)	KEPES protection[a] (%)
1930	9.4	4.9	−2.5
1931	12.2	4.5	+36.4
1932	16.4	5.9	+77.3
1933	28.2	5.9	+41.4
1934	26.6	5.7	+43.4
1935	26.2	5.5	+23.2
1936	6.3	5.8	+0.1
1937	14.2	6.6	−7.7

[a] Average support price/(import price + tariff).

Source: AOS, *Epi tou georgikou mas provlimatos* (Athens, 1939), 150, 178.

[15] D. Pournaras, *I oikonomiki thesis ton agroton* (Athens, 1932); also AOS, *Ta metra pros epavxisin tis enchoriou sitoparagogis* (Athens, 1934), 30.

[16] *E* 31, 2 Aug. 1930; Ypourgeion tis Georgias, *Pepragmena*, pp. 47–56; IBA, Larissa, YR 1929/30, 2; IBA, Tripolis, YR 1929/30, 1.

TABLE 9.4. *Wheat harvests, yields, and cultivated area*

Period (average)	Cultivated area (000 hectares)	Yields (kg./ha.)	Harvests (000 tonnes)
1928–32	563	604	340
1933–7	804	886	712

Source: AOS, *Epi tou georgikou mas provlimatos* (Athens, 1939), 132–7.

at the Ministry of Agriculture in 1923. Based at first in Thessaly, they later extended operations into Macedonia and Thrace. The initial tests suggested that use of Italian and Australian strains could better the performance of local wheats by more than 50%.[17] They were more resistant to pests and ripened earlier, thus avoiding much of the driest summer weather. After the 1930 harvest, when many growers were left without seed for the following year, the state financed large imports of seed from Italy, Cyprus, and Turkey.[18] By 1932 the new strains were being widely used in parts of Macedonia, while in Epiros, where the previous year's harvest had been blighted by scoriasis and in some cases completely wiped out, the introduction of Cypriot wheat led to greatly increased yields, due largely to earlier ripening.

In general the peasants belied their conservative reputation by responding readily to the opportunities offered by the combination of guaranteed prices and higher yields. Use of the new varieties spread rapidly. However, these improvements were chiefly confined to the plains, and productivity gains were less striking in the hills. They were also effected despite a counterproductive KEPES policy of buying in the new 'Montana' wheat at a lower price than traditional strains. But the success of the scheme in the north of the country led the Director of the Crop Improvement Centres to predict—correctly as it turned out—in 1934 that harvests of 750,000 tonnes would eventually be achieved.[19] An expansion of the cultivated area coincided with a definite, if variable, improvement in yields—so that average harvests between 1933 and 1937 were twice the level of the 1928–32 average.

Although the incentives provided by KEPES support buying had been felt as world prices fell between 1927 and 1931, they actually intensified thereafter. Imported wheat prices rose after 1931, but they

[17] *E* 157, 1 Jan. 1933. [18] *E* 132, 10 July 1932.
[19] *OE 1934* (Athens, 1935), 223.

failed to rise to the full extent of the drachma depreciation—thanks partly to a deliberate government policy of advancing exchange for cereal purchases at a low rate.[20] KEPES support prices, on the other hand, rose sharply in 1932, thereby increasing the level of protection of domestic producers. Although there is no archival evidence to explain this policy, one plausible explanation is that it formed part of an attempt by the Liberal Government to counter the effects of the crisis on the agricultural sector on the eve of the autumn general election. But it is equally likely that the financial crisis had strengthened forces in favour of an effective stimulus to wheat growers. Between 1931 and 1935, in the period when its intervention provided a high degree of protection, KEPES became a major force in the Greek wheat market. Its purchases amounted at their peak to almost one-third of the entire harvest.[21]

However, the wheat support price was never raised above the level at which it had been set in 1932. KEPES price support acted counter-cyclically, cushioning producers at times of falling world prices and reducing the margin of protection when world prices began to rise. The economist Nikos Mousmoutis noted that agricultural producer prices generally continued to be influenced far more by imported wheat price movements than they were by the trend in KEPES prices, which suggests that, apart from preserving the incomes of cereal farmers, KEPES may have had a relatively restricted impact on the agricultural sector as a whole.[22]

Greece's success in massively expanding wheat production at the height of the crisis had few parallels in Europe. Statistically, of course, it started from a very low base. Nevertheless, improvements in yields and output were successfully made at a critical time as a result of the sort of effective state intervention and support which was so lacking elsewhere in the economy. Comparing averages for 1926–30 and 1931–5, the cultivated area and consumption of wheat alone both increased by one-third, whilst production almost doubled. Over the same period production actually fell in Yugoslavia and Romania, whilst elsewhere in Europe it grew relatively slowly.

Yet, within the country, the very success of the response gave rise to a fierce policy debate. Self-sufficiency in cereals now seemed feasible, or

---

[20] *E* 132, 10 July 1932.
[21] *E* 288, 7 July 1935.
[22] *AOI* (1937), vol. C, 230–43.

virtually so—but was it desirable? From the late 1920s onwards, peasant farmers had turned from the high-value crops, such as tobacco, whose prices had fallen heavily, towards cereals, and especially wheat. The protection accorded to wheat encouraged peasants to restrict cultivation of other cereal crops in its favour.[23] Had the process now perhaps gone too far?

By 1933 these developments were viewed with alarm by some commentators, who argued that peasants were producing wheat without adequate preparation of the soil at the risk of its eventual impoverishment.[24] In a work published in 1934, the conservative George Kyriakos, later Metaxas's Minister of Agriculture, proposed restricting *cereal* cultivation to some 500–550,000 hectares—about one-third of the current level—and directing producers towards higher-value crops such as fodder crops, sugar beet, rice, and cotton. It was generally observed that in many areas smallholders had abandoned the traditional two-field fallow rotation for the continuous cultivation of wheat. In Larissa, for example, the pressure of indebtedness forced peasants to plant cereal crops continuously. A local observer reported that the 'lands are weakened from repeated cultivations with no reinforcement from chemical manures'.[25]

The critics believed that permanent improvements in yields would be slow to filter through. The remarkable yields of 1932–4 were attributed —with some justification—to favourable weather conditions. More permanent improvements, they went on, depended upon the adoption of deep-ploughing techniques, the use of fertilizers, and the adoption of rotations incorporating more intensively cultivated crops. The expansion of the early 1930s had not been part of the systematic programme demanded in the last years of the Liberal Government; rather it had led to 'anarchy'. Policy-makers should aim to reduce the cultivated area devoted to wheat, while at the same time increasing yields permanently.[26]

The opposing view was put most forcefully by Ioannis Papadakis, the Director of the Crop Improvement Centres. Attacking Kyriakos, he argued that smallholders behaved rationally: if wheat brought in a low income compared with other crops, why had they not switched to the

---

[23] *OT*, 18 July 1933; *OE 1935* (1936), 80.
[24] *E* 230, 27 May 1934.
[25] G. Kyriakos, *I georgiki politiki tou kratous* (Athens, 1934); X. Zolotas, *Agrotiki politiki* (Athens, 1934), 140–2; IBA, Volos, YR 1933/4, 3.
[26] *OA*, 8 June 1934; 25 Aug. 1934.

latter? The answer was that for a number of reasons they were not such an attractive proposition; rice, for example, required heavy investment in irrigation channels before it became viable. Fodder crops suffered from poor climatic conditions rather than backward cultivation techniques.[27] Papadakis also attacked the view that continuous cultivation impoverished the soil. Here too he asserted that peasant farmers knew what they were doing. Contrary to the received wisdom, it was *not* certain that in the short run continuous cultivation was harmful. In Greek conditions yields were affected much more by the weather than by the soil. In the longer term, Papadakis accepted that rotation allowed higher yields. His argument, however, was that in cases where continuous cultivation had taken over fallow land the drop in yields had not been such as to rule out income gains. Given that estimated wheat yields during continuous cultivation were 70% of those during two-year rotation, it was economically rational in conditions where land was scarce and labour cheap to switch to continuous cultivation. Papadakis pointed out that the peasants' rapid adoption of the new types of wheat suggested that they were not as resistant to change as many experts claimed. If they ignored the experts' advice—to support more livestock, for example—it was because they derived a higher income from planting land with wheat for their own consumption than from growing maize to feed their animals.[28]

He stressed, however, that he accepted the need to encourage more intensive farming.[29] In his view the two were not mutually exclusive since the expansion of wheat had largely been at the expense of other cereals, leaving land more suitable for other crops untouched. The reason that peasants were reluctant to return to traditional cash crops, such as tobacco and cotton, was simply lack of demand for them. As for fodder crops, he pointed out that in 1933 there had been an increase in *both* wheat and clover in the very areas where KEPES was active. Given the central importance of wheat in most agricultural incomes, however, it was right for the state to concentrate its efforts there. Yields had increased in tandem with the expansion of the cultivated area and these increases had been attained with a minimum of investment.

Given the paucity of evidence, particularly concerning rotation systems and peasant behaviour, it is not easy to make a judgement on the validity

[27] *E* 216, 18 Feb. 1934; *OE 1934* (1935), 190 ff.; V. Ganosis, *Peri tis ektheseos tou kyriou Kyriakou eis tin Akadimian* (Athens, 1934), *passim*.

[28] *OE 1934* (1935), 200.   [29] *E* 216, 18 Feb. 1934.

of such views. The critics of expansion included many conservative opponents of what they saw as the Venizelist policy of supporting cereal production on the new smallholdings; prone to base their arguments upon the agricultural experience of other European countries, their views may have been right in the long run but were weakened by their insistence on the basic irrationality of peasant behaviour and by their advocacy of other crops—rice, clover—which required heavy investment in irrigation projects before they were viable in the Greek context. Papadakis and others who sympathized with his views seem to have paid closer attention to the specific conditions of Greek agriculture. They had, after all, presided over a remarkable 'revolution': their successful introduction of new wheat strains had proved an extremely cost-effective means of raising rural incomes. Yet the success was perhaps short-term: there is evidence, based on area studies, that, as Kyriakos had feared, the successful introduction of 'Montana' wheat had discouraged the cultivation of higher value crops. In the plain of Serres, for example, the expansion of cotton cultivation had been restricted for this reason.[30]

The chief problem with wheat farming was its basic inappropriateness to Greek conditions, where land was scarce and labour plentiful. If specialization in many cash crops implied a capital base which Greek smallholders lacked, monocultivation of wheat, on the other hand, implied an acreage which they lacked as well. Case-studies reveal the drawbacks. In the Macedonian hill village of Lefkon in the early 1930s, nearly 85% of the cultivated area was devoted to cereals, half alone to wheat.[31] Yet the total cereal harvest contributed less than half of the gross annual agricultural product, whilst it was estimated that the men worked only 74 days in the year. In a similar village nearby, the area devoted to cereals was over 90% of the total and cereals constituted three-quarters of the (low) gross agricultural product. The author of the study estimated that gross family incomes could have been doubled if the area devoted to cereals had been reduced to less than half the total.[32] Diversification, it was argued, increased farmers' incomes and reduced the vulnerability of their enterprises. When heavy early spring rains in 1936 led to the partial failure of the wheat crop, wheat growers in several regions who had virtually abandoned other crops, were forced to seek assistance from the Agricultural Bank in order to feed their families.[33]

[30] E. Panagos, in *DATE*, 2(4) (1937), 352–84.
[31] N. Anagnostopoulos, *O kampos ton Serron* (Athens, 1937), 218–22.
[32] Ibid. 204, 211.   [33] *DATE*, 2(4) (1937), 368.

TABLE 9.5.　*Lending by the Agricultural Bank*

Year	Total lending (million drs.)	Short-term loans (million drs.)	% of short-term loans for	
			Cereals, tobacco, olives, currants, grapes	Cotton, vegetables, fodder, misc.
1930	1,306	1,289	89	7
1931	1,354	1,318	84	12
1932	1,126	1,105	76	17
1933	1,364	1,337	80	13
1934	1,932	1,884	88	11
1935	1,917	1,837	85	12
1936	2,885	2,737	80	15
1937	3,873	3,558	78	15
1938	4,009	3,592	76	15
1939	4,317	3,899	79	15

Source: Agrotiki Trapeza tis Ellados, *To ergon mias dekaetias (1930–39)* (Athens, 1940), 229–33.

This event highlighted the risks of over-specialization which Kyriakos and others had warned against.

However, their prescriptions could only be carried out if the state was prepared to channel greater resources into agricultural investment and make concessions on the debt owed by farmers to the state, which had not been affected by the earlier moratoria. Many high-value crops could not be cultivated until irrigation and drainage works had been undertaken. This occurred only partially. The funds which the Agricultural Bank extended to farmers increased substantially during the 1930s, but as Table 9.5 shows, the bulk of the Bank's funds were employed in financing the three traditional props of Greek agriculture—cereal, tobacco, and currants. Between them they accounted for over three-quarters of all short-term loans. The proportion directed towards newer crops remained unchanged for most of the decade. Medium- and long-term loans, the bulk of which were utilized for infrastructural improvements, or supplying machinery and livestock, were never more than 10% of the Bank's total advances.

High levels of indebtedness hindered farmers from making long-term investments themselves. Roughly three-quarters of all farmers were in debt by 1936, owing on average just under the equivalent of the average annual net income from farming.[34] However, despite the political importance of the debt issue, it would be wrong to conclude that there was no improvement in the position of the farming population after 1932. The suspension of private debts was followed in 1933 and 1934 by measures to scale down debts owed to the state by beneficiaries of the land reform. Finally Metaxas introduced a more sweeping moratorium on peasant debts after he seized power in 1936. But even before then the peasants had clearly benefited from the agricultural prosperity of the early 1930s. The proportion of defaults on Agricultural Bank loans fell from a high of 33.7% in 1932 to a low of 10.9% in 1935.[35] Consumption of basic foodstuffs rose in the same period: for example, comparing 1928–30 and 1935, we find that per capita consumption of meat rose by 15%, cheese by 27%, wheat by 10%, and potatoes by 32%.[36] Just as the crisis years after 1928 had reduced trade between rural areas and the towns, so the recovery increased it again, to the benefit of domestic producers.

It ought to be stressed that a number of reformers had been aware of this possibility and justified the state encouragement of wheat cultivation accordingly. Thus, in June 1932, Venizelos had been told by Kalligas, a senior civil servant in the Ministry of Agriculture that, because of the close connection of the urban and rural economies, high wheat prices could *not* be said to benefit one class at the expense of another, or to reflect a 'one-sided interest in the farmers'; on the contrary, encouraging a better agricultural performance would benefit the entire economy. Papadakis took a similar view: at the end of 1934 he argued that the state support of cereal producers would boost rural purchasing power, help merchants and manufacturers in the towns, and stem the influx of labour from the fields. Many business men, particularly in the smaller market towns, agreed. From Farsala, a small town in Thessaly, the local union of tradesmen (*panepangelmatiki enosis*) wrote to Venizelos at the height of the crisis, urging him to help the farmers, since 'the agricultural crisis is a crisis for us too'.[37] With the record harvests of 1932–3, the situation improved dramatically. In 1934 one leading annual survey noted that 'formerly, even in the recent past, domestic

---

[34] B. Alivizatos, *Kratos kai georgiki politiki* (Athens, 1938), 518–19; also, *E*, 26 Feb. 1933, 23 Apr. 1933, 20 Jan. 1935, 14 July 1935.

[35] Agrotiki Trapeza tis Ellados, *To ergon mias dekaetias (1930–39)* (Athens, 1940), 125.

[36] *OE 1939* (Athens, 1940), 304–5.

[37] Kalligas–Venizelos, 27 June 1932, AEV 173/128, *E*, 18 Dec. 1934; Panepangelmatiki enosis Farsalon–Venizelos, 18 July 1932, AEV 173/73.

industry for the most part served the needs of the urban population alone and consequently the market for its products was restricted. Today it has been broadened remarkably to include the rural population.' In Volos local manufacturers of agricultural machinery were working 15 hours daily to meet demand from the Thessaly hinterland. An observer in Salonika reported that 'the industrial movement in nothern Greece during the calendar year 1934 has been more active as compared with that of the previous year . . . thanks to the improved consumption as a result chiefly of the good crops of the last years'.[38] Thus, for all its long-term problems, the Greek agricultural sector recovered sufficiently to act as a stimulus for domestic manufacturing.

Industrial Growth

Industry recovered extremely rapidly from 1933 onwards, at a rate of over 9% in the first year alone. Between 1932 and 1937 growth averaged over 8% annually, well above the levels attained in the late 1920s (see Table A1.4). The view that this was a period of high profits for industry is supported by the published results of limited-liability companies: profits as a percentage of share capital increased from an average of 7% during 1930–2 to over 13% in 1933 and an average of over 11% during 1934–7. Some major firms did even better than this: Charilaos's Wine and Spirits Company—the most important wine producer in Greece—saw profits rise as a percentage of *total* liabilities from 5% during 1930–2 to 23% in 1933 and 16% in 1934. Behind this improvement was industry's ability to exploit its quasi-monopoly position in the Greek market, which enabled business men to pass on increases in raw material and fuel costs to the consumer. In addition, low land prices and the prospect of growth in tourism thanks to the depreciation of the drachma contributed to what one business man described as an 'unbelievable' building boom, especially in the coastal area around Athens. A review of industry in 1934 noted that 'our industry today is enjoying a period of exceptional prosperity and unusual activity'.[39]

Yet, as Ivan Berend has remarked, inter-war economic development in the Balkans saw a 'relatively fast rate of industrialization' take place

[38] *OE 1933* (Athens, 1934), 608; IBA, Volos, YR 1933/4. 5; IBA, Salonika, YR 1934/5, 2.

[39] *OE 1933* (1934), 607; *DEVE/A*, Oct. 1936; FO 371/16765 C7723/2, Cavendish-Bentinck–FO, 21 Aug. 1933; FO 371/16766 C9957/2, Ramsay–FO, 2 Nov. 1933.

within 'the constraints of old and obsolete structural frameworks'.[40] So far as we can tell, on the basis of imperfect data, it is unlikely that a high proportion of these profits were reinvested to modernize or expand industrial plant. While the value of new industrial investment between 1932 and 1936 came to around 620 million drachmas, the profits of the *leading* industrial concerns alone came to at least 2,000 million drachmas.[41] The lack of reinvestment is scarcely surprising, since—as we shall see—official policy after 1932 was to *discourage* further industrial investment, on the grounds that firms created in such conditions were unlikely to be internationally competitive. This self-fulfilling prophecy was certainly borne out to the extent that industrial exports remained negligible during the 1930s—around 5% of total exports. For the two leading manufacturing sectors—textiles and chemicals—more than half of their high growth rates was due simply to increasing import-substitution, rather than to any increase in the size of the market. For manufacturing as a whole the conclusion is even less equivocal: on aggregate the high rate of growth can be explained entirely by import-substitution (Table 9.6). For a more detailed examination of what such growth entailed, let us look in detail at textiles, the critical sector in the recovery.

In the 1920s the textile industry grew rapidly, helped by the abundance of cheap labour, to become the most important branch of manufacturing in Greece. According to the 1930 census, out of a total labour force in manufacturing of 233,000 it employed over 47,000 workers, of whom most were women, working for rather small firms. Many of its problems were shared by other industries in Greece: technological backwardness, the predominance of small, inadequately financed, family-owned units, excessive competition, which reduced profitability despite tariff protection. Firms were concentrated in the Athens area—by 1931 they produced two-thirds of cotton thread output—and this problem grew worse over time.[42] However, the cotton manufacturers had several advantages over other industries. Not only did the high level of textile imports before 1932 increase the potential for import-substitution; but perhaps more importantly, raw materials could be produced locally. Cotton cultivation spread remarkably after 1932: between 1928–32 and

---

[40] I. Berend, 'Balkan Economic Development', *Economic History Review*, 29(3) (May 1984), 268–71.

[41] N. Anastasopoulos, *Istoria tis ellinikis viomichanias*, iii (Athens, 1947), 1,580.

[42] MNE, *Elliniki viomichania* (Athens, 1931), 141–54.

TABLE 9.6. *Industrial growth due to import-substitution*

(1)	1929–31 (average) (2)	1936 (3)	Compound average annual growth		
			Overall (4)	Due to import-substitution[a] (5)	Due to market growth ((4) − (5)) (6)
Textiles	(1) 55.7	72.6	9.7	5.4	4.3
	(2) 1,778.3	2,830.7			
Engineering	(1) 26.4	28.9	4.0	1.8	2.2
	(2) 264.6	322.7			
Construction	(1) 84.7	97.7	4.3	2.9	1.4
	(2) 389.4	480.5			
Food/drink	(1) 91.6	86.1	1.8	−1.2	3.0
	(2) 1,306.9	1,426.9			
Chemicals	(1) 64.2	79.3	8.3	4.3	4.0
	(2) 866.3	1,289.6			
General average[b]	(1) 63.1	82.9	5.6	5.6	0.0
	(2) 6,036.0	7,933.1			

Notes: Row (1): % share of total consumption; row (2): actual output at constant (1930) prices (million drs.).
[a] i.e. implicit growth rate in row (1).   [b] All sectors except electricity.
Source: My calculations from data in *OE 1939* (Athens, 1940).

1933–7 the cultivated area doubled and the crop of unginned cotton quadrupled. The result was that whereas in 1922 Greek manufacturers had relied on domestically produced cotton for only one-third of their requirements, in 1935 they obtained two-thirds in this way; over the same period their consumption of ginned cotton rose from 5,610 to 21,843 tonnes annually.[43]

The combination of import restrictions, the drachma devaluation, and the agricultural revival enabled firms to enjoy the benefits of the investments made before 1932, but provided no incentives to invest or modernize further. As stated in the report of the Supreme Economic Council: 'While the cotton industry showed a perceptible development in the period to 1932 and an improvement of production, in the last few years [i.e. 1932–6]—despite favourable conditions—it has shown relative stagnation ... with only a *quantitative* increase in output.'[44] Profits and output rose, together with some increase in the labour force, while mechanical capacity grew more slowly. Profits of limited-liability textile companies rose from a low of 5.1% in 1931 to a seven-year high of 13.2% in 1933. The growth of the labour force—unparalleled in any other branch of manufacturing—was eased by the fall in real wages. An increasing number of apprentices were taken on at wages below the official minimum, whilst even adult workers were paid just above the minimum wage. A 10-hour day was common. Manufacturers also gained from the slow rise in raw cotton prices after 1933. Even in 1932/3 when cotton prices shot up thanks to the drachma devaluation, Greek textile manufacturers successfully passed on most of the price rise to their consumers.

Despite such favourable conditions, the technological level of the industry remained very low. The Supreme Economic Council's investigation of the cotton industry found in 1936 that at least one-third of the existing machinery was in need of immediate replacement, and most of it was at least 30–40 years old. Restrictions imposed by the Ministry of the National Economy obstructed imports of replacement machinery, and also blunted competition and enabled established manufacturers to take advantage of their monopoly position. The consequence was that the industry as a whole remained uncompetitive in foreign markets

---

[43] Organismos Vamvakos, *Ta pepragmena tis protis eptaetias tou O.V. (1931–37)* (Athens, n.d.), 52, 54.
[44] AOS, *Erevna kai gnomodotisis epi ton viomichanion vamvakos* (Athens, 1937), 8; a useful survey of the main textile firms may be found in *EX*, 26 Nov. 1933–22 July 1934.

TABLE 9.7. *Textile industry indices* (1932 = 100)

Year	Output at constant (1930) prices		Cotton manufacturing			
	Textiles	Cotton thread	Spooled cotton thread	Labour force	Nominal wages[a]	No. of spindles in use	No. of looms in use
1932	100	100	100	100	100	100	100
1933	120	124	118	108	105	99	114
1934	140	146	137	121	110	103	118
1935	135	134	126	130	114	106	122
1936	147	150	136	135	117	106	127

[a] Simple arithmetical average of data in AOS source, p. 13.

Sources: 'Output at constant (1930) prices': my own calculations from data in *AS* 1933, 1937. 'Cotton manufacturing': AOS, *Epi ton viomichanion vamvakos* (Athens, 1937) 13–19.

despite exceptionally cheap labour costs.[45] Antiquated equipment and the shortage of skilled workers discouraged textile firms from moving into the production of finer yarns: of the 262,000 spindles operating in 1935, only 19,328 could produce relatively fine-quality yarns (nos. 42 and above). Only 10–15% of the capital stock fitted in the years 1930–3 was suitable for this task. To be fair, the fault did not lie entirely with the manufacturers since the generally primitive ginning facilities in the countryside also hindered the production of finer yarns.[46] By 1936 the concentration of firms in the production of coarse yarns led to fierce competition in this area and calls for intervention by the state to tilt production towards finer yarns.

The problem that left to itself the market might ignore the more expensive end of the range had been discussed as early as 1933. The argument was that existing specific tariffs were too low, discouraging the domestic production of finer yarns. Industrialists complained of French 'dumping' in Greek markets and demanded higher tariffs. They complained of the state's indifference to industrial problems, and its acquiescence in the widespread public sentiment that industry was no more than a 'necessary evil'.[47] In fact, though the incidence of the tariffs on yarns gave greater protection to coarse yarns than to fine ones, the real problem was that those few Greek producers of fine yarns—just four or five firms—who had installed more modern equipment before 1932, were attempting to block the proposed mass import of new looms in order to preserve their own predominant position.[48] The Government's reaction to this dispute was to refer the problem to the Supreme Economic Council, which in its 1937 report advocated a combination of tariff reform and controls over production costs in order to modernize the industry and turn it into a viable exporter. It was noted that neither the favourable climate of 1933–5 nor the increased competition of 1935–6 had led to modernization or improvements in quality. The recent competition between integrated—combined spinning and weaving—firms and straight weaving concerns, reliant upon their competitors for their yarns, had forced the latter to cut prices and quality in an effort to survive. In this sector, at least, one of the most dynamic elements in the industrial recovery, fast rates of growth seem to have been accompanied by a gradual deterioration in the quality of plant and equipment.

[45] Ibid. 8–14.   [46] Ibid. 17–18, 27.
[47] *OT*, 22 Jan. 1933, 2 Aug. 1936, 16 Aug. 1936; *OA*, 1 Dec. 1934, 9 Mar. 1935.
[48] *OT*, 21 Sept. 1936.

This was surely not the outcome that proponents of industrial 'rationalization' had had in mind in the 1920s when they had stressed the need to curb competition. The main features of industrial growth in the 1930s were determined by a policy which countenanced state intervention to restrict further industrial investment but shrank from intervening in the labour market or from controlling prices. Unlike agriculture, where the Populist Government could (and did) rely on the administrative machinery set up by its predecessors, industry posed unprecedented problems after 1932 for the state.

Prices, Profits, and Labour

Initially industrialists reacted sympathetically to the Liberal Government's decision to defend the drachma, and supported the government policy on import controls, obviously aware of the benefits such a policy would offer them.[49] However, they were opposed to the monetary policy that accompanied the authorities' defence of the gold standard, arguing that the commercial banks' excessive contraction of credit was forcing some firms into bankruptcy and generally hindering manufacturers' ability to take advantage of import restrictions. From October 1931 to April 1932 the Chambers of Commerce attacked the high level of interest rates and urged Venizelos to adopt a more relaxed monetary stance. Their arguments were presented in a contradictory fashion: on the one hand they asserted that expanding the money supply would not lead to inflation; yet they claimed that economic recovery depended upon raising prices and hence increasing purchasing power. Venizelos, however, remained opposed to such views.[50]

At the same time there occurred the first signs of an incipient conflict between merchants and industrialists. These two groups, jointly represented in the Chambers of Commerce, did not always work harmoniously together. Industry resented the merchants' traditional preference for stocking imported rather than domestic goods; the merchants, now facing supply difficulties, found that many Greek manufacturers were arranging their own retail and distribution outlets, bypassing the merchants. Many merchants had been badly hit by the moratorium on peasant debts and demanded the assistance of the Populist Government to prevent—in the words of one spokesman in the Senate—'big capital profiting at the expense of small capital'. This

---

[49] *OT*, 24 Nov. 1931; *EV*, 16 Jan. 1932.
[50] *DEVE/A*, Oct. 1931, Mar. 1932.

conflict, muted at first, was to develop into a more rancorous affair after 1932.[51]

Acceptance of the need for import controls soon diminished as manufacturers found themselves facing increasingly severe supply problems of their own. By keeping stocks low during 1931 they had remained liquid, and avoided bookkeeping losses as wholesale prices fell. However, this also meant that they soon reached a point where their stocks had to be replenished.[52] As firms faced growing difficulties and in some cases were forced out of business through their inability to obtain vital raw materials from abroad, the Ministry of the National Economy's failure to make import controls responsive to the needs of industry came to be seen as part of a more general failure of policy.[53]

The Tsaldaris administration retreated from its predecessor's mild encouragement of industry and based its own policy on a purported dichotomy between 'viable' and 'unviable' concerns. From this perspective an industry's reliance on imported inputs was proof of its 'unviability'. It was an idea which had been discussed during Venizelos's premiership in the context of the 'rationalization' debate, when spokesmen for industry insisted on the need to encourage mergers, 'cleansing' industry of 'unviable' firms.[54] But as elsewhere in Europe mergers were basically a defensive response by established firms to new competition; this was also true for cartels, such as that among wine exporters in 1930, or among the country's leading three cement producers in 1932. They were therefore unlikely to lead to the improved competitiveness which the Government desired. In an article in *Ergasia*, Petros Garoufalias, a former Director-General of the Ministry of the National Economy, had argued against the 'viable/unviable' distinction, warning that 'an industrial policy which tends to preserve antiquated machinery and relies on lower and lower wages, burdening consumption, will spell disaster for the economy. That is the nature of our industrial development at the moment.'[55]

Nevertheless, such prophetic warnings had little impact. For the Populists the vocabulary of 'viability' linked industry's problems with the broader economic and demographic dilemmas facing Greece. Doubtful about the wisdom of pursuing autarky, they envisaged only a restricted

[51] *DEVE/A*, Jan. 1932; G. Kakoulides in *ESG*, 20 Sept. 1933, 571; *OA*, 20 Oct. 1934.
[52] *DEVE/A*, Apr.–May 1932.
[53] *OT*, 4 June 1933; FO 371/15966 C2092/462, 'Monthly Report from H. M. Consul at Salonica', 7 Mar. 1932.
[54] *Near East and India*, 10 Apr. 1930.   [55] *E*, 8 Aug. 1931.

degree of industrialization, and laid down inhibiting balance of trade considerations as criteria. Tsaldaris, in his opening statement as Prime Minister in April 1933, stressed that industries which used domestically produced raw materials would be looked on with special favour.[56] His Minister for the National Economy, George Pesmazoglu, was particularly committed to this line. Summarizing the Government's policy one year later, he made clear his belief that industrialization did not provide a long-term solution to Greece's demographic problem. As a primarily agricultural and commercial country, it should only permit industrial expansion 'upon full and minute reflection'. Industrial growth could provide but a temporary palliative for unemployment, which would only be permanently reduced through emigration. According to Pesmazoglu, Greece was a country without an 'industrial character' and as such, its industrial sector did not offer 'the likelihood of the broadest development'. Although the existing anomalous conditions made high profits possible, there was a danger that excessive investment in new plant would create further protectionist pressures precluding a swift return to free-trade principles.[57]

Thus the policy of import restrictions as practised by the Tsaldaris administration was a quite deliberate attempt to hold back industrial development. A survey of conditions in 1933 reported that in response to 'the demand for the establishment of new industries . . . the state issued the desired permits with extreme restraint, and instituted restrictions on imports of machinery, very wisely aiming to avoid excessive competition in the future when the existing import restrictions are lifted . . . If industry is kept as far as possible within the existing limits it will be secure in the face of any threatening change of circumstances.' Between 1931 and 1934 imports of machinery fell by one-third despite the increases in profits and output.[58] There were fears that the policy resulted in inflated import prices, though the evidence offered earlier in this work suggests such fears were exaggerated. But domestic prices may have been raised as a result of firms being forced to maintain stocks at low levels, requiring constant reprovisioning. This would obviously have created uncertainties—both as to whether stocks would be replenished, and, if so, at what price—which themselves may have led manufacturers to raise their own prices in compensation.[59]

The Government's rather lukewarm attitude to industry provoked

[56] *OT*, 9 Apr. 1933.   [57] *VE*, July 1934; also *OT*, 26 July 1936.
[58] *OE 1933* (1934), 608; *DEVE/A*, Feb. 1936, 5–6.
[59] *OA*, 4 Aug. 1934, 20 Oct. 1934.

criticism and resentment. The 'viable'/'unviable' dichotomy came under attack from a senior civil servant at the MNE itself.[60] Industrialists too, many of whom had been calling for the sort of curbs on the formation of new companies which the Tsaldaris Government introduced, disliked the rigidity of the Government's views. Andreas Chadzikyriakos, a leading business magnate, complained that the dichotomy provided an unworkable base on which to erect an industrial policy: examining the dependence of various branches of manufacturing upon imported raw materials, he concluded that overall only one-seventh to one-eighth of the total raw materials employed by industry were imported. This was surely, he argued, too small a proportion to feature largely in the industrial policy of the Government. The industrial progress of a country, he concluded, was exclusively the affair of entrepreneurs, who alone could judge a firm's prospects, capable as they were of turning an 'unviable' industry into a 'viable' one.[61]

The greatest criticism was reserved for the Government's reluctance to view industrial policy outside the narrow bounds of balance of payments considerations. 'Industrial development—indispensable to Greece because of her population density in relation to the cultivable land—is destined to save the country, since the doors of emigration in all directions have been closed,' wrote George Stringos, President of the Piraeus Chamber of Commerce and a former Senator. Referring to the Populists' nostalgia for the pre-war era, he went on: 'The return to that epoch seems most unlikely, and perhaps we should not even wish for it.'[62] Stringos did not answer, however, the question of what role the state should play in promoting industrialization. Here the economic crisis helped polarize opinion: when late in 1932 *Ergasia*, a journal set up two years earlier with the support of the Liberal Government, carried a series of articles entitled 'Can and should we draw up a long-term plan for industrial development?', it aroused a mixed response. Some industrialists, such as Nikolaos Kanellopoulos, founder of the enormous Chemical and Fertilizer Company, resisted the idea of planning, though they wanted further state encouragement of entrepreneurs. Others, however, insisted that the essential components of industrial development—a more reliable supply of domestically produced inputs, cheaper credit, increased industrial exports—could all best be achieved by state intervention. The results of the essentially entrepreneurial growth of the 1920s had underlined the point that unrestricted investment did not

---

[60] *OT*, 4 June 1933.   [61] *OT*, 9, 16, 24 Apr. 1933.
[62] Bank of Athens, *Bulletin Économique et Financier*, 122 (Dec. 1935), 2,437.

TABLE 9.8. *Price and wage indices* (1928 = 100)

Year (1)	Industrial wholesale prices (2)	Fuel wholesale prices (3)	Nominal wages (4)	(2)/(3) (5)	(2)/(4) (6)	Real wages ((4)/cost-of-living index) (7)
1929	107	103	n.a.	104	n.a.	n.a.
1930	98	100	100.2	98	98	111.2
1931	86	94	n.a.	91	n.a.	n.a.
1932	108	114	96.8	95	112	106.9
1933	128	119	n.a.	108	n.a.	n.a.
1934	123	113	102.4	109	120	103.4
1935	122	115	103.0	106	118	103.0
1936	126	114	108.0	111	117	103.9

n.a. = not available.

Sources: Cols. (2) and (3): AOS, *EO 1935* (Athens, 1936); *EO 1937* (Athens, 1938); col. (4): MNE. *Apografi ton ypallilon kai ergaton ton viomichanikon kai emporikon epicheiriseon kai imeromisthia axton* (Athens, 1940).

necessarily lead to the most efficient allocation of resources. Pesma-zoglu's policy satisfied neither the *laissez-faire* business world nor the étatists. He was accused of possessing a 'static, pre-war conception of the Greek economy' and there were calls for his resignation at meetings of the Athens Chamber of Commerce and Industry. By 1935 the étatists were underlining the social implications of the passive nature of the Government's industrial policy: the discouragement of new industrial investment served to protect existing factory owners, as did the mainten-ance of high tariffs and import quotas. In these circumstances they had been able to recoup considerable profits, despite high interest rates and the high price of raw materials.[63]

Industrialists retorted that their high profits in 1933–5 were neces-sary to wipe out the losses incurred during the crisis. But public opinion was turning in favour of price controls on manufactured goods. Civil servants had for some time argued that high levels of protection would do nothing to improve industrial efficiency unless allied to some form of price control. Tsouderos noted in 1935 that 'complaints are heard from every quarter that the prices of certain goods of home production . . . are increasing continuously without there having occurred any correspond-ing increase either in the price of raw materials or in other costs affecting home production . . . Neither society nor the state can possibly tolerate with passivity the continuance of such a movement.'[64] By early 1935 the Tsaldaris Government had become aware of the populist appeal of a move against 'profiteering' industrialists. In July it announced plans to introduce legislation providing for state control of the production costs of domestically produced goods.

This provoked a violent reaction from the business lobby against what it described as the 'party state': the MNE was, according to Nikolaos Kanellopoulos, 'continuing to restrict that entrepreneurial freedom which was the basis of the bourgeois state' and its new proposals would lead to an 'unprecedented bolshevism'. Another industrialist described the measures as 'anti-productive and anti-liberal' and insisted that their only result would be to bring industrialists into disrepute with 'the popular masses'.[65] Outside the business world, however, the reaction was less hostile. Citing the example of what Mussolini had done in Italy,

---

[63] *E*, 23 Oct.–11 Dec. 1934; *VE*, Nov. 1934; *E*, 17 Feb. 1935, 21 July 1935; *OT*, 4 Mar. 1934.

[64] *VE*, Sept. 1935; *Ploutos*, 5 Aug. 1934; *E*, 17 Feb. 1935; Bank of Greece, *The Economic Situation in Greece and the Bank of Greece in 1934* (Athens, 1935), 39.

[65] *VE*, June 1935; *OT*, 7 July 1935; *E*, 21 July 1935; *OT*, 14 July 1935.

Antonios Bernaris, whose 1933 book on post-war developments in the Greek economy was a fierce attack on the managerial incompetence of the political élite, now wrote that the state was quite justified in intervening on behalf of the 'social economy' especially in view of the benefits industry had already derived from the state's actions. But Bernaris criticized the proposed legislation as unworkable, since it presupposed similar production costs for different firms producing the same good. The basic aim was correct, but the plan was flawed by its dependence upon an 'agoranomic' conception of consumer protection rather than upon stimuli to increased competitiveness. Leading policy-makers remained confined mentally at least within the world of the small market town, unable to make the transition to the new demands imposed by industrialization on a national scale. In the end, since the scheme required a larger and more competent supervisory bureaucracy than actually existed in Greece at the time, it is scarcely surprising that it went the way of most other measures designed to force the state into a more active role against the business world.[66] Even in early 1937, after Metaxas had taken control, Tsouderos, Governor of the Bank of Greece, was still vainly seeking the 'more practical spirit which should predominate among industrialists in fixing the prices of their products' and proposing the introduction of wide-ranging price controls if 'industrialists insisted in refusing to understand where their true interests lie'.[67]

Labour relations—increasingly embittered and violent after 1932 —were where the political élite of the 'good bourgeois world' (as one Populist deputy put it) reacted with greatest uncertainty. The rapid growth of manufacturing output was dependent upon cheap labour costs: real wages fell around 13% between 1930 and 1935, kept down by the availability of unskilled labour. Indeed working-class incomes were extremely low throughout the inter-war period: according to a study of the position in 1938—which cannot differ substantially from that a few years earlier—the average worker's annual income amounted to only 15,109 drachmas, compared with a farmer's of 19,218 drachmas or the income of a member of the liberal professions at 59,029 drachmas. Given the country's highly regressive tax structure, post-tax income disparities would have been greater still. An official survey of working

---

[66] *E*, 18–25 Aug. 1935; K. A. Kanellopoulos, *Ai koinonikes asfaliseis* (Athens, 1934), 5–6.

[67] Bank of Greece, *The Economic Situation in Greece and the Bank of Greece in 1936* (Athens, 1937), 15–16.

conditions found badly fed and underpaid workers confined to dark, unhygienic workshops and factories.[68] In general, workers in manufacturing were poorly organized, and in a weaker bargaining position than the tobacco workers, seamen, or utilities and transport workers: strikes by manufacturing workers were relatively uncommon before 1936 and they remained unprotected by the sort of insurance and benefit schemes which the latter groups had gained. The most thorough contemporary study of unemployment in inter-war Greece painted a grim picture of the living conditions of the urban proletariat, emphasizing that the post-1932 rise in wages was outstripped by the cost of living; once unemployed, most workers faced a 'truly tragic situation'. High population growth, the migration of workers from the fields into the towns, and the drying up of employment in the public sector after its rapid expansion during the Liberal administration—all these contributed to the growth of a destitute urban work-force. Although reliable unemployment statistics are unavailable, it may be worth citing an estimate of the numbers of employed manufacturing workers, according to which this work-force actually diminished—despite the growth in output—by 12% between 1929 and 1933–4; the number of tobacco workers declined over the same period by 35%.[69] The position was especially bad outside the capital since the gradual concentration of industry in the Athens–Piraeus area shifted employment opportunities out of the provincial towns. To give but one graphic example, virtually all the cigarette factories in northern Greece closed or moved south so that between 1925 and 1934 the contribution of the New Provinces to total cigarette production fell from 36% to 4%.[70] 'What have we to show—as society and state—up to now in the field of unemployment benefit?' asked a leading contemporary expert in 1935. 'To this question we can only answer that we have addressed the problem of unemployment through weak and tentative measures, taken under the pressure of events, without serious, systematic and comprehensive study of the problem and without the conviction that we can solve it, thereby

---

[68] G. Nezis, 'Katanomi tis daneiakis epivarynseos en ti propolemiki Elladi', *Nea oikonomia*, 2(1) (Nov. 1947), 10–16; *MA*, 20 June 1935.

[69] S. Kladas, *I anergia en Elladi* (Athens, 1935), 28, 30; GPEK, Kavalla, *Deltion*, June 1938, 16.

[70] Kladas, *I anergia*; *MA*, 27 June 1935; N. Anastasopoulos, *Istoria tis ellinikis viomichanias*, p. 1,581; G. Burgel, *Croissance urbaine et développement capitaliste: Le "Miracle" athènien* (Athens, 1981), 142–62, 218; AOS, *To zitima tis synkentroseos ton viomichanion en Elladi* (Athens, 1940); FO 371/20392 R1436/1110, 'Conditions in Patras for February 1936'; *VE*, Oct. 1935.

ignoring the enormous social disturbances which an increase in unemployment may produce.'[71]

Although Venizelos had urged employers to accept labour legislation as a 'bulwark against revolutionary theories of the class struggle', his Government had not made the issue a priority. Spokesmen for industry had argued that such legislation was 'unsuitable for Greek conditions' where worker–employer relations were governed by 'the old patriarchal sincerity and by a deeper common humanity, cultivated in the fertile soil of mutual respect'. The Liberal Government actually published proposals for a bill on social insurance at about the time the *Idionymon* was passing through Parliament, but in the face of business pressure these were dropped, despite the strong protests of the trades union leadership.[72] In December 1930 Venizelos himself spoke out strongly against unemployment benefit schemes which 'would empty the countryside, empty the fields and invite all those who didn't feel like working into the towns to come and sign on'. He never wavered in his view that unemployment benefit was a luxury Greece was too poor to afford, whilst the Liberals only introduced legislation on social insurance in the summer of 1932 after Papanastasiou's brief stay in power had publicized the issue.[73]

Neither in the case of unemployment benefit, nor on labour issues generally, did the Tsaldaris Government show any sign of advancing beyond the hesitancy of its predecessors. On the contrary, one of its first acts in the spring of 1933—despite Tsaldaris's rhetoric to the working classes of Piraeus in his pre-electoral speeches in support of the 'social state'—was to repeal the social insurance legislation which had been passed the previous year. This appears to have been for the entirely trivial reason that Stefanopoulos, the Populist Under-Minister for the National Economy, wished to gain the credit for introducing a similar scheme; thus one year later the Populists brought in a measure which differed little from that they had repealed. Defending it before Parliament in July 1934, Pesmazoglu described social insurance as a 'promise which all parties have given to the workers', while the Populist deputy who introduced the committee report affirmed that such legislation was

[71] Kladas, *I anergia*, p. 33.

[72] S. Stefanou (ed.), *Ta keimena tou El. Venizelou*, iv: *1930–36*, 190–1; *OA*, 4 Jan. 1930, 18 Jan. 1930; D. Livieratos, *Koinonikes agones stin Ellada (1927–31)* (Athens, 1987), 151; C. Chadziiosif, 'I venizelogenis antipolitefsis sto Venizelo', in Mavrogordatos and Chadziiosif (eds.), *Venizelismos*, p. 444.

[73] Stefanou (ed.), *Ta keimena*, iv. 410; *MA*, 22 Aug. 1930, 3 Sept. 1930, 12 Dec. 1930; 21 June 1932.

necessary to give the Republic 'genuine social content'. Although on paper the new legislation provided for a national network of insurance centres, in practice little was achieved amidst the constitutional turmoil of the following months. Three years later, Fotylas wrote that the 1934 legislation was only then about to be implemented; for him, writing during the Metaxas dictatorship, and for Varvaressos, his mentor, the social policies of the governments of the Republic had been 'empirical and spasmodic'.[74]

In labour disputes, both employers and workers typically continued to appeal for government support, but Tsaldaris, a man with more caution and far less authority than Venizelos, was the wrong sort of character for such situations. His weak intervention in the tobacco workers' strike in July 1933 revealed his discomfort in the role of mediator and in the debate on the provisional legislation brought in to settle the dispute, he made clear his basic reluctance to involve the state in labour arbitration:

It must not be thought that the basic inclination of the Government as it emerges from this legislation is to intervene in regulating issues where the free will of the citizen ought to prevail . . . I think that the regulation of how many workers the employer should take on, what wage he should give . . . constitutes excessive intervention [by the state] and may have unfavourable results.[75]

Unprepared to provide legislative reform or effective political mediation, the Greek state relied increasingly on force. In northern Greece there was tension between the mainly Venizelist population and the followers of the extremist General Kondylis in the police and gendarmerie. But in Old Greece too local authorities used the gendarmerie to break up strikes, or allowed local employers to take matters into their own hands. A couple of examples must suffice to demonstrate how violent such disputes could become: in August 1935 workers at the port of Irakleion in Crete went on strike, demanding an eight-hour day, higher wages, and union rights. Clashes with the police led to several deaths and caused the conflict to escalate until, for a brief period, the workers seemed to have gained control of the town. The authorities' response was to send in troop reinforcements and declare martial law. Later that month, the trouble spread to the province of Messenia, which

[74] G. Vouros, *Panayis Tsaldaris* (Athens, 1955), 296; P. Kanellopoulos, *I zoi mou* (Athens, 1985), 37; FO 371/20392 R1432/1432, 'Annual Report for 1935', Waterlow–Eden, 26 Feb. 1936; *MA*, 16–17 June 1934, 25 July 1934; D. Chadzigiannis, *Epi tou nomoschediou peri koinonikon asfaliseon* (Athens, 1934), 65; S. Kladas, *I ergatiki mas politiki kai nomothesia* (Athens, 1945), 75–6; N. Fotylas, *Koinoniki politiki* (Athens, 1937), 386.

[75] *ESV*, 2 Sept. 1933, 609.

was also put under martial law after rioting currant growers, mounted and armed, cut railway lines, burned warehouses, and besieged small groups of gendarmes. In the port of Kalamata workers came out on strike to support them. In May of the previous year there had been another strike in Kalamata, involving workers in the docks and flour-mills. After police shot two demonstrators, their bodies were carried through the town by a crowd which hurled stones at a bank building and sacked the house of a wealthy industrialist. Another two workers were shot by troop reinforcements before the disturbances ended and fright-ened shopkeepers reopened their shops.[76]

The weakness of the authorities led factory owners to look after themselves as best they could. The Wine and Spirit Company had a factory in Kalamata and when the authorities refused to guarantee the factory's safety during a strike in June 1934, the Company organized its own tough but successful counter-measures to keep the business working normally. Charilaos, its Managing Director, reminded the Athens Chamber of Commerce of 'the need for firm measures by employers in confronting such actions in similar demonstrations of anarchism'.[77] Afterwards the Chamber passed a motion 'expressing the hope that the labour policy of the Government will make it possible on the one hand to quell the sporadic confrontations with communism by supporting law-abiding workers, and on the other to achieve harmonious relations between workers and employers'.[78]

Fascism offered one way to reach this goal. Kondylis, who would seize power in the autumn of 1935, made much of his meeting with Mussolini that summer, hailing him as 'the greatest man of the present epoch' who had 'achieved a magnificent task, having disciplined a lively people . . . and having solved the problem of the cooperation of capital and labour'. Charilaos toured Western Europe and on his return contrasted the flourishing state of Germany, which had followed Mussolini in cutting unemployment benefits and promoting public works projects, with France, whose poor performance was attributed to her reluctance to leave the gold standard as well as to her extravagant provisions for the unemployed. But the political implications of this stance were spelled out by Venizelos, during preliminary discussions on the introduction of

---

[76] D. Koutsoulakis, *I defteri dekaetia tou KKE: 1929–39* (Athens, 1984), 120; G. Andrikopoulos, *I dimokratia tou mesopolemou* (Athens, 1987), 157; *MA*, 10 May 1934, 25 Aug. 1935; FO 371/19508 R5543/34, Walker–FO, 9 Sept. 1935.

[77] *DEVE/A*, Dec. 1934, 30; MNE, *Ekthesis somatos epitheoriseos ergasias, 1934* (Athens, 1936), 36.   [78] *DEVE/A*, Dec. 1934, 35.

compulsory arbitration. The former Prime Minister praised Fascism for having solved the problem of industrial relations through the establishment of the corporatist state, but insisted that since he believed in parliamentary democracy, and since 'we in Greece do not want a Fascist state, we cannot solve the problem that way'.[79]

In one sense Venizelos's comments were quite justified: political organizations of an openly Fascist character—like the 'Steelhelmets' or Skylakakis's 'Organization of the National Sovereign State'—remained marginal to the Greek scene. A German diplomat was perhaps right to note that 'the Greek people is patriotic, but the State and the necessity of offering whatever sacrifice is necessary for their State—these ideas are foreign to them'. But might there not be a 'third way' between totalitarianism and the existing parliamentary order for Greece? Leading constitutionalists argued that the 'crisis of democracy' could only be surmounted by reorganizing the parties, reducing the power of their leaders, and incorporating a wider range of social groups into the political process, using social legislation or some form of corporatism to transform 'political democracy' into 'social democracy'. Venizelos himself held that effective government required a strengthening of the executive at the expense of the legislature, along the lines of the notorious Article 48 of the Weimar Constitution, and his hard-line former lieutenant, Constantine Zavitsianos, shortly to become Finance minister under Metaxas, echoed such thoughts. Charilaos criticized the Populists' abolition of the Senate in 1935, widely hailed as a proto-corporatist body, where the presence of representatives of the professional classes had moderated 'party passions'. There were also several attempts to form a political 'third force': the Venizelist Kafandaris tried in 1932, calling for the creation of a 'third situation' (*triti katastasis*) to unify the bourgeois world; out of the anti-Venizelist camp the young Kanellopoulos emerged in 1935 to try a similar venture, with equal lack of success.[80]

[79] Andrikopoulos, *I dimokratia*, p. 150; *DEVE/A*, May 1935, 4–5; S. Stefanou (ed.), *Eleftheriou Venizelou politikai ypothikai anthologitheisai apo ta keimena avtou*, ii (Athens, 1969), 347.

[80] *DEVE/A*, Apr.–May 1936; Eisenlohr–Neurath, 9 May 1934, cited in G. Andrikopoulos, *Oi rizes tou ellinikou fasismou* (Athens, 1977), 56–7; G. Paschos, 'I politeiologiki skepsi stin Ellada kata tin periodo 1930–35', in Mavrogordatos and Chadziiosif (eds.), *Venizelismos*, pp. 345–68; C. Sarandis, 'The Emergence of the Right in Greece (1922–1940)', D.Phil. thesis, Oxford University, 1979, 404–9; *MA*, 21 June 1932, 25 May 1933, 3 Feb. 1935; D. Goula, *Georgios Kafandaris* (Athens, 1982), 36–8; G. Mavrogordatos, *Stillborn Republic: Social Coalitions and Party Strategies in Greece 1922–1936* (Berkeley, Calif., 1983), 334–42.

The Greek political élite itself proved unable to plot a new course between a failed paternalism and a solution along Fascist lines; this would prove fatal since it had lost the legitimacy to implement the first and lacked the belief in a strong state necessary for the second. All that was left was a defensive conservatism—common to both major parties —which emerged with particular clarity over the labour question. Panayis Vourloumis, the former Liberal Minister for the National Economy, arguing for social insurance in an article he published in 1934, felt obliged to insist that it was not 'a socialist measure. Bismarck introduced it to combat socialist ideas . . . It is the conservative measure *par excellence* of bourgeois societies.' In that equation of conservatism and the bourgeois world one can discern the outlines of a new, more ideological politics emerging in Greece, to which the 'national schism' had scant relevance.[81]

When the Republic—and with it the whole constitutional issue—was abolished by General Kondylis's *coup d'état* in favour of the King towards the end of 1935, the social question remained unresolved. Kondylis's administration issued several important decrees concerning labour arbitration which passed unnoticed amidst the welter of proclamations issued by the new Regent. They were the work of a young LSE-trained graduate, George Kartalis, at the Ministry of the National Economy. But the collective bargaining procedures which he introduced were not initially accepted by either employers or workers, and neither the new Ministry of Labour nor the new Sub-Ministry of Food Market Control had sufficient personnel to implement the checks on working conditions and prices for which they had been established. When the Kondylis Government fell, and the elderly business magnate Kanellopoulos took over the Ministry of the National Economy, these interventionist initiatives were jettisoned. By 1936 price increases of essential foodstuffs, fuelled by rising world prices, were provoking increasingly bitter labour disputes.[82] In April 1936 one observer described the wave of strikes as having attained the proportions of 'a recent epidemic . . . in the past two months'.[83] He attributed them chiefly to 'rising prices and lagging wages' as well as to the lack of any sign that the Government intended to 'remedy a state of affairs whereby the majority of Greek workers lived upon the borderline of starvation and received

---

[81] A. Liakos, 'Apo kratos fylax eis kratos pronoia?', *O Politis*, 78(6) (Apr. 1987), 34–40.

[82] S. Kladas, *I ergatiki mas politiki kai nomothesia* (Athens, 1945), 77–8; USNA 868.00/935, MacVeagh–State Dept., 14 Nov. 1935; *OE 1935*, pt. 4, 226.

[83] FO 371/20386 R2124/89, Waterlow–FO, 9 Apr. 1936.

little or no assistance from the State'.[84] The former Venizelist General Mazarakis-Ainian, increasingly disillusioned with the factionalism of the political world, noted with some understatement in his diary: 'Poor administration and frequent changes of government have not allowed the time for a systematic study of the needs of the proletariat.'[85] The second deficiency, if not necessarily the first, was remedied by the *coup d'état* engineered by the King and his Prime Minister, Metaxas, on 4 August 1936. Metaxas had already made clear his proclivity for authoritarian solutions to the labour question by announcing his intention to implement Kondylis's decree concerning compulsory arbitration in industrial disputes. With the establishment of the dictatorship grandiose plans for turning Greece into a corporatist state were prepared.

To sum up, though import-substitution benefited both agriculture and industry, it had rather different effects in the two sectors. In both cases output rose as did prices—with little effective government control. In both cases the chief stimulus was the shift in relative prices after Greece left the gold standard. Although many peasants remained encumbered by debt, their economic position generally improved compared with the crisis years of 1929–32. Domestic industry benefited too, but few of the benefits reached the workers. The development of manufacturing after 1932 led neither to technological improvement nor to an increase in international competitiveness, but rather reinforced the oligopolistic features of Greek industry—with the economic and social consequences that have been described. Established businesses were strengthened by the Populist Government's policy of curbing industrial expansion; they also gained from the Government's reluctance to impose labour legislation from above. The Government relied chiefly on liberal use of the *Idionymon* law, police, and gendarmes to keep the peace, and by the time it got around to introducing its own version of labour legislation it was in no position to implement it.

Inflation affected neither the bulk of the peasantry, who could retreat to some form of self-sufficiency, nor industrialists, who passed on higher input prices to the consumer. But it did hit the vulnerable urban classes—workers, civil servants, artisans. The US Commercial Attaché asserted that while the farmers were 'as well off by 1934 as before the depression', industrial workers, day labourers, and junior civil servants

---

[84] FO 371/21143 R3166/94, 'Annual Econ. Report (A) for 1936', 29 Apr. 1937.
[85] A. Mazarakis-Ainian, *Memoires* (Thessaloniki, 1979), 373.

were '10–20% worse-off' as prices rose. As the recovery progressed, it became obvious that, in the words of a leading official in the Ministry of the National Economy, the Greek Republic was far from being an 'economic democracy or a state of the economically and socially weaker popular classes'.[86] This of course was nothing new: what had changed was its effect on the legitimacy of the existing order. Behind the social unrest after 1932 lay not economic stagnation, but the Greek political élite's reluctance to admit that the state, by its action or inaction, defined who derived the benefits from growth in a closed economy.

[86] Karl L. Rankin Papers, Box 3, 'Annual Econ. Report for Greece, 1934', 15 Jan. 1935; Kladas, *Ergatiki mas politiki*, pp. 79–80.

V

TOWARDS DICTATORSHIP

10

ECONOMIC ASPECTS OF
POLITICAL COLLAPSE

Greece is passing today, slower perhaps than any other country, the period of tendencies towards the left, from which other countries have already come out, either by the patriotic co-operation of the political parties for imposing a conservative policy, or by the strong hand of some illustrious personality, who could lead the popular masses to the road of national salvation and progress. In Greece, however, I see neither a politician of such superior political conscience, nor the strong man who would have the required qualifications for sweeping away the present shocking state of affairs.

(Theodoros Lekatzas, 5 December 1933)

Here as elsewhere the central problem is how to combine a managed economy successfully with a party system inherited from the age of *laissez-faire*.

(S. Waterlow, 8 April 1936)

In 1929 the former Finance Minister, George Kofinas, wrote an article entitled 'The Greek Miracle', in which he stated that 'despite the great and disproportionate burdens which the advent of the War threw upon Greece, and despite the excessively weighty taxation which the Greek people have had to endure . . . the public and private economy of the country today inspires optimism for its economic future'.[1] For a few years the despair and nihilism which had swept the country in the wake of the Asia Minor disaster were replaced by a mood of confidence. American and British financiers competed for contracts. The League of Nations lent its authority to plans for the reconstruction of the economy. Greece joined the gold standard, and embarked on ambitious projects to increase agricultural production and reduce her chronic trade deficit.

---

[1] *Hellas Jahrbuch*, 1929, cited in C. Chadziiosif, 'Apopseis gyro apo tin "viosimotita" tis Ellada kai to rolo tis viomichanias', *Afieroma ston Niko Svorono*, 2 (1986), 339.

For Venizelos, the 'productive works' would solve Greece's post-war demographic problem and stem the drift into the cities. He was certainly not the only one who, as a later critic put it, wore 'rose-coloured' spectacles in those years.[2]

Nor was this optimism immediately dispelled after 1929. Until the financial crisis, the Liberal Government argued that Greece was relatively unaffected by the international recession, and that indigenous factors such as poor harvests and excessive competition in industry were more important than external forces in causing such economic difficulties as were admitted to exist. Thanks to the lack of heavy industry, and to the primitive state of agriculture, the transmission of shocks from the international economy was muted. So ran the official argument, which we can also find espoused by politicians in other Mediterranean countries around this time.[3]

This exaggerated confidence even led the Venizelos Government to pat itself on the back for its handling of the public finances. The Liberal Budget committee chairman asserted in March 1931 that 'despite the worldwide crisis and all the special circumstances in Greece, such as successive droughts, it is an unarguable fact that our public finances present an amazing stability and firmness, a matter upon which we are certainly entitled to pride ourselves'.[4] And this in the same month when three-quarters of the latest Greek government loan offering had been left with the underwriters in London! The Government failed to appreciate the precarious balance of payments position, which made the country's adherence to the gold standard vulnerable to any cessation of capital inflows. As the central bank's foreign exchange reserves fell, it tried in vain to contract the money supply. Its failure saved Greece from serious deflation but made abandonment of the gold standard inevitable.

The financial crisis of 1931–2 marked the end of the Liberal Government's strategy of financing development through the London money market and thereby brought about the collapse of the Government itself. Venizelos never recovered from the dent to his reputation caused by the inglorious outcome of his self-proclaimed 'battle for the drachma'. His fierce defence of the gold standard, imitated dutifully by most other politicians, and his unfortunate trust in some *deus ex machina* (in the form of a new foreign loan) that would bring him political

---

[2] Finlayson–Niemeyer, 26 Nov. 1932, AET 46/163.
[3] J. Harrison, *An Economic History of Modern Spain* (Manchester, 1978), 127
G. Toniolo, *L'economia dell'Italia fascista* (Bari, 1980), 139.
[4] S. Kostopoulos, in *ESV*, 12 March 1931, 947.

salvation, both betrayed a fundamental inability to adapt to rapidly changing circumstances. It would be wrong to criticize him too harshly for this; after all, politicians in many other countries also believed that the British decision to abandon gold might be reversed.[5] But for Venizelos, who had always stressed the political importance of optimism, the heavy depreciation of the currency which ended the long 'battle for the drachma' had dire political costs: it weakened his claims to competent leadership and made his professions of confidence ring hollow. He was accused of having replaced the pessimism of his predecessors not with sound management, but with an exaggerated picture of Greece as a 'country of miracles'.[6] What, according to an unsympathetic critic in 1930, had he brought to the country?

A strong psychological encouragement, without any objective and self-sustaining basis to survive after him—just a purely personality-based psychological encouragement in his own name and for himself.[7]

The financial crisis made this sort of assessment more convincing. Indeed it was not of course just in Greece that the stability of the currency was bound up with political prestige. In Spain, for example, Primo de Rivera had suffered similarly, whilst at an earlier point in Italy political considerations weighed heavily in Mussolini's handling of the 'battle of the lira'. The primary difference with these figures was that, for better or worse, Venizelos was part of a parliamentary tradition. His failure, in a country where charismatic leaders were pivotal, contributed to the crisis of parliamentarianism.[8]

The irony was that when the drachma was allowed to depreciate, the economy soon began to respond. The Bank of Greece managed the abandonment of gold without provoking a domestic banking crisis. Domestic prices were slow to follow the rise in the drachma price of

---

[5] The point is argued for Germany in K. Borchardt, 'Could and Should Germany have Followed Great Britain in Leaving the Gold Standard?', *Journal of European Economic History*, 13(3) (Winter 1984), 471–99; for Latin America see Thorp (ed.), *Latin America in the 1930s*, pp. 23–4; for Colombia, where events followed a very similar course to Greece, see Antonio Ocampo, 'The Colombian Economy in the 1930s', in Thorp (ed.), *Latin America*, pp. 127–33.

[6] FO 371/15961 C3724/324, Ramsay–Sargent, 30 Apr. 1932; A. Bernaris, *I diarthrosis kai ai prospatheiai prosarmogis tis ellinikis oikonomias* (Athens, 1933), 40.

[7] K. Karavidas, 'Sosialismos kai koinotismos', in K. Karavidas, *To provlima tis avtonomias* (Athens, 1981), 37.

[8] S. Ben-Ami, *Fascism from Above* (Oxford, 1983), 334–55; R. Sarti, 'Mussolini and the Industrial Leadership in the Battle of the Lira, 1925–1927', *Past and Present* (May 1970), 87–112.

imported goods, thus providing a strong stimulus to domestic producers, who were also insulated by the imposition of import and exchange
controls from world price deflation. Relative price movements encouraged a shift of resources, especially in agriculture, from export items to
importables. Tsouderos, the Governor of the Bank of Greece, noted in
his annual report for 1932 that 'the emancipation of a country from the
gold standard has its practical side' and he argued that the year's
changes had 'fundamentally influenced the very texture of our economy,
and indeed constitute a historical stage in its future evolution'.[9]

In the next three years, contemporary observers were struck by the
rapidity with which Greece recovered from the crisis. The trough seems
to have occurred in the second half of 1932, and by early 1933 the
upswing was evident. 'Greece reached the low point of the economic
depression in the closing weeks of 1932,' reported the US Commercial
Attaché in Athens. 'Soon after the beginning of 1933 the outlook
changed. By the end of March the political situation had cleared and in
subsequent months the country's economic progress was continuous.'
During 1933, according to Tsouderos, Greece showed a 'remarkable
recovery from the crisis', whilst Zolotas wrote that the upswing took
place 'with astonishing ease and swiftness'. By 1935 a British observer
was remarking that in the provinces 'a perceptible atmosphere of
prosperity prevails compared to two or three years ago'.[10]

This upturn was closely connected with the radical change in
Greece's economic relations with the outside world. Her default on her
foreign debt meant that henceforth development would have to be
financed out of her own resources. The collapse of trade encouraged the
trend towards self-sufficiency, or 'autarky'. In itself this was not a new
aim: the pursuit of autarky had been a policy of governments ever since
the *Entente* blockade during the First World War. Moreover, few people
thought in terms of complete self-sufficiency; the emphasis, after 1932
as it had been before, was on the need to boost wheat production and,
more generally, to reduce the trade deficit in foodstuffs. But as
Diomedes, the former Governor of the Bank of Greece, wrote in 1935,
Greece was unused to looking inward and relying on her own resources,

[9] Bank of Greece, *The Economic Situation in Greece and the Bank of Greece in 1932*
(Athens, 1933), 11.
[10] Karl L. Rankin Papers, Box 3, 'Annual Economic Report for Greece (1933)',
Athens, 10 Jan. 1934; 'Annual Report of the Governor of the Bank of Greece for 1933',
MA, 17 Feb. 1934; N. Mousmoutis, 'To oikonomikon varometron', *EKDO* (1934),
129–42; X. Zolotas, *Katefthynseis tis oikonomikis mas politikis* (Athens, 1936), 16; FO
371/19516 R646/646, Waterlow–FO, 22 Jan. 1935.

to create 'greater self-reliance *vis-à-vis* the outside world'. According to him this would involve a shift from an individualism, well suited to the Greek temperament, to new principles, which required the co-ordinated action of the 'social organism'. It was necessary 'to attempt to achieve "autarky" even if we disagree with it in theory'.[11]

After 1932 Greek consumers turned increasingly to cheap, domestic-ally produced goods and in both agriculture and industry the share of imports in overall consumption dropped. This, combined with the high growth rates achieved domestically, meant that the early 1930s could be regarded as a success from the economic point of view. The new American Ambassador, Lincoln MacVeagh, reported back to Washing-ton early in 1934 that 'the operation of a planned economy such as Greece has never known has thus, beyond any question of doubt, proved itself a material success in one short year'; and he went on to extol the political benefits that the Populist Party were reaping as a result.[12] But the pivotal question which this raises is: if the recovery was such a success, why did Greek democracy die an ignominious death some two years later? More generally, what was the relation between politics and economics in Greece after the 1929–32 crisis?

Part of the answer is that MacVeagh, who was writing directly to Roosevelt at the time of the New Deal, could not help viewing Greek affairs through American spectacles. His assertion that Greece was 'an example of a country operating almost completely under the principles of a planned economy' was wildly off the mark. The Tsaldaris Govern-ment, which was in power for most of the upswing, could take little of the credit for the country's economic performance. It adopted—with little conviction but still less idea of anything better—the measures and institutions it inherited from its predecessors. It suffered the existence of the Bank of Greece much as Venizelos had done, and the increasingly prominent role played in the economy after 1932 by that institution reflected its desire to prove itself in the eyes of the Populist Government as much as any distinct monetary policy on the part of the latter. The six-monthly import quotas introduced as an emergency measure in 1932 continued to cast uncertainty over commercial dealings right

---

[11] A. Diomedes, 'Meta tin krisin', *EKDO* (1935), 129–55; cf. C. Evelpides, *Theoria kai praxis agrotikis politikis kai oikonomias* (Athens, 1939), 298–310; P. Kanellopoulos, *Ai koinonikai asfaliseis kai o nearos ellinikos nomos* (Athens, 1932).

[12] MacVeagh–Roosevelt, 2 Mar. 1934, cited in J. Iatrides (ed.), *Ambassador MacVeagh Reports: Greece 1933–1947* (Princeton, NJ, 1980), 23.

through to the end of the Republic in 1935. Like the Liberal Government, but less excusably, the Tsaldaris administration failed to take any measures to promote exports or to link them with imports through clearings—the 1936 crisis over the Greco-German clearing was just the most obvious consequence of this passive approach. The default on the foreign debt brought the budget massive windfall savings, but there does not seem to have been any discussion of how to make the best use of them. So far as agriculture was concerned, one observer noted that 'development has hitherto been more due to the efforts of the cultivators themselves than to a planned government policy'. And this was still truer where industry was concerned, where the Government's lack of any policy beyond tariff protection was manifest and politically more troubling since it produced an uneasy dependence, as one critic noted, on the goodwill of the industrialists.[13]

This lack-lustre performance was in part due to Tsaldaris himself —an essentially well-meaning, provincial lawyer with none of Venizelos's charisma, energy, or vision. His caution and reluctance to commit himself were legendary. Venizelos once burst out in a moment of annoyance that he 'has to think for half an hour before putting one foot in front of the other'.[14] But much more important than Tsaldaris's personal shortcomings were the ideological predilections of the Greek political élite. Neither Populists nor Liberals found it easy to abandon the *laissez-faire* principles they had grown up with for a step in the dark towards the planned economy.

Even before 1932 the politicians of the Republic, with few exceptions, had been unsure what the economic priorities of the state should be. Speaking to a gathering of young Liberals in 1929, Venizelos encouraged them to work for a 'modernized state' which would improve the 'social order'; at the same time, he reminded them, they should not be impatient, or reject all pre-war values:

What we chiefly seek through the gradual improvement of the social order is a juster distribution of the annual national income . . . Don't forget that any effort towards a juster distribution must take into account the sincere attempt of everyone to increase the national income as much as possible.[15]

[13] FO 371/21143 R3166/94, 'Annual Report: Economic (A) for 1936', 29 Apr. 1937; E, 17 Feb. 1935.

[14] Quoted in B. Lazaris, *Politiki istoria tis Patras*, ii (Athens, 1986), 284.

[15] S. Stefanou (ed.), *Ta keimena tou El. Venizelou*, iv: *1930–1936* (Athens, 1984), 169; cf. P. Papastratis, 'Apo ti megali idea sti Valkaniki Enosi', in Mavrogordatos and Chadziiosif (eds.), *Venizelismos*, 430–2.

Fairer distribution of higher output—which came first? It was essentially in the pursuit of the latter that the 1928 Liberal Government had shaped its economic strategy, confining the role of the state to raising loans abroad and supporting the stabilization programme. Venizelos remarked characteristically that 'the state is believed to be all powerful. But in economic affairs its actions are limited.'[16] Thus as the same time as the Liberals encouraged an awareness of the need for a 'modern state' they also shrank from what it implied. This fear of intervening in the economy was even more pronounced among the Populists who took power in 1933. The anti-Venizelism which held their camp together was—in the words of an opponent—a 'negative and sterile political ideology', which lacked even Venizelos's commitment to change. Quite typical of this outlook was the response of the elderly Populist Finance Minister, Loverdos, to charges that he had failed to introduce substantial tax reforms into the 1933/4 Budget: 'Unfortunately today things are tending by themselves so far along new paths, that woe to the minister whose thirst for innovation and radical changes adds to this chaos.'[17]

Did 1932 mark a permanent break with the past—or just a hiatus before a revival of economic liberalism? Few mainstream politicians, with the exception of Alexandros Papanastasiou and his followers, were willing to contemplate the first possibility. Konstantine Angelopoulos, a leading economic voice in the Populist Party, believed that the lack of independently minded politicians and civil servants made increased involvement by the state in the economy undesirable: policy would end up being made by parties on the basis of special electoral interests or by 'plutocratic' monstrosities like the NBG.[18] Others justified their opinions on the basis of the country's supposed natural endowments. Their belief, as the economist Stefanides defined it, was that 'the economic future of Hellenism lies not so much in the production of goods, as in commerce and emigration abroad'.[19] This was an accurate reflection of the view of the Tsaldaris Government, notably its Minister for the National Economy, George Pesmazoglu, and explains the latter's lack of enthusiasm for industry. Pesmazoglu felt that industrialization was

---

[16] Stefanou (ed.), *Ta keimena tou El. Venizelou*, iv. 182–3.

[17] A. Mazarakis–Ainian, *Memoires* (Thessaloniki, 1979), 367; Ministry of Finance, *Psifistheis genikos proypologismos, 1933–34*, i (Athens, 1934), 9–10.

[18] K. Angelopoulos, *Politikoi agones: 1892–1934*, iii (Athens, 1934), 80.

[19] D. Stefanides, *I thesis tis viomichanias en ti koinoniki mas oikonomia* (Thessaloniki, 1938), 41.

merely a temporary expedient to solve Greece's demographic problems until emigration again became possible. Politicians criticized the poor use made of the protection afforded to industry but were not prepared to consider greater state control over the sector. One conservative Liberal observed that 'the industrialization of a large part of the economy can only be carried out rapidly and effectively by a wealthy [*sic*] Socialist State. We are not Russia, nor do we intend a policy of sovietization.' By 1935 most Liberal and Populist Party politicians confined themselves to warning industrialists to use their large profits to modernize their equipment—without providing any incentive for them to do so.[20]

The politicians' apathetic response left academics and civil servants unimpressed. For the technocrats the trend towards autarky presented the Greek state with an unprecedented challenge—to replace the market as the arbiter of both economic development and social equity. The Supreme Economic Council warned in 1932 in its first published report that 'only a stable and well-directed economic policy can prevent great internal anomalies and economic disturbances'.[21] One financial journalist wrote: 'Greece presents the spectacle of a partisan state, which takes a succession of *ad hoc* measures to solve questions under pressure from organized groups, heeded according to their voting strength. Now we have the opportunity, with the extension of the state's influence, to work out and apply a carefully researched state policy, which will regulate economic activity.'[22] Such visions were largely unrealized in the lifetime of the Republic. One factor was the experts' lack of power, faced with a general hostility, sustained by profound cultural influences, to any enhancement of the state's role. Apart from the Bank of Greece, few other institutions were able to shape official policy. Reforms suggested and drawn up within the Ministry for the National Economy on labour legislation and the organization of foreign trade were opposed by powerful vested interests. For the business world, the advocates of planning were 'bureaucratic, pedantic young graduates entirely lacking in real experience'.[23] Followers of the political theorist Dragoumis, like Kostas Karavidas, felt confirmed in their view that grandiose hopes for economic reform through state planning

---

[20] L. Makkas, *To ellinikon provlima kai to schedion mias lyseos* (Athens, 1933), 16; N. Anastasopoulos, *Istoria tis ellinikis viomichanias*, iii (Athens, 1947), 1,439.

[21] AOS, *Gnomodotisis epi tou dynatou tis rythmiseos tou exoterikou emporiou tis Ellados* (Athens, n.d.), 15.

[22] T. Galanis, 'To kratos kai pistotiki organosis', *E*, 7 Apr. 1935.

[23] *VE*, Sept. 1935.

were based on West European models unsuitable for Greek conditions. Karavidas, who worked at the Agricultural Bank, elaborated his nostalgic vision of a Greece centred around local communities rather than a centralized state in a series of works, culminating in *The Communal State*, published in 1935. Others looked beyond the chaotic inefficiency of the Republic to more authoritarian solutions. The right-wing politician George Merkouris, having left the Populists to found his own unsuccessful National Socialist Party, provided a systematic discussion of Fascist thinking in his book, *The Corporatist State*, which appeared in 1936. Some form of étatism, usually with an anti-parliamentarian flavour, was increasingly acceptable to apolitical 'experts'. Their changing expectations could perhaps be charted in the career of a young man like Babis Alivizatos: trained in economics with a doctorate from Paris, author of a classic study of the land reform and close to the social-democratic Papanastasiou in the 1920s, he moved up the university ladder in the mid-1930s before accepting a senior position under Metaxas at the Ministry of Agriculture in 1936. Ignored by their political masters, the technocrats had little cause to mourn the passing of the Republic.[24]

The second part of the answer to the rosy picture painted by MacVeagh in 1934 can be supplied by showing how quickly the authority of democratic political institutions crumbled in the face of constitutional turmoil and social unrest. A prominent Venizelist Alexandros Pallis had emphasized in December 1931 that Greece should not worry about the economic effects of the crisis; it was its impact on social tranquillity that needed attention:

What I think is indispensable is to preserve that spirit of solidarity among the different classes—bourgeois, workers, farmers—which was so admirably displayed at the difficult time of the refugee settlement and which—I hope—will not fail us during this period of new trials.[25]

Unfortunately the effects of the crisis were just the opposite—at both the élite and the mass level. Having suffered a defeat in the 'battle for the drachma' Venizelos tried to reassert his authority over the Venizelist camp through an engineered confrontation with his opponents, insisting

---

[24] See M. Psalidopoulos, *I krisi tou 1929 kai oi ellines oikonomologoi* (Athens, 1989), 350–473; 'Morfes oikonomikis skepsis stin Ellada, 1936–1940', in H. Fleischer and N. Svoronos (eds.), *I Ellada, 1936–1944* (Athens, 1989), 98–144; N. Inglesis, *Odigos ton Anonymon Etaireion, 1937–38*, ii(ii) (Athens, 1939), 3.

[25] *Les Balkans*, 17–18 (Feb.–Mar. 1932), 289.

that the Populists could not be admitted to government until they officially recognized the Republic. As one senior republican bitterly remarked, whenever Venizelos felt threatened, he raised the constitutional question.[26]

These tactics suited the extreme royalists on the right wing of the anti-Venizelist camp and when a Populist Government was formed with their support in March 1933 they kept the constitutional issue alive. With the Venizelist camp disintegrating into its separate factions, and Tsaldaris a hostage to the Right, there was increasing discussion of the failure of parliamentarianism, fanned of course by Hitler's success in Germany. The examples of Hitler and Mussolini seemed to recommend an authoritarian solution to Greece's political problems. Although the defects of parliamentarianism had been debated in the 1920s, they were underlined by several vain attempts by Venizelos to strengthen the powers of the executive at the expense of the Chamber. In 1934 he observed that the parliamentary system was ill-adapted to promote the sort of state intervention in economic affairs which the problems that had emerged since the crisis required.[27] That January the anti-Venizelist newspaper *Kathimerini* invited a series of contributions on the topic of 'Dictatorship or Parliamentarianism?', prompting an article by Metaxas on the bankruptcy of democracy, and a similar offering by Admiral Chadzikyriakos, who was actually Minister for the Navy at the time![28] In June a debate in the Chamber on modifications to the electoral law turned into a discussion of the crisis of parliamentary democracy itself. The Venizelist George Papandreou conjured up a picture of a country in transition:

> The liberal economy gives way to state socialism, to the managed economy. And the free, easy-going, anarchic State gives way to the managed, strong and just State . . . Right yields and leads to Duty.[29]

As such language suggests, many Liberals shared some of the central values of authoritarianism. Others moved beyond theory: on the anti-Venizelist side both Metaxas and Kondylis dreamed of seizing power; indeed they are reported to have had several private discussions on the subject in the summer of 1934. Venizelos was no doubt aware of similar

---

[26] Mazarakis–Ainian, *Memoires*, p. 338.

[27] N. Alivizatos, *Les Institutions politiques de la Grèce à travers les crises, 1922–1974* (Paris, 1979), 22.

[28] G. Vouros, *Panayis Tsaldaris* (Athens, 1955), 357.

[29] G. Papandreou, *Politika keimena*, i (Athens, n.d.), 243.

schemes within his own camp. Then, proclaiming the need to defend the Republic, in March 1935 the old statesman led an abortive and ill-planned rebellion, which petered out after several days fighting in northern Greece. He was forced to flee, humiliated, into exile for the last time. 'The revolution lacked an ideological objective,' wrote Dafnis. 'There was no programme, no aim. Some—a few—believed that democracy [*dimokratia*] was in danger, or rather the Republic [*avasilevftou dimokratias*], others supported their private interests, others aimed at social reform, while others finally hoped to set up a pure dictatorship to release Greece from the corruption [*miasma*] of the political world.' Observers reported that 'there seems to have been very little popular feeling aroused, either for or against the movement'.[30]

It was the end of an era, for Venizelos had dominated Greek politics since he first became premier in 1910. Although on his return in 1928 he was a more conservative figure than he had been in his early years, he could not be accused of lacking the 'mental force' and 'strong will' that he believed essential to successful government.[31] The fact as well as the manner of his departure undermined the legitimacy of parliamentarianism. In his wake he left a fragmented, defensive Liberal opposition as well as a political élite bereft of any charismatic figures. As MacVeagh remarked: 'One cannot work up much enthusiasm for Tsaldaris, Kondylis or Metaxas.'[32]

After the failure of Venizelos's revolt, there followed an anti-Venizelist backlash as republican sympathizers were purged from the civil service and the Army. Power now swung towards the extremists in the anti-Venizelist camp, particularly when the Liberal Party abstained from the general elections in June, thereby weakening still further the prestige of Parliament. The following month General Kondylis, the unscrupulous and ambitious former Venizelist on whom Tsaldaris had relied for two years, declared to an astonished public that he now favoured a return of the monarchy. There was no indication of any strong popular feeling for the King but this did not deter Kondylis from overthrowing the Tsaldaris Government in October and rigging a plebiscite to legitimize King George's return.

---

[30] Bodosakis Athanasiades, untitled memoirs, p. 141; T. Veremis, *Oi epemvaseis tou stratou stin elliniki politiki 1916–1936* (Athens, 1977), 218; B. Lazaris, *Politiki istoria tis Patras*, ii (Athens, 1986), 309; G. Dafnis, *I Ellas metaxy dyo polemon: 1923–1940*, 2 vols. (Athens, 1955), ii. 350; Iatrides (ed.), *Ambassador MacVeagh Reports*, p. 41.
[31] S. Stefanou (ed.), *Ta politika keimena tou El. Venizelou*, i: *1909–1914* (Athens, 1981), 96.   [32] Iatrides (ed.), *Ambassador MacVeagh Reports*, p. 41.

Kondylis was a great rival of Metaxas, and his strong-arm tactics and dictatorial dreams give his activities in retrospect the air of a trial run for the 4 August regime. Announcing the forthcoming plebiscite, Kondylis also spelled out the measures he planned to introduce: they included restricting movement from the countryside into the towns, job creation schemes and social security legislation. In the circumstances, this was of course mostly window-dressing—of interest chiefly for the reflection it offered of contemporary public concerns; but all too real was the new brutality shown by his supporters in the gendarmerie and Army against the Venizelist opposition. Papanastasiou and Papandreou were deemed 'dangerous to the public peace' and deported. Improving on the *Idionymon*, Kondylis's regime outlawed the propagation of any ideas intended not only to 'change the existing social order' but even to 'excite the passions for any purpose whatsoever'. When the Liberal leader Sofoulis visited Salonika to address a republican rally on the eve of the plebiscite he was prevented from speaking and the crowd was dispersed by cavalry charges. Other republican rallies planned for Athens were repeatedly banned. Kondylis was soon to depart from the scene with his hopes unrealized, but his followers and their methods did not.[33]

Once the King returned to Greece, after the plebiscite had given a ludicrous 97% vote in his favour, the old political divisions began to lose much of their significance. With the disappearance of the constitutional issue there was no longer any need for Leftist voters to vote Liberal in the belief that 'the Republic of Venizelos is a lesser evil than the Monarchy' as they reportedly had done in 1933.[34] Venizelos himself advised his supporters from his exile in Paris to accept the King. The long-term outlook for the Populist Party was not much better either: with Venizelos's departure from Greece, and then his death in March 1936, anti-Venizelism lost its *raison d'être*. Demanding that the two main camps co-operate and work out a comprehensive social and economic programme, George Vlachos wrote in *Kathimerini*: 'Let the parties get together, but not on the ancient issues of Venizelism and anti-Venizelism. Let them discuss what should be done to create a new state on the ruins of the old.' But on what basis? To answer this question, to

---

[33] USNA 868.00/929, MacVeagh (Athens)–State, 31 Oct. 1935; cf. V. Lazaris, *Politiki istoria tis Patras*, iii (Athens, 1989), 13.

[34] *MA*, 12 Oct. 1935; FO 371/19508 R6115/34, Walker–Eden, 7 Oct. 1935; A. Elefantis, *I epangelia tis adynatis epanastasis* (Athens, 1976), 223.

identify the new political currents that were to wash away the residues of the *dichasmos*, we must move outside the political world of Athens.[35]

Beyond the constitutional disputations and the factionalism of the political élite, the abandonment of the liberal economic order also intensified social discontent. We have argued here that simple correlations between economic slump and political crisis do not apply to the Greek case; rather, there was an economic upswing of impressive dimensions, and both this upswing and the preceding crisis presented challenges of government to an élite which could not meet them. It was economic *growth* which taxed the capacities of the existing system and pointed the way to an eventual realignment of political forces.

Successive governments had neglected the towns for the countryside, where they hoped to encourage a way of life far removed from the pernicious influence of urban 'parasites'. While the refugee resettlement programme, combined with the public works in northern Greece, had been designed to address the problem of rural resettlement, little had been done for city-dwellers. In 1930 the outgoing chairman of the Refugee Settlement Commission had warned that further expenditure of 900 million drachmas would be required for housing and equipment; by 1937 it was estimated that only 62 millions had been spent to this end, while town-based refugees remained in squalor. Once the chance of borrowing abroad disappeared, it emerged that Greek politicians lacked any other ideas for improving the standard of living of the masses. The reorganization of the banking system—it was suggested—could have stemmed or even reversed the flow of workers from the fields into the towns by channelling funds into agriculture and away from small merchants or real-estate speculators. But this implied taking on the National Bank of Greece, with its stranglehold over commercial credit, and the politicians of the Republic lacked the will to do this.[36]

Widespread urban poverty ensured a cheap labour supply for industry but also raised new political problems. By 1935 there was extensive public disquiet at the profits amassed over the previous three years by Greek manufacturers and at the growing antagonism in labour relations; the Government's unwillingness to intervene more forcefully in industrial affairs aroused criticism and commentators increasingly stressed,

[35] J. Koliopoulos, *Palinorthosis, diktatoria, polemos: 1935–1941* (Athens, 1985), 30; USNA 868.00/981, MacVeagh (Athens)–State, 16 June 1936.

[36] FO 371/23768 R7282/94, 'Annual Report Economic (B) for 1937', 1 Nov. 1937; T. Galanis, *Trapezikai meletai* (Athens, 1946), 119.

not the inefficiencies brought about by the recovery, but the lack of social justice. When Xenophon Zolotas argued that such intervention was necessary to set the industrial sector on a more competitive footing since 'the recent development of industry has generally lacked any permanence or stability', he was criticized in a review for divorcing his economic prescriptions from the political context. In an article entitled 'Towards a New Economic Policy', one journalist called for 'a "new economy" with greater fairness in economic and social relations'. A reviewer of a book on industrial policy by the former Minister for the National Economy, Pesmazoglu, criticized him for having been responsible for a policy which resulted in 'the clearest indications of a swift concentration of wealth in the hands of a few'. The reviewer attacked the view that all that was needed to produce economic growth was capital, and called instead for the emergence of 'an educated class of policy-makers with independent morals'. Even the Populist Party—out of government—echoed the new mood with a call in the spring of 1936 for a 'more just organization of our economic and social life'.[37]

In 1936, as working-class protest gathered force, the major political parties were first marginalized and then pushed into a position of supporting anti-communist repression. This came about largely as a consequence of the political deadlock produced by the general election in January in which Venizelists and anti-Venizelists won almost equal numbers of seats, leaving the Communist Party holding the balance of power. While Liberals and Populists negotiated the formation of a new government, the death of Demertzis in April forced the King to select a new caretaker Prime Minister. He picked Ioannis Metaxas, a stalwart of the anti-Venizelist Right, and a man of known anti-democratic sympathies, who had just been appointed Minister of Army Affairs under Demertzis. In the January elections Metaxas's party had won only 4% of the votes and seven seats. Deeply humiliated by this result he can hardly have suspected that three months later he would be invited to become premier.

Once in power, Metaxas quickly turned to the repressive measures of his predecessors to quell the spreading urban unrest. On 4 May, tobacco workers in Kavalla struck once more, including among their chief demands full liberty of association and an end to 'the state of terror'. Shopkeepers and artisans closed their shops in sympathy, arguing that

---

[37] X. Zolotas, *Katefthynseis tis oikonomikis mas politikis* (Athens, 1936), 23; *E*, 2 Feb., 17 May, 16 June 1936; G. Mavrogordatos, *Stillborn Republic* (Berkeley, Calif., 1983), 114.

'the tobacco worker's wage is the source of life for the commercial professions and the other classes of eastern Macedonia and Thrace'. The moderate local newspaper *Tachydromos* declared the urgency of 'regulating the relations between labour and capital through the intervention of the state', a task which was being hindered by the state's unwillingness to solve 'this gigantic social problem'. As if to bear out the truth of these remarks, the local Prefect responded with the 'old methods'—arresting and deporting among others senior officials of local merchants' guilds.[38]

Similar events on a more startling scale took place in Salonika four days later. As MacVeagh subsequently reported, 'from the organised centres of tobacco-picking, particularly from Cavalla, it has indeed been inevitable, under the prevailing policy of *laissez-faire*, that communistic influence should extend to the miserably low-paid workers of the textile and other industries of Salonica'. After declaring a strike on 29 April and presenting their demands to the Governor-General, workers there had waited over a week to learn the Government's views. On the morning of 8 May, large crowds gathered in the streets by the tobacco warehouses and a committee was appointed to urge the Governor-General to accept the strikers' demands. However, the police blocked access to the Governor's house and clashes broke out. The next day the crowds were larger, with textile workers, bakers, printers, dockers, and others supporting the tobacco workers, while the police were strengthened by Army units. In the ensuing clash they opened fire on the strikers, killing 12 and wounding over 200. With no light or communications, the city was paralysed for several days before the Government capitulated to the demands of the workers. Although this ended the Salonika strike, unrest continued in various towns for much of the summer. On June 3 police in the port of Volos fired on demonstrators during a strike of tobacco, metal, and textile workers, killing one and wounding six.[39]

Foreign observers stressed the economic causes of these events. According to the British Consul in Salonika the unrest stemmed from 'the real distress of the working classes' with 'the increases in the cost of living reducing the value of already low wages'.[40] Later he wrote that the

[38] *Tachydromos tis Kavallas*, 5–6 May 1936.
[39] Iatrides (ed.), *Ambassador MacVeagh Reports*, p. 86; FO 371/20389 R3310/220, encl. Lomas (Salonika)–Walker, 27 May 1936; ibid. R3312/220, Walker–Eden, 3 June 1936; ibid. R4354/220, Walker–Eden, 14 July 1936.
[40] FO 371/20389 R3310/220, Walker–FO, 'Report of H.M. Consul at Salonica', 2 June 1936.

May disturbances 'would have occurred even without the existence of communist propaganda . . . and unless a general rise in wages among the working-classes is accompanied by a proper system of Health and Unemployment Insurance, serious troubles are likely to recur in the future'.[41] MacVeagh noted that 'the extent to which the organisation of the tobacco-pickers has strengthened them *vis-à-vis* their employers . . . has not gone unobserved by their brothers engaged in less fortunate occupations, particularly in Salonica where a large industrial city is in the making under the eyes of a Government which persists in seeing little else in politics but the spoils and pays little heed to economic factors till these get the upper hand'.[42]

Greek politicians, on the other hand, insisted that the unrest was politically inspired. The sudden political prominence of the Communists after the January election, together with the sense of ideological polarization in Europe generally may have contributed to this perspective, though as a British observer noted 'the habit of regarding all discontent among the working class as of communist origin is too deeply ingrained to be easily eradicated'.[43] According to MacVeagh, the politicians in Athens debated the causes of the unrest 'in terms of Venizelism and anti-Venizelism, according to the time-honoured formula . . . losing sight altogether of its fundamental significance'. To Metaxas, worried by the growing unrest and with the additional headache of a likely harvest failure, it was evident that 'the aims of the leaders of the strike movement were political and subversive'. Quietly he consolidated his position, appointing a close associate, Theodoros Skylakakis—a Nazi sympathizer—as Minister of the Interior. When anti-Venizelists put their opponents on the defensive by describing them as 'Venizelo-communists', even progressive figures such as Papanastasiou and Papandreou felt it necessary to defend themselves by making public warnings against the threat of communism.[44] By doing so, of course, they played straight into the Prime Minister's hands, a favour which the latter badly needed, since by early summer there was little sign that his interim administration had won much popularity.

---

[41] FO 371/20389 R4354/220, Walker–FO, 'Report of H.M. Consul at Salonica for June', 14 July 1936.

[42] Iatrides (ed.), *Ambassador MacVeagh Reports*, p. 84.

[43] FO 371/20389 R3310, Walker–FO, 2 June 1936, cited in J. Kofas, *Authoritarianism in Greece* (New York, 1983), 21–3.

[44] Iatrides (ed.), *Ambassador MacVeagh Reports*, p. 87; J. Koliopoulos, *Greece and the British Connection 1935–1941* (Oxford, 1977), 43.

'Dissatisfaction with the Government is steadily increasing and poorer people one and all regard the Greek Government as a gang of thieves,' reported one observer, as the Chamber of Deputies adjourned for its summer recess.[45] Following an official announcement that the Government would shortly implement compulsory arbitration procedures in labour disputes, trade union leaders declared on 27 July that a 24-hour general strike would take place in protest. This provided the King and Metaxas with a pretext for embarking upon a course of action which they seem to have already decided was necessary. Parliament was indefinitely suspended and martial law declared on 4 August: there was little protest. Several communist and republican figures were arrested and strict Press censorship was imposed. General Mazarakis-Ainian confided to his diary: 'I feel two things, on the one hand, profound sadness for the state to which this poor country has been reduced, where its premier can declare himself dictator without the least drop of blood being shed, without the slightest opposition; . . . on the other hand, a deep resentment against the politicians whose incapacity and partisan rivalries have led us to dictatorship.'[46]

The Metaxas regime quickly presented itself as a unifying force in Greek society which would bring into being—echoing the title of the regime's leading ideological organ—the New State. In his first address, on 4 August, Metaxas declared that he had acted in order to preserve the 'social state' from its two enemies: communism and party faction; his Government would be 'entirely beyond parties'. At the end of the month he announced that economic development would henceforth be 'more co-ordinated and totally systematized': a long-term plan was to be elaborated to help achieve autarky. Metaxas even offered an economic theory for the collapse of parliamentary democracy: once the state became involved in economic management, the parliamentary system lost its justification, since the stakes for which parties competed were raised, leading the good relations which had prevailed between them when parliamentarianism worked effectively to degenerate into bitter conflict. And there were many others, by no means all of them fascists, who believed that parliamentarianism had failed to adapt to the contemporary needs of Greek society.[47]

[45] FO 371/20389, 'Report of H.M. Consul at Salonica for June 1936', cited in Kofas, *Authoritarianism in Greece*, p. 26.
[46] Mazarakis-Ainian, *Memoires*, p. 374.
[47] J. Metaxas, *Logoi kai skepseis 1936–1941*, i (Athens, 1969), 9–10, 20–9.

The heterogeneous group of figures which made up the Government in its early days reflected the broad extent of the disaffection with party politics. The former President of the Federation of Greek Industrialists, Andreas Chadzikyriakos, was appointed Minister for the National Economy; the conservative ex-Liberal, Konstantine Zavitsianos, who as Venizelos's Interior Minister had been responsible for the 1929 *Idionymon* legislation, became Finance Minister; Alexandros Koryzis, Deputy-Governor of the National Bank of Greece, was responsible for Public Assistance and Welfare; George Kyriakos, a rather undistinguished and conservative agriculture expert, was appointed Minister of Agriculture, with, as one of his advisers, the young Paris-trained university professor Babis Alivizatos. The Junior Minister for Labour, Aristides Dimitratos, was a former trade union leader, while the leader of the Youth Movement, Alekos Kanellopoulos, was the son of another prominent industrialist. Varvaressos refused ministerial office but remained at the Bank of Greece, where he succeeded Tsouderos as Governor in 1939. A combination of business men, bankers, and technocrats under the leadership of a rather conservative and not notably charismatic military man, this was a similar sort of coalition of experts and professors to that found in other authoritarian regimes of the day. Few members of this Government—other than key figures in security and propaganda departments—had been associated with Metaxas before. What, apart from ambition, united them was not Fascism—after all the regime never succeeded in creating a mass party to support it—but the conviction that democracy had failed in Greece and had left society disunited and pessimistic.

But was authoritarianism any more effective as an approach to the country's problems? In September Metaxas told the conservative paper *Kathimerini* that Greece would be organized on the basis of the Turkish, Italian, and German examples—thereby unwittingly bearing out the remark George Papandreou had made more than two years earlier that a dictatorship in Greece would probably not correspond to 'an internal, organic necessity' of the country, but be no more than mimicry of other regimes.[48] Though as time went on Metaxas would stress the specifically Greek character of his regime, Papandreou's prophecy touched a raw nerve, and as late as 1939 pro-regime constitutionalists were still defensive on this point. In November Finance Minister Konstantine

---

[48] G. Andrikopoulos, *I dimokratia tou mesopolemou* (Athens, 1987), 235; Papandreou, *Politika keimena*, p. 238.

Zavitsianos, revealing plans to turn the country into a corporatist state, announced that events since 1922 had proved the bankruptcy of both the parliamentary form of government and economic liberalism, which according to him had been unable 'to adjust themselves to the new social and economic synthesis which emerged from the war'. Late 1936 and early 1937 saw a spate of articles on the need for the modern state to act as 'arbiter and regulator of conflicting individual interests'. Writers praised the replacement of *laissez-faire* by the move towards a planned economy. Nor was it just self-serving mediocrities and admirers of totalitarian regimes abroad who expressed such views. Varvaressos, perhaps the most influential of contemporary Greek economists, looked forward to the chance to shape a new role for the modern state between, on the one hand, the apathy induced by the liberal belief in the primary of the market, and, on the other, the extremes of socialism with its apparent acceptance of class conflict. After years of haphazard and ill-thought-out intervention, the state could now elaborate its policies with the aim of encompassing 'the entire social problem'.[49]

Any evaluation of the achievements of the Metaxas regime, which lasted from 1936 until the dictator's death in January 1941, must wait until we possess a detailed study of the regime's domestic policies. It is, however, clear that together with a new emphasis on the role of the state came legislation on a variety of issues—social insurance, compulsory labour arbitration, peasant debt relief—which had in most cases been prepared but not implemented by earlier governments. At the same time many familiar economic difficulties continued to plague Metaxas: problems associated with the Greek–German clearing led to the resignation of Zavitsianos, whilst Chadzikyriakos too resigned in 1937 after Metaxas echoed earlier appeals to Greek industrialists to curb price increases. For all the regime's rhetoric about national regeneration and a return to the values of ancient Greece, the dictator remained committed to the defence of the 'bourgeois order', though in his search for popular support this was extended to include not only the farmers, but workers too. Metaxas (like Venizelos) called for the co-operation of capital and labour, but combined this with a distinctly anti-Venizelist attack on 'plutocracy'. This does not seem to have won him much backing among the lower classes. Popular discontent was repressed by harsh police methods, and according to one observer all that kept the regime in power was 'no positive force, but relief from past troubles and disgust with the discarded politicians'.[50]

This perhaps provides an appropriate note on which to end a story of passivity and missed opportunities. A study of the Greek experience of the inter-war economic crisis reveals the complexity of the links between economics and politics—more particularly, between the crisis of economic liberalism and the collapse of parliamentary democracy. Greece's defeat by Turkey in 1922 ended the era of irredentism, disoriented the political élite, and set the tone of nostalgia and pessimism which was present throughout the Republic's lifetime; Alexandros Papanastasiou was quite correct when he noted in 1929 that the Liberal Government's proposed anti-communist legislation indicated a 'lack of confidence in our own ideals'.[51] The two major parties looked back to the past to reaffirm their identity—politically to the 'national schism', economically to the pre-war world of free trade and labour flows. This was particularly true of the anti-Venizelists, who gained power at just the time when the trend towards autarky increased demands for the state to take a more assertive role in the economy. The view that existing political allegiances and passions no longer corresponded to social needs was nicely summarized by Sir Sydney Waterlow, the British Ambassador, who wrote in April 1936:

> As new issues take shape, new lines of cleavage may be expected gradually to cut across the old, turning old hatreds into new channels, blurring the sharp edges of the two fronts and making new combinations possible in time. Here as elsewhere the central problem is how to combine a managed economy successfully with a party system inherited from the age of laissez-faire. Perhaps the problem is insoluble: it may well be that parliamentary government will break down altogether.[52]

The new polarization which emerged as Greece's politicians fought for the leadership of a modernizing mass society was to become visible with stark and brutal clarity only in the next decade through the violent years of occupation and civil war. Little was obvious in the 1930s beyond the evident shakiness of existing political structures; not by chance was King

---

[50] A. Kyros, in *Neon Kratos* (Jan. 1937), cited in N. Psyroukis, *O fasismos kai i tetarti Avgoustou* (Athens, 1977), 87; FO 371/21143 R3166/94, Waterlow–Eden, 'Annual Report, Economic (A) on Greece for 1936', 29 Apr. 1937, 2; Sarandis, 'Emergence of the Right', pp. 381–445; cf. G. Andrikopoulos, *Oi rizes tou ellinikou fasismou* (Athens, 1977), 25–7.

[51] G. Anastasiadis, G. Kontogiorgis, and P. Petridis (eds.), *Alexandros Papanastasiou: Thesmoi, ideologia kai politiki sto mesopolemo* (Athens, 1987), 165.

[52] FO 371/20389 R2033/220, Waterlow–Eden, 8 Apr. 1936.

George struck by the fact on returning to Greece that he encountered only 'old and sick men' as party leaders.[53] And just as economic changes contributed to the sense of a political world in transition, so too politics had an important effect on Greece's response to the world economic depression. The backward character of her economy did *not* condemn her to prolonged stagnation. On the contrary, as the Greek case shows, a backward economy possesses certain recovery mechanisms of its own which help explain why Greece's upswing after 1932 was unusually rapid. Yet in the hands of an uncertain political élite the recovery itself became linked to the crisis of parliamentarianism and in many respects made the economy more uncompetitive and technologically backward.

[53] *DGFP*, ser. C, vol. iv (Washington, DC, 1962), 911.

11

BOURGEOIS DILEMMAS

I do not believe that our economic and social evolution has been such that the major issues facing the country are best served when we are divided into classes and form class parties . . . I believe it is an economic and social necessity that we remain organized in national parties.

(Venizelos, 21 December 1929)

The Greek social classes do not yet have a class consciousness . . . But the 'national parties' Venizelos talked about also do not exist: they emerge around a leader [*archigos*] and disappear with him; they have no programmatic tradition, no organization.

(*Peitharchia*, 29 December 1929)

The position of the two major bourgeois parties was not inexplicable. They felt, deep down, that Metaxas had provided the only possible solution for the unification of the bourgeois world.

(Gregorios Dafnis, *I Ellas metaxy dyo polemon*)

In Greece during the 1920s the prestige of parliamentary institutions was bound up with the success of economic liberalism and the allure of Western money-markets. When international capitalism collapsed, most emphatically in 1931, the political values associated with it in Greece suffered too. In the 'battle for the drachma' Venizelos defiantly tied himself to the mast of a sinking ship, dragging Greek liberalism down with him. Thus the economic crisis of 1929–32 proved to be an important turning-point for Greek politics. And yet it is possible to imagine a different outcome. This book has, after all, argued that economic recovery came early in Greece. A more reformist programme which would have given the institutions of the Republic 'genuine social content' was not unfeasible. Moreover, the configuration of political forces in Parliament was apparently well suited to ensure the preservation of bourgeois rule, with two large parties, the Liberals and the Populists, surrounded by smaller partners, with *no* socialist party and only a small communist party out on the political margin. Why then, despite the upswing after 1932, could parliamentary democracy not ride out the transition to a new form of economic development? And what can this failure tell us about the political priorities of the Greek élite?

In 1931 the Venizelist journalist Georgios Ventiris published a lengthy and highly sympathetic study of the first decade (1910–20) of Liberal rule in Greece. Ventiris saw Venizelos's ultimate goal as the foundation of what he called the 'bourgeois national state'.[1] Though we may doubt the usefulness of seeing those years as marking the moment when the Greek bourgeoisie gained political power, we must acknowledge the energy and vision of the early Liberal administrations. Before the First World War the main opponent of Venizelos's new Liberal Party had been the former governing groups, with their ties to certain large landowners. Collectively they formed the *tzakia*—the leading families —or alternatively, *palaiokommatismo*—'old partyism'. Against these supposed conservatives the Venizelists' mission was active, reformist, and heroic—building new state institutions, planning for territorial expansion.

But the Great War transformed Greek politics in two ways. In the first place it led to the republican–royalist *dichasmos*, which became the dominant and overpowering feature of the political landscape. And yet, at the same time, through industrial and urban growth, it introduced new social forces into Greek life which ultimately threatened *both* parties, royalist and republican, and led them to emphasize their common character. The war brought the spectre of Bolshevism and the language of class, pitting the bourgeois world against the threat from below. Social change, in other words, was turning the *dichasmos* into an anachronism. The idea of a 'bourgeois national state' had lost its triumphal ring and acquired defensive, increasingly beleaguered overtones by the time Ventiris came to write his account.

'I belong unmistakably to the bourgeois class,' Venizelos admitted in 1933, but he insisted that this was not true of the Liberal Party as a whole.[2] He and his followers feared the very thought of politics stratified along class lines and tried to preserve their claim to speak for all those who had the interests of the nation at heart. In vain did Venizelist

---

[1] G. Ventiris, *I Ellas tou 1910–1920*, i (Athens, 1931), 74–89.
[2] S. Stefanou (ed.), *Eleftheriou Venizelou politikai ypothikai anthologitheisai apo ta keimena avtou*, ii (Athens, 1969), 346.

progressives point out that the real threat to the parliamentary system lay in precisely such attitudes, that even the Liberal Party, far from being a 'national party', was built around the personality of its leader, that the best antidote to 'class parties' was social reform.[3] Indeed it would turn out that neither the charisma of Venizelos himself nor the appeal to the old loyalties of the national schism were sufficient to prevent these post-war social pressures emerging as political realities. When Alexandros Papanastasiou, always a sensitive observer of Greek society, altered the name of his party from the Republican Union to the Farmer-Worker Party in the summer of 1931, his action suggested that the constitutional issue had been superseded by more material concerns as a focus for political action. But here, as so often, Papanastasiou was ahead of the game. Liberals and Populists were much slower to reach the same conclusion. And when they did there were few who followed Papanastasiou's reformist lead. Indeed by 1935 even Papanastasiou himself was arguing that the best method of protecting the 'social state' involved excluding the communists from Parliament.[4] Inter-war bourgeois politics had less and less in common with the progressive ideals of the pre-war Liberal Government.

The 1920 elections suggested early on that Venizelos would find it difficult to keep the urban workers under his leadership. Two years later, defeat at the hands of Kemal's forces put an end to dreams of realizing the Great Idea. The overwhelming influx of refugees from Asia Minor now set domestic reconstruction at the top of the political agenda and reaffirmed the rationale for Venizelos's original strategy for preserving social peace: land reform. Creating a large group of peasant smallholders would not only win a new constituency, or so he hoped, over to Venizelism; as importantly, it would weaken the chances of a combined mass movement from below of workers and peasants—just the combination, of course, that in Italy Gramsci believed essential to any overthrow of bourgeois rule.

The nightmare of such a coalition haunted political élites after 1918 throughout much of Europe, and their economic policies often reflected various strategies for preventing its realization. The path pursued by Greece's Liberals may be contrasted with that chosen by some of their contemporaries, engaged in a similar modernization effort elsewhere. Ataturk in Turkey, Bethlen in Hungary went a different route, concen-

---

[3] *Peitharchia*, 29 Dec. 1929, 5 Jan. 1930, 15 Mar. 1931.

[4] G. Anastasiadis, G. Kontogiogis, and P. Petridis, *Alexandros Papanastasiou: Thesmoi, ideologia kai politiki sto mesopolemo* (Athens, 1987), 118.

trating their efforts on industrial growth, and using a heavy hand in the rural areas to force the farming population into acquiescence. In Romania, Bratianu's Liberals also sought to industrialize, but were handicapped by strong peasant opposition within a more democratic polity.[5] These comparisons may help to clarify the underlying rationale for the Liberal land reform in Greece. It was difficult for democratic regimes to bear the social costs of rapid industrialization. For a largely agrarian society, modernization and capital accumulation within a democratic framework implied giving priority to agriculture over industry. This route may have involved a slower rate of growth than one which squeezed the rural sector dry, but it opened up new political possibilities. To put it simply, the land reform, together with foreign loans, purchased peasant backing for Venizelist rule, pushing industrialization into second place.

In this strategy the state was inevitably brought in to oversee changes in the agricultural sector, and was sucked in further as the slump in wheat prices forced it to come to the aid of the new farmers with various support schemes. Nor perhaps should one stress the *political* rationale alone: not just in Greece, but in many other agrarian countries as well, bourgeois élites were committed to promoting national economic development, and this naturally made them readier to involve the state in the economy than was the case in Britain or France. There was a good deal in common between Venizelos's liberalism and that outlined by the Romanian liberal Stefan Zeletin in *Burghezia romana*, the economic blueprint he published in 1925.[6] But side by side with this nationalist component, particularly in the 1920s, lay a commitment to *laissez-faire* so far as commercial and financial arrangements were concerned. Thus economic liberalism in a country like Greece pulled in several directions at once.

By the late 1920s the Greek authorities had negotiated a solution to the war debts dispute, paving the way for a period of entrepreneurial growth based on the encouragement of foreign and domestic investors.

[5] K. Boratav, 'Kemalist Economic Policies and Etatism', in A. Kazancigil and E. Ozbudun (eds.), *Ataturk: Founder of a Modern State* (Hamden, Conn., 1981), 165–90; A. Janos, *The Politics of Backwardness in Hungary: 1825–1945* (Princeton, NJ, 1982), 219; I. Berend and G. Ranki, *Hungary: A Century of Economic Development* (New York, 1974), 132; J. Rothschild, *East Central Europe between the Two World Wars* (Seattle, 1988), 298–304.

[6] D. Chirot, 'Neoliberal and Social Democratic Theories of Development: The Zeletin–Voinea Debate Concerning Romania's Prospects in the 1920s and its Contemporary Implications', in K. Jowitt (ed.), *Social Change in Romania: 1860–1940* (Berkeley, Calif., 1978), 31–53.

The cultivation of export crops, notably tobacco, assumed virtually speculative proportions in parts of northern Greece. Concessions to the wheat producers became part of an overall project for economic reconstruction which, with American, French, or British capital, would secure the Liberals' right to political leadership. Since Greece, unlike most countries in Eastern Europe, was a wheat importer on a massive scale, it could be argued that this was the most sensible form of import-substitution available.

A policy of financing development through foreign assistance suited an élite whose commitment to state intervention outside agriculture was weak. Industrial investment was left to the private sector. The result was a patchwork of family firms which relied on cheap labour and antiquated machinery—an unpromising basis for an industrialization effort. Nor were the few larger concerns necessarily more efficient: their success stemmed as much from privileged access to political and financial power as from entrepreneurial dynamism. In industrial relations, Venizelos's paternalistic approaches and appeals were less and less successful. Basing industrialization on cheap labour made ruling groups reluctant to enforce minimum wage legislation; deflation and the slump made the problem worse. Politically, the urban labourer could not easily be brought into the existing party system via the patronage networks which operated in the countryside. Seeing the hand of Moscow behind each labour protest, the increasingly nervous bourgeois politician turned to repression.

In fact the reliance on foreign funds was not due just to a lack of capital within the country; as great a problem was the poor distribution of what capital there was. We have seen how some observers criticized the Greek credit system for channelling existing funds into speculative areas, notably import stocks, rather than into manufacturing or long-term agricultural credit. Heavy borrowing also reflected the political impotence of the state, or, more precisely, the inability of Greek politicians to tap available capital *within* Greece and use it on the state's behalf. Domestic taxation remained extremely regressive. Capital flight was a chronic problem which the commercial banks did little or nothing to check. The Greek bourgeoisie held large sums in Zürich, London, and elsewhere: as much as one-third of the loan capital raised abroad by the Venizelos Government after 1928 was subscribed by Greek subjects![7] Unable to tax this money, the Greek state could only gain

---

[7] Ministère des Affaires Étrangères, *La Grèce et la crise mondiale* (Athens, 1933), 37.

access to it through borrowing. These fiscal constraints indicated the low domestic toleration for Liberal economic policies.

There was no hint of weakness, however, in Venizelos's pronouncements: his vision of Greece's economic future was exuberant and upbeat, as he laid out how, with enlightened foreign help, both agriculture and industry would expand enough to provide employment for a rapidly growing population. He would, he promised during his triumphal progress through the country in 1928, transform Greece and make her 'unrecognizable'. The deepening depression gave his words a new meaning; by 1931 his insistent optimism flew in the face of reality.

Defeat in the 'battle for the drachma' cost the Liberals dearly. Former supporters were alienated as a result of the débâcle—merchants, who resented the new trade controls, workers thrown out of a job as factories closed for lack of raw materials, refugee farmers who were burdened by a debt they felt the state should have assumed. The Venizelist hold over northern Greece was shaken by the collapse of the tobacco trade. From this point onwards, Venizelism no longer sufficed to unite a rather disparate coalition, and on the Left in particular more radical political parties were greatly strengthened.

The crisis thus exposed great fissures in the supposedly classless façade of Venizelism. To be sure, the appeal to inter-class harmony had always sounded a little strained. Traces of class tensions had been evident in Greece even before the refugees pitched their tents amid the classical ruins of Athens; with the onset of depression the signs became inescapable. Alexandros Diomedes, in his first speech as Governor of the new central bank in 1929, alluded to 'this merciless struggle' and to 'the growing tension which, especially in recent years, has developed in social and economic differences'.[8] Gradually, the political élite moved to close ranks. As the crisis began to threaten the success of the Liberal economic project, Venizelos himself suggested—how seriously it is difficult to judge—the formation of a bourgeois anti-communist coalition which would unite parties on both sides of the *dichasmos*. Tsaldaris, too, began to speak a new sort of political language. 'There are no longer Republicans and Royalists, Venizelists and anti-Venizelists,' he wrote just before his death. 'There is only the great majority of the Greek people on the one side, faithful to their age-old national traditions, following at the same time the development of world conditions, never

[8] Bank of Greece, *Report for the Year 1928 of the Governor of the Bank of Greece* (Athens, 1929), 27.

rejecting progress and the benefits one can derive from it. On the other side, there is a minority seeking to overthrow the social order ... confusing progress with disorder, corruption and immorality.'[9] Anti-communism was turning into a new unifying motif for bourgeois politics.

In 1932 this still lay some way in the future. The more immediate short-term outcome of the crisis, and a direct consequence of Venizelos's failure to persuade the Populists to come into government with him, was the revival of the *dichasmos*. No less fierce than a decade earlier, its significance this time was different: what it represented now was chiefly a desperate effort by Venizelos to prevent the disintegration of the old Venizelist bloc.

Venizelos's gamble failed, but who gained? Both the Agrarians and the Communists performed well in the 1933 general election. Neither, however, received more than 5% of the vote. At their high point in 1935—with the Liberals abstaining—the Communists polled just under 10%, and saw their support slump seven months later. In retrospect, the main significance of the gains on the Left was *not* that these parties became a serious threat to the political mainstream. It was rather that the disintegration of the Venizelist camp increased the power within the bourgeois political world of the anti-Venizelist Populist Party. Its leadership, headed by the ineffectual Tsaldaris, was suddenly confronted with the task it had managed to avoid for so long—that of elaborating a coherent socio-economic policy. It was no longer possible for the Populists to trail after Venizelos, as they had done before the crisis.[10]

What the Populists produced turned out to be quite inappropriate to the new conditions—an ideology which rejected the stress on national economic development nurtured by Venizelos, and clung desperately to the values of *laissez-faire*, anti-state individualism. The tone was pessimistic, the manner passive: Greece's own resources were too limited to sustain an adequate standard of living and therefore nothing should be done which might obstruct an eventual return to an open economic order. As Bernaris acidly noted, the over-optimistic Venizelos had been succeeded by advocates of the 'Greece cannot live' school:

---

[9] Cited in D. G. Kousoulas, *Revolution and Defeat: The Story of the Greek Communist Party* (London, 1965), 51.

[10] USNA 868.00/626, Skinner (Athens)–State, 15 Jan. 1930; 868.00/652, Skinner (Athens)–State, 20 July 1931.

what was lacking in both cases, he went on, was 'an economic effort directed and undertaken by the *politikos kosmos* [political world]'.[11]

The justice of this remark can only be appreciated if the *economic* effects of the crisis are clearly understood. The world crisis did *not* condemn Greece to prolonged recession, but on the contrary opened new doors and set new challenges. Depreciation, default, good agricultural performance, and impressive short-term industrial growth together offered a model of how a largely market-led recovery based on the domestic economy could emerge after 1932 in the underdeveloped world. If it is wrong to exaggerate the dimensions of this upswing—and I hope I have made clear the inefficiencies and obstacles that soon emerged—it would also be wrong to ignore what it meant for politics and the role of the state.

Out of the recovery, and for all its limitations, there arose a new configuration of economic relationships within the country. The state was drawn into allocative decisions through quotas and clearing arrangements. Civil servants at the Ministry of the National Economy constructed new machinery of intervention, sufficient to excite the hostility of import merchants as they tried to gain control over trade flows. The gold standard system with its largely automatic adjustment mechanisms was replaced by a new, more discretionary and complex set of monetary arrangements, in which the Bank of Greece played a more assertive role *vis-à-vis* the private sector. In agriculture, the Populists allowed Venizelist institutions such as the Agricultural Bank, KEPES, and the Cotton Institute to expand their operations. The Ministry of Agriculture supervised what was probably the most effective form of technology transfer possible in the early 1930s in Greece—the provision of new strains of seed to farmers. This, combined with devaluation and continued state purchasing, pushed wheat production to the point where some commentators argued that the country was now growing too *much* rather than too little of its own cereal supply.

Greek politicians had acknowledged the need to pursue some form of economic self-sufficiency from 1914 onwards. In the 1920s it looked as though the best way to achieve this was through an economic liberalism which supported native entrepreneurs and attracted the foreign investor. But international trade and capital flows dried up during the depression. In such circumstances, the move towards autarky implied

[11] A. Bernaris, *I diarthrosis kai ai prospatheiai prosarmogis tis ellinikis oikonomias* (Athens, 1933), 59–60.

new relationships between state and society. Autarky, to put it simply, favoured domestic producers over consumers. A loose monetary policy had helped protect the country from the sort of deflationary pressures suffered elsewhere under more orthodox banking regimes; however, after 1933 a similar policy led before long to alarming price rises. As business men and import merchants cashed in and their profits rose, workers and urban consumers generally demanded state intervention to protect wages and salaries: *laissez-faire* under autarky, in other words, produced blatant distributive inequalities which the state was expected to rectify. How could this be achieved amid the chaos of Greek party politics? A rational economic order now seemed to depend, not on a market of free individuals, but on planning by enlightened technocrats. The independence of the legislature would have to be sacrificed for the sake of a decisive executive. Hence the collapse of international institutions encouraged a shift in social values: individualism seemed out-moded and less appropriate to these new conditions than more collective or communal ideals. Kantian idealists like the young Kanellopoulos, social reformers like Alexandros Svolos, advocates of a return to the land like Karavidas, and of course any number of tough, right-wing disciplinarians—all these and many more coincided in their views at least on this point.

If the Tsaldaris Government did not seem a promising initiator of such a decisive shift, neither—especially after the failed 1935 rebellion —did the Venizelists. Not only did the *dichasmos* between the two camps seem increasingly anachronistic; their obsession with it and corresponding lack of interest in, or understanding of, those problems facing the country which could not be reduced to its terms gradually undermined their political legitimacy. This was precisely what motivated Kafandaris and Kanellopoulos in their unsuccessful attempts to bridge the divide and find a new party mould for bourgeois politics. Personal feelings for or against Venizelos remained extraordinarily intense, but they provided no guarantee of widespread support for democracy itself. There was little popular reaction either to the Venizelist rebellion in 1935 or to Metaxas's establishment of the 4 August regime the following year. Pervasive public disaffection with the parliamentary system was one reason why Metaxas's rule was never seriously challenged.[12]

For important groups within the political élite, authoritarian rule promised to be an advance on what preceded it: many would-be social

---

[12] G. Dafnis, *I Ellas metaxy dyo polemon 1923–1940*, 2 vols. (Athens, 1955), ii. 466.

reformers and economic planners—civil servants in the economics ministries, members of the National Bank and the Supreme Economic Council—thought that the unstable party system of the Republic had obstructed their attempts to shape a more just and rational economic order.[13] Anti-communists (as many Venizelist as anti-Venizelist), uninterested in socio-economic reform but concerned about issues of public order and with diminishing confidence in the ability of the existing parties to protect their interests, saw Metaxas as the guarantor of the bourgeois state against 'anarchy' from below.[14] This was the sort of coalition which underlay, not just Metaxas's regime, but also that in Poland and Bulgaria after 1935, and of Vargas in Brazil from 1930. Preserving bourgeois rule had meant imposing an authoritarian regime from above.

Our conclusion must be that for most bourgeois politicians and their associates in the state apparatus, parliamentary democracy was in the last resort dispensable. Like their Romanian and Italian counterparts, Greek Liberals—their illustrious leader included—did not turn out to be committed democrats.[15] Their commitment to parliamentary sovereignty, which had brought them into conflict with the Crown in their early years in power, began to wane between the two world wars. When the economic crisis altered popular attitudes towards politics and fuelled demands for a more interventionist state, they opted more readily for repression than for reform. Further work will be necessary before we can assess the continuities of personnel and policies before and after 1936 with any accuracy. There was some rather ineffectual plotting against Metaxas. However, at least as powerful a motive in political circles for conspiracy against the dictatorship as the pursuit of democratic ideals was the resentment of established personalities at being excluded from power.[16]

Their resentment against Metaxas reflected disagreements over means rather than ends, since they shared with him an acceptance of the fundamental need to defend the bourgeois order. As Koliopoulos has remarked: 'Metaxas was a product and representative of the Greek political system; only he played the game more roughly than was

---

[13] M. Psalidopoulos, 'Morfes oikonomikis skepsis stin Ellada, 1936–1940', in H. Fleischer and N. Svoronos (eds.), *I Ellada 1936–1944: Diktatoria, katochi, antistasi* (Athens, 1989), 98–144.

[14] Relevant here is an interesting article by D. H. Close, 'I astynomia sto kathestos tis 4is Avgoustou', in Fleischer and Svoronos (eds.), *I Ellada 1936–1944*, pp. 77–91.

[15] Cf. J. Koliopoulos, *Greece and the British Connection: 1935–1941* (Oxford, 1977), 11–12.   [16] Dafnis, *Metaxy dyo polemon*, ii. 466.

conventionally expected.'[17] Nowhere was the substantial convergence
of aims between the dictator and his predecessors more strikingly
evident than in the programme for constitutional reform secretly drawn
up by representatives of the old parties in January 1937. This included
provisions to replace strikes and lock-outs by compulsory arbitration,
monitoring of the Press, and parliamentary sessions of no more than
three to four months annually. *Both* communism and Fascism would be
outlawed.[18] With the possible exception of the last clause, such details
do not suggest that life under a new coalition government would have
differed sharply from that under Metaxas.

The dictatorship ended with Metaxas's death in 1941. But this event
no more signalled the demise of bourgeois values and rhetoric in Greek
politics than the earlier collapse of democracy had done. Subsequent
events would confirm the striking resilience of the 'political world' as its
members became more accustomed to using the new motifs of mass
politics that had entered the public arena in the 1930s. The calls for a
political order devoted to greater egalitarianism which had first become
audible in those years re-emerged more loudly during the resistance to
the wartime German occupation when even the new leader of the
Populist Party, Tsaldaris's cousin Constantine, echoed the prevailing
mood among the suffering Greek population by pledging to work after
Liberation for 'social justice'.[19] In 1945 Kyriakos Varvaressos tried
briefly to implement a brave programme for socio-economic reform, but
failed not least because it required—in the words of one onlooker—'a
large degree of "étatisme" at a moment when Greece bears little
resemblance to an "état"'.[20] Varvaressos's departure, and the escalation
of the civil war, opened the way for less disinterested politicians to draw
on the other dominant motif of the inter-war years, anti-communism.
The way forward for the Greek bourgeois élite, as Tsaldaris was among
the first to sense, was to profit from the tensions of the Cold War:
anti-communism would not operate in the absence of foreign economic
support, as had been the case in the 1930s; it would instead secure
it—and on an unprecedented scale. The Truman Doctrine and the
Marshall Plan proved him right and maintained the old political world in
power.

---

[17] Koliopoulos, *Greece and the British Connection*, p. 46.
[18] Dafnis, *Metaxy dyo polemon*, ii. 441.
[19] Populist Party manifesto of Sept. 1943, in USNA RG 226/80220, Berry (Istanbul)–
State, 21 June 1944.
[20] Cited in G. Alexander, *The Prelude to the Truman Doctrine* (Oxford, 1982), 132.

'The political life of Athens . . . tends to become artificial and to be more concerned with parties and political combinations than with social problems,' wrote a former British Ambassador to Greece. 'I knew that men like Papandreou, Sofianopoulos, Kanellopoulos, Kafandaris etc., were leaders of parties, but it never occurred to me to ask these party leaders what they really stood for, nor would it occur to them to offer an explanation . . . This kind of thing is the great defect of political life. In a world which is changing so rapidly and where one country after another has been in the throes of a social upheaval, the Greek political world remains unaffected. It is inconceivable that this can continue. Sooner or later, Greek political life will be forced to undergo a radical change.'[21] This could easily be a description of politics in the inter-war years—but it is not. When Rex Leeper wrote this account, at the end of the 1940s, Greece had already undergone one social upheaval during the German occupation and subsequent civil war. It would have to go through another between 1967 and 1974 before democracy was established there on a new basis.

[21] R. Leeper, *When Greek Meets Greek* (London, 1950), 212–13.

APPENDIX 1: TABLES

TABLE A1.1. *Agriculture*

Year	Cultivated area (000 ha.)		Indices of agricultural output			
	Greece	New Greece[a] as % of total	1911 prices (1914 = 100)	1928 prices (1928 = 100)	Non-export crops[b] (1928 prices)	Export crops[c] (1928 prices)
1911[d]	864.6	n.a.	(71)	—	—	—
1914[e]	1,336.6	32.2	100	n.a.	—	—
1915[f]	1,074.0	n.a.	n.a.	n.a.	—	—
1916[f]	1,221.5	n.a.	n.a.	n.a.	—	—
1917[g]	1,361.8	n.a.	78	n.a.	—	—
1918[g]	1,415.6	n.a.	86	n.a.	—	—
1919[e]	1,389.5	34.6	74	n.a.	—	—
1920[e]	1,319.3	31.8	74	n.a.	—	—
1921[e]	1,232.4	34.7	70	n.a.	—	—
1922	1,245.3	40.6	75	n.a.	—	—
1923	1,269.0	31.7	73	n.a.	—	—
1924	1,467.1	40.0	73	80	81	77
1925	1,465.5	41.3	88	90	85	95
1926	1,623.3	41.9	95	91	95	87
1927	1,520.1	44.5	89	90	88	92
1928	1,597.4	45.6	93	100	100	100
1929	1,544.6	48.4	89	97	92	102
1930	1,788.9	46.7	n.a.	100	98	100
1931	1,931.9	47.1	n.a.	93	105	80
1932	1,921.0	47.7	n.a.	120	141	100
1933	2,081.1	48.7	n.a.	141	178	103
1934	2,144.5	48.7	n.a.	137	168	107
1935	2,190.9	48.5	n.a.	137	163	110
1936	2,315.6	48.6	n.a.	125	147	103
1937	2,415.5	48.4	n.a.	179	219	138

n.a. = not available.

[a] New Greece = Macedonia, west Thrace, Epiros, Crete, Aegean Islands.
[b] Non-export crops comprise cereals, pulses, legumes, cotton, 'other industrial plants', olive oil (80% of total output), olives (50% of total harvest).
[c] Export crops comprise tobacco, must/grapes, currants, olive oil (20% of total output), olives (50% of total harvest).
[d] Old Greece only, excluding Thrace.
[e] Excluding Thrace.
[f] Excluding Thrace and Macedonia.
[g] Excluding Thrace and the nomes of Serres and Drama.

Source: AS 1933 (1934), *1938* (1939); A. Boyazoglu, *Contribution à l'étude de l'économie rurale de la Grèce* (Paris, 1931); *OE 1939* (1940).

TABLE A1.2. *Public finances (millions current drachmas)*

Year	Total revenues	Total expenditure	Official deficit/ surplus ((2) − (3))	Ordinary revenues (OR)	Implicit deficit/ surplus ((5) − (3))	Public debt	Public debt service (PDS)	PDS/OR (%)
(1)	(2)	(3)	(4)	(5)	(6)	(7)	(8)	(9)
1911	235	181	+54	138	−43	n.a.	n.a.	n.a.
1912	172	208	−36	127	−81	1,172	57	45
1913	300	262	+38	122	−140	1,217	n.a.	n.a.
1914	559	486	+73	221	−265	1,383	n.a.	n.a.
1915	438	386	+52	232	−154	n.a.	n.a.	n.a.
1916	314	238	+76	230	−8	n.a.	n.a.	n.a.
1917	443	317	+126	263	−54	n.a.	n.a.	n.a.
1918/19	1,251	1,446	−195	288	−1,158	2,432	n.a.	n.a.
1919/20	1,129	1,354	−225	562	−792	2,434	n.a.	n.a.
1920/1	1,654	1,683	−29	924	−759	4,553	n.a.	n.a.
1921/2	1,623	2,258	−635	1,287	−971	11,469	n.a.	n.a.
1922/3	5,158	3,383	+1,775	2,666	−717	12,594	n.a.	n.a.
1923/4	3,992	4,951	−959	3,299	−1,652	18,766	1,023	31
1924/5	5,757	5,510	+247	4,685	−825	29,482	1,302	28

1925/6	8,066	6,843	+1,223	5,668	−1,175	35,842	1,579	28
1926/7	9,440	8,690	+750	7,023	−1,667	38,029	2,925	42
1927/8	8,997	7,771	+1,226	8,807	+1,036	36,973	2,260	26
1928/9	10,552	9,450	+1,102	9,058	−392	38,038	3,688	41
1929/30	18,730[a]	18,358	+372	9,242	(−9,116)	38,602	3,329	36
1930/1	11,394	11,176	+218	9,013	−2,163	41,310	3,300	37
1931/2	11,077	11,099	−22	8,552	−2,547	43,039	3,027	35
1932/3	9,144	9,117	+27	7,779	−1,338	43,161	1,898	24
1933/4	8,476	7,706	+770	8,147	+441	42,687	1,320	16
1934/5	9,237	8,746	+491	9,061	+315	44,985	1,484	16
1935/6	10,647	10,049	+598	10,232	+183	47,363	1,810	18
1936/7	13,214	12,683	+531	10,130	−2,553	49,630	1,859	18

n.a. = not available.

[a] Official figures include for accounting purposes proceeds and uses of 1924 Refugee Loan and other foreign loans contracted before 1929.

Sources: cols. 2 and 3: AS, various; col. 5: 1911–18. E. Tsouderos, Le Relèvement économique de la Grèce (Paris, 1920), 67, 89; 1919–22: K. Kostis, I Elhniki Trapeza en Mikri Asia (1919–22) (Athens, 1984), 113; 1923/4–1936/7: A. Angelopoulos, To dimosion chreos tis Ellados (Athens, 1937), 54, 206–7; col. 7: 1912–14: Tsouderos, Relèvement, pp. 76–8; 1918–36: L.N. Public Debt, 1914–1946 (New York, 1946), 71 (1918–26: converted into paper drachmas from gold equivalents of data in X. Zolotas, I Ellas eis to stadion tis exviomichaniseos (Athens, 1926), 157); col. 8: Angelopoulos, Dimosion chreos, pp. 54, 206–7.

TABLE A1.3.   *Exchange rates and prices (annual averages)*

Year	£: drachmas[a]	$: drachmas[a]	Swiss franc: drachmas[a]	Wholesale price index[b]	Cost-of-living index[c]
1914	25.16	5.17	0.995	100	100
1915	25.03	5.27	0.995	n.a.	117
1916	24.63	5.19	0.989	n.a.	159
1917	24.60	5.17	1.092	n.a.	256
1918	24.82	5.17	1.203	n.a.	366
1919	24.32	5.51	1.066	n.a.	323
1920	34.07	9.44	1.576	n.a.	351
1921	70.38	18.17	3.190	n.a.	398
1922	166.54	36.67	6.900	n.a.	636
1923	296.44	64.00	11.600	n.a.	1,181
1924	247.35	56.08	11.220	n.a.	1,235
1925	312.62	64.76	12.530	n.a.	1,414
1926	386.51	79.56	15.41	n.a.	1,633
1927	368.55	75.82	14.65	n.a.	1,790
1928	375.00	77.06	14.87	1,720	1,868
1929	375.00	77.07	14.90	1,811	1,923
1930	375.00	77.08	14.96	1,646	1,682
1931	375.00	77.38	15.06	1,471	1,671
1932	472.97	133.68	26.07	1,766	1,773
1933	595.96	144.97	34.83	1,997	1,904
1934	543.94	108.36	34.91	1,969	1,937
1935	529.15	108.43	34.99	2,003	1,956
1936	539.26	108.71	32.62	2,038	2,027
1937	550.00	111.39	25.58	2,281	2,189
1938	550.00	111.00	25.55	2,227	2,172

n.a. = not available.

   [a] Exchange rates cited at Athens, 1914–27 National Bank of Greece; 1928–38 Bank of Greece.
   [b] Based on prices in Athens and Piraeus area.
   [c] 1914–30 'old series' based on 106 towns; 1931–8 'new series' based on 44 towns. (The inclusion of official prices for a number of items leads the index to understate the rate of price inflation at times of rising prices.)

Sources: *AS*, various issues.

TABLE A1.4. *Indices of industrial growth rates (1928 = 100)*

Year	Gross output			Net output (without electricity)
	At 1930 prices	At 1930 prices (without electricity)	AOS Index	
(1)	(2)	(3)	(4)	(5)
1921	n.a.	62.1	60.3	60.4
1922	n.a.	65.5	69.4	64.0
1923	n.a.	64.6	62.7	66.0
1924	n.a.	75.9	80.7	83.4
1925	83.6	84.5	88.9	89.7
1926	81.9	83.4	84.6	86.1
1927	92.5	92.1	94.4	92.8
1928	100.0	100.0	100.0	100.0
1929	104.3	102.9	101.8	102.1
1930	109.5	103.2	105.3	104.4
1931	112.1	103.3	108.9	105.4
1932	107.8	97.7	102.7	100.6
1933	120.6	111.0	111.8	112.0
1934	138.5	128.1	127.5	133.5
1935	139.3	127.1	143.2	131.6
1936	149.6	134.9	141.7	138.9
1937	160.0	140.9	153.9	143.9
1938	171.6	148.3	168.1	148.5
1939	174.2	145.7	179.0	146.1

Notes: the AOS index as reported annually in *OE* is described as a volume index, but no information is supplied regarding its construction. The other calculations are my own; they are based on output data of over 80 items published annually in *AS*. To the volume data I have added (1) an estimate of shipbuilding which I obtained by deflating the drachma value of this activity by movements in the drachma/sterling exchange rate, (2) for 1921–2, an estimate of the value of leather manufactures cited in DOT, *Report on Industrial and Economic Conditions in Greece to 1922* (London, 1923), 35. Data of electricity production date from 1925. Col. 5 is based on col. 3: gross output figures for each branch have been converted into estimates of net output on the basis of information (which refers to 1928) in MNE, *Elliniki viomichania*. I assume that the ratios between net and gross output in each branch remained unchanged over the complete time series.
    n.a. = not available.

Sources: *OE 1939* (1940); *AS*, various issues; MNE, *Elliniki viomichania* (1931).

TABLE AI.5. *Balance of trade data*

Year	Export values[a]	Import values[a]	Emigrant remittances[a]	Export volume[b]	Import volume[b]	Export prices[b]	Terms of trade[b]	Capacity to import[b]
1911[c]	141	174	n.a.	n.a.	n.a.	n.a.	n.a.	n.a.
1912	146	158	n.a.	n.a.	n.a.	n.a.	n.a.	n.a.
1913	119	178	n.a.	n.a.	n.a.	n.a.	n.a.	n.a.
1914	179	319	61	n.a.	n.a.	n.a.	n.a.	n.a.
1915	218	289	71	n.a.	n.a.	n.a.	n.a.	n.a.
1916	155	399	72	n.a.	n.a.	n.a.	n.a.	n.a.
1917	110	204	65	n.a.	n.a.	n.a.	n.a.	n.a.
1918	297	734	126	n.a.	n.a.	n.a.	n.a.	n.a.
1919	764	1,522	361	n.a.	n.a.	n.a.	n.a.	n.a.
1920	682	2,177	770	n.a.	n.a.	n.a.	n.a.	n.a.
1921	944	1,764	1,060	n.a.	n.a.	n.a.	n.a.	n.a.
1922	2,489	3,170	817	n.a.	n.a.	n.a.	n.a.	n.a.
1923	2,544	6,076	2,007	n.a.	n.a.	n.a.	n.a.	n.a.
1924	3,266	8,039	2,112	n.a.	n.a.	n.a.	n.a.	n.a.
1925	4,574	10,177	2,283	n.a.	n.a.	n.a.	n.a.	n.a.

Year								
1926	5,440	9,967	2,848	101	74	86	80	81
1927	6,040	12,600	2,552	105	98	94	91	96
1928	6,331	12,417	2,412	100	100	100	100	100
1929	6,960.	13,276	2,931	102	106	114	113	115
1930	5,799	10,524	3,135	95	100	100	118	112
1931	4,165	8,763	2,356	82	99	83	115	94
1932	4,576	7,870	1,455	84	91	90	130	109
1933	5,155	8,426	1,724	84	74	94	102	86
1934	5,474	8,831	982	84	76	101	109	88
1935	7,095	10,766	1,131	81	92	111	117	115
1936	7,384	11,847	1,806	86	105	128	142	122
1937	9,546	15,548	2,334	89	131	n.a.	n.a.	n.a.
1938	10,149	14,759	1,892	84	134	n.a.	n.a.	n.a.

n.a. = not available.

a Millions current drachmas.
b 1928 = 100.
c Old Greece only.

Sources: 1911–17: E. Tsouderos, *Le Relèvement économique de la Grèce* (Paris, 1920), 204; 1918–38: *AS*; last five cols.: my calculations from data in *OE 1939* (1940), table 19.

APPENDIX 2: DEBT DEFAULT
ON THE PERIPHERY

The Greek experience of default should be put in perspective. If we take default to cover unilateral reductions in debt servicing by the debtor as well as outright repudiation then we can find many examples of this phenomenon among debtor nations after 1929. Scholars have stressed the burden of indebtedness before the crisis but have paid less attention to the benefits that accrued from default, though this may be less due to ethical qualms than to the extreme difficulty of finding reliable data. Despite data problems I have thought it worth while to attempt crude estimates of savings from debt default for the countries listed below. Latin American countries were large (and early) defaulters on dollar loans, while Greece was one of the worst defaulters (in percentage terms) in Europe.

Column 6 in Table A2.1 provides one measure of a country's ability to repay its debts on the eve of the crisis: Greece emerges as the most unrealistic debtor of this group, though the disparity between her export earnings and her foreign debt would be somewhat mitigated if invisible earnings were taken into account. However, savings on the scale which accrued to Greece (columns 3 and 4 for alternative measures) were found in at least half a dozen countries of central/Eastern Europe, and in several important Latin American states as well. Default acted as an important adjustment mechanism in many debtor countries, cushioning the effects of falling exports and budget revenues.

TABLE A2.1. *Savings from debt default on the periphery*

Country	Total savings, 1931–5 (millions national currency unit)	(2) as % of export earnings 1931–5	(2) as % of total government expenditures 1931–5	Date of suspension of foreign debt service	Export earnings/ total value of foreign debt, 1928–30
(1)	(2)	(3)	(4)	(5)	(6)
Greece	4,131[a]	18.1	11.0	1932	21.3
Czechoslovakia	—	—	—	—	356.4
Hungary	117[b]	7.4	2.4	1931–2	69.9
Poland	—	—	—	—	67.5
Romania	11,726[c]	19.1	13.6	1932	33.6[d]
Bulgaria	2,323[e]	19.3	11.1	1932	36.8
Yugoslavia	3,182[f]	16.6	6.0	1932	545.7
Argentina	—	—	—	—	186.3
Brazil	971[g]	6.6	7.4	1931	291.5
Chile	701[h]	19.1	—	1931	77.1
Mexico	126[i]	5.3	10.0	1928	53.2
Peru	97[j]	7.6	17.3	1931	118.3

[a] Derived from Table 7.4, col. 1.

[b] Net balance of Foreign Creditors' Fund (1935, Foreign Credits Cash Office), 30.6.32–30.6.35. These sums underestimate total savings from default.

[c] Difference between foreign debt service as entered in the Budget for 1931 and that for subsequent years (1932–35/6).

[d] 1929–30.

[e] Difference between foreign debt service paid in 1931–2 and subsequent years (1932/3–35/6).

[f] Difference between foreign debt service paid in 1930–1 and subsequent years (1931–5).

[g] Untransferred portion of foreign debt service employed as special funds.

[h] No foreign debt service in these years; gains estimated equivalent to six times the domestic debt service 1932–5 (this was the average ratio of foreign debt service to domestic debt service in 1929–31).

[i] Foreign debt interest arrears 1931–5.

[j] Difference between 1930 *public* debt service and that for subsequent years. These sums overestimate total savings from default.

Sources: M. Jackson and J. Lampe, *Balkan Economic History 1550–1950* (Bloomington, Ind., 1982), 480–1; B. Mitchell, *European Historical Statistics 1750–1970* (London, 1976), 304–6, 376–9; LN, *Public Debt, 1914–1946* (New York, 1946); LN, *Public Finances, 1928–1935* (Geneva, 1936); LN, *Public Finances, 1928–1937* (Geneva, 1938).

BIBLIOGRAPHY

Primary Sources

Unpublished

AET (Bank of Greece, Athens: Archive of Emmanouil Tsouderos).
AEV (Benaki Museum, Athens: Archive of Eleftherios Venizelos).
AKV (Bank of Greece, Athens: Archive of Kyriakos Varvaressos).
Bodosakis Athanasiades, untitled memoirs, in author's possession.
FO (Public Record Office, Kew, London: Foreign Office files): 286: Consular;
    371: General and Political
IBA (St Antony's College, Oxford: Ionian Bank Archive).
Karl L. Rankin papers, Seeley Mudd Library, Princeton University.
USNA (National Archives, Washington, DC): State Department files: 868.oo,
    Greece (Internal), 868.ooB, Greece (Commercial); OSS files: RG 226.

Newspapers and Periodicals

AOI (*Agrotiki Oikonomia*)
AOKE (*Archeion Oikonomikon kai Koinonikon Epistimon*)
Balkans, Les
Banker, The
Bank of Athens, *Bulletin Économique et Financier*
DATE (*Deltion tis Agrotikis Trapezas tis Ellados*)
DEVE/A (*Deltion Emporikou kai Viomichanikou Epimelitiriou/ton Athinon*)
E (*Ergasia*)
Economist, The
EKDO (*Epitheorisis Koinonikis kai Dimosionomikis Oikonomias*)
EV (*Eleftheron Vima*)
EX (*Efimeris tou Chrimatistiriou*)
Financial Times, The
GD (*Georgikon Deltion*)
GPEK (Grafeion Prostasias Ellinikon Kapnon), Kavalla, *Deltion*
GPEK (Grafeion Prostasias Ellinikon Kapnon), Thessaloniki, *Deltion*
MA (*Messager d'Athènes*)
Near East and India
OA (*Oikonomologos Athinon*)
OT (*Oikonomikos Tachydromos*)

P (*Ploutos*)
Peitharchia
Proia
Stafidikon Deltion
Tachydromos tis Kavallas
Times, The
VE (*Viomichaniki Epitheorisi*)

Parliamentary Debates

ESG (*Efimeris ton Syzitiseon tis Gerousias*)
ESV (*Efimeris ton Syzitiseon tis Voulis*)
PSV (*Praktika ton Synedriaseon tis Voulis*)

Other Published Sources

Agrotiki Trapeza tis Ellados, *To ergon mias dekaetias: 1930–1939* (Athens, 1940).
Angelopoulos, K., *Politikoi agones: 1892–1934*, iii (Athens, 1934).
AOS (Anotaton Oikonomikon Symvoulion), *EO* (*Elliniki oikonomia*) (Athens, various years).
—— *Gnomodotisis epi tou dynatou tis rythmiseos tou exoterikou emporiou tis Ellados* (Athens, n.d.).
—— *To exoterikon emporion tis Ellados kai ai symvaseis antallagis emporevmaton* (Athens, 1933).
—— *O timarithmos chondrikis poliseos en Elladi* (Athens, 1933).
—— *Ta metra pros epavxisin tis enchoriou sitoparagogis* (Athens, 1934).
—— *Oi deiktai tis oikonomikis drastiriotitos tis Ellados kata ta eti 1928–1934* (Athens, 1935).
—— *Peri tou tropou tis rythmiseos ton meta tis Germanias emporikon synallagon* (Athens, 1936).
—— *Erevna kai gnomodotisis epi ton viomichanion vamvakos* (Athens, 1937).
—— *Epi tou zitimatos tou kapnou* (Athens, 1938).
—— *Epi tou georgikou provlimatos tis choras* (Athens, 1939).
—— *To zitima tis synkentroseos ton viomichanion en Elladi* (Athens, 1940).
ASO (Avtonomos Stafidikos Organismos), *Ekthesis* (Patras, various years).
Bank of Greece (Trapeza tis Ellados), *Dyo simeomata epi tou proschediou nomou: 'Peri anonymon etaireion kai trapezon'* (Athens, 1930).
—— *Report for the Year of the Governor of the Bank of Greece* (Athens, 1929–31).
—— *The Economic Situation in Greece and the Bank of Greece* (Athens, 1932–8).
Chadzigiannis, D., *Epi tou nomoschediou peri koinonikon asfaliseon* (Athens, 1934).
Corporation of Foreign Bondholders, *Annual Report of the Council for 1932* (London, n.d.).
DGFP (*Documents on German Foreign Policy*), ser. c, vols. iv–v (Washington, DC, 1962–5).

DOT (Department of Overseas Trade), *Report on Industrial and Economic Conditions in Greece to April 1922* (London, 1923).

——*Report on Industrial and Economic Conditions in Greece in 1923 and 1924* (London, 1925).

——*Report on Industrial and Economic Conditions in Greece in 1925* (London, 1927).

——*Report on Economic Conditions in Greece, 1932–3* (London, 1934).

——*Report on Economic and Commercial Conditions in Greece in April 1937* (London, 1937).

Eisigiseis tis eidikis proparaskevastikis epitropis epi tou stafidikou zitimatos (Athens, 1936).

GPEK (Grafeion Prostasias Ellinikon Kapnon), Kavalla, *To ergon tou Grafeiou Prostasias Ellinikon Kapnon Kavallas kata tin dekaetian 1926–35* (Kavalla, 1937).

GPEK (Grafeion Prostasias Ellinikon Kapnon), Thessalonikis, *To kapnikon zitima* (Thessaloniki, 1929).

HMSO, *Report for the Year 1906 on the Trade of the Consular District of Salonica* (London, 1907).

——*Report for the Year 1909 on the Trade and Agriculture of the District of Piraeus* (London, 1910).

——*Report for the Year 1909 on the Trade of the District of Thessaly* (London, 1910).

——*A Handbook of Greece,* i: *The Mainland of Old Greece and Certain Neighbouring Islands* (London, 1920).

——*Report on Commercial and Industrial Conditions in Greece in 1919* (London, 1920).

I istoriki periodeia tou prothypourgou kyriou Eleftheriou Venizelou ana tin voreion Ellada kai to Ayion Oros (Thessaloniki, 1932).

Iatrides, J. (ed.), *Ambassador MacVeagh Reports: Greece 1933–1947* (Princeton, NJ, 1980).

Institouton Vamvakos, *To Institouton Vamvakos kai ton dietes ergon avtou* (Athens, 1934).

LN (League of Nations), *Greek Refugee Settlement* (Geneva, 1926).

——*Balance of Payments and Trade 1927–29* (Geneva, 1930).

——*The Agricultural Crisis,* i (Geneva, 1931).

——*Report of a Mission Sent to Greece* (London, 1933).

——*Review of World Trade* (Geneva, 1934).

——*World Production and Prices 1925–33* (Geneva, 1934).

——*Public Finances 1928–35* (Geneva, 1936).

——*Public Finances 1928–37* (Geneva, 1938).

——*Public Debt 1914–1946* (New York, 1946).

——*Financial Committee: Procès-Verbal* (Geneva, various years).

——*International Trade Statistics* (Geneva, various years).

Mazarakis-Ainian, A., *Memoires* (Thessaloniki, 1979).

Metaxas, J., *Logoi kai skepseis 1936–1941*, i: *1936–38* (Athens, 1969).
Ministère des Affaires Étrangères, *La Grèce et la crise mondiale* (Athens, 1933).
Ministry of Agriculture (Ypourgeion Georgias), *Etisia georgiki kai ktinotrofiki statistiki tis Ellados* (Athens, various years).
——*Ta pepragmena tou Ypourgeiou Georgias kata tin televtaian tetraetian 1928–1932* (Athens, 1932).
Ministry of Finance (Ypourgeion Oikonomikon), *Ta pepragmena tis diarkous epitropis tou dasmologiou kata ta eti 1932–1935* (Athens, 1936).
——*Psifistheis genikos proypologismos 1933–34*, i (Athens, 1934).
MNE (Ypourgeion Ethnikis Oikonomias), *H elliniki viomichania* (Athens, 1931).
——*To kapnikon zitima* (Athens, 1931).
——*Apografi ton katastimaton ton viomichanikon kai emporikon epicheiriseon* (Athens, 1934).
——*Apografi ton ypallilon kai ergaton ton viomichanikon kai emporikon epicheiriseon kai imeromisthia avton* (Athens, 1940).
——*AS (Annuaire Statistique)* (Athens, various years).
——*Ektheseis kai pepragmena somatos epitheoriseos ergasias* (Athens, various years).
——*Minaion deltion eidikou emporiou tis Ellados* (Athens, various years).
NBG (Ethniki Trapeza tis Ellados), *OE (Oikonomiki epetiris tis Ellados)* (Athens, various years).
——*Report of the Governor of the National Bank of Greece* (Athens, various years).
Pangalos, T. (ed.), *Archeion Theodorou Pangalou*, i: *1925–1952* (Athens, 1974).
Papandreou, G., *Politika keimena*, 2 vols. (Athens, n.d.).
Stefanou, S. (ed.), *Eleftheriou Venizelou politikai ypothikai anthologitheisai apo ta keimena avtou* (Athens, 1969).
——*Ta keimena tou Eleftheriou Venizelou*, i: *1909–1914* (Athens, 1981).
——*Ta keimena tou Eleftheriou Venizelou*, iii: *1920–1929* (Athens, 1983).
——*Ta keimena ton Eleftheriou Venizelou*, iv: *1930–1936* (Athens, 1984).
US Department of State, *FRUS (Foreign Relations of the United States)* (Washington, DC, various years).
Vouli ton Ellinon, *Ekthesis epi tou nomoschediou 'Peri anonymon etaireion kai trapezon'* (Athens, 1931).

Secondary Sources

Unpublished

Maddison, A., 'Growth, Crisis and Interdependence, 1929–38 and 1973–83', OECD, Paris, 1985.
Notel, R., 'International Capital Movements and Finance, 1919–1949', no. 20, Papers in East European Economics, held at the Oxford Institute for Economics and Statistics, 1972.

Pryor, Z., 'Czech Economic Development between the Two World Wars', no. 11, Papers in East European Economics, held at the Oxford Institute for Economics and Statistics, 1972.

Sarandis, C., 'The Emergence of the Right in Greece: 1922–1940', D. Phil. thesis, Oxford University, 1979.

Spigler, I., 'Some Aspects of Public Finance of East European Countries between the Two World Wars', no. 15, Papers in East European Economics, held at the Oxford Institute for Economics and Statistics, 1972.

Teichova, A., 'The Potential and Actual Exploitation of Natural Resources and Industrial Structure, 1919–1949', no. 41, Papers in East European Economics, held at the Oxford Institute for Economics and Statistics, 1974.

Published

Adanir, F., 'Tradition and Rural Change in Southeastern Europe during Ottoman Rule', in D. Chirot (ed.), *The Origins of Backwardness in Eastern Europe* (Berkeley, Calif., 1989), 131–76.

Agriantoni, C., *Oi aparches tis ekviomichaniseos stin Ellada ton 19^0 aiona* (Athens, 1986).

Aivaliotakis, N., *O kampos tis Messinias kai ai oreinai lekanai avtou* (Athens, 1942).

Aldcroft, D., *From Versailles to Wall Street, 1919–1929* (London, 1977).

Alejandro, D., 'Latin America in the 1930s', in R. Thorp (ed.), *Latin America in the 1930s* (London, 1984).

Alivizatos, B., *I metapolemiki exelixis tis ellinikis georgikis oikonomias kai ep'avtis epidrasis tis agrotikis politikis* (Athens, 1935).

——*Kratos kai georgiki politiki* (Athens, 1938).

——*I georgiki Ellas kai i exelixis tis* (Athens, 1939).

Alivizatos, N., *Les Institutions politiques de la Grèce à travers les crises, 1922–1974* (Paris, 1979).

Altsitzoglou, F., *Oi giakades kai o kampos tis Xanthis* (Athens, 1941).

Anagnostopoulos, N., *O kampos ton Serron* (Athens, 1937).

Anastasiadis, G., Kontogiorgis, G., and Petridis, P. (eds.), *Alexandros Papanastasiou: Thesmoi, ideologia kai politiki sto mesopolemo* (Athens, 1987).

Anastasopoulos, N., *Istoria tis ellinikis viomichanias*, vol. iii (Athens, 1947).

Ancel, J., *La Macédoine: Son évolution contemporaine* (Paris, 1930).

Andreades, A. (ed.), *Les Effets économiques et sociales de la guerre en Grèce* (Paris, 1928).

Andreopoulos, G., 'The IFC and Anglo-Greek Relations (1928–1933)', *Historical Journal*, 31(2) (1988), 341–64.

Andreou, A., *I exoteriki emporiki politiki tis Ellados 1830–1933* (Athens, 1933).

——*I dasmologiki epivarynsis eisagomenon eidon* (Athens, 1947).

Andrews, K., *Athens Alive* (Athens, 1979).

Andrikopoulos, G., *Oi rizes tou ellinikou fasismou* (Athens, 1977).

——*I dimokratia tou mesopolemou* (Athens, 1987).

Angelopoulos, A., *I ammesos forologia en Elladi* (Athens, 1933).

—— *To dimosion chreos tis Ellados* (Athens, 1937).

Arliotis, K., *Istoria tis Ethnikis Ktimatikis Trapezis tis Ellados* (Athens, 1979).

Arrighi, G. (ed.), *Semiperipheral Development: The Politics of Southern Europe in the 20th Century* (Beverly Hills, Calif., 1985).

Aschenbrenner, S., *Life in a Changing Greek Village* (Dubuque, Ia., 1986).

Avramides, A., *To ellinikon emporion* (Athens, 1935).

Bacon, L., and Schloemmer, F., *World Trade in Agricultural Products* (Rome, 1940).

Bakalbasis, A., *Ta ellinika kapna en ti evropaiki kapnagora* (Athens, 1930).

Basch, A., *The Danubian Basin and the German Economic Sphere* (London, 1944).

Ben-Ami, S., *Fascism from Above: The Dictatorship of Primo de Rivera in Spain: 1923–1930* (Oxford, 1983).

Benaroya, A., *I proti stadiodromia tou ellinikou proletariatou* (repr. Athens, 1986).

Berend, I., 'Balkan Economic Development', *Economic History Review*, 29(3) (May, 1984), 268–71.

—— *Hungary: A Century of Economic Development* (New York, 1974).

—— and Ranki, G., 'L'Evolution économique de l'Europe orientale entre les deux guerres mondiales', *Annales ESC*, 33 (1978), 389–405.

Bernaris, A., *I diarthrosis kai ai prospatheiai prosarmogis tis ellinikis oikonomias* (Athens, 1933).

Bloomfield, A., *Monetary Policy under the International Gold Standard: 1880–1914* (New York, 1959).

Boratav, K., 'Kemalist Economic Policies and Étatism', in A. Kazancigil and E. Ozbudun (eds.), *Ataturk: Founder of a Modern State* (Hamden, Conn., 1981), 165–90.

Borchardt, K., 'Could and should Germany have Followed Great Britain in Leaving the Gold Standard?', *Journal of European Economic History*, 13(3) (Winter 1984), 471–99.

Boyazoglu, A., *Contribution à l'étude de l'économie rurale de la Grèce* (Paris, 1931).

Bristoyiannis, D., *La Politique de la Banque Nationale de Grèce* (Paris, 1928).

Burgel, G., *Croissance urbaine et développement capitaliste: Le 'Miracle' athénien* (Athens, 1981).

Burks, R. V., 'Statistical Profile of the Greek Communist', *Journal of Modern History*, 27(2) (June 1955), 153–8.

Cairncross, A., and Eichengreen, B., *Sterling in Decline* (Oxford, 1983).

Campbell, J. K., *Honour, Family and Patronage* (Oxford, 1964).

Cassimatis, L. P., *American Influence in Greece, 1917–1929* (Kent, Ohio, 1988).

Chadziiosif, C., 'Apopseis gyro apo tin "viosimotita" tis Ellados kai to rolo tis viomichanias', in *Afieroma ston Niko Svorono*, vol. ii (Rethymno, 1986), 330–68.

Chadzivasileiou, N., *Katefthynseis tis exoterikis emporikis mas politikis* (Athens, 1936).

Charitakis, G., *Ellinikis viomichanias* (Athens, 1927).

Chasiotis, S., *Ta kalliergitika systimata en Elladi* (Athens, 1936).

Childs, F. C., *The Theory and Practice of Exchange Control in Germany* (The Hague, 1958).

Christides, C., *Emporikoi sympsifismoi kai antallagai* (Athens, 1937).

Christodoulopoulos, P., *Pistotiki politiki kai periodikai kriseis* (Athens, 1930).

Cliadakis, H., 'The Political and Diplomatic Background to the Metaxas Dictatorship, 1935–36', *Journal of Contemporary History*, 14 (1979), 117–38.

Collier, D. (ed.), *The New Authoritarianism in Latin America* (Princeton, NJ, 1979).

Comes, O., 'Delle razze dei tabacchi', in Reale Istituto d'Incoraggiamento di Napoli, *Atti*, ser. 6, vol. 57 (Naples, 1906), 74–306.

Dafnis, G., *I Ellas metaxy dyo polemon: 1923–1940*, 2 vols. (Athens, 1955).

de Cecco, M., *Money and Empire: The International Gold Standard 1880–1914* (Oxford, 1974).

Ta deka eti tis Trapezis tis Ellados, 1928–1938 (Athens, 1938).

Dertilis, G., *Koinonikos metaschimatismos kai stratiotiki epemvasi, 1880–1909* (Athens, 1977).

Dertilis, P. B., *La Reconstruction financière de la Grèce et la Société des Nations* (Paris, 1929).

Diamantopoulos, T., *Oi politikoi dynameis tis venizelikis periodou* (Athens, 1988).

Diomedes, A., *Meta tin krisin* (Athens, 1935).

Doulis, T., *Disaster and Fiction: Modern Greek Fiction and the Asia Minor Disaster of 1922* (London, 1977).

Dritsa, M., *Viomichania kai trapezes stin Ellada tou mesopolemou* (Athens, 1990).

du Boulay, J., *Portrait of a Greek Mountain Village* (Oxford, 1979).

Eddy, C., *Greece and the Greek Refugees* (London, 1931).

Eichengreen, B., 'Inflazione e ripresa economica negli anni '20', *Rivista di Storia Economica*, 3(3) (Oct. 1986), 269–303.

——and Sachs, J., 'Exchange Rates and Economic Recovery in the 1930s', *Journal of Economic History*, 45(4) (1985), 925–46.

Elefantis, A., *I epangelia tis adynatis epanastasis* (Athens, 1976).

Ellis, H. S., *Exchange Control in Central Europe* (Cambridge, Mass., 1941).

ETVA (Ethniki Trapeza Viomichanikis Anaptyxis), *Elliniki viomichania apo ton 19° eis ton 20° aiona* (Athens, 1985).

Eulambio, M., *The National Bank of Greece* (Athens, 1924).

Evelpides, C., *I exelixis tis georgikis kriseos* (Athens, 1935).

——*To ethnikon eisodima* (Athens, 1937).

——*Theoria kai praxis agrotikis politikis kai oikonomias* (Athens, 1939).

——*I georgia tis Ellados* (Athens, 1944).

Filaretos, D., *Dia tou kapnou i anastatheropoïisis ton ellinikon oikonomikon* (Athens, 1932).

Fleischer, H., and Svoronos, N. (eds.), *I Ellada 1936–1944: Diktatoria, katochi, antistasi* (Athens, 1989).

Fotylas, N., *Koinoniki politiki* (Athens, 1937).

Freris, A., *The Greek Economy in the Twentieth Century* (Athens, 1986).

Galanis, T., *Trapezikai meletai* (Athens, 1946).

Ganosis, V., *Peri tis ektheseos tou kyriou Kyriakou eis tin Akadimian* (Athens, 1934).

Garon, S., *The State and Labor in Modern Japan* (Berkeley, Calif., 1987).

Gerth, H., and Wright Mills, C. (eds.), *From Max Weber* (New York, 1958).

Geshkoff, T., *Balkan Union* (New York, 1940).

Goula, D., *Georgios Kafandaris* (Athens, 1982).

Hanisch, T., 'The Economic Crisis in Norway in the 1930s', *Scandinavian Economic History Review*, 26(2) (1978), 145–55.

Harrison, J., *An Economic History of Modern Spain* (Manchester, 1978).

—— 'The Interwar Depression and the Spanish Economy', *Journal of European Economic History*, 12(2) (Autumn 1983), 295–322.

Herzfeld, M., *The Poetics of Manhood* (Princeton, NJ, 1985).

Hirschon, R., *Heirs to the Greek Catastrophe* (Oxford, 1989).

Hope-Simpson, J., 'The Work of the Refugee Settlement Commission', *Journal of the Royal Institute of International Affairs* (1929), 583–604.

Iatrides, J. (ed.), *Greece in the 1940s: A Nation in Crisis* (London, 1981).

Inglesis, N., *Odigos ton Anonymon Etaireion, 1937–38*, vol. ii (Athens, 1939).

Jackson, M., 'Comparing the Balkan Demographic Experience: 1860–1970', *Journal of European Economic History*, 14(2) (Autumn 1985), 223–72.

—— and Lampe, J., *Balkan Economic History: 1550–1950* (Bloomington, Ind., 1982).

James, H., *The German Slump: Politics and Economics 1924–1936* (Oxford, 1986).

Janos, A., *The Politics of Backwardness in Hungary: 1825–1945* (Berkeley, Calif., 1982).

Jecchinis, C., *Trade Unionism in Greece* (Chicago, Ill., 1967).

Jowitt, K. (ed.), *Social Change in Romania: 1860–1940* (Berkeley, Calif., 1978).

Kaiser, D., *Economic Diplomacy and the Origins of the Second World War* (Princeton, NJ, 1980).

Kallitsounakis, D., *O kapnos* (Athens, 1931).

Kanellopoulos, K., *Ai koinonikai asfaliseis* (Athens, 1934).

Kanellopoulos, P., *Ai koinonikai asfaliseis kai o nearos ellinikos nomos* (Athens, 1932).

—— *I zoi mou* (Athens, 1985).

Kapsalis, T., *La Balance des comptes de la Grèce* (Lausanne, 1927).

Karamanlis, K., *O Eleftherios Venizelos kai oi exoterikes mas scheseis 1928–1932* (Athens, 1986).

Karavidas, K., *Agrotika* (Athens, 1931).

—— *To provlima tis avtonomias* (repr. Athens, 1981).

Kaser, M. (ed.), *The Economic History of Eastern Europe*, vol. i (Oxford, 1985).

Kemp, T., 'The French Economy under the Franc Poincaré', *Economic History Review*, 24(1) (1979), 82–99.

Kerner, R. J., and Howard, H. N., *The Balkan Conferences and the Balkan Entente: 1930–1935* (Berkeley, Calif., 1936).

Kindleberger, C., *The World in Depression: 1929–1939* (London, 1973).

Kirkilitsis, A., *Ai trapezai en Elladi* (Athens, 1934).

Kirtsis, A., 'O Alexandros Papanastasiou kao oi theories koinonikis metarrythmisis', *Ta Istorika*, 5(9) (Dec. 1988), 339–52.

Kitroeff, A., 'Continuity and Change in Contemporary Greek Historiography', *European History Quarterly*, 19(2) (Apr. 1989), 269–98.

Kladas, S., *I anergia en Elladi* (Athens, 1935).

——*I ergatiki mas politiki kai nomothesia* (Athens, 1945).

Kofas, J., *Authoritarianism in Greece: The Metaxas Regime* (New York, 1983).

Koliopoulos, J., *Greece and the British Connection 1935–1941* (Oxford, 1977).

——*Palinorthosis, diktatoria, polemos: 1935–1941* (Athens, 1985).

Kordatos, J., *Eisagogi eis tin istorian tis ellinikis kefalaiokratias* (repr. Athens, 1972).

Kostis, K., *Oi trapezes kai i krisi, 1929–1932* (Athens, 1986).

——*Agrotiki oikonomia kai Georgiki Trapeza* (Athens, 1987).

——and Veremis, T., *I Ethniki Trapeza en Mikri Asia (1919–1922)* (Athens, 1984).

Koulas, T., *I epivarynsis ton foron epi tis stafidos* (Athens, 1948).

Kousoulas, D., *Revolution and Defeat: The Story of the Greek Communist Party* (London, 1965).

Koutsoulakis, D., *I defteri dekaetia tou KKE: 1929–1939* (Athens, 1984).

Kypriades, S., *I organosis tis sitoparagogis mas* (Athens, 1931).

Kyriakos, G., *I georgiki politiki tou kratous* (Athens, 1934).

Ladas, S., *The Exchange of Minorities: Bulgaria, Greece and Turkey* (New York, 1932).

Lambrou, G., and Jannides, M., *Ta anatolika kapna* (Kavalla, 1939).

Lazaris, V., *Politiki istoria tis Patras*, vols. ii–iii (Athens, 1986–9).

Lee, C., 'The Effects of the Depression on Primary-Producing Countries', *Journal of Contemporary History*, 4 (1969), 139–55.

Leon, G., *Greece and the Great Powers* (Thessaloniki, 1974).

——*The Greek Socialist Movement and the First World War* (New York, 1976).

Liakos, A., 'L'Apparition des organisations de Jeunesse: Le Cas de Salonique', in *Actes du Colloque International: Historicité de l'Enfance et de la Jeunesse* (Athens, 1986), 512–38.

——'Apo kratos fylax eia kratos pronoia?', *O Politis*, 78(6) (Apr. 1987), 34–40.

——'O Eleftherios Venizelos kai to Diethnes Grafeio Ergasias', *Synchrona Themata*, 31 (Oct. 1987), 40–6.

——'Problems on the Formation of the Greek Working Class', *Études Balkaniques*, 2 (1988), 43–54.

Livieratos, D., *Koinonikes agones stin Ellada (1927–1931)* (Athens, 1987).

Lyde, L., and Mockler-Ferryman, A., *A Military Geography of the Balkan Peninsula* (London, 1905).

Lyttelton, A., *The Seizure of Power: Fascism in Italy 1919–1929* (Princeton, NJ, 1988).

McNeill, W., *The Metamorphosis of Modern Greece* (Chicago, Ill., 1978).

Maier, C., *Recasting Bourgeois Europe: Economic Stabilisation in France, Germany and Italy in the Decade after World War 1* (Princeton, NJ, 1975).

Makkas, L., *To ellinikon provlima kai to schedion mias lyseos* (Athens, 1933).

Marasli, A., *Istoria tis Patras* (Patras, 1983).

Martin, P., *Greece in the Twentieth Century* (London, 1913).

Mathaiou, S., 'I efimerida "Kampana"', *Mnimon*, 10 (1985), 212–35.

Mavrogordatos, G., *Stillborn Republic: Social Coalitions and Party Strategies in Greece 1922–1936* (Berkeley, Calif., 1983).

——and Chadziiosif, C. (eds.), *Venizelismos kai astikos eksynchronismos* (Irákleion, 1988).

Mavrogordatos, M., and Chamoudopoulos, A., *Makedonia: dimografiki kai oikonomiki meleti* (Thessaloniki, 1931).

Maximos, S., *Koinovoulio i diktatoria?* (repr. Athens, 1975).

Mazower, M., 'The Greek Economy and the Interwar Depression', *Rivista di Storia Economica*, 2(2) (1985), 175–93.

——'Economic Diplomacy between Great Britain and Greece in the 1930s', *Journal of European Economic History*, 17(3) (Winter 1988), 603–19.

Mears, E. G., *Greece Today: The Aftermath of the Refugee Impact* (Stanford, Calif., 1929).

Milios, G., 'O Marxismos sto mesopolemo kai o Serafeim Maximos', *Theseis*, 26 (Jan.–Mar. 1989), 102–20.

Miller, W., *Greece* (London, 1928).

——'Greece since the Return of Venizelos', *Foreign Affairs*, 7(3) (Apr. 1929), 468–77.

Milward, A., and Saul, S. B., *The Development of the Economies of Continental Europe: 1850–1914* (Cambridge, Mass., 1977).

Mitchell, B., *European Historical Statistics 1750–1970* (London, 1976).

Mitrany, D., *Marx against the Peasant* (Chapel Hill, NC, 1951).

Montague Bell, H. T., *The Near East Yearbook and Who's Who, 1927* (London, 1927).

Morgan, O. S., *Agricultural Systems of Middle Europe* (New York, 1933).

Morgenthau, H., *I was Sent to Athens* (New York, 1929).

Neal, L., 'The Economics and Financing of Bilateral Clearing Agreements: Germany 1934–38', *Economic History Review*, 24(4) (1979), 391–404.

Newbigin, M., *The Geographical Aspect of Balkan Problems* (London, 1915).

Nezis, G., 'Katanomi tis danciakis epivarynseos en ti propolemiki Elladi', *Nea Oikonomia*, 2(1) (Nov. 1947), 10–16.

Nicolson, H., *Peacemaking 1919* (New York, 1931).

Nikolaides, D., *Oi kindynoi tis stafidos* (Patras, 1934).

Notaras, M., *I agrotiki apokatastasis ton prosfygon* (Athens, 1934).

Noutsos, P., 'Ideologikes synistoses tou kathestotos tis 4is Avgoustou', *Ta Istorika*, 5 (June 1986), 139–51.

Pallis, A., 'Racial Migrations in the Balkans during the Years 1912–1924', *Geographical Journal*, 69 (1925), 315–31.

—— 'The Greek Census of 1928', *Geographical Journal*, 73 (1929), 543–8.

Pamuk, S., *The Ottoman Empire and European Capitalism: 1820–1913* (Cambridge, 1987).

Pegios, G., *Apo tin istoria tou syndikalistikou kinimatos tis Kavallas, 1922–1953* (Athens, 1984).

Pelt, M., 'Greece and Germany's Policy towards South-Eastern Europe, 1932–1940', *Epsilon*, 2 (1988), 55–77.

Pentzopoulos, D., *The Balkan Exchange of Minorities and its Impact upon Greece* (The Hague, 1962).

Pepelasis, A., 'The Legal System and Economic Development of Greece', *Journal of Economic History*, 19(2) (June 1959), 173–98.

Petropulos, J., 'The Compulsory Exchange of Populations: Greek–Turkish Peacemaking, 1922–1930', *Byzantine and Modern Greek Studies*, 2 (1976), 135–61.

Polychronis, L., *Skepseis epi tou georgikou mas provlimatos* (Athens, 1931).

Polyzos, N., *Essai sur l'émigration grecque* (Paris, 1947).

Pournaras, D., *I oikonomiki thesis ton agroton* (Athens, 1932).

Ta prota peninta chronia tis Trapezis tis Ellados (Athens, n.d.).

Protecdicos, D., *Greece Economic and Financial* (London, 1924).

Psalidopoulos, M., *I krisi tou 1929 kai oi ellines oikonomologoi* (Athens, 1989).

Psyroukis, N., *O fasismos kai i tetarti avgoustou* (Athens, 1977).

Pyrris, N., *La crise monétaire en Grèce* (Paris, 1934).

Pyrsos, G., *Symvoli eis tin istorian tis Trapezis tis Ellados*, vol. i (Athens, 1936), vol. ii (Athens, 1946).

Raupach, H., 'The Impact of the Great Depression in Eastern Europe', *Journal of Contemporary History*, 4 (1969), 77–85.

Riginos, M., 'Oi diakymanseis ton viomichanikon imeromisthion stin Ellada, 1912–1936', *Ta Istorika*, 5 (June 1986), 151–76.

Rigos, A., *I B' elliniki dimokratia: Koinonikes diastaseis tis politikis skinis* (Athens, 1988).

RIIA (Royal Institute of International Affairs), *The Balkan States*, vol. i: *Economic* (London, 1936).

—— *The Problem of International Investment* (London, 1937).

Rothschild, J., *East Central Europe between the Two World Wars* (Seattle, 1988).

Salamone, S., *In the Shadow of the Holy Mountain* (New York, 1987).

Sarti, R., 'Mussolini and the Industrial Leadership in the Battle of the Lira, 1925–27', *Past and Present* (May 1970), 87–112.

Sideris, A. D., *I georgiki politiki tis Ellados 1833–1933* (Athens, 1934).
Simonides, V. M., *O Avtonomos Stafidikos Organismos kai ai ergasiai tou kata to proton etos 1925–1926* (Athens, 1927).
Skliros, G., *Ta synchrona provlimata tou ellinismou* (Alexandria, 1919).
Starr, J., 'The Socialist Federation of Saloniki', *Jewish Social Studies*, 7 (1945), 323–35.
Stavrianos, L. S., *The Balkans since 1453* (New York, 1958).
Stefanides, D., *I eisroi xenon kefalaion kai ai oikonomikai kai politikai tis synepeiai* (Thessaloniki, 1931).
——*I thesis tis viomichanias en ti koinoniki mas oikonomia* (Thessaloniki, 1938).
Stefanopoulos, O., *Meleti peri tis viomichanias ton oinon en Elladi* (Athens, 1932).
Synchrona Themata, 35–7 (Dec. 1988).
Theodorou, N., 'Georgooikonomiki meleti epi tessaron antiprosopeftikon chorion tou lofodous tmimatos tis periferias Katerinis', *GD* 5 (1939), 49–210.
Theotokas, G., *Argo* (Athens, 1987).
Theseis gia ton Pan. Kanellopoulo (Athens, 1982).
Thorp, R. (ed.), *Latin America in the 1930s* (London, 1984).
Toniolo, G., *L'economia dell'Italia fascista* (Bari, 1980).
Treves, A., *Le migrazione interne nell'Italia fascista* (Turin, 1976).
Tsouderos, E., *Le Relèvement économique de la Grèce* (Paris, 1920).
Tsoukalas, K., *Koinoniki anaptyxi kai kratos: I synkrotisi tou dimosiou chorou stin Ellada* (Athens, 1981).
van der Wee, H. (ed.), *The Great Depression Revisited* (The Hague, 1972).
Veloudis, G., *Germanograecia: Deutsche einflüsse auf die neugriechische Literatur (1750–1944)*, 2 vols. (Amsterdam, 1983).
Venezis, E., *Chronikon tis Trapezis tis Ellados: 1928–1952* (Athens, 1955).
——*Emmanouil Tsouderos* (Athens, 1966).
Ventiris, G., *I Ellas tou 1910–1920*, 2 vols. (Athens, 1931).
Veremis, T., 'The Officer Corps in Greece, 1912–1936', *Byzantine and Modern Greek Studies*, 2 (1976), 113–34.
——*Oi epemvaseis tou stratou stin elliniki politiki: 1916–1936* (Athens, 1977).
——*Oikonomia kai diktatoria* (Athens, 1982).
——and Dimitrakopoulos, O. (eds.), *Meletimata gyro apo ton Venizelo kai tin epochi tou* (Athens, 1980).
——and Goulimi, G. (eds.), *Eleftherios Venizelos: koinonia, oikonomia, politiki stin epochi tou* (Athens, 1989).
Vergopoulos, K., *Le Capitalisme difforme* (Paris, 1977).
——*Ethnikismos kai oikonomiki anaptyxi* (Athens, 1978).
Vouros, G., *Panayis Tsaldaris* (Athens, 1955).
Warriner, D., *Land Reform in Principle and Practice* (Oxford, 1969).
Zolotas, X., *I Ellas eis to stadion tis ekviomichaniseos* (Athens, 1926).

——*Nomismatika kai synallagmatika fainomena en Elladi: 1910–1927* (Athens, 1928).

——*I daneiaki epivarynsis tis Ellados* (Athens, 1931).

——*Nomismatikai meletai* (Athens, 1932).

——*Agrotiki politiki* (Athens, 1934).

——*Katefthynseis tis oikonomikis mas politikis* (Athens, 1936).

INDEX

Printed in the United Kingdom
by Lightning Source UK Ltd.
113519UKS00001BA/11